THE *Fairy* ARTIST'S FIGURE DRAWING BIBLE

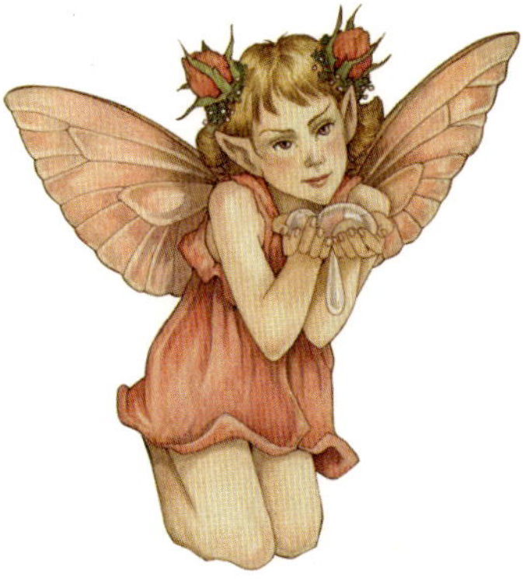

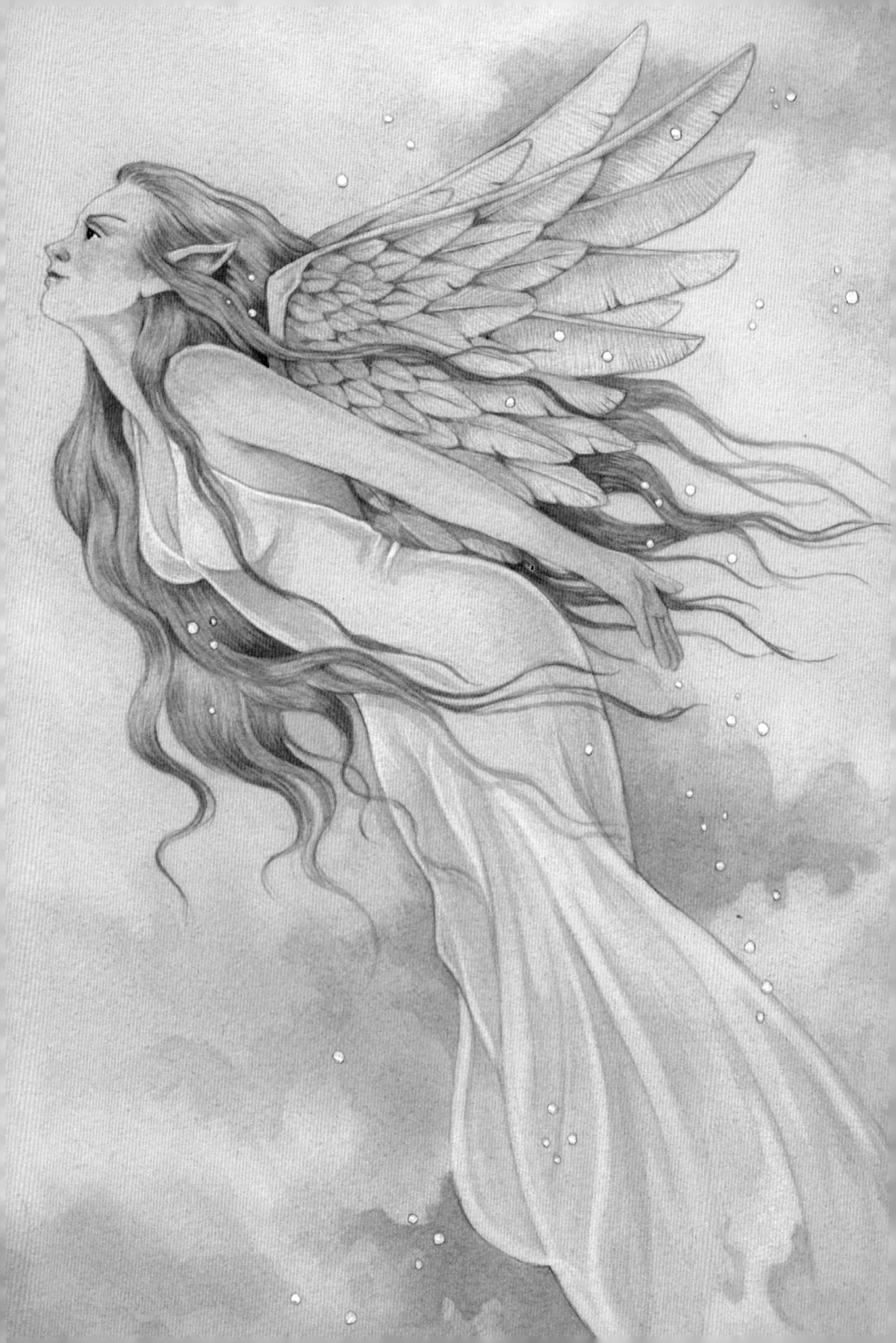

THE *Fairy* ARTIST'S FIGURE DRAWING BIBLE

READY-TO-DRAW TEMPLATES AND
STEP-BY-STEP RENDERING TECHNIQUES

LINDA RAVENSCROFT

BARRON'S

A QUARTO BOOK

First edition for North America published in 2009 by Barron's Educational Series, Inc.

All inquiries should be addressed to:
Barron's Educational Series, Inc.
250 Wireless Boulevard
Hauppauge, NY 11788
www.barronseduc.com

ISBN-10: 0-7641-6201-2
ISBN-13: 978-0-7641-6201-5
Library of Congress Control Number: 2009922388
QUAR.FDB

Conceived, designed, and produced by
Quarto Publishing plc
The Old Brewery
6 Blundell Street
London N7 9BH

Project editor: Chloe Todd Fordham
Art editor: Emma Clayton
Designer: Tanya Devonshire-Jones
Additional text: Sheila Coulson
Photographer: Andrew Atkinson
Additional illustrations: David Wenzel
Proofreader: Liz Dalby
Art director: Caroline Guest
Creative director: Moira Clinch
Publisher: Paul Carslake

Color separation by Modern Age Repro House Ltd, Hong Kong
Printed in China by Midas Printing International Limited

10 9 8 7 6 5 4 3 2 1

Contents

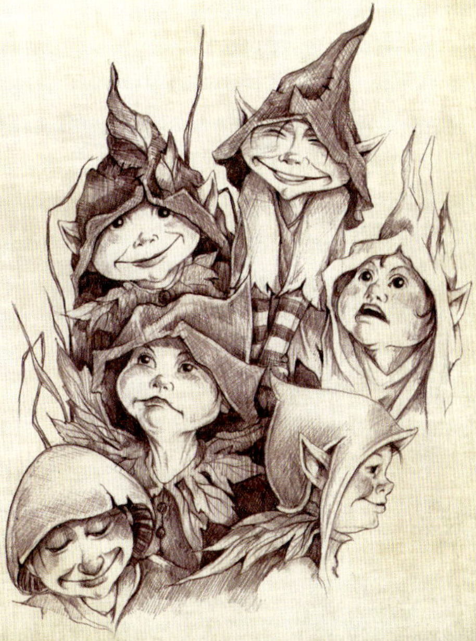

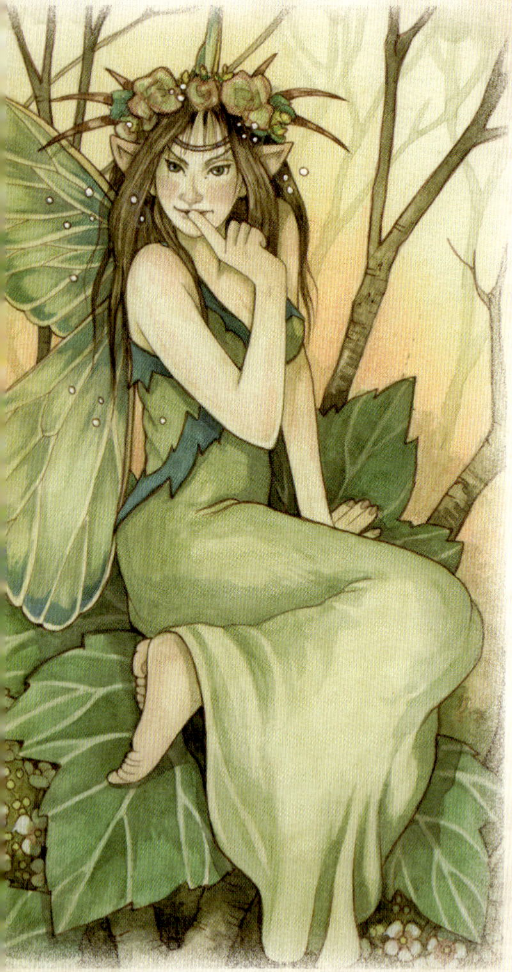

Introduction

This book will guide you through some of the best-known characters of the fairy realm—from evil Goblins and Sorceresses to playful Gnomes and Flower Spirits. Learn techniques essential to the fairy artist, such as how to construct fairy anatomy and wings, how to apply paint, and how to work with color, value, and composition. Build on these techniques to copy the fairy images in the character directory (pages 86–237)—or start to create characters of your own using the costume ideas, character variations, and the gallery (pages 238–251) as inspiration.

Whether you want to paint fairy images just for fun or for more serious fine-art pieces, I hope that the projects and information in this book will offer some inspiration and help to get you in the mood for creating some truly original art!

Anatomy and costume
Learn how to construct the head, body, and fairy wings following basic step-by-step illustrations—then adorn the anatomical underdrawing with lavish costume ideas.

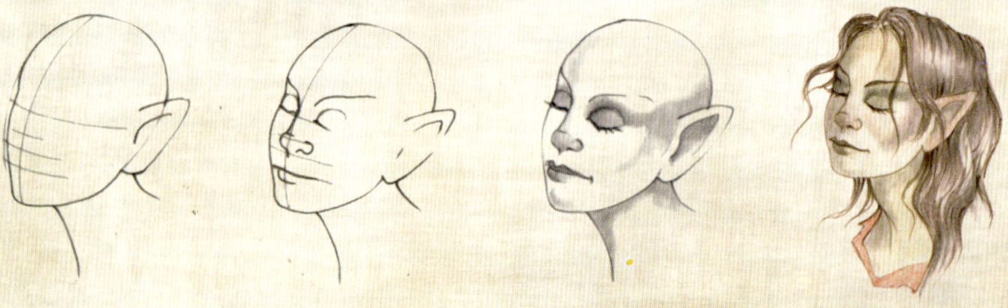

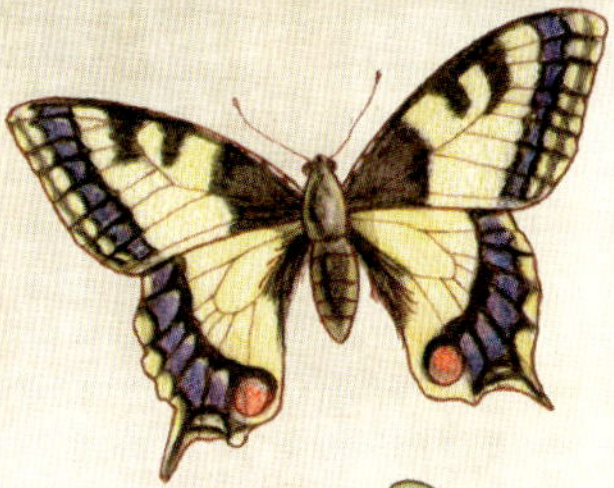

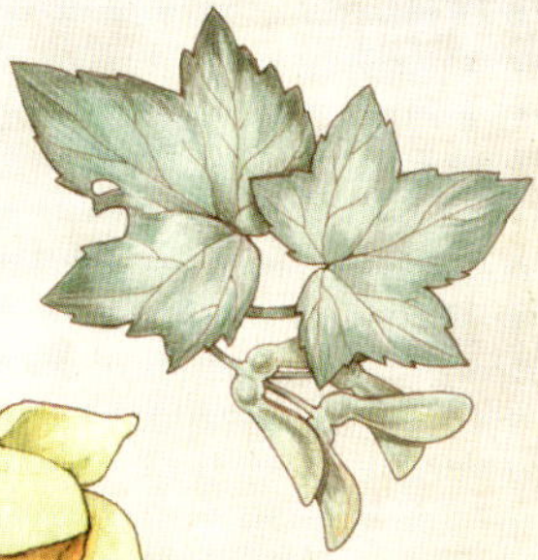

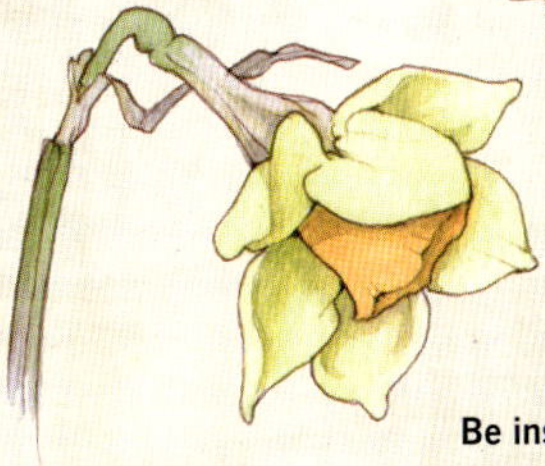

My personal faerie ethos is heartfelt; my thoughts are for the protection of our world and all its flora and fauna, especially the hope of a brighter future for our children, but I do the occasional painting just for fun too! Fairy and fantasy art is the perfect genre to express such personal feelings; I hope that you can find your own "fairy characters" through which you can express your dreams.

Shine brightly!

Linda Ravenscroft

Be inspired
This book is packed full of still-life sketches from the natural world that will help you to set your fairy in context.

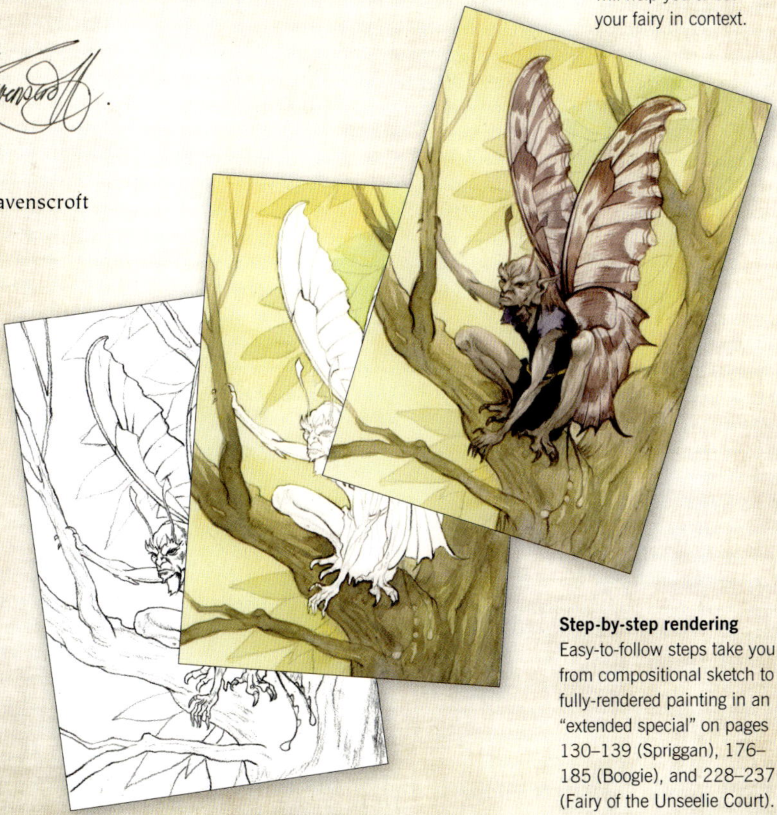

Step-by-step rendering
Easy-to-follow steps take you from compositional sketch to fully-rendered painting in an "extended special" on pages 130–139 (Spriggan), 176–185 (Boogie), and 228–237 (Fairy of the Unseelie Court).

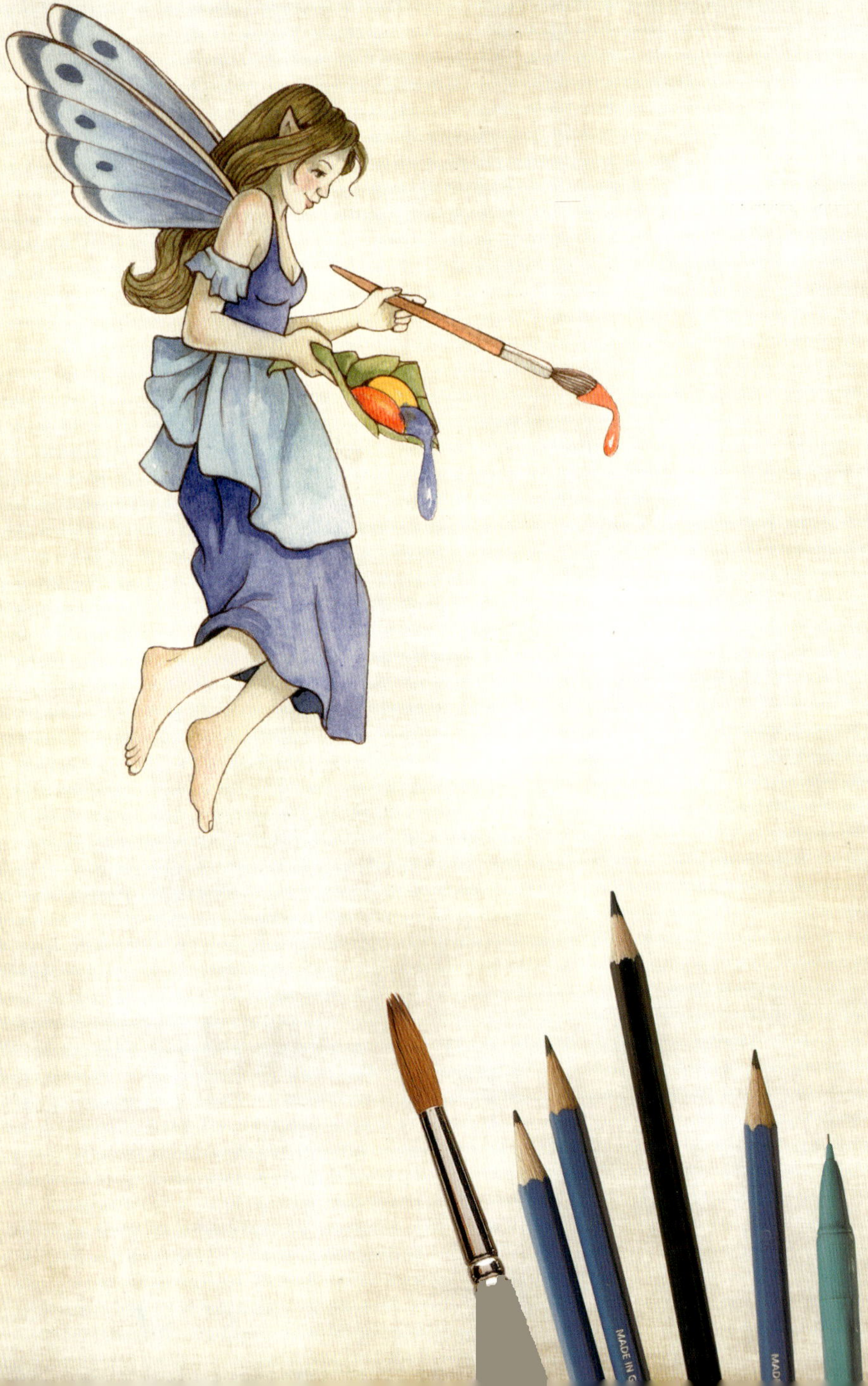

Part 1

Getting started

This chapter introduces you to a wide variety of media, and shows you the techniques you can use and the varied effects that can be achieved. With this knowledge you can make informed creative decisions from the outset. But before you start, explore the suggested sources of inspiration to fire up your imagination with plenty of fairy character ideas.

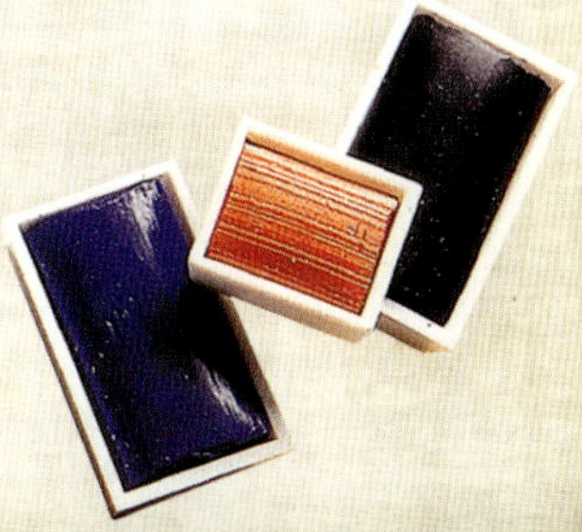

Sources of inspiration

FINDING INSPIRATION IN THE WORK OF OTHERS IS A LEGITIMATE AND EFFECTIVE WAY TO KICK-START YOUR IMAGINATION. THE FAIRY WORLD HAS FASCINATED ARTISTS AND WRITERS FOR CENTURIES. MODERN COMPUTER TECHNIQUES MAKE IT A POPULAR GENRE FOR MOVIES AND VIDEO GAMES, AND THERE IS A WEALTH OF THOUGHT-PROVOKING MATERIAL TO BE INSPIRED BY.

Artists of the fairy world

William Blake (1757–1827)

The 18th century British artist William Blake was a poet and visionary with a profound fascination for the gothic world. He believed that imagination was man's most valuable faculty and immersed himself in mythology, legend, and fairy folklore. In *Oberon, Titania and Puck with Fairies Dancing* he depicts the fairies as free-spirited and graceful elementals dancing with delight in a softly-lit woodland glade. In contrast to this, he created a personal mythology peopled with darker and more brutal characters.

Henry Fuseli (1741–1825)

Working at the same time as Blake, Fuseli produced a very different take on fairy imagery, producing an altogether darker version of the same *Midsummer Night's Dream* scenes. He paints more dramatic spectacles, populated with strange and demonic fairy creatures of all shapes and sizes hiding and cavorting in the shadows. He uses powerful tonal contrasts for added dramatic effect, and this darkly romantic approach was to influence later Victorian fairy illustration.

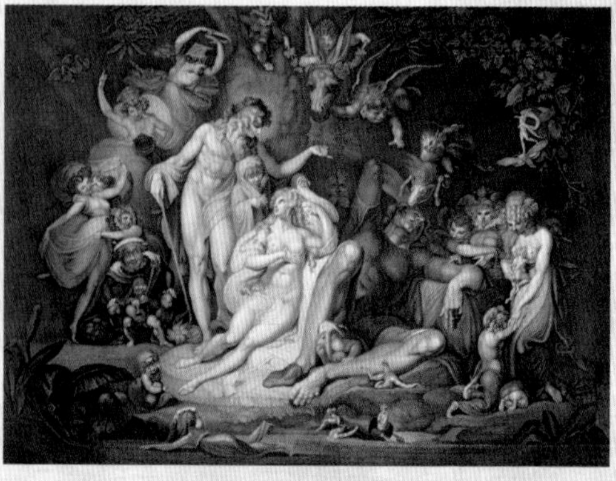

A Midsummer Night's Dream, Act IV, scene i, engraving
Henry Fuseli

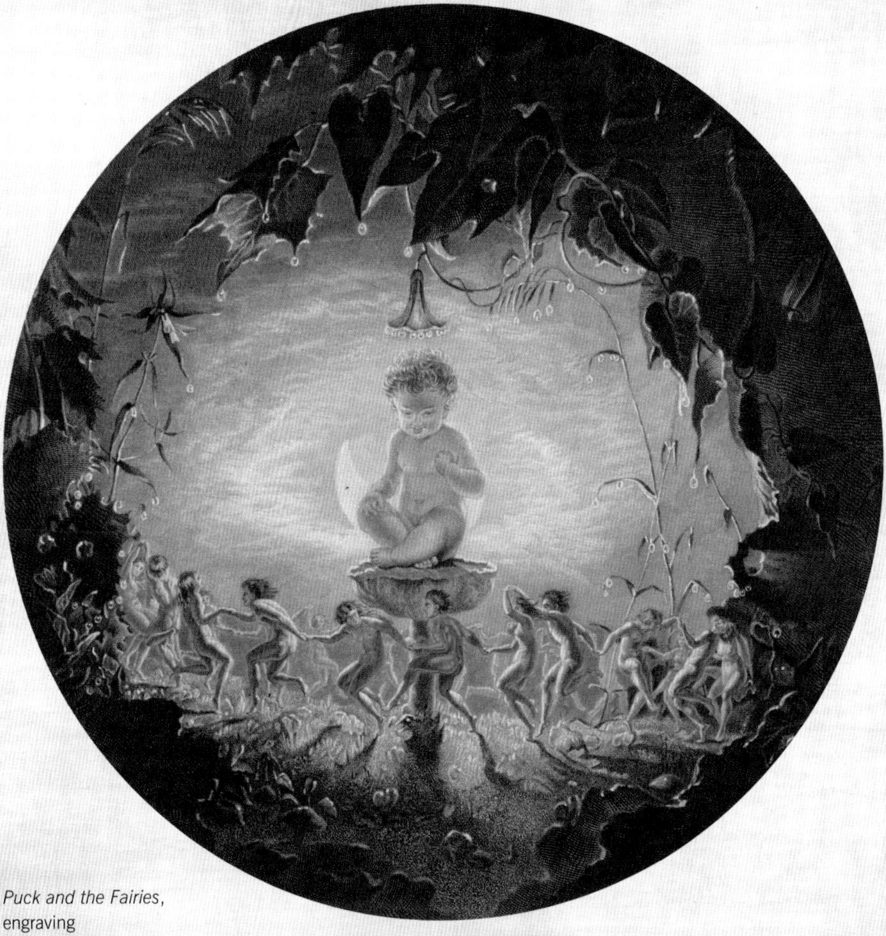

Puck and the Fairies,
engraving
Richard Dadd

Richard Dadd (1817–1886)

A Victorian painter in the Romantic tradition, Dadd is best known for his depiction of fairies and the supernatural. Two early works, *Puck* and *Titania Sleeping* established his reputation as a fairy painter. He spent a large part of his life in a psychiatric hospital, where he produced his famous *Fairy Feller's Master-stroke* and *Contradiction: Oberon and Titania*. These both display obsessive and breathtaking detail and are filled with hosts of tiny creatures, both fairylike and grotesque—the product of a fevered imagination.

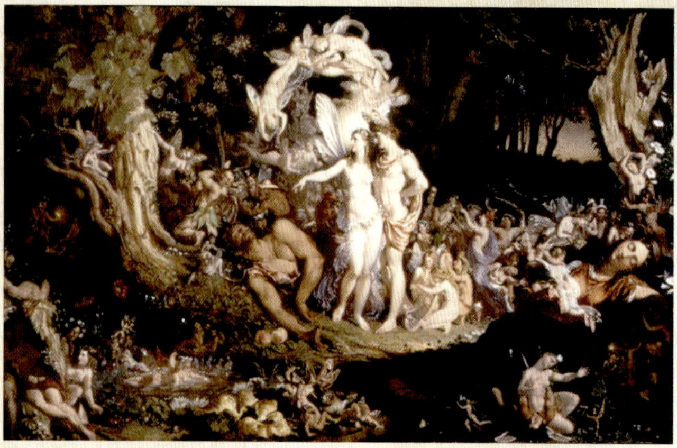

The Reconciliation of Oberon and Titania
Joseph Noel Paton

Joseph Noel Paton (1821–1901)

Like many Victorian artists, Paton was drawn to fairy folklore. His painting *The Quarrel of Oberon and Titania*, and its companion piece *The Reconciliation of Oberon and Titania*, won critical acclaim in the 1850s. Both canvases burst with a mêlée of exuberant, cavorting fantasy characters, all painted in exquisite detail. He exploits their variation in size to disturbing effect, from tiny elves and fairies to more impressive fairy monarchs and on to huge human beings. There are all sorts of goings on—not all pleasant—that provide a rich source of inspiration for countless fairy compositions.

Arthur Rackham (1867–1939)

Arguably the most famous and prolific British illustrator of the 19th and early 20th century, Rackham illustrated many classic fairy stories and tales of the underworld. His haunting and dreamlike evocations of fairies and sprites remain popular today with fans of the genre. His intricate and flowing line work and subdued palette add enchantment and mystery to every character from benign and graceful winged fairies to the darker inhabitants of fairyland, and his style continues to influence fairy artists today.

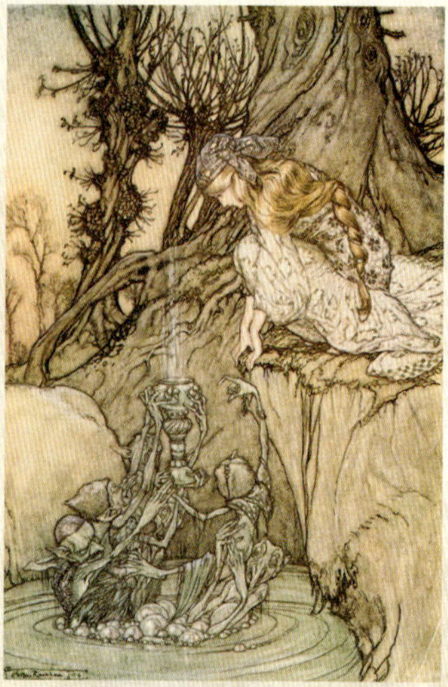

Arthur Rackham's Book of Pictures: The Magic Cup (1913)
Arthur Rackham

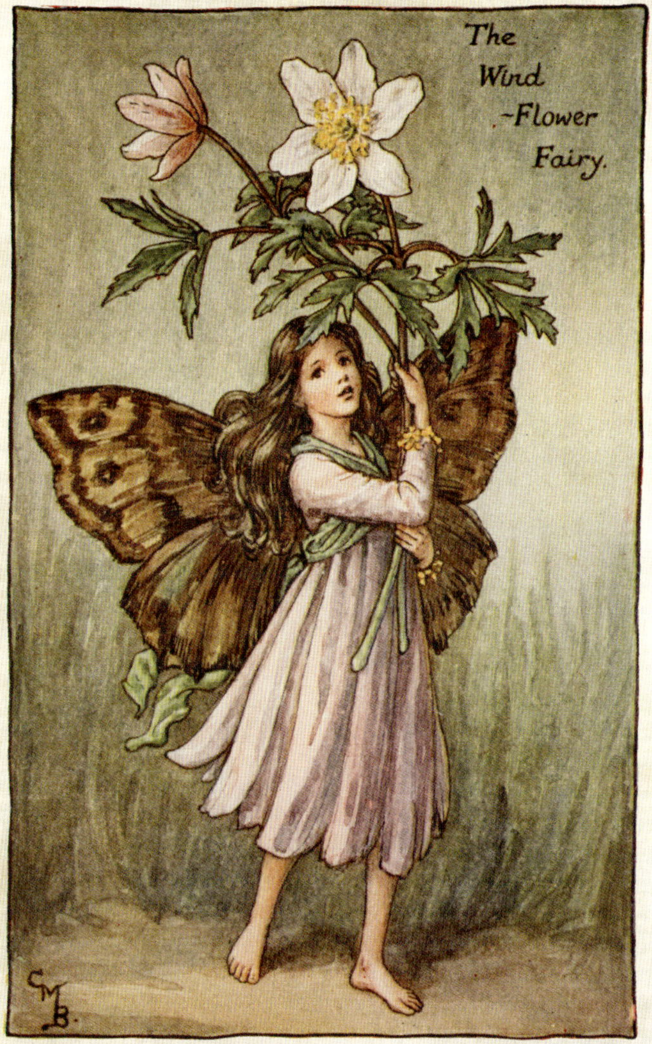

The Wind-Flower Fairy, color lithograph
Cicely Mary Barker

Cicely Mary Barker (1895–1973)

Cicely Mary Barker illustrated the most famous children's fairy books in the world. Working in the first half of the 20th century, her enchanting flower fairies found an immediate appreciative audience, and they are still in print and popular today with children and adults alike. The images are pretty and appealing, with each fairy cleverly characterized by the flower he or she represents. They are beautifully rendered—there are no nasty intruders here to disturb the gentle country idyll and yet the images avoid cliché.

Edmund Dulac (1882–1953)

Working in the first half of the 20th century, Dulac produced beautiful, romantic, jewel-like images to illustrate fairy tales and stories such as those of Hans Christian Anderson, and Shakespeare's *The Tempest*. He was a master of composition and color and a consummate draftsman. His images are always decorative, elegant, and dramatic. Even the ugly bad guys are given the same sensitive treatment as his gentler fairies and sprites.

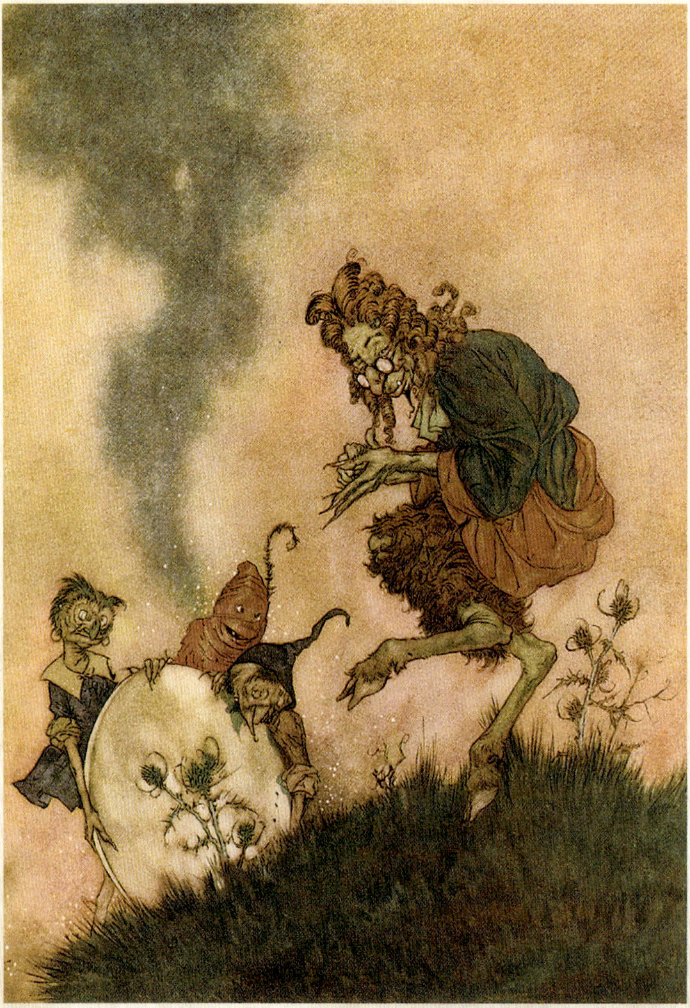

From *The Snow Queen* (1911): *"One day he was in a high state of delight."* **Edmund Dulac**

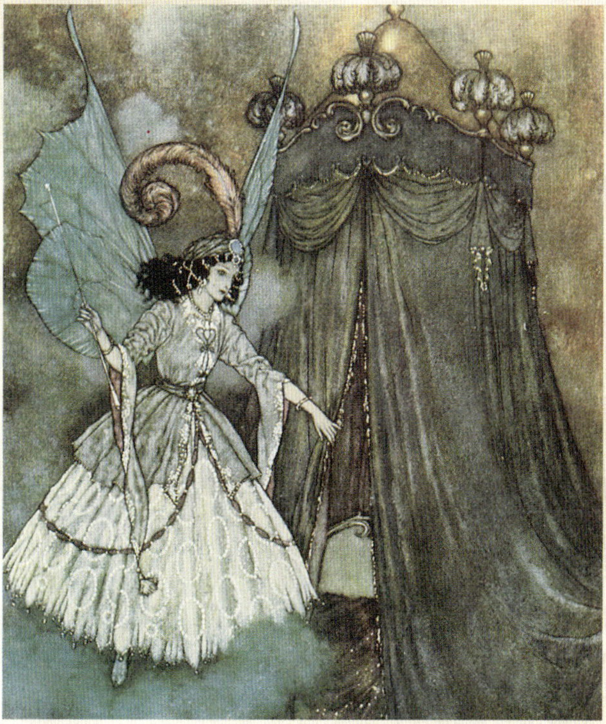

From *Beauty and The Beast* (1911): *"She found herself face to face with a stately and beautiful lady."*
Edmund Dulac

Margaret Tarrant (1888–1959)

As a contemporary of Cicely Mary Barker, Margaret Tarrant tackled similar subject matters but in a different style. She illustrated many children's books of fairy stories and nursery rhymes, and drew engaging Pixies, Goblins, Flower Fairies, and woodland folk. She painted imaginary fairy abodes, and groups of fairies at play together in enchanted landscapes. Her style is now regarded as somewhat stereotypical and her work has often been imitated, but nevertheless it provides a fertile source of ideas for modern fairy artists.

Alan Lee (1947–)

Alan Lee presents a very different take on the fairy world. In the late 1970s, his book *Faeries*, produced with fellow artist Brian Froud, introduced a faerie population of dark, alien creatures, and ugly changeling characters alongside some more traditional fairy images. More recently he illustrated *The Lord of the Rings* with drawings that aim to set a mood and then invite the viewer to use his or her imagination. On the strength of the images, he was invited to be a concept artist for the movie series.

See also: The gallery, pages 238–251.

Writers

William Shakespeare (1564–1616)

A Midsummer Night's Dream contains some of the best-known fairy characters of all time. Titania, Oberon, and Puck have become part of fairy tradition, while Shakespeare transformed the mischievous evil-minded fairies of ancient English folklore into enchanting creatures with a strong connection to nature, who dance, sing, and gently tease. Their names—Cobweb, Moth, Pease Blossom, and Mustard Seed—conjure benign and playful characters. In *The Tempest*, Ariel is a spirit of the air who becomes Prospero's fairy servant, while Caliban is a mysterious, deformed creature bent on evil.

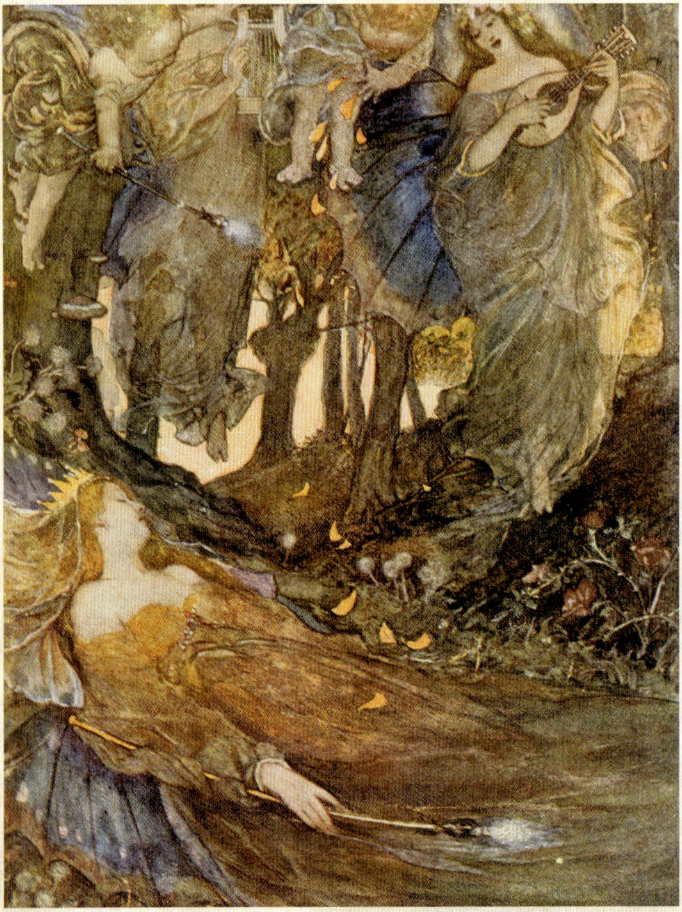

Nineteenth century illustration of Titania from *A Midsummer Night's Dream*
N.M Price

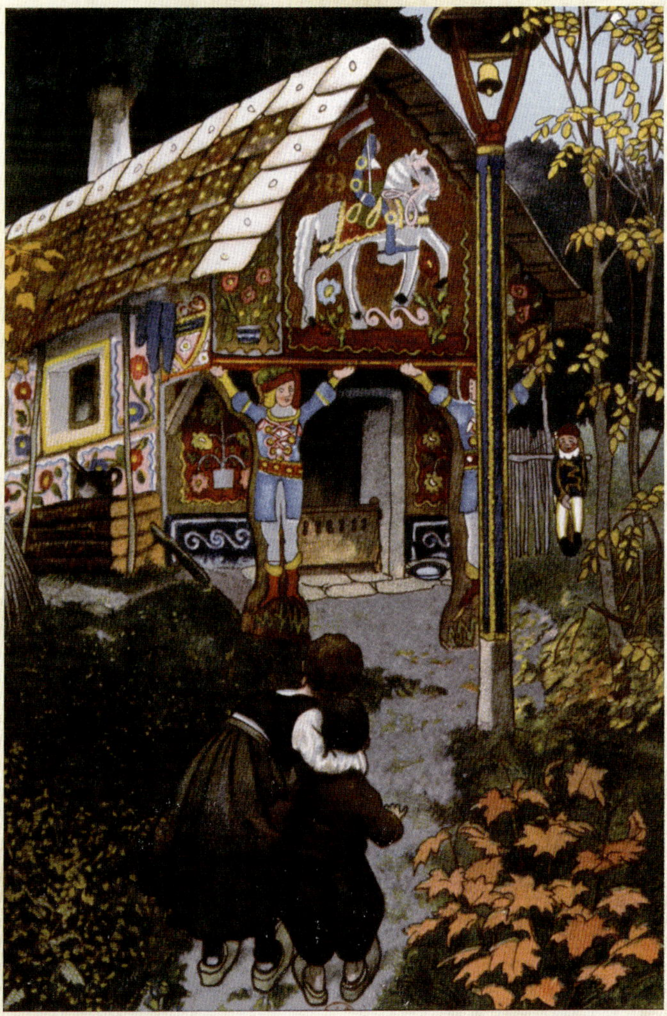

Hansel and Gretel at the witch's gingerbread house, a German illustration, c. 1900

Grimm's Fairy Tales (1812)

The Brothers Grimm first published their world famous collection of German and French fairy tales in 1812. The stories tell of strange and scary happenings, of Princes and Princesses in castles, Witches in the forests, Giants and Dwarfs, and weird and wonderful animals. The stories have been illustrated many times, adapted for movies and television, and animated. In 1969, David Hockney illustrated six of the most gruesome stories with moody descriptive drawings, including the well-known characters of Rapunzel and Rumpelstilzkin.

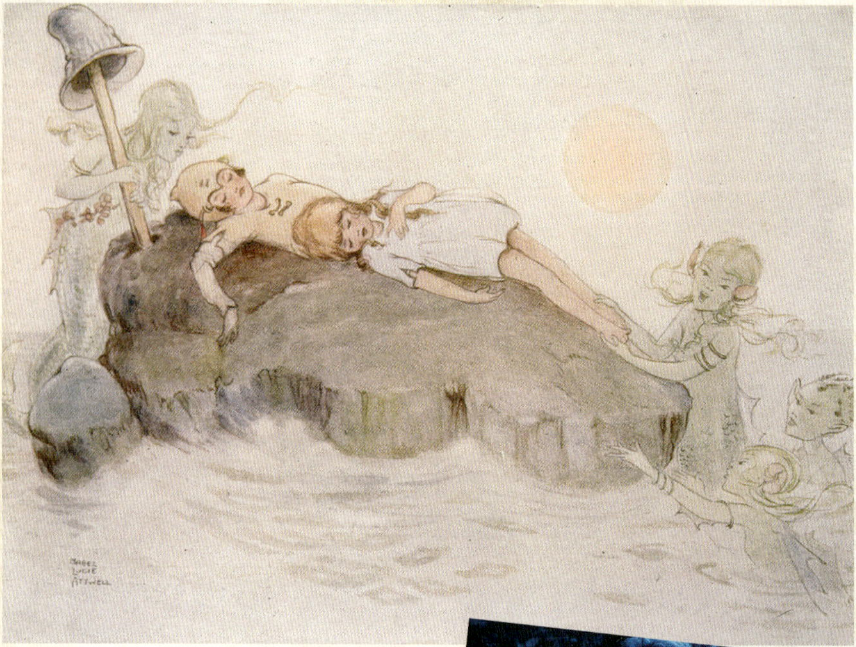

A Mermaid Caught Wendy, illustration from *Peter Pan* by J.M. Barrie
Mabel Lucie Attwell

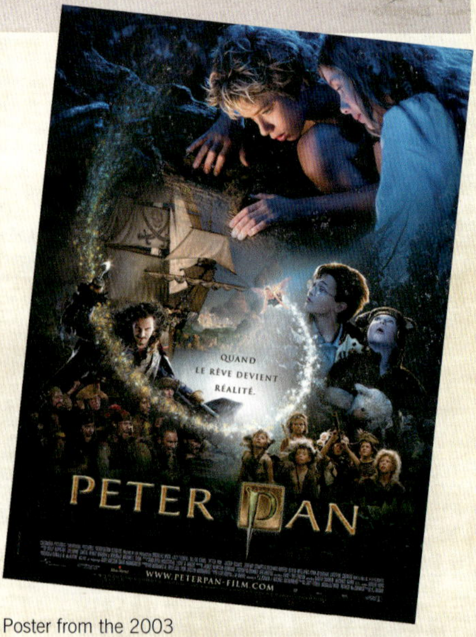

Poster from the 2003 movie *Peter Pan*, directed by P.J. Hogan

J.M. Barrie (1860–1937)

Peter Pan is another classic that has captivated children for decades, and Tinkerbell is one of the best-known fairies in the world. As Peter's sidekick, she alternates between vindictive mischief and helpful kindness, as becomes a standard in the fairy world. A sprinkling of her fairy dust enables people to fly, and she depends on our belief to survive. She has been characterized in numerous ways in illustrations and animated movies, and on stage she is often appears as a spot of bright dancing light.

Edith Nesbit (1858–1924)

Edith Nesbit is considered to be the first modern writer for children and the inventor of the children's adventure story. She wrote about real children in the real world encountering magical adventures and imaginary worlds, rather than creating out-and-out fantasies. They fly on magic carpets, travel through time, explore enchanted castles, and encounter a plague of dragons. A hundred years after their first publication, her exuberant stories have lost none of their appeal and are full of entertaining fantasy imagery.

J.R.R. Tolkein (1892–1973)

Lord of the Rings is an epic novel that has become the most influential fantasy text of all time. Men, accompanied by other humanoid beings such as Elves, Hobbits, Dwarfs, and Orcs—and numerous other creatures—populate the world of Middle Earth (many of the characters have become fantasy archetypes). The book continues to kindle works of art, music, theatre, and of course has made it to the big screen as well. It is the most fertile source of inspiration for fantasy and fairy artists.

C.S. Lewis (1898–1963)

The seven fantasy novels that make up *The Chronicles of Narnia* are a children's literary classic. Narnia is a place full of mystery and magic, where good and evil battle it out and animals talk. Traditional British and Irish fairy tales lend characters and ideas alongside beings from Greek and Roman mythology. The stories have been adapted for radio, television, stage, and screen, so there's no shortage of visual imagery to flesh out the characters.

Philip Pullman (1946–)

Pullman's trilogy of fantasy novels, *His Dark Materials* follows the adventures of two children through a series of parallel worlds. They endure truly epic events that are deeply rooted in philosophy, theology, and the spiritual. They encounter awesome adversaries, make staunch and unexpected allies, and meet witches and fairies in their journey toward enlightenment.

Susanna Clarke (1959–)

The Ladies of Grace Adieu is a recent addition to the list of essential reading for fantasy fans. This collection of dark, enchanted stories is set in fairy-ridden 19th century England. Mischievous fairies cause havoc to unsuspecting humans, who have to deal with such challenges as endless paths through sinister dark woods and houses that change their appearance without warning.

Eoin Colfer (1965–)

The *Artemis Fowl* series has taken the children's adventure world by storm. Set firmly in the modern hi-tech world, they embrace fairy magic and myth in an imaginary underworld populated with technically sophisticated Elves, Gnomes, Goblins, Trolls, and Fairies. Good combats evil in thrilling adventures and daring battles of magic and wits, and there are plenty of innovative ideas to give you a fresh look at the standard fairy genre.

Tools and materials

A WIDE VARIETY OF ART MATERIALS ARE AVAILABLE, AND MANY CAN BE PURCHASED FAIRLY CHEAPLY. TAKE TIME TO SAMPLE DIFFERENT TOOLS TO DISCOVER THOSE THAT FEEL MOST NATURAL, AND THAT BEST SUIT YOUR STYLE AND FAIRY SUBJECT.

1

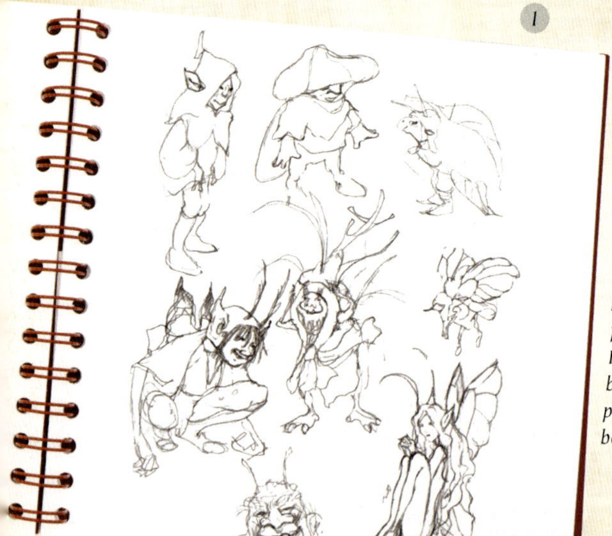

Sketchbook (1)

A serious artist is never without a sketchbook—ideas can strike at any time and need to be noted down there and then. Sketchbooks come in a bewildering array of shapes and sizes, and contain different papers to suit all media. To help you choose, get advice from other artists and your art supplier. Hard covers offer good protection; ring-bound spines open flat and provide a place to clip your pen. A pocket-sized book is easy to carry around.

2

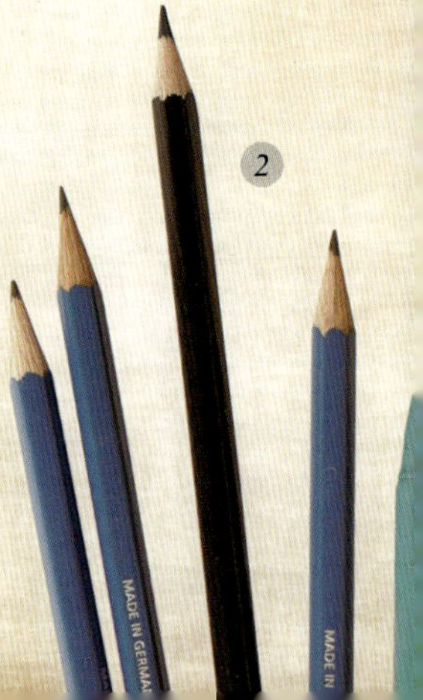

Pencils (2)

Inexpensive, adaptable, and transportable, graphite pencils are essential in an artist's toolbox. An HB pencil is a good basic choice for both rough sketches and finer details. Experiment with a range of pencil grades to see which suit you best (see pages 40–41). Mechanical pencils give a constant line weight without the need for sharpening. However, most artists prefer creating their own points to achieve different marks.

3

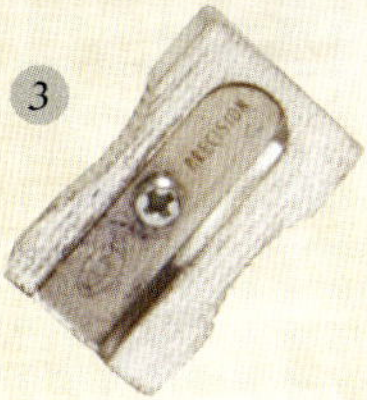

Pencil sharpener (3)

Sharpen pencils with a craft knife or scalpel to create exactly the tip you require—for safety always cut away from the body with light strokes. Pencil sharpeners give a consistent sharp point but tend to break the delicate graphite. Collect pencil shavings in a cup or container to keep your workspace clean.

4

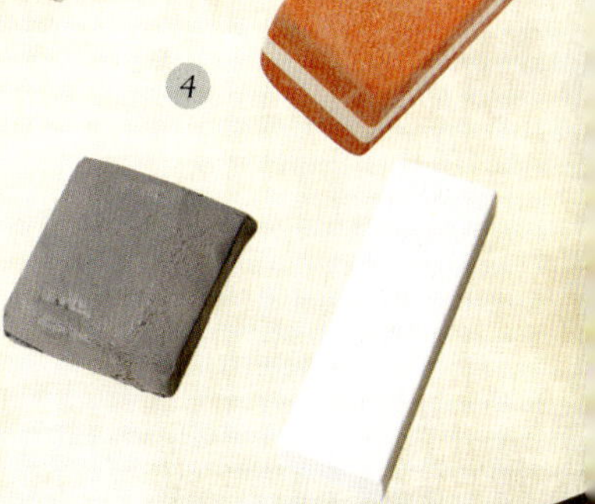

Erasers (4)

Erasers are correctives, but they can also refine pencil lines, and "draw" into shaded areas. Plastic erasers lift the most graphite, but can also damage the paper if used with excessive force; putty erasers can be molded into different shapes to correct elaborate designs. Clean your erasers regularly by cutting away dirty areas with a craft knife or rubbing on clean paper.

Watercolors (5)

Watercolors can be difficult to control, but the results are unique and spectacular, with bright, vivid colors and wonderful textures that make this the number one preferred medium for fairy artists. Paints are available in two main grades: artist's and student's colors, both of which are available in tube (good for broad washes) and pan (great for painting on location) formats. Artist's quality contain a higher proportion of pure pigment, and will yield more vibrant colors. *See page 50–51 for more on watercolor technique.*

Gouache (6)

Gouache is opaque watercolor, used to pick out special effects on wings, or to create highlights. As with watercolor, there is a wonderful array of colors to choose from, which will create a dazzling matte finish if used over watercolor or acrylic paint. Gouache, like watercolor, can be used thinly to lay washes, but it has a slightly more chalky appearance because the lighter tones contain a white pigment.

5

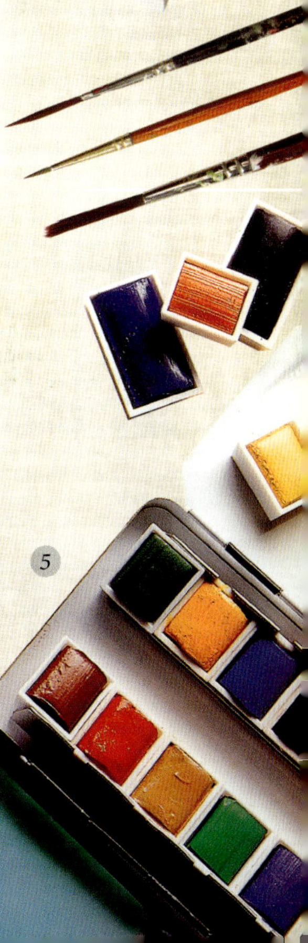

6

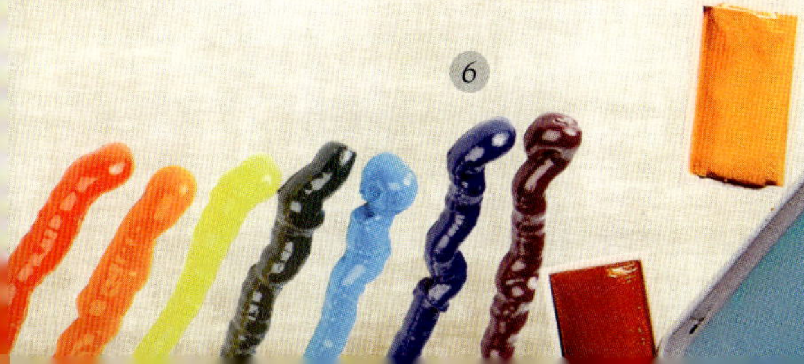

7

Colored pencils (7)

Colored pencils are a favorite among fairy artists, and their soft and subtle texture makes them an ideal medium for drawing delicate colored wing designs. They are great for beginners: fun, clean, and easy-to-use, they are an inexpensive way to introduce color to your work. Try combining with acrylic paint to add fine detail and color.

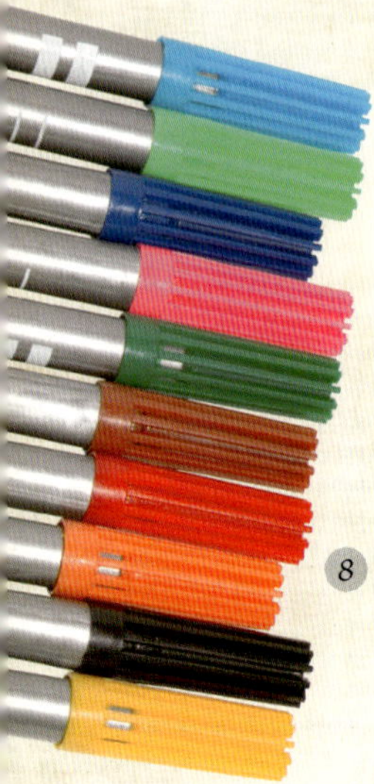

8

Markers (8)

Ink in marker pens is delivered through a porous tip of felt or nylon. It may be opaque or transparent, and tips come in various sizes and shapes. Marker pens give the artist convenient access to bright, mess-free, consistent colors, great for concept and compositional work.

Pastels (9)

Different kinds of pastels create different effects, though they can all create broad swathes of color. Soft pastels (dry and chalky) will smudge and blend easily for softly shaded effects or broad line work; hard pastels and pastel pencils are suitable for more precise marks and details; water-soluble pastels can combine line work with wash effects; oil pastels create broad lines and large, textured areas of intense color. All are highly pigmented.

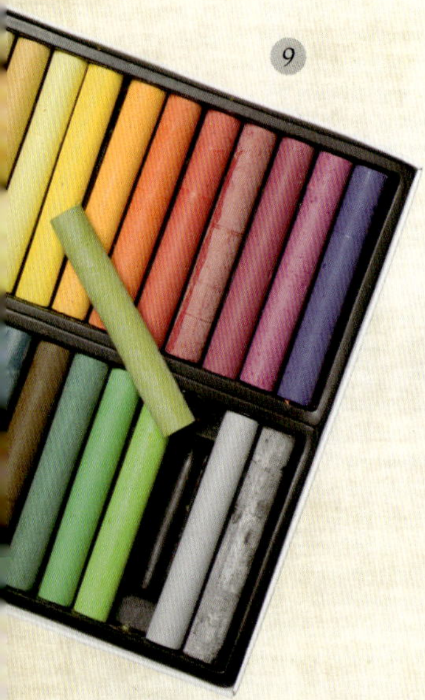

9

Acrylics (10)

Acrylic paints are bright, odorless, easily-mixed, and versatile. Although they are water-based and diluted with water, they are impermeable once dry which makes them easy to manipulate, and perfect for building up color. Retarders are available to prolong drying time, and gels can be mixed with acrylics to change their appearance.

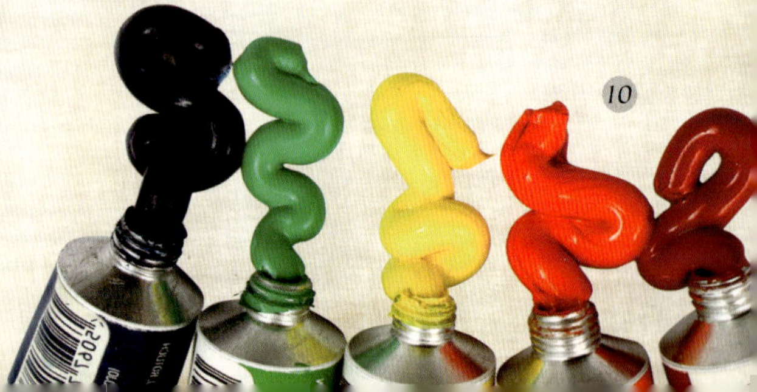

10

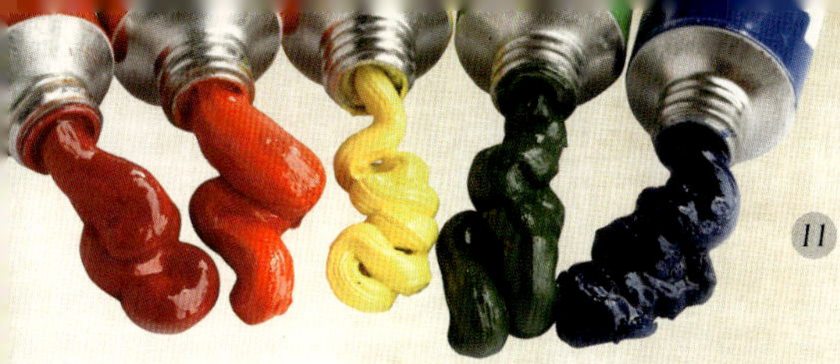

11

Oil paints (11)

Oils have a long history and are still regarded by many artists as the premier medium. However, they are expensive, require the use of toxic solvents, and are slow-drying. They are dense, heavy, and thick and tricky to manipulate successfully. Experiment with them, but you may decide that, for you, they are unsuited to the delicacy of fairy subjects.

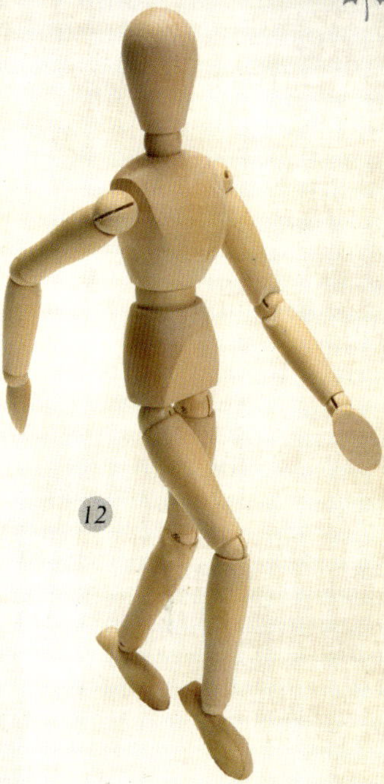

12

Mannequin (12)

Wooden mannequins can be purchased cheaply from art supply stores and are useful for experimenting with fairy poses (see pages 60–63). More expensive mannequins, showing accurate anatomical details, will help you visualize characters in three dimensions.

Airbrush (13)

A tool rather than a medium, an airbrush uses compressed air to spray paint in a fine mist. The atomized medium can be applied in thin layers, allowing very subtle gradients of color that are great for creating moody fairy landscapes. The airbrush can cover large areas quickly, but often requires masking fluid or film to achieve hard edges and protect any fine detail.

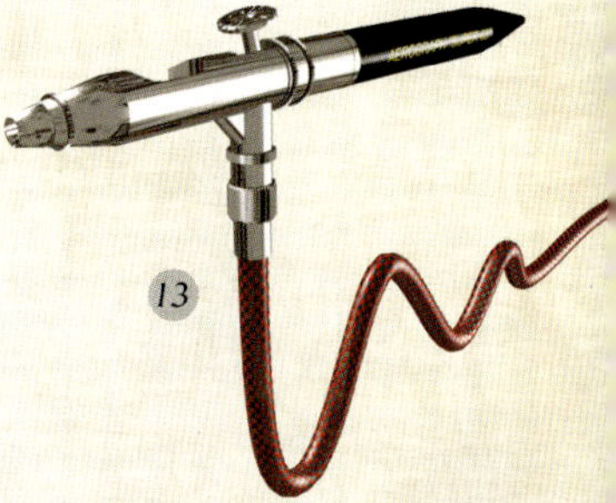

13

Camera (14)

In 1917 two girls supposedly produced photographic evidence of fairies dancing in their backyard in Cottingley in the UK. These pictures aroused much public interest but proved to be a hoax. However, a camera is an invaluable tool for collecting reference material of scenes for fairy settings or poses and faces that you might use in your work. An inexpensive digital camera is adequate for this purpose.

14

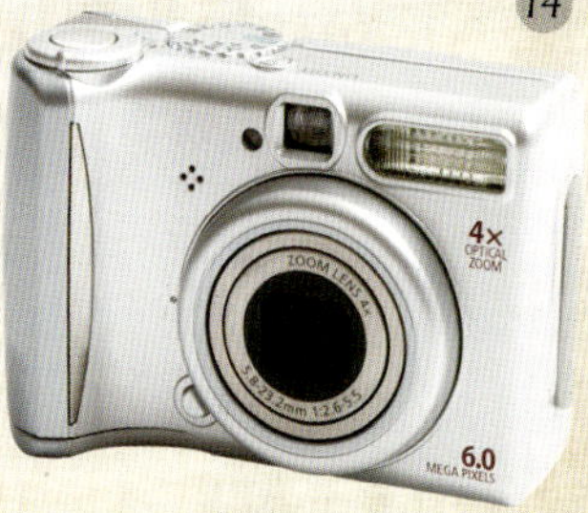

Lighting

If possible, choose a workspace with plenty of natural light. When light is poor, or at night, use an adjustable lamp fitted with a daylight bulb—this gives a more natural light that doesn't distort color values. If working digitally, make sure your screen is free from glare.

Choosing your media

WITH SO MANY MEDIA OPTIONS AVAILABLE, YOU NEED TO EXPERIMENT TO FIND WHICH ONES SUIT YOUR SUBJECT AND STYLE BEST. YOU CAN USE THEM ALONE OR CREATE EXCITING MIXED-MEDIA EFFECTS, OR COMBINE TECHNIQUES FOR EVEN MORE CREATIVE OPTIONS.

Pencil

Graphite pencils are the most versatile drawing medium of all. They are graded to produce endless variations of tone and line. Standard drawing pencils are encased in wood; thick graphite sticks are great for bold lines and large areas of tone.

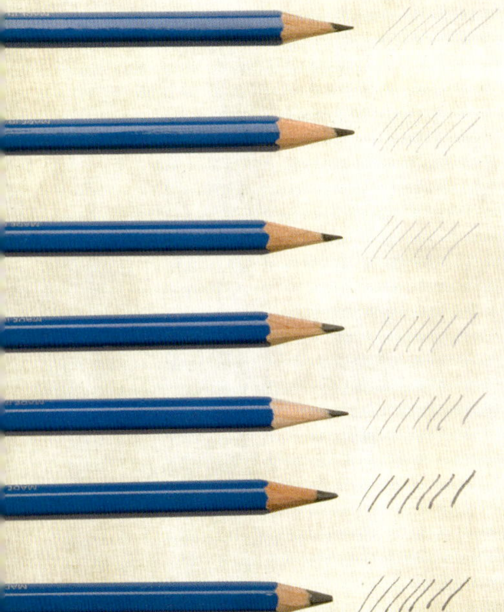

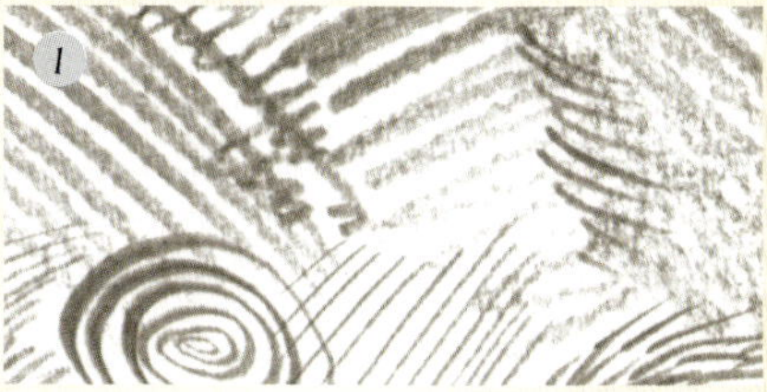

Expressive lines (1)

Cross-hatching is a standard technique for any monochrome medium. Lay hatching lines in one direction, then increase tonal depth with more lines crossing over the first set. Use the edge as well as the point of your pencil to get expression in your lines.

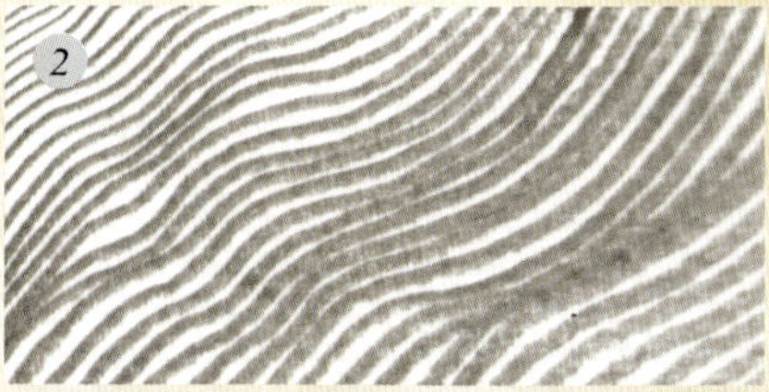

Describing three-dimensional forms (2)

This technique can feel more natural than cross-hatching. Rather than making single strokes, keep the pencil on the paper all the time, using a loose zigzagging motion. Create dark and light tones by adjusting the pressure and overlaying the marks.

3

Shading (3)

Gradations are best created using a soft pencil and starting with the darkest values. Soften the gradations even further by blending the lines with a finger. Change the tone by varying the pressure on the pencil.

4

Eraser shading (4)

You can lighten tones, create highlights, or reclaim areas by lifting out pencil marks with a kneaded eraser molded to an appropriately sized point. Use stroking or stippling motions depending on the desired effect.

5

Pencil grades (5)

You can increase the tonal range by combining different grades of pencil: hard for light areas and soft for dark ones. Lay the soft pencils over the hard ones, or use different grades for each area of a drawing.

Adding color to pencil work

Colored pencils are an ideal way to add color without paint. Some are waxy, some chalkier; both create line work and shaded effects while watercolor pencils can produce washes as well.

Blending by hatching

By using different colored pencils and making hatching strokes in a uniform direction, you can create subtle and expressive color changes and blends. As with graphite, you can vary the depth of tone by increasing the pressure on the pencil.

Rubbing

Create softly blurred effects by blending colored pencil with a cotton swab, a rolled paper stump, or a clean finger. You can burnish successive layers to create completely smooth gradations. The chalkier the colored pencil, the easier this is to do.

Water-soluble pencils

Also known as watercolor pencils, these allow you to combine watercolor techniques with line work. You can either lay down lines and then spread them with a clean, wet brush, or draw on wet paper to create blurred linear effects.

Dark pencil into light paint

Pale watercolor or acrylic washes can be worked into darker colored pencils, picking out and enhancing details and textures. You can also use light pencils over dark washes and build up layers of wash and pencil for deeper effects.

Ink

Many types of drawing pens and inks are now available, so experiment first to see how each performs—fiber-tipped and technical pens deliver a constant line, while traditional "nibbed" pens give varied lines. Some drawing inks are permanent so lines can't be erased, while colored inks add yet another dimension. These are transparent and can be overlaid on the page or mixed in a palette for different tones.

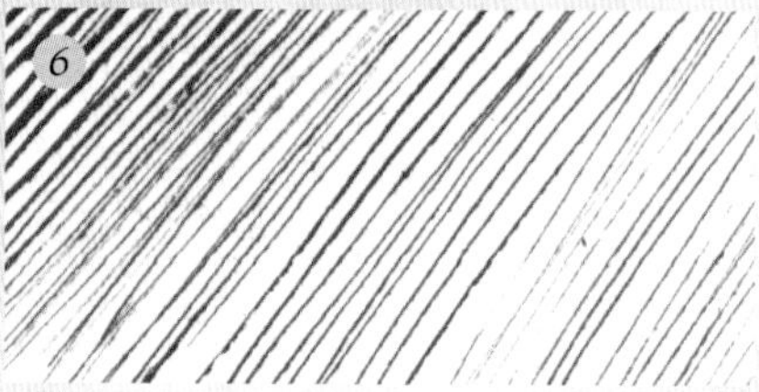

Dip pens (6)

The irregular quality of lines made with a dip pen conveys a strong sense of movement. Experiment with different textures of paper to create interesting variations in your drawings.

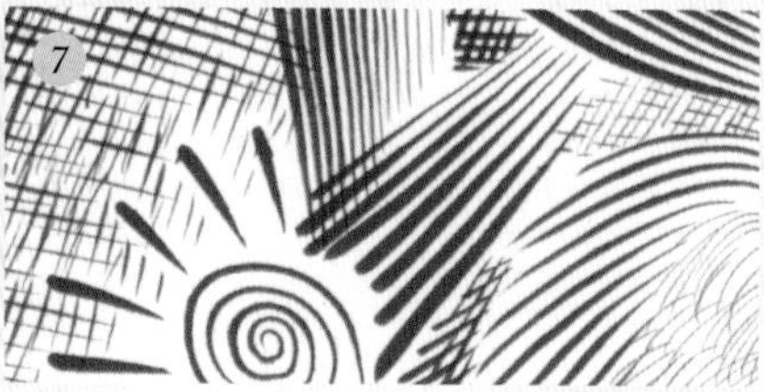

Brush and ink (7)

Drawing with a brush produces fluid lines that can be fine or broad depending on the size of the brush and weight of the stroke. Achieve light tones by "starving" the brush of ink at the end of a stroke.

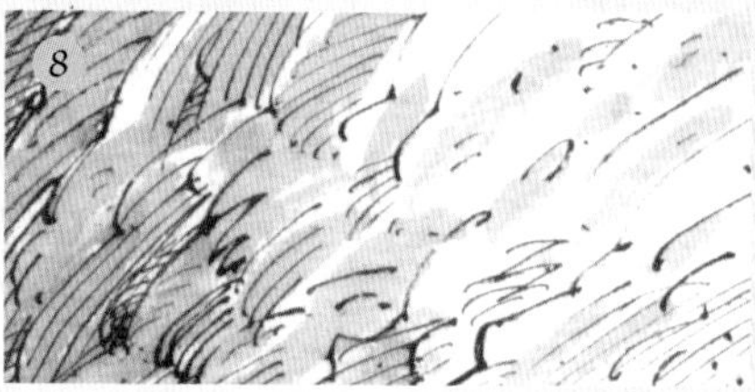

Ink and wash (8)

A full range of values can be created using waterproof ink on paper. Once it has dried, go over an ink drawing with ink washes to establish all the midtones.

Adding color to ink

You can add color to black ink outlines with colored inks, or mix media and use watercolors instead.

Line and wash

The classic technique is to draw the ink lines first and then add color to create all but the darkest shades. This can feel more spontaneous than creating a wash and drawing over it to describe shape and form.

Layering colors

Waterproof inks, including strongly pigmented acrylic ones, enable you to add successive layers of ink wet-on-dry without compromising the dry colors beneath. If you work quickly, you can blot out wet ink with a tissue for soft highlights and mottled effects.

Acrylic

Acrylic is the newest painting medium, using synthetics rather than natural oils to support the pigment. It is water-soluble, quick-drying, waterproof when dry, light fast, and can be applied to any surface. You can add mediums that thicken, thin, or texture the paint, and it can mimic both oil and watercolor in performance and effects. This is the most versatile, user-friendly, and cost-effective addition to the artist's repertoire.

Layering washes (9)

To achieve soft, watercolor-like washes, acrylic paint must first be diluted with water. Because acrylic is completely waterproof once dry, you can build up successive layers of washes to create complex color effects, working either wet-in-wet or wet-on-dry.

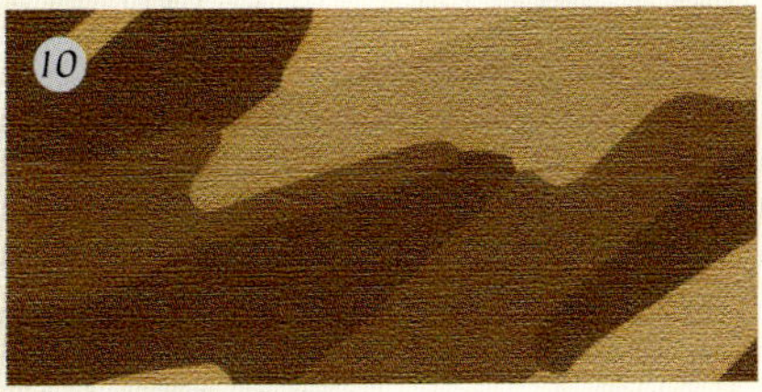

Flat wash (10)

Acrylic paint has a uniform, matte finish, and even the most opaque color will be somewhat translucent, allowing you to build up colors and values gradually in layers.

Lifting out (11)

Interesting effects can be created by lifting out color while it's drying, with paper towels, sponges, or cloth, particularly on canvas or other non-absorbent grounds.

Impasto (12)

Thick, undiluted acrylic can mimic the look of oil paint, allowing for application with a stiff brush or palette knife.

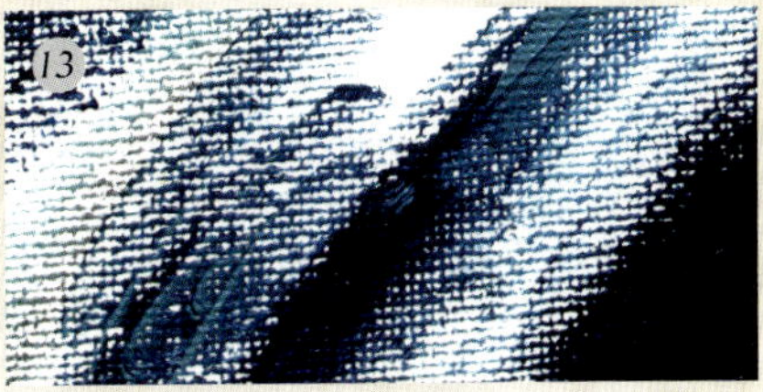

Dry brushing (13)

Wipe most of the paint off your brush with a rag; once the brush is mostly dry, drag it across the canvas. Paint will adhere to the "peaks" of the textures, allowing colors beneath to show.

Watercolor

Translucent watercolor is a popular medium for fairy subjects. It can be diluted in thin washes for delicate tonal effects, or used more thickly for solid colors and fine details. It remains water-soluble when dry, so a light touch is required—adding too many layers of paint and overworking it will muddy the colors. It can be unpredictable, but there are numerous simple techniques that create a wide range of beautiful effects.

Controlled wet-in-wet (14)

To achieve interesting and soft color transitions within one controlled area, lay the first color and then drop in more paint while still wet. It will flare out within the wet area but not onto the surrounding dry paper.

Lifting out (15)

You can create intriguing patterns by dropping a loosely crushed tissue onto wet paint. Leave it for a second to soak up the paint, then lift it off carefully.

Sponging off (16)

Patterns and textures can be created by lifting out wet paint with a dry or damp sponge. A damp sponge will give a soft pattern, while a dry sponge will create a more defined pattern.

Flat wash (17)

Uniform areas of color can be created by applying fluid color evenly to an area of your painting. Wet paper will increase your working time.

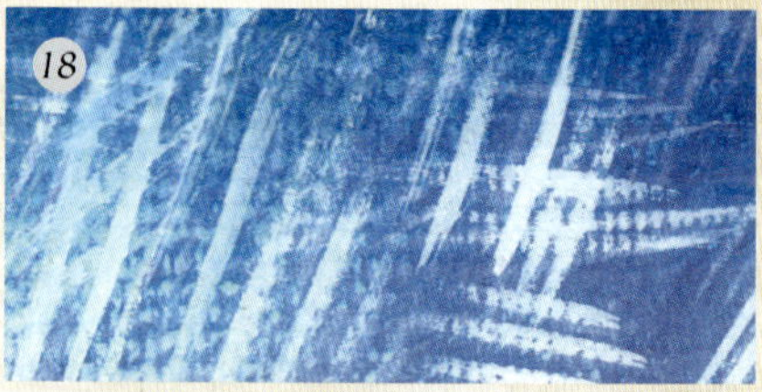

Opaque highlights (18)

Use opaque white watercolor to build up highlights over a dry watercolor wash.

See also: Basic watercolor techniques, page 50.

Glazes (19)

Applying one color over another dry color allows light to shine through both layers of color. Here, blue is consecutively applied over yellow.

Wet onto damp paper (20)

Dripping water onto semi-dry paint causes the color to "run away," creating blotches that might be ideal for rock or foliage textures or for creating atmospheric sky effects.

Graded wash (21)

On wet paper, apply paint in large, even strokes, gradually diluting the paint with water on the paper to create your gradation.

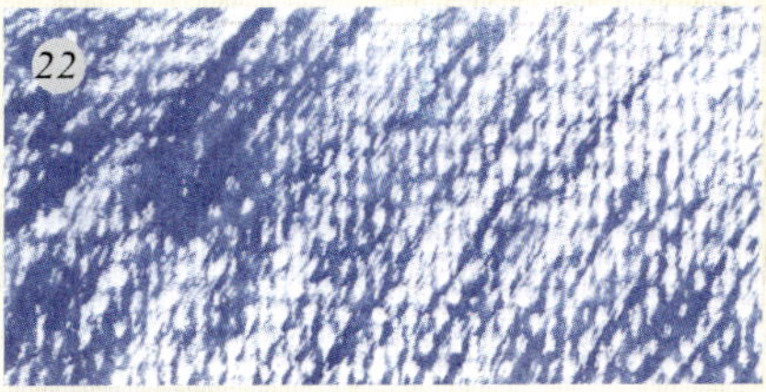

Dry brushing (22)

This method, often used for foliage, involves using very little paint on the brush and dragging it lightly over the support so that the color does not puddle or sink into the surface. It creates a broken, stippled look without disturbing the paint layers beneath it.

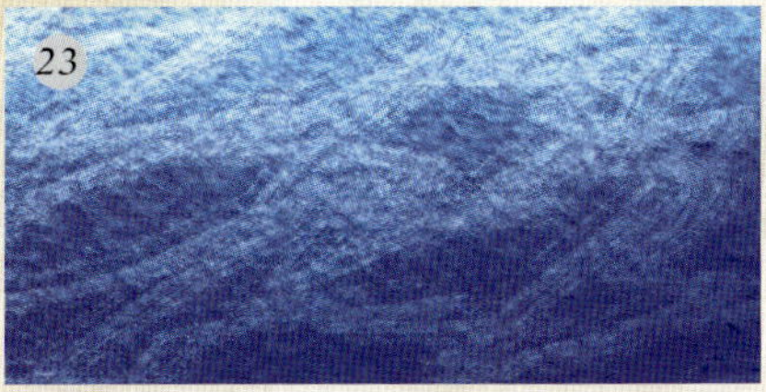

Scrubbing out (23)

Midtones and highlights can be created by scrubbing out paint once it has dried. Use clean water and a soft brush to create subtle effects, or a stiffer brush to create sharper lights.

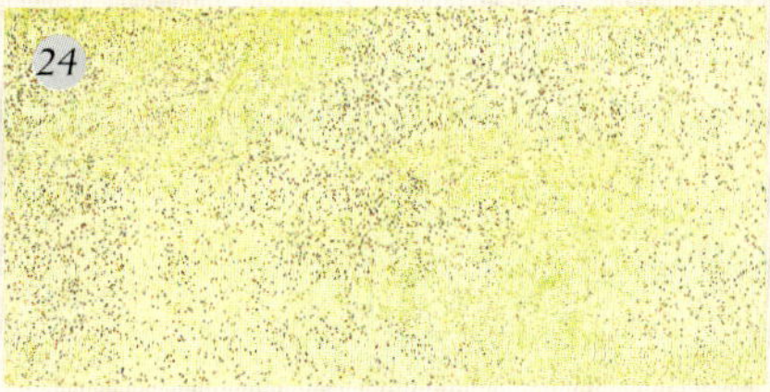

Salt wash (24)

Sprinkling salt into an area of wet paint will create interesting textures and variations in value as the salt soaks up the water. Allow the paint to dry, then brush off the salt.

Working digitally

COMPUTERS AND COMPUTER SOFTWARE OFFER A WIDE RANGE OF POWERFUL AND CONVENIENT TOOLS. IN FACT, COMPUTERS HAVE TRANSFORMED THE COMMERCIAL ART WORLD. LESS THAN A DECADE AGO, ART CREATED USING A COMPUTER WAS UNUSUAL; NOW IT IS FAST BECOMING THE STANDARD.

Many young artists find the digital environment more familiar and comfortable than traditional media. Even work created using traditional media becomes digital before publication, as most printing processes are now digital.

It is important to recognize that a computer is merely a tool, and although computer software gives access to many new ideas for the creation of art, the principles of art still apply; you must understand these if your work is to be successful, whatever medium you choose.

1

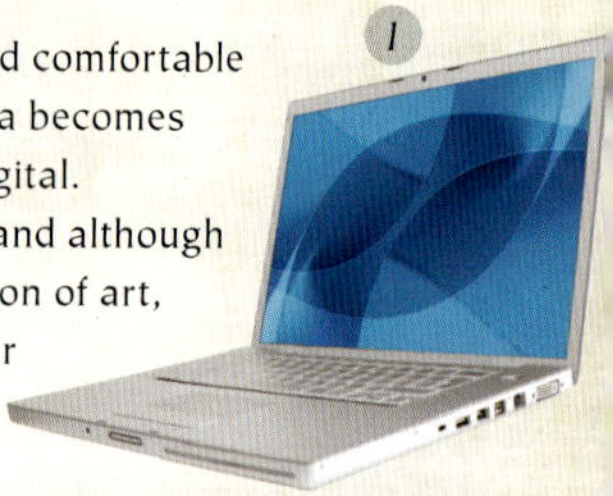

Laptop computer (1)

For artists who do not make daily use of a computer, a laptop is a good choice. It occupies a minimum of desk space, and can be put away when not in use. Their portability makes them ideal as digital sketchbooks—carry spare battery packs if you use your laptop in this way, and invest in a sturdy carrying bag with storage for extra equipment.

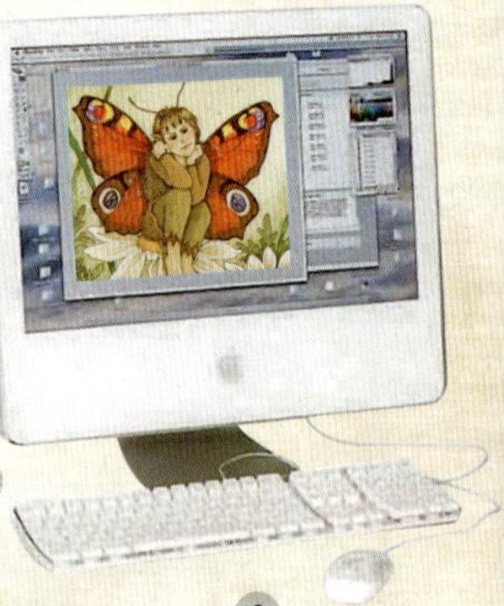

2

Desktop computer (2)

Art software is not demanding, and most modern desktop computers will happily run a painting application. A quality graphics card is important. System RAM has the greatest bearing on the performance of art packages. Look for a minimum of 1GB.

3

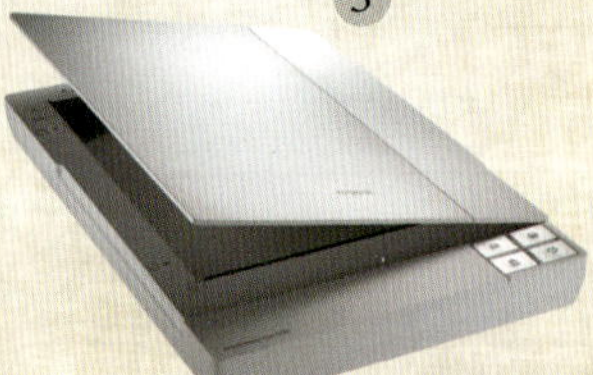

Scanner (3)

Whether you simply wish to scan pages from your sketchbook for a digital piece, or you want to digitize a finished traditional artwork to adjust it ready for print, a scanner is essential equipment for the digital artist.

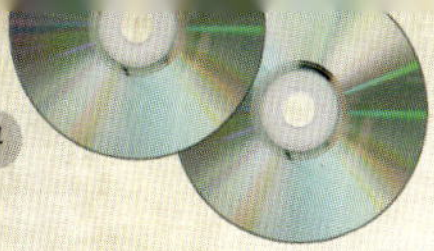

4

Monitor (not shown)

Your monitor is the interface between you and your art. Choose the best quality display you can. CRT displays offer the best level of contrast, but LCD panels take up less space. Check that your display is properly calibrated to ensure colors are displayed accurately.

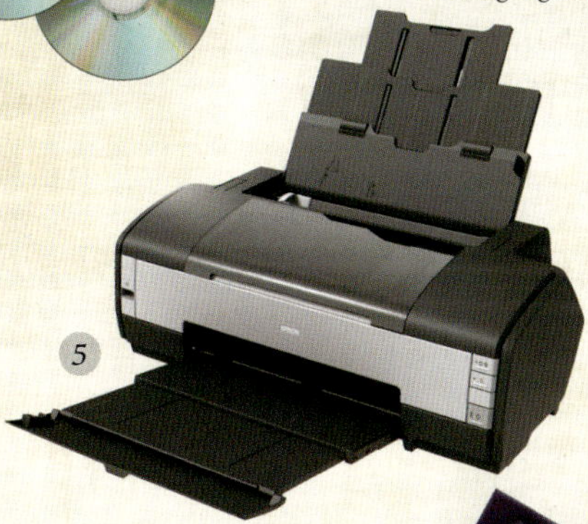

5

Organization (not shown)

Many files may be created during the production of a digital artwork. Organize your files carefully to avoid losing or accidentally deleting important data. Keep a consistent folder structure and use a sensible naming convention for your files so that your work can be easily identified.

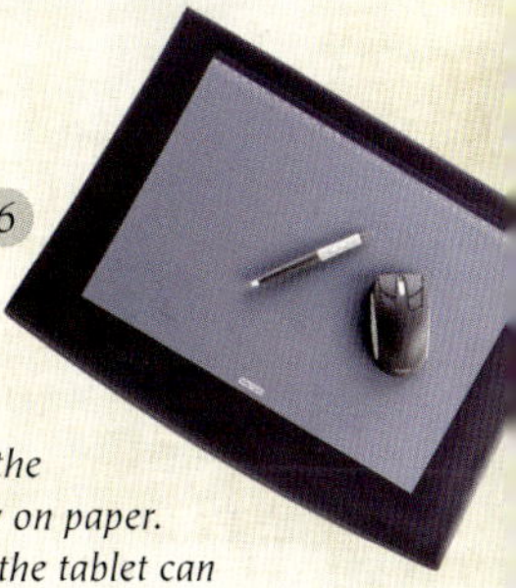

6

Security (4)

Make frequent backups of your digital work and store them safely. Ensure you have up-to-date antivirus software installed.

Printer (5)

Good quality inkjet photo printers can be purchased cheaply. Experiment with different papers to get results you like. If you intend to sell prints of your work, you may find professional reproduction more economical.

Graphics tablet (6)

Use a stylus (or "pen") to draw on a graphics tablet in the same way as you would draw on paper. Depending on the hardware, the tablet can read pressure, angle, rotation, and other parameters from the stylus and feed this information to the art software. Tablets are available in a variety of sizes. Hardware is also available that integrates this technology with a flat-panel display, allowing the user to draw directly onto the screen.

Programs and software

There's plenty of digital art software available to the digital fairy artist. *Photoshop* is the longest-established and best-known, but *Corel Painter, Paint Shop Pro, ArtRage,* and *Autodesk Sketchbook Pro* are equally good applications. Consult their websites, or talk to a store manager to find the program that's best for you.

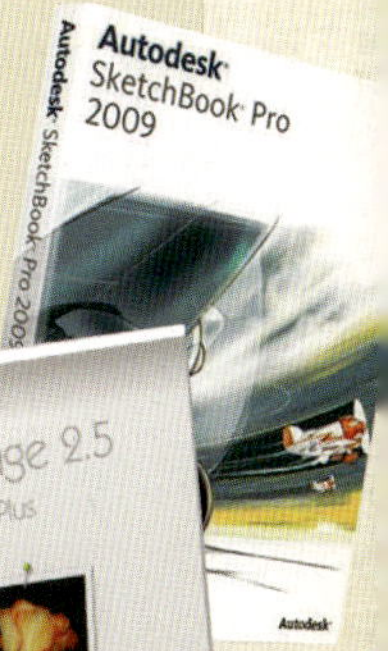

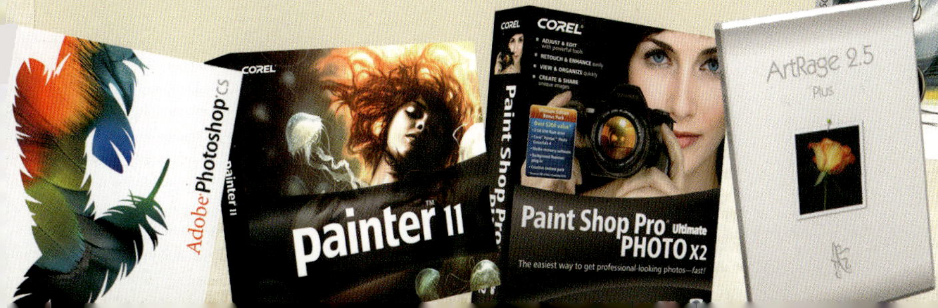

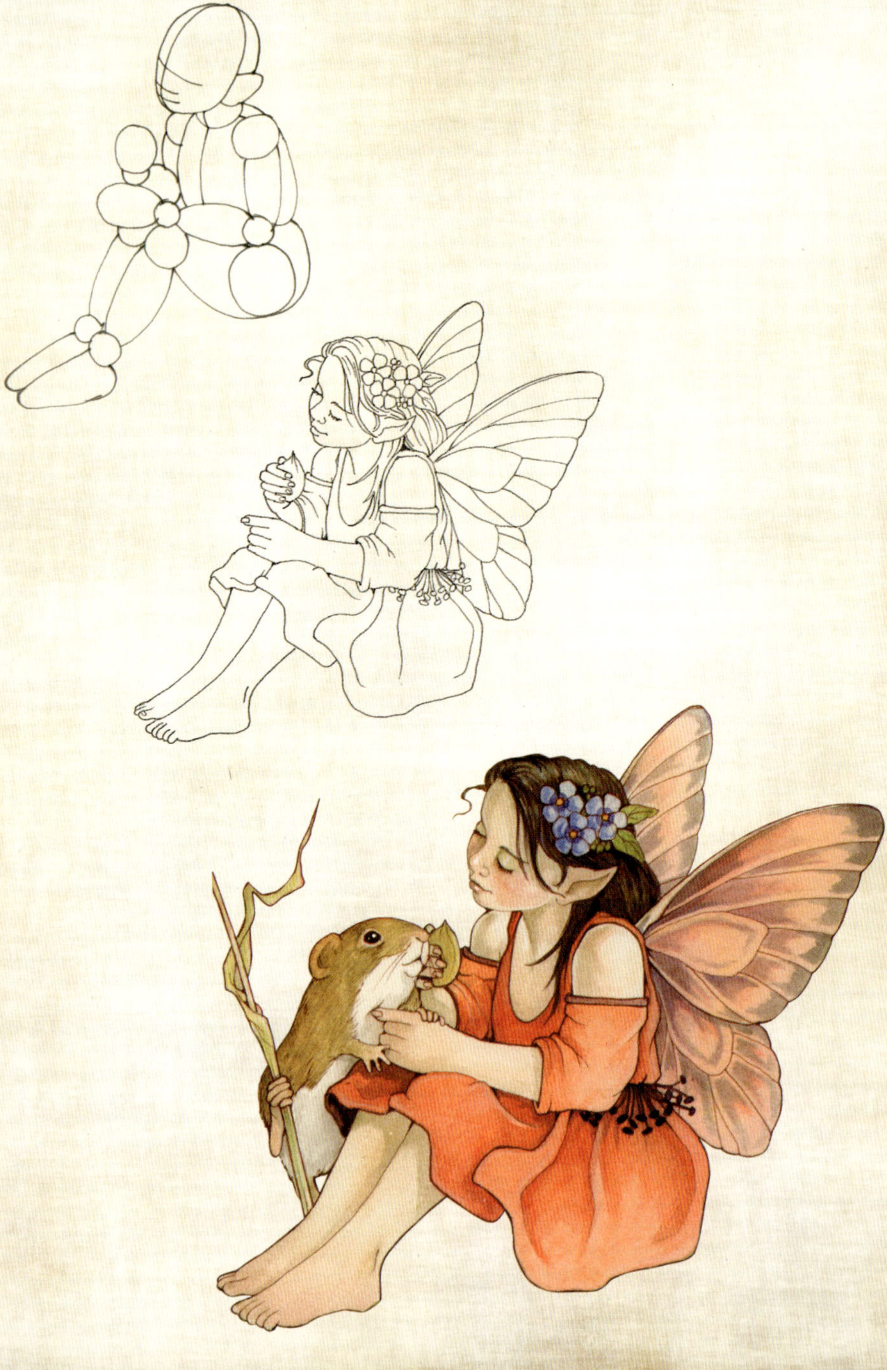

Part 2

From sketch to finished picture

The journey from initial sketch to fully resolved original painting takes in many considerations and crucial decisions. The following pages will help you to understand the importance of composition, color, and tone; to collect ideas and use them effectively to design your character; and to render the finished painting in carefully planned stages for an image that will inform and entertain your audience.

Storytelling

FAIRIES AND FAIRYLAND ARE ELUSIVE AND INVISIBLE CONCEPTS ROOTED IN ANCIENT MYTHS AND LEGENDS. AS A FAIRY ARTIST, THIS MEANS THAT YOU ARE AT LIBERTY TO EXERCISE YOUR CREATIVE IMAGINATION AND POPULATE YOUR FAIRY WORLD WITH FIGURES ENTIRELY OF YOUR OWN INVENTION.

Drawing something that can't be seen presents a unique challenge, and to really "speak" to your audience your fairies must appear to be utterly credible, living and breathing creatures. Your starting point must be reality, and from there your mythical concepts can blossom into enchanting and believable characters.

Using nature

Nature will provide you with all the raw material you'll need to create not only convincing fairy characters but also their worlds. Look at insects, butterflies, birds, flowers, and trees. Examine hedgerows, fields, and woodlands. Sketch from life or photos, and keep a scrapbook of magazine cuttings and "found" items. You'll build a precious personal reference library filled with whatever inspires you.

Make a record of anything that catches your eye, from a single item to a complete setting. Filled with information, your sketchbook will be a constant source of inspiration and ideas.

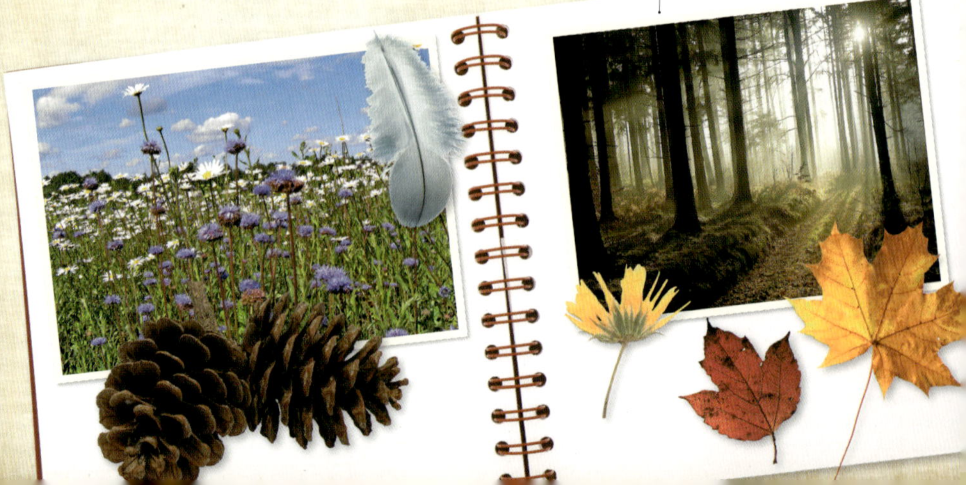

Visual language

While writers use words, artists communicate with a rich and varied visual language. Consider, for example, the connection between color and mood, and the different messages conveyed by flowing lines and angular staccato marks. Facial expressions, body language, and the interaction between characters speak volumes. These all provide visual signals that are universally understood and influence your viewer's response.

Avoid stereotype

Composition, color, technique, style, medium, shape, movement, and pose all work together to create a narrative in this atmospheric painting by Patricia Ann Lewis-MacDougall. Harness these tools to engage your audience in the story, but consider carefully and make sure the language you use conveys the right messages. Try to be original—simply reproducing the archetypal fairy may produce bland images.

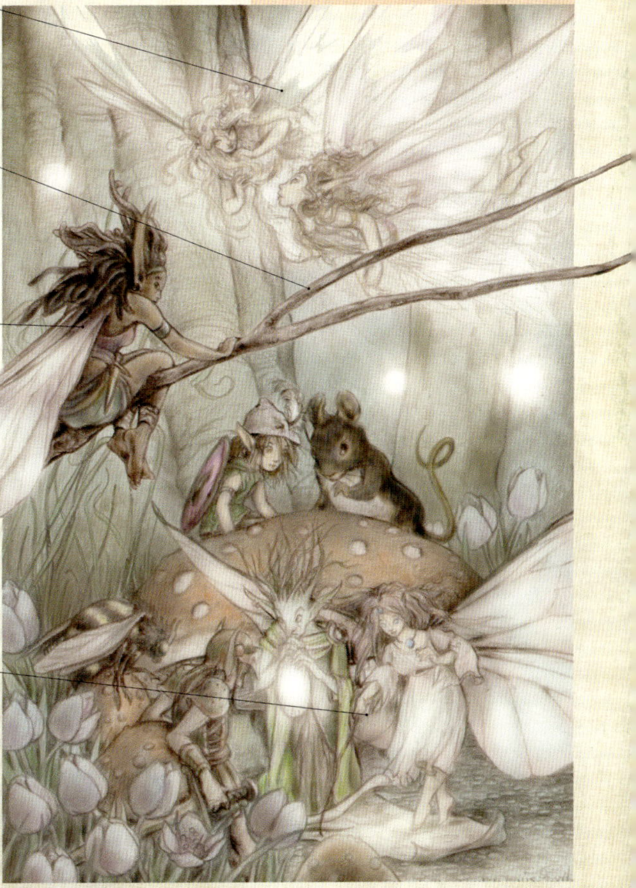

If the gaze wanders upward, two pale ethereal creatures deep in conversation return us to the unfolding story below.

Here the artist bisects the picture area to focus the eye on the foreground activity. Stronger colors and careful detail make the eye linger here to "read" the narrative.

This character turns her back to the audience. Her silhouette acts as a full stop, preventing the eye from wandering offstage left. She glances over her shoulder, aware of us, the audience, behind her but directs our eyes back down to the main focus of the composition.

The artist has used the conventions of winged folk but these are no pretty fairy stereotypes. They are an intriguing, slightly disturbing group of characters that appear to be engaged in important business. As such, they hold the interest and invite further study to unlock their story.

Copying your image

THE FOLLOWING TECHNIQUES ARE INVALUABLE IF YOU WISH TO COPY THE FAIRY TEMPLATES IN THE CHARACTER DIRECTORY.

Making an exact copy with graphite paper

This is a nice, easy method of transferring your traced images onto paper. It will create an almost exact copy of the image you wish to reproduce, though in order to achieve the best results remember to draw over your lines as accurately as possible, and keep an eye on the drawing as you progress, just to make sure that you have all the lines traced out.

You will need:

- Good quality tracing paper
- Ready-coated graphite paper. If you can't find this, make your own. Take a piece of copier paper and rub an HB graphite stick all over one side so it is coated with powder. Re-coat it after each use for clear copies.
- Masking paper
- HB and 4H pencils
- Low-tack masking tape
- Drawing paper

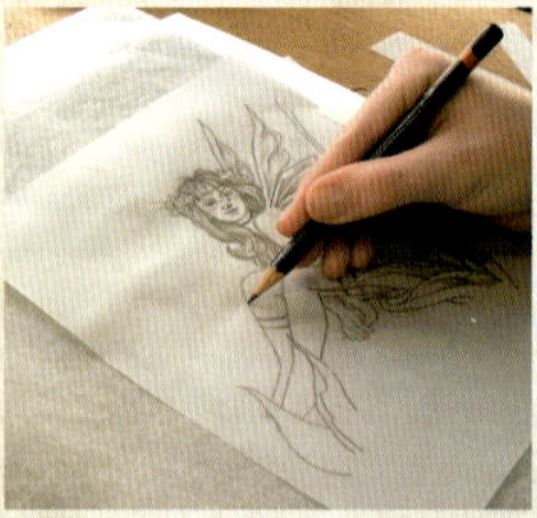

1 Secure the image. Place the graphite sheet under the tracing paper and, with a sharp 4H pencil, draw over the original. If the graphite messes up the paper beneath, erase any fogging when the tracing is complete.

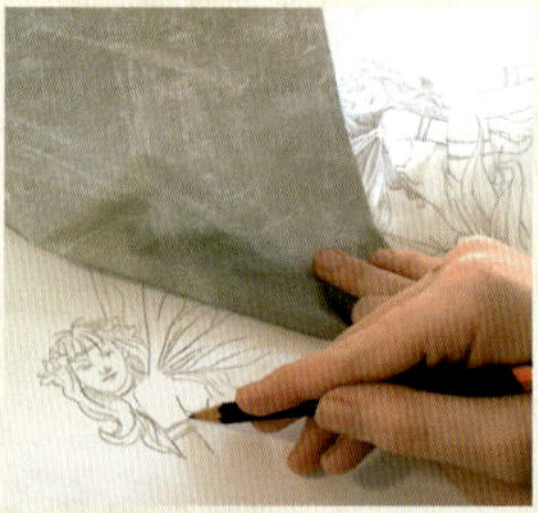

2 Remember to lift the sheets to check your work every so often as you progress. If the image is very faint, it might help to go over some of the lines while you still have the paper secured.

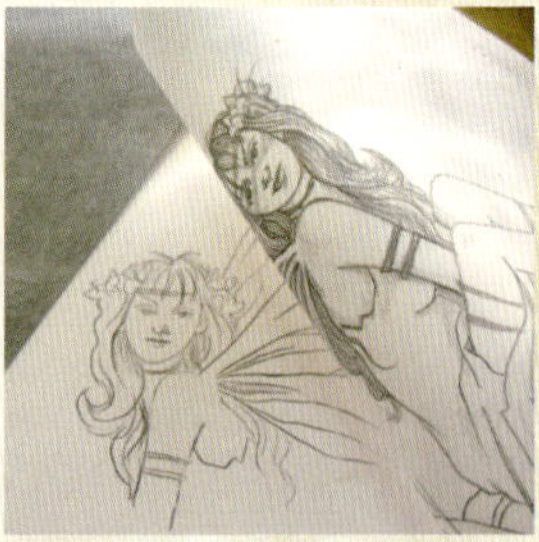

3 Here you can see how the image appears on your drawing board. The copy should be almost the same as the original. When you are happy with your image, carefully remove the tracing sheet and graphite paper.

Using a grid

A grid is a handy way to reproduce images that you want to enlarge or reduce. Of course you can also use it to create same-size copies.

1 Onto an acetate sheet, using a ruler and fine-line pen, draw a grid of 1-inch (2.5-cm) squares large enough to cover the picture you want to reproduce.

2 Secure the picture to a piece of paper or cardboard with small pieces of masking tape. Lay the acetate grid over it and secure that in place, too.

3 On your drawing paper, use an HB pencil to draw a faint grid with the same number of squares. For a same-size copy use the same size squares. To enlarge the image use bigger squares, and to reduce it use smaller squares.

4 Now copy the information in each square, one square at a time. Concentrate and work slowly and you will end up with an accurate facsimile of the original. As long as your grid lines are very faint they will be covered later by your paint. Any that remain outside the picture area can be erased carefully when the painting is complete.

You will need:

- Sheet of clear acetate large enough to cover the image and overlap a little on each of the sides
- Permanent, fine-line pen
- Ruler
- HB pencil
- Drawing paper
- Spare sheet of paper
- Low-tack masking tape

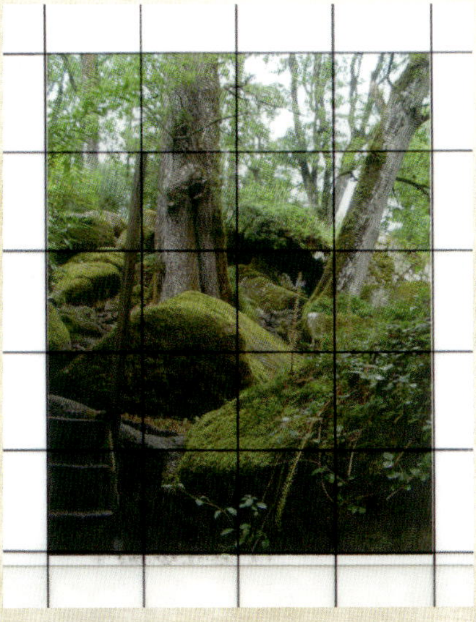

Photograph with an acetate grid

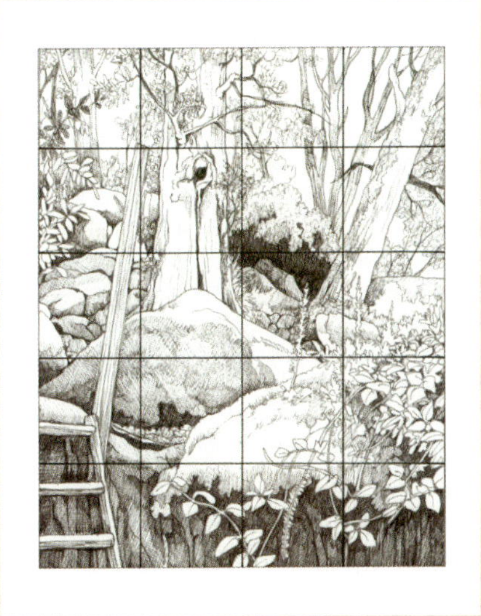

Pencil sketch extrapolated from the gridded photograph

Composition

COMPOSITION IS THE BALANCED ORGANIZATION OF THE ELEMENTS WITHIN A PICTURE AREA. YOU SHOULD ARRANGE THE SHAPES TO LEAD THE EYE AROUND THE IMAGE AND BRING THE ATTENTION OF THE VIEWER TO THE FOCAL POINT.

For every image there are many compositional options to consider. You must choose the shape or "format" and decide on the main focus. You must decide what other elements to include, and where to place them effectively so they lead the eye in the right direction. Your composition must be energetic and balanced. A series of thumbnail sketches will help you to explore all the options and make your final choices.

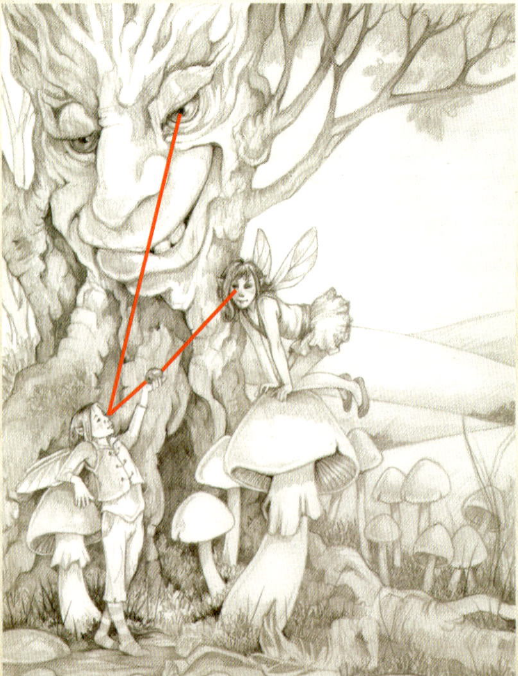

This dynamic composition keeps the viewer involved. The eye, led by the empty space, is drawn first to the tree face, following its glance down to the Elf. From there the gaze travels up his arm to the apple, and on to the fairy—and begins the circular journey once again. Within the composition there are several cropping opportunities for different, equally successful images—as shown by the examples opposite.

CENTRALLY PLACED FOCAL POINTS

Balance is essential in a composition. This is most easily achieved by placing the focal point centrally. However, perfect balance can be static and unexciting as the eye always wants somewhere to go. In this instance the central figure reaches upward. The eye doesn't wander off but follows the backward-leaning arc of his body, and remains engaged with the story.

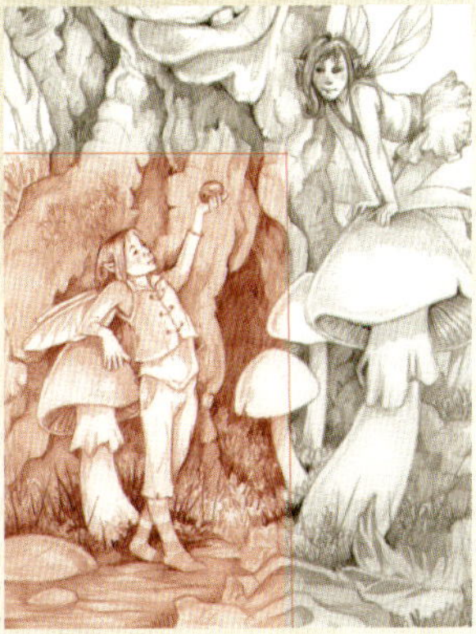

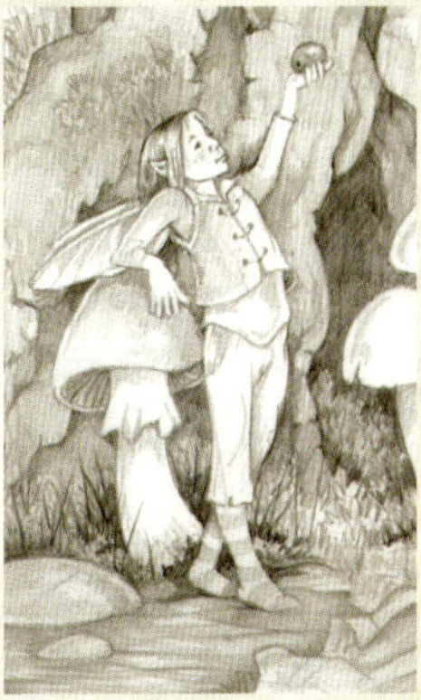

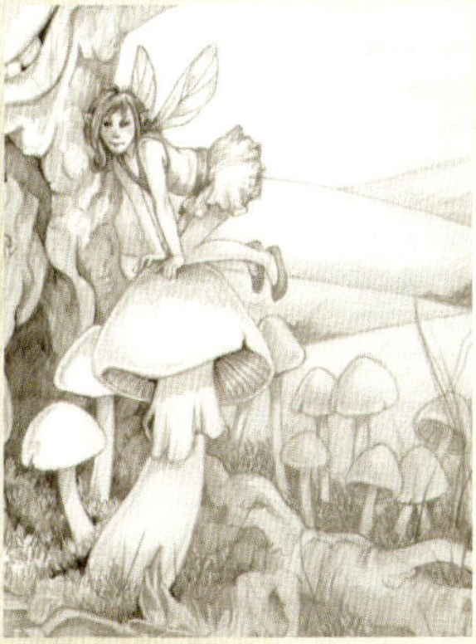

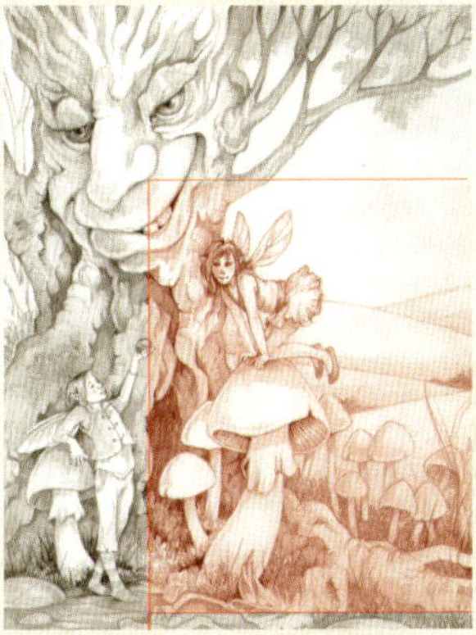

OFFSET COMPOSITION

Placing elements off-center creates energy and movement within a composition. Here a small part of the whole image is cropped to create a similar offset composition. The fairy's gaze invites the viewer in to explore her home, while the distant landscape offers an intriguing sense of a world beyond the borders of the image.

READING YOUR COMPOSITION

In a composition, strong lines act as a map to guide the viewer's eye around the image. Used effectively they enable the viewer to "read" the story, manipulating the gaze toward focal points, and preventing it from wandering out of the picture area. Here the lines of the large toadstool, the crouching fairy, and the standing Pixie create a continuous oval that keeps the eye moving.

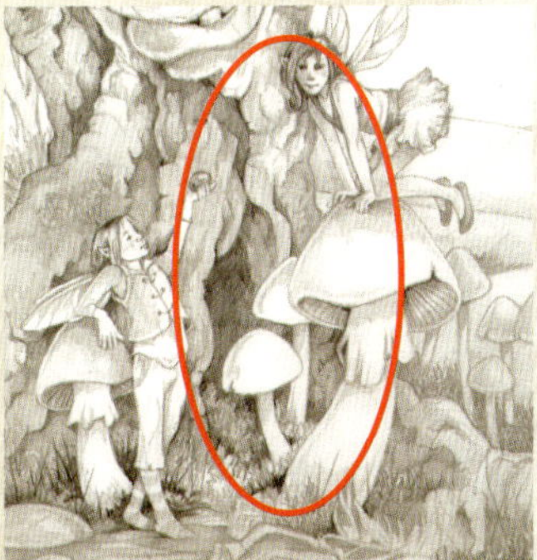

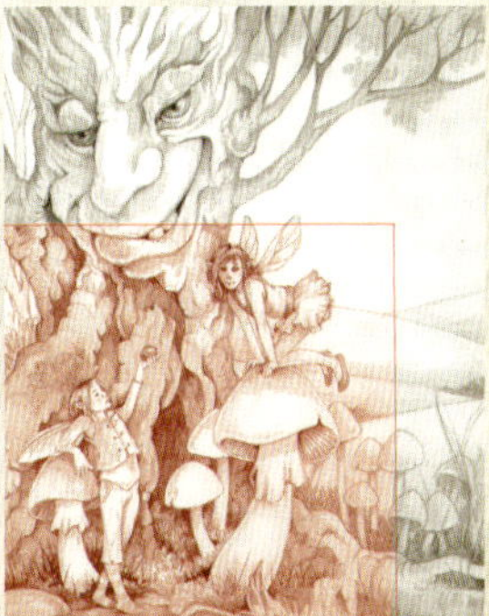

Sketching

WITH THE COMPOSITION DECIDED, YOU SHOULD BEGIN TO SKETCH. REFINE THE COMPOSITION, MAKE SENSE OF ANY ABSTRACT SHAPES, AND ADD SIGNIFICANT DETAILS.

Sketching the figure

Pose a mannequin to sketch out your image or copy photographs, splitting the anatomy into simple shapes before fleshing them out.

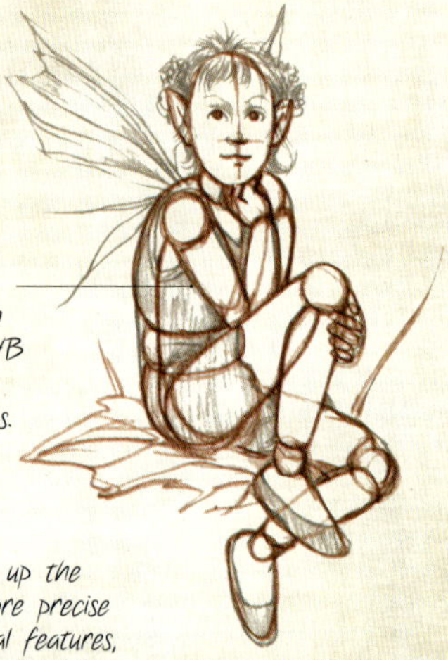

1 Represent the figure with simple shapes first. Here these are shown in red for clarity. In reality, use an HB pencil lightly so the underlying shapes will be hidden as your sketch develops. Suggest the wings, face, and hair.

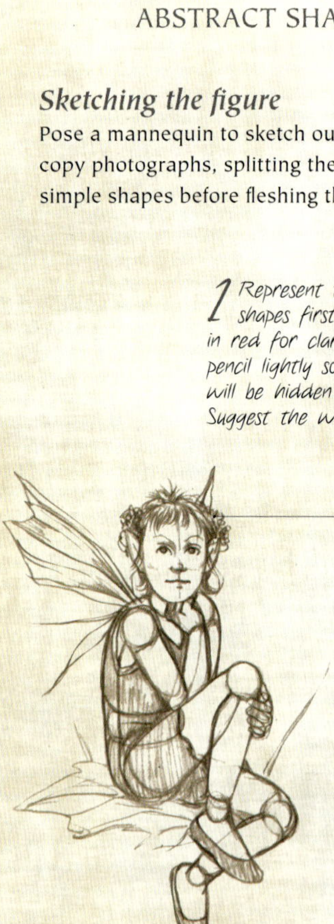

2 Continue working up the figure, adding more precise character to the facial features, darkening the hair, and adding detail to the wings. Work on the clothes, making sure they drape over the body to indicate the three-dimensional forms beneath.

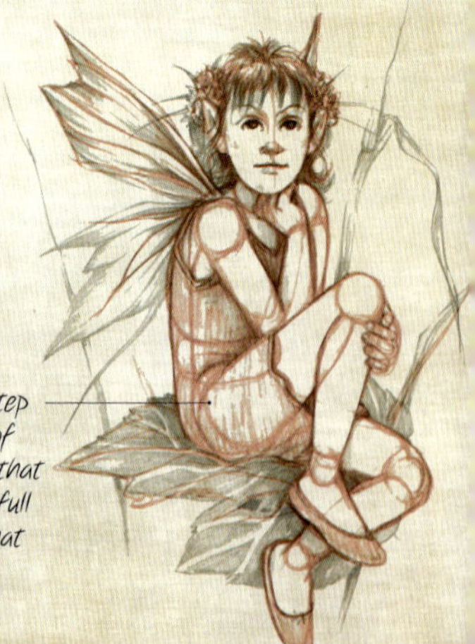

3 Here the initial sketch in step 1 overlays the next stage of the drawing in step 2. Notice that the developing drawing makes full use of the underlying shapes that were the starting point for constructing the figure.

Choosing your materials

Softer pencils allow you to build up tone as well as line, and can be used either over or under watercolor washes to add texture and depth, perhaps on the body or wings of the fairy, or on additional features such as trees, toadstools, and various other accents and accessories from fairyland. Harder pencils are best for intricate design features—for example, a woven basket, the bark of a tree, or a complex facial expression or wing construction.

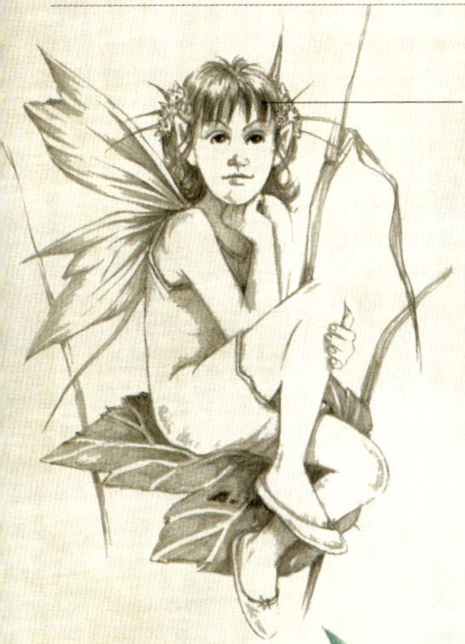

4 Now that everything is well established, continue with the HB pencil adding sensitive shading to round out the forms of the face and body and describe the wings and leaf. These significant details begin to bring the fairy to life.

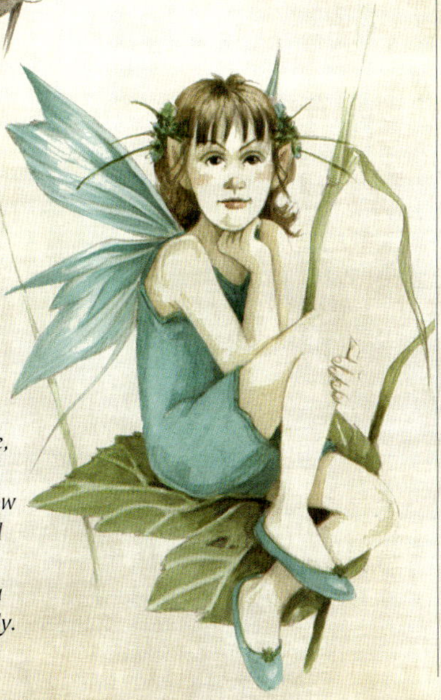

Sketching with color

At this stage you can use your sketch to explore the color palette you want to use, adding light washes to your drawing to see how they "read." The pencil shading beneath adds tonal depth to help you plan your finished study.

Grades of pencil

Pencils are made in different grades, and are marked with a number and letter classification, with "B" standing for black and "H" standing for hard. The higher the number, the harder or softer the pencil, with 9B being very soft, and 9H being very hard indeed.

1. Medium soft pencil (2B)

For sketching and trying out ideas, a 2B pencil is ideal, as it combines flexibility with a sympathetic, soft mark. You will find it too dark for preliminary drawings for paintings, as the pencil marks will show through the paint.

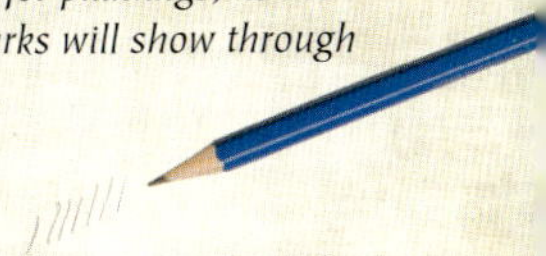

2. Soft pencil (6B)

A 6B pencil is ideal for making really dark marks and building up solid areas of near-black. It smudges easily, so keep your hand off your drawing or protect it with a piece of spare paper.

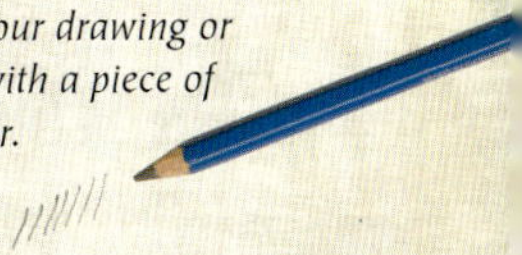

3. HB pencil

An HB pencil is a good all-around drawing tool. It is soft enough for initial light sketches and composition planning as marks are easily erased. It creates a wide range of shaded tones for initial sketches and it is also hard enough to retain a point for drawing finer details such as face and hair.

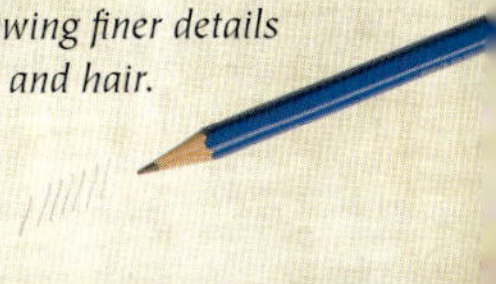

Understanding value

THE NEXT STEP IS TO ESTABLISH THE ARTWORK'S VALUES. VALUE—ALSO REFERRED TO AS TONE—DEFINES FORM, SEPARATES SHAPES AND PLANES, IMPARTS DEPTH, AND CONTROLS FOCUS; THESE ARE ALL ESSENTIAL ELEMENTS IN THE CONSTRUCTION OF A SUCCESSFUL IMAGE.

Value contrasts

In a composition, value contrasts control the viewer's gaze. Areas of high tonal contrast draw the eye first—think of a bright moon in a dark sky. In an image with a constant tonal value (such as a dark wood with minimal light) the elements will blend and lack focus. So reserve the highest value contrasts for the most important elements in the design to create a focal point.

In addition, darker values recede and bright values advance. Thus, values that darken toward the background will create a sense of recession and depth, throwing out a lighter figure. Remember, though, that strong tonal contrasts suggest bright light, while more subtle values indicate diffused light—think of the difference between a sunny day and a dull cloudy one.

Background tonal values

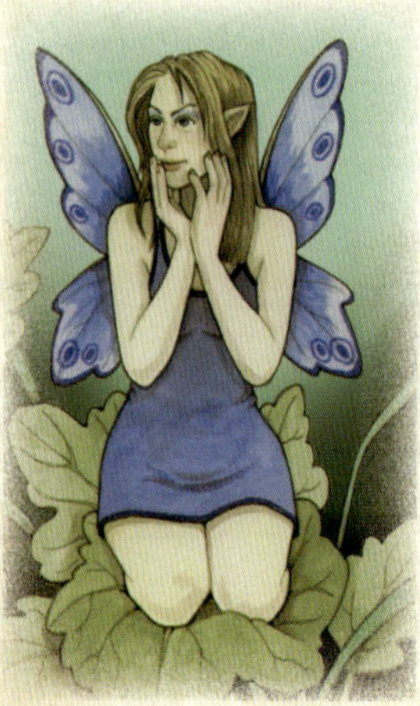

High value contrast
The high value contrast between the fairy and the background separates the two planes in the image and the outline of the figure is easy to read.

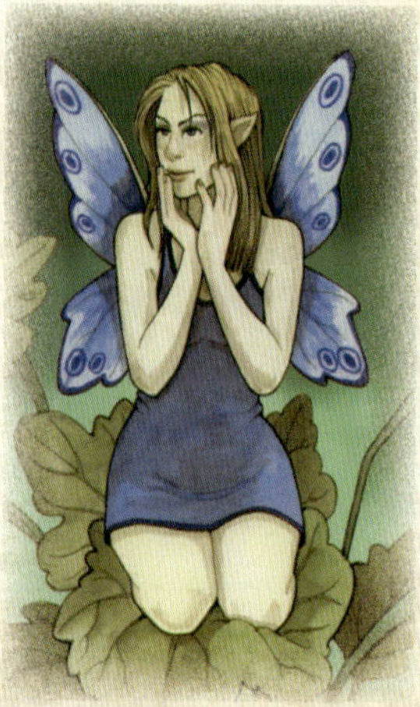

Low value contrast
Here the figure and background share the same value and merge into a single plane in spite of the color difference. The outline of the figure is less obvious.

Establishing a light source

Value is governed by the direction and intensity of the light. Many artists find it helpful to make a purely tonal study before adding color to pinpoint the light source.

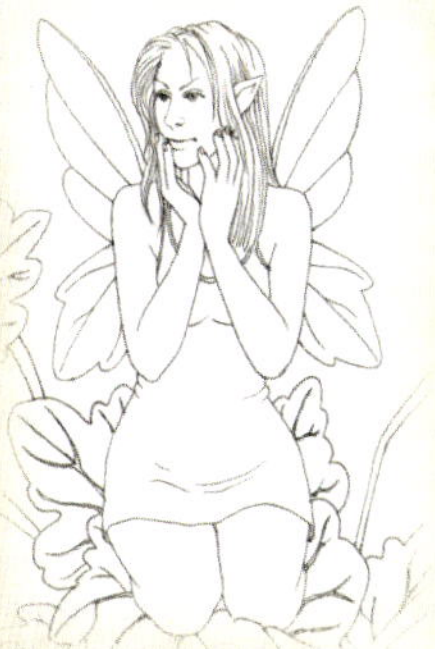

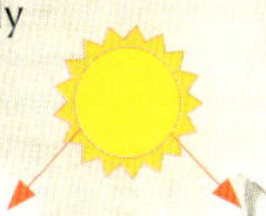

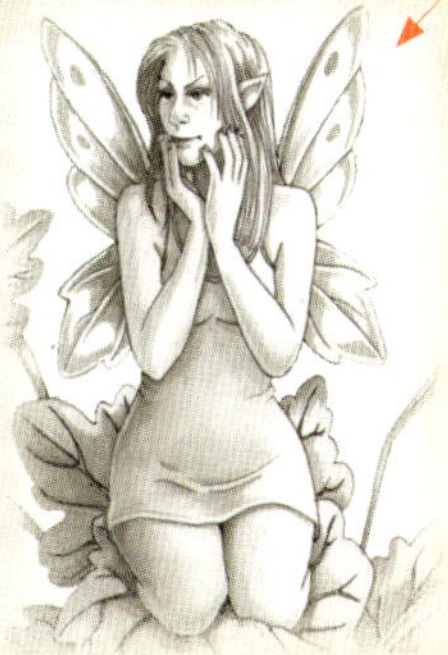

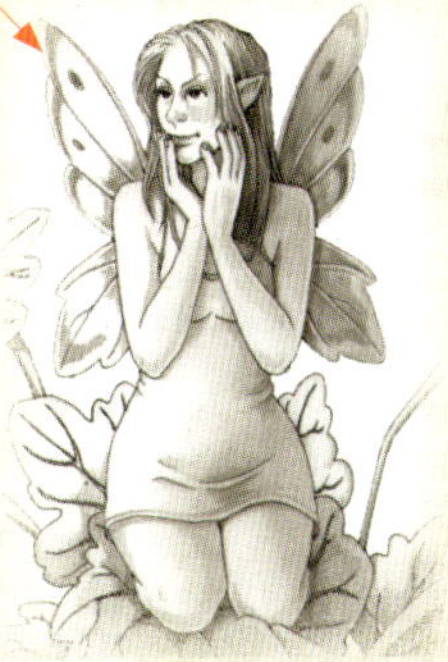

Drawn in line only, the figure looks flat, and there is little sense of form and space.

Shading the darker values rounds out the figure creating a sense of volume. The high right light source casts deepest values on the left side of the figure.

Here the light comes from the left, so the right-hand side of the figure is deepest in value. The figure's shadow falls to the right on the leaf.

Seeing tone as color

With the values established it's easier to translate tone into color. Every color has a value—darker values of a color are called shades; lighter values are known as tints.

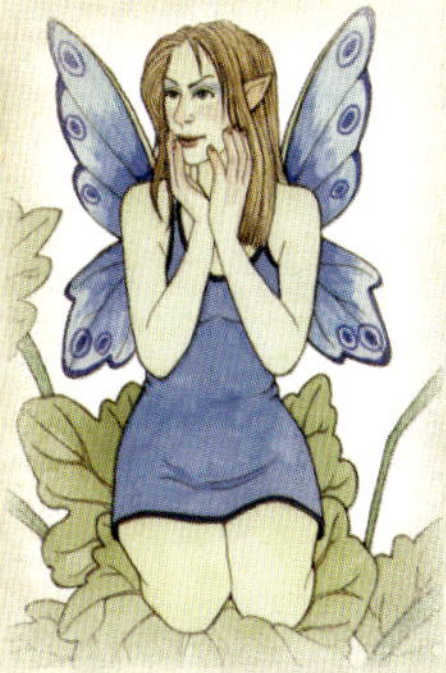

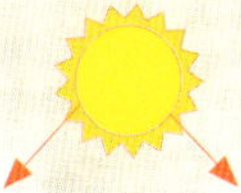

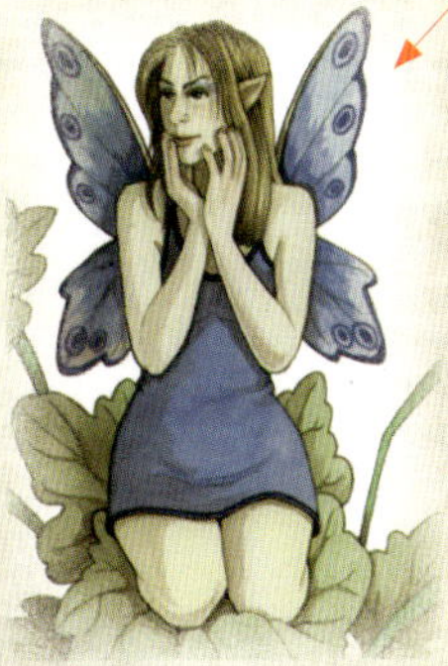

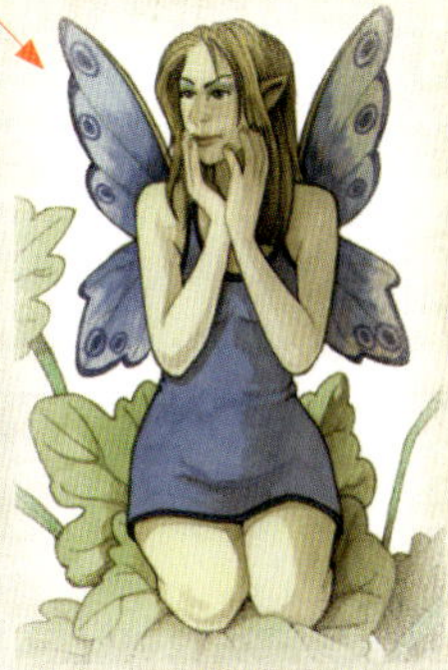

With no directional light to cast shadows and indicate form, both the figure and the background look flat and unexciting.

The right-hand light source casts shadows to the left. The darker shades create volume and make the wings stand out from the shoulder plane.

The light changes direction, altering the position of the shadows. The lightest tints are reserved for the areas that face the light.

Understanding color

WHILE THE PLACEMENT OF VALUE HAS A DRAMATIC IMPACT ON ANY ARTWORK, COLOR HAS A SUBTLE YET SIGNIFICANT INFLUENCE ON THE MOOD AND EMOTION OF AN IMAGE.

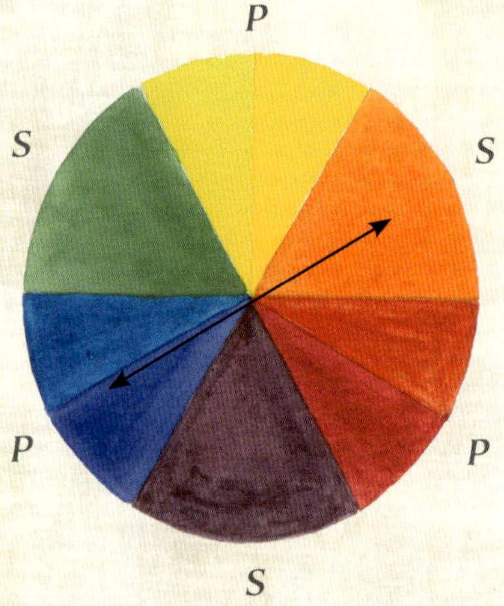

Color wheel

The relationship between colors is shown using the color wheel. Red, yellow, and blue are the primary colors (marked "P" on the diagram). When two of these pigments are mixed together, they produce the appropriate secondary colors (marked "S"). Red and yellow make orange. Red and blue make purple. Blue and yellow make green.

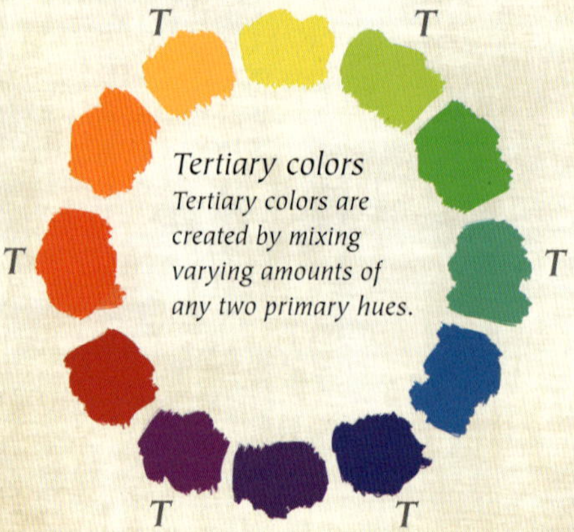

Tertiary colors
Tertiary colors are created by mixing varying amounts of any two primary hues.

Working digitally

Note that the color wheel is valid for digital artwork as well as traditional media. Digital color models may vary, but colors can be "mixed" with predictable results by overlaying hues with varying levels of opacity. Be aware, however, that this method can lead to a reduction in the saturation of the resulting color.

Complementary colors

Complementary colors lie opposite each other on the color wheel. They enhance each other's brightness and create a dynamic effect when used adjacent to each other. A few bright red berries among foliage, for example, will bring the green to life, or you might try touches of orange on a blue gown to give extra interest to a fairy's clothing.

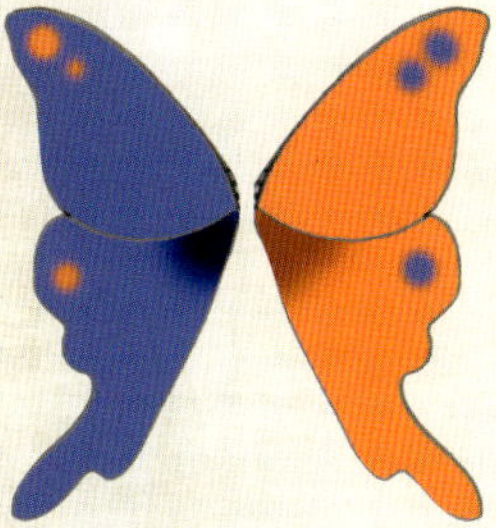

Blues always sing out more loudly when oranges are nearby. Each color borrows vitality from the other.

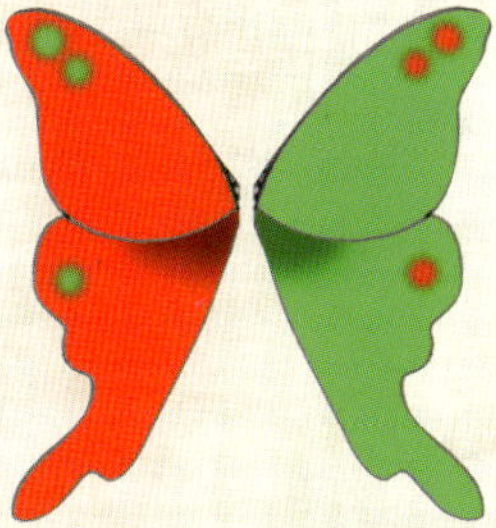

The vibrant pairing of green and red is a classic. Think of eye-catching scarlet poppies in a green hedgerow.

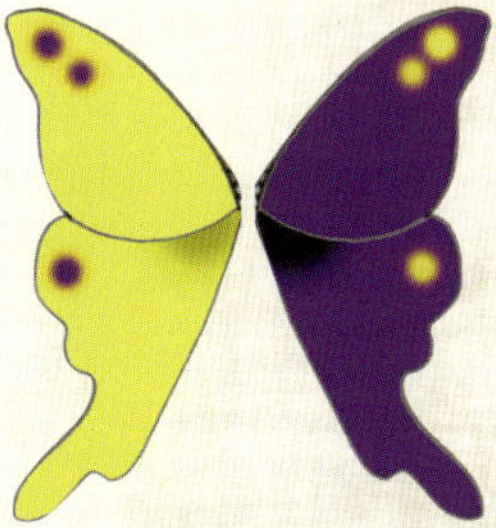

Yellow becomes quite dazzling when paired with purple, while mere spots of yellow are enough to make purple glow.

Harmonious colors

Harmonious colors lie next to each other on the color wheel. Used together they create quiet partnerships with none of the pulsating vibrancy of paired complementary colors. On the contrary, when used in a painting, harmonious colors produce a calming image even if the colors themselves are strong and vivid—placed alongside each other they are soothing to the eye with no startling "jumpy" effects.

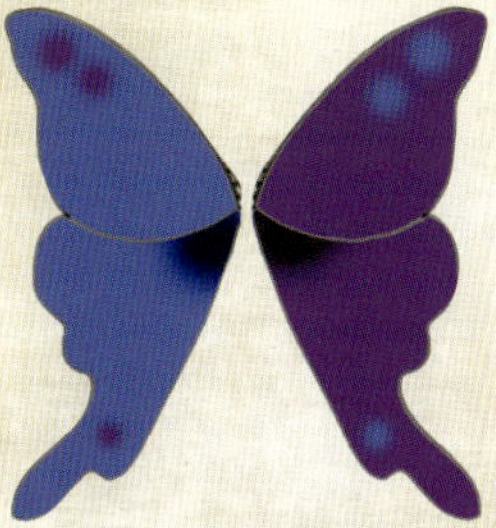

Blue and purple, from the same color family, make harmonious companions however strong the intensities.

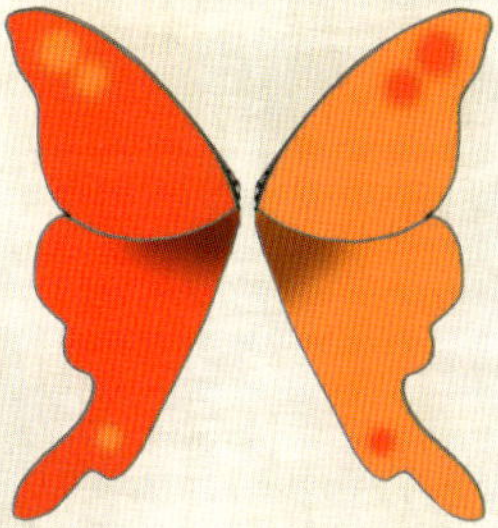

Placed together, warm orange and red appear more muted without their complementaries.

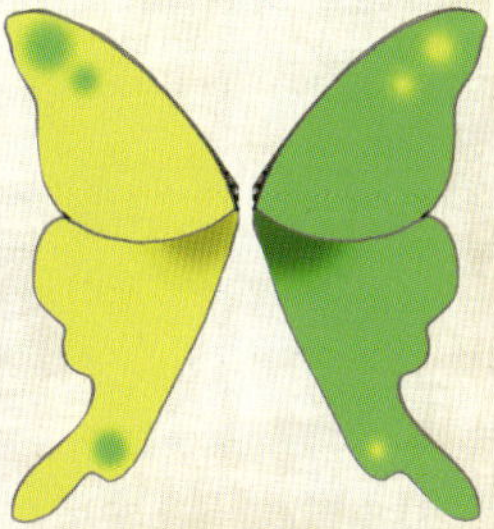

Yellow, though still bright, loses its electrifying quality when partnered with green.

Mood

Colors have strong symbolic meanings, and make a powerful contribution to the mood and atmosphere of an artwork. For example, red is often associated with danger or conflict. Green and blue can impart a calm, tranquil atmosphere. Colors also have an association with temperature: red, orange, and yellow are warm colors; blue, cyan, and green are cool.

Color scheme

Think about your image. What will the viewer expect to see? Traditional fairy art deals largely with natural and earthy colors, such as greens, browns, and yellows, but you must decide whether a more unusual color scheme would be more fitting for a more unusual fairy specimen. Color is a subjective experience, and you should take risks. Even from a monotone value sketch, certain assumptions about a color scheme can be made and you must choose whether to work with the audience's expectations, or against them.

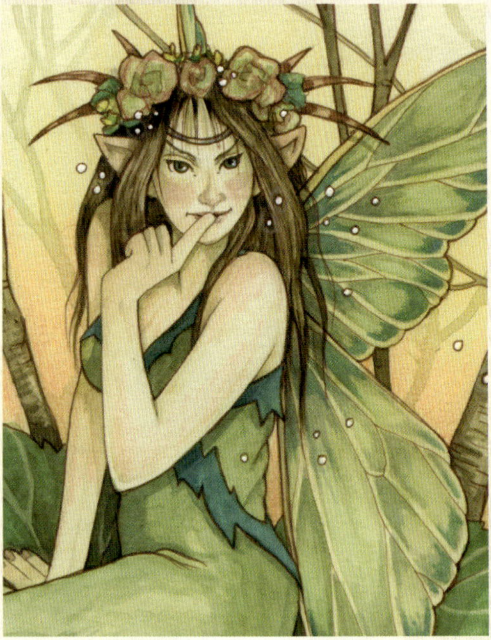

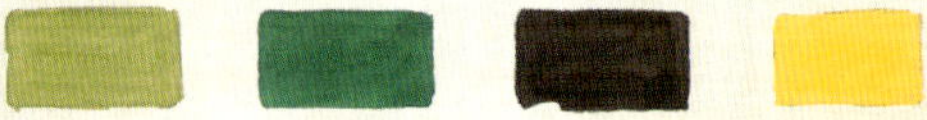

COLOR SCHEME FOR A SUMMER FAIRY

The greens and yellows used for the fairy's costume suggest high summer, while the complementary oranges and browns draw attention to her hair and warm skin tones.

FLOWER PALETTES

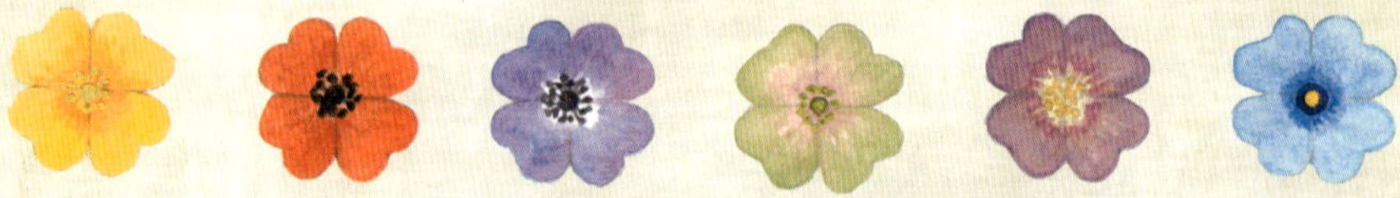

Paint buttercups and daffodils with cadmium yellow and lemon yellow with a touch of orange.

Poppies and geraniums use cadmium red and alizarin crimson, with Payne's gray and purple madder.

Mixes of ultramarine, purple, and violet are used for anemones, lavender, and bluebells.

For young flowers, combine olive green and rose madder.

Mix magenta and purple for red campion flowers, deepening the magenta toward the center.

Soft mixes of cobalt blue and ultramarine create forget-me-nots, with darker mixes toward the flower centers.

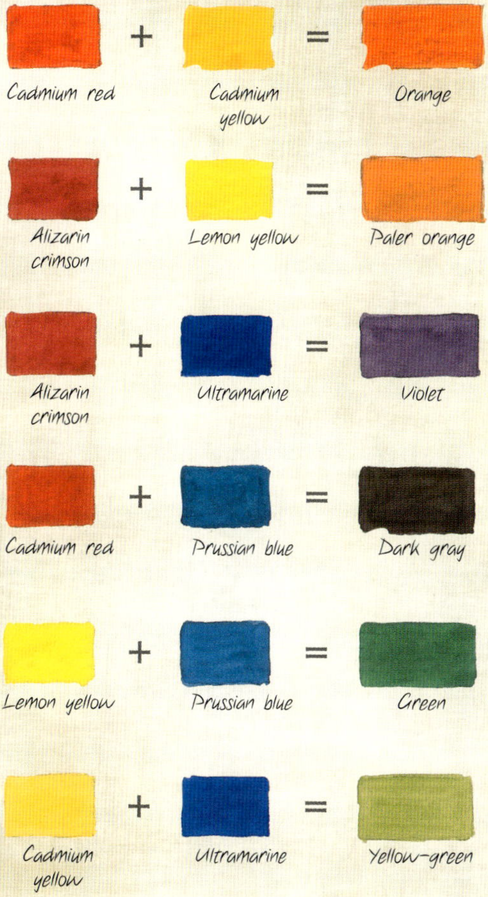

Modifying hues

If a color is very strong, it can look artificial and will, in some cases, not be ideal for painting natural subjects such as fairy habitats. If you want to modify a hue quite subtly, try adding small touches of the more subdued earth colors such as muted browns and yellows. For example, mix burnt sienna into green, and yellow ocher in mauve.

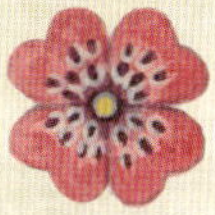

Foxgloves and orchids are created with rose madder, magenta, and purple. Highlight with white gouache.

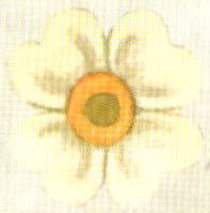

Apply washes of raw umber and olive green for daisies and narcissi, then add orange and olive green centers.

Use mixes of cadmium red, cadmium yellow, and lemon yellow for sunflowers, with sepia for the center.

Light sources

The light source may influence the color scheme. Neutral light reveals a surface's natural (or "local") color. A strongly colored light will visibly tint all the surfaces it illuminates. Consider, for example, how perceived colors are different during bright daylight or a vivid sunset, for example.

Seasonal palettes

FAIRIES ARE CLOSELY ASSOCIATED WITH NATURE AND THE SEASONS. PALETTES CAN BE CHOSEN TO REFLECT THIS.

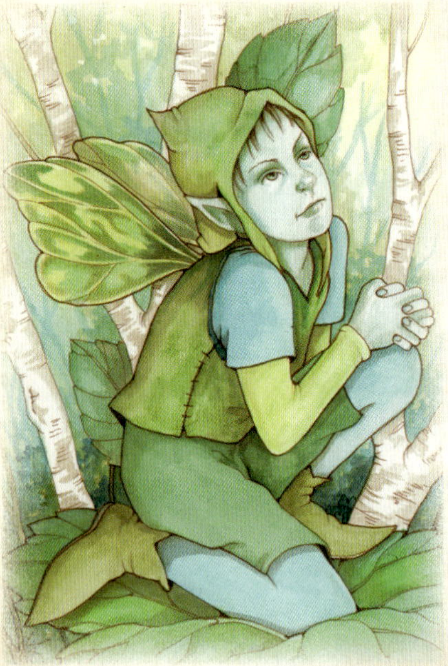

- Deep olive green
- Hooker's green
- Veridian
- Transparent turquoise
- Green-gold
- Sap green

SPRING
Bright greens and blues speak of the new growth and freshness of spring and reflect the colors of young leaves. The skin tones have a blue tinge, suggesting there is still a chill in the air.

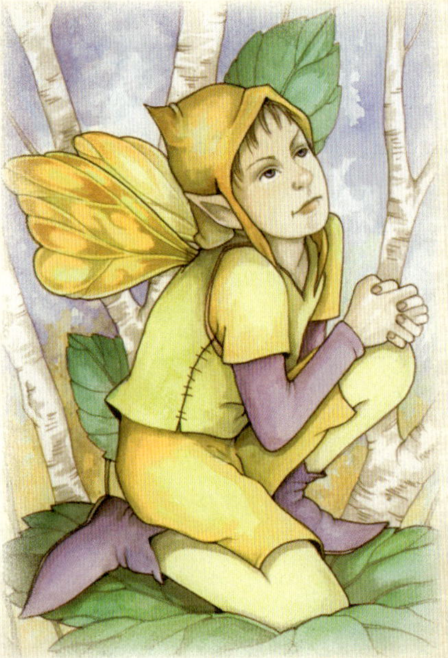

- French ultramarine
- Cadmium orange
- Violet
- Cobalt green
- Lemon yellow

SUMMER
Summer colors are reminiscent of clear blue skies and warm sunny days, with abundant brightly colored flowers and lush green fields. The heat of the sun warms the skin tones.

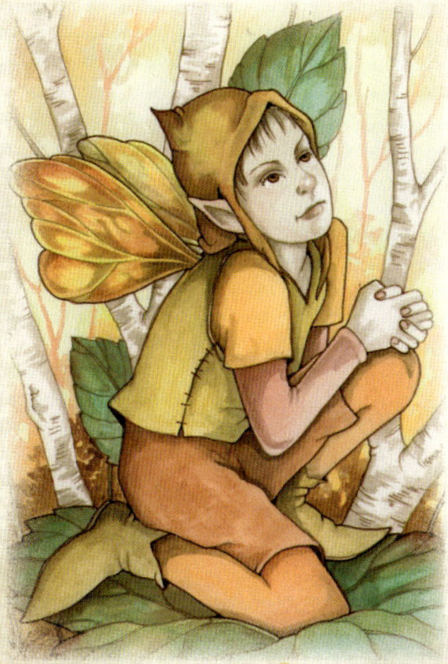

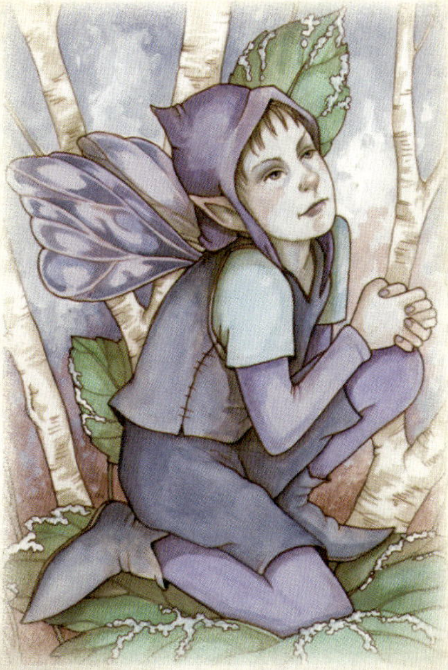

Cadmium red

Cadmium orange

Venetian red

Yellow ocher

Lemon yellow

Indian red

Sap green

Payne's gray

Ultramarine violet

Cobalt blue

Permanent magenta

Cobalt green

FALL

The mellow fruitfulness of fall when the leaves change color is suggested with warm reds and burnished golden yellows. There is still a hint of green left behind by the passing summer.

WINTER

Cool blues and lilacs reflect the chill of winter and white gouache adds the touches of Jack Frost's icy fingers on the leaves. Faces become pale and noses glow red.

Basic watercolor techniques

WATERCOLOR IS THE PREFERRED MEDIUM FOR MOST FAIRY ARTISTS AS IT IS SUBTLE—LIKE THEIR SUBJECTS. HERE ARE SOME BASIC TECHNIQUES TO GET YOU STARTED.

Flat wash

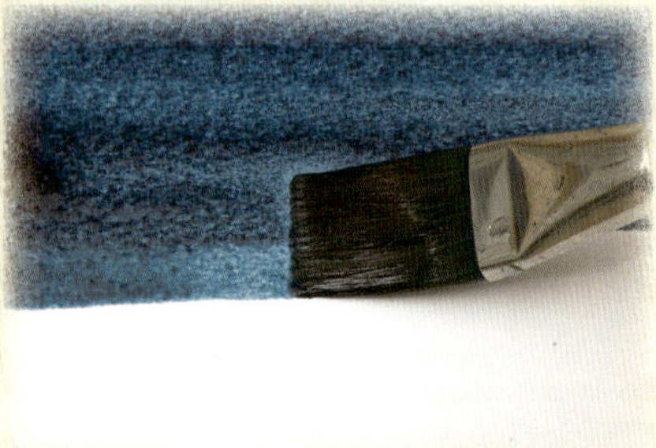

1 Tape your paper to a board or flat surface. Starting with a wide, flat brush, load enough diluted color (in this case, Winsor blue and Venetian red) to make one stroke across the top of the paper.

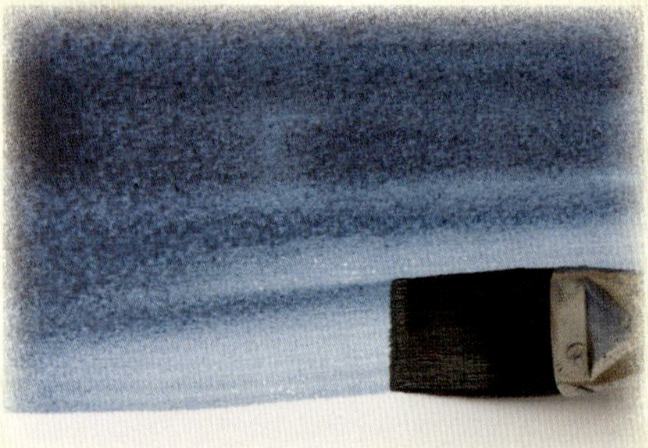

2 Continue down the paper quickly, not allowing the paint to dry between strokes. Work back over uneven lines if necessary to even out any discrepancies in the wash.

3 Continue down to the base of the paper, tilting the paper downward to encourage even flow of the pigment before it settles.

4 Here the paint has dried to a flat, even finish. Some pigments will granulate and produce a grainy effect. Get to know the paints in your palette before applying them.

Graduated wash

Graduated washes use water to dilute the pigment between strokes for a gradual thinning and lightening of color.

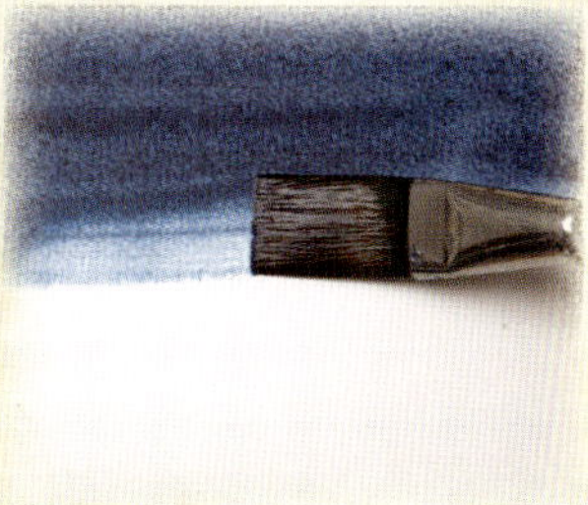

1 Using the same Winsor blue and Venetian red, mix as for the flat wash, laying down a couple of brushstrokes, left to right, across the top of the paper.

2 Continuing down the paper, add less pigment and more water until the final brushstroke is just water.

3 Lay the paper flat for the wash to dry. If you tilt it, the stronger pigment will run down into the lighter areas.

Variegated wash

The variegated wash simply blends two or more colors together in a manner that produces a seamless transition between them. The wider the flat brush, the fewer the number of strokes, and the better the gradation.

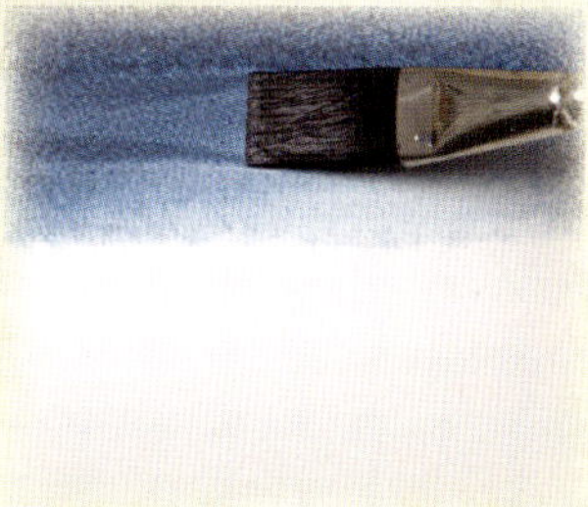

1 Brush blue paint from left to right across the top of the paper, moving down almost to the center.

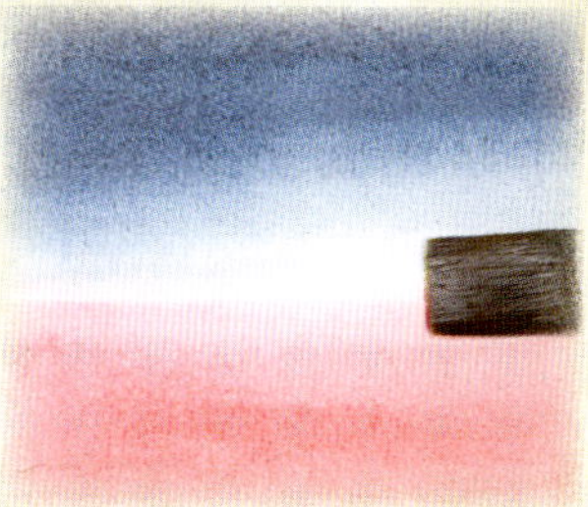

2 Rinse the brush before washing pink across the base of the paper. Stroke with the brush where the two colors meet to help blend them.

3 While the paint is still wet, gently tilt the paper upward, downward, and sideways to allow the paint to flow and blend.

Rendering

THOROUGH PREPARATORY WORK GIVES YOU A SOLID UNDERSTANDING OF THE ART IN PROGRESS, AND THE CONFIDENCE THAT ALL THE AVAILABLE OPTIONS HAVE BEEN COMPLETELY EXPLORED. IT IS NOW TIME TO BRING ALL THESE ELEMENTS TOGETHER, AND PAINT THE FINAL PIECE.

You will need

- Paper—hot pressed smooth 140lbs
- HB and 2H graphite pencils
- Fine sepia pen (0.01 nib)
- Wash brush
- Brushes no. 4 and no. 1
- Selection of watercolor paints
- White gouache
- Colored soft pencils in chromium orange and cadmium red

Follow these steps to take a piece of work from exploratory sketch to final painting. This mixed-media sequence begins with a carefully detailed ink underdrawing. The image develops and takes life with broad watercolor washes followed by more detailed passages. Finally, colored pencil and opaque white gouache add depth and sparkle to the finished fairy figure.

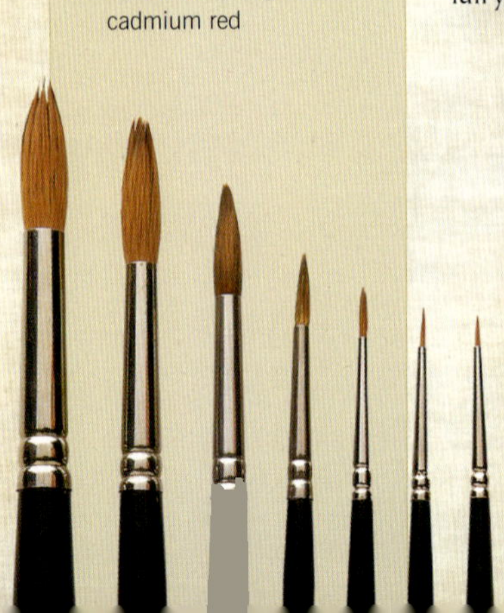

Step-by-step rendering

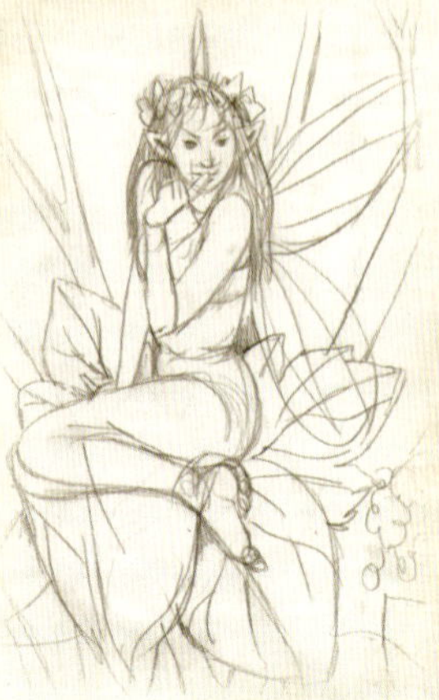

1 Sketch the figure lightly with an HB pencil, using underlying shapes to build the figure. Use this structure to create a basic outline. Add facial features and background indications.

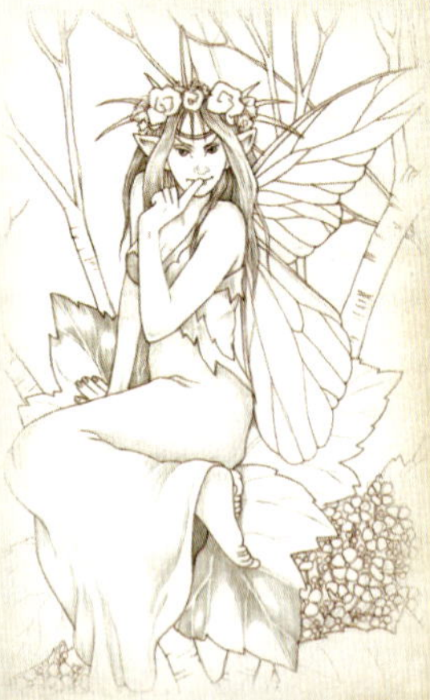

5 When the sepia ink is absolutely dry, carefully remove the graphite lines with a soft eraser, leaving just the ink lines. Be gentle with the eraser to protect the paper surface.

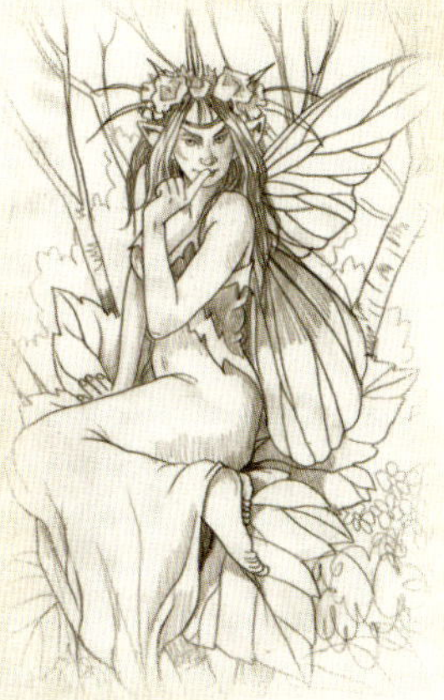

2 Continue working lightly with the HB pencil. Resolve the background and the wings; add detail to the face, hair, and headdress; work up the gown, shading where it drapes around the body.

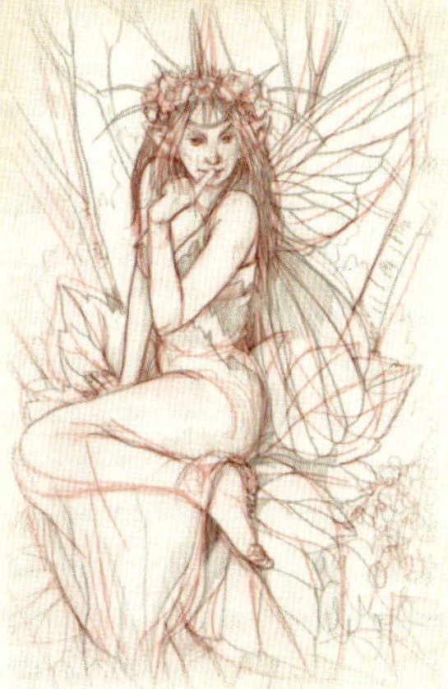

3 Here steps 1 and 2 are overlaid to demonstrate how closely the developed drawing follows the guidelines of the vital initial structure created in step 1.

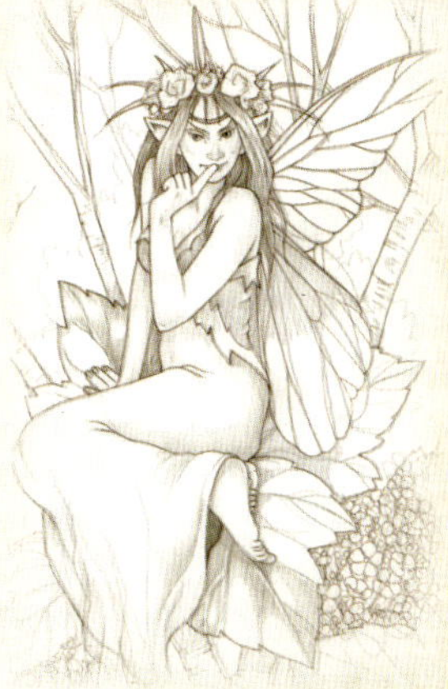

4 Use a fine sepia pen to draw around the sketched image, including the face and head, the wing patterns, and the background indications. Keep the pen lines fluid and smooth.

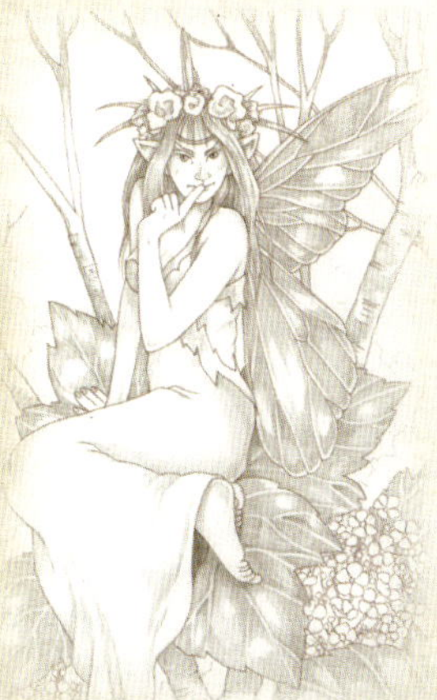

6 With the HB pencil, add shading to round out the forms and create a sense of depth. Use the harder 2H pencil for the finest details of face, hair, and headdress.

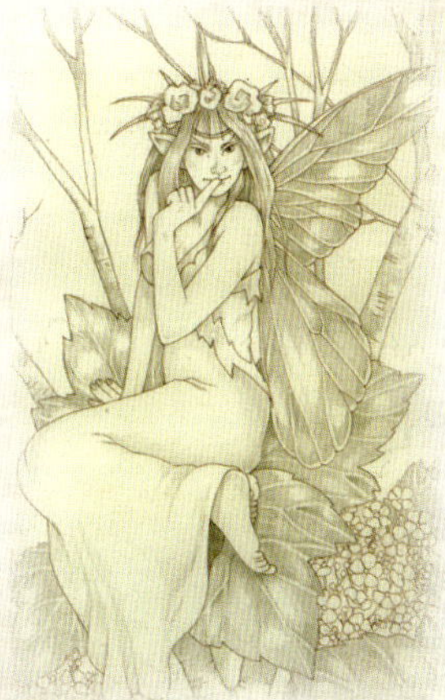

7 Now the drawing is fully established it's time to start adding color. With a large wash brush, apply a thin wash of raw umber over the entire picture area.

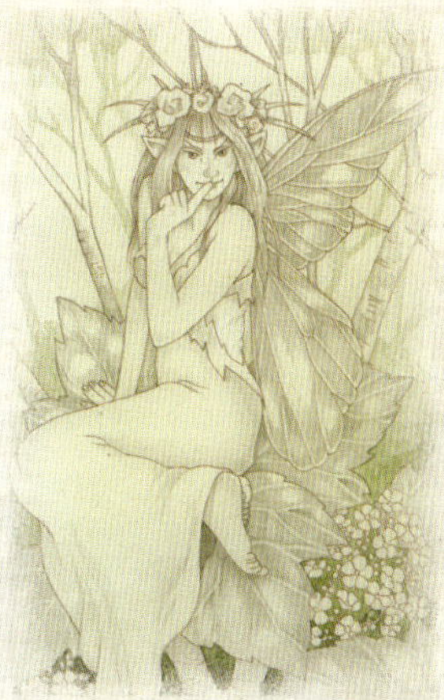

8 Add a wash of olive green to the background behind and under the leaves to give a sense of recession. Use the same color to pick out shadow areas among the flowers.

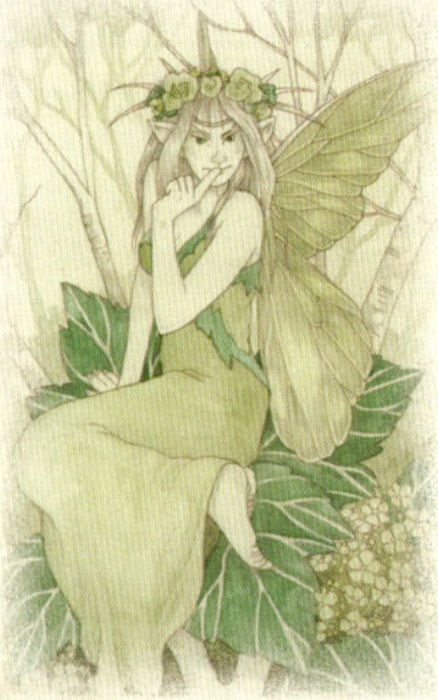

9 Add an olive green wash to the fairy's dress and wings. Then use a wash of Hooker's green for the dress trim, headdress, and large leaves, taking care to paint around the veins on the leaves.

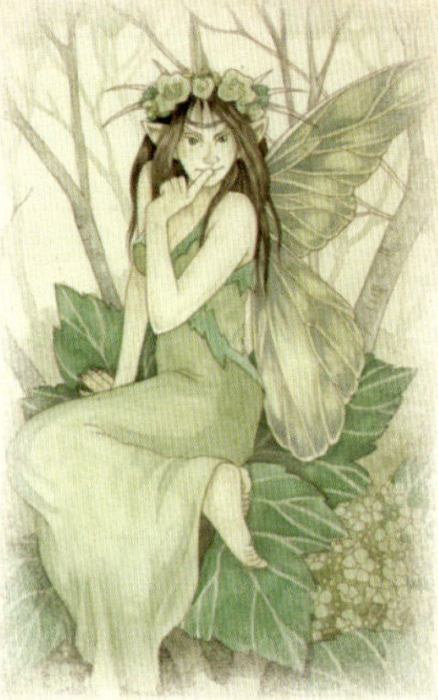

10 Add a light wash of Payne's gray to the shading on the wings. Then use the fine brush to apply washes of raw umber to the hair.

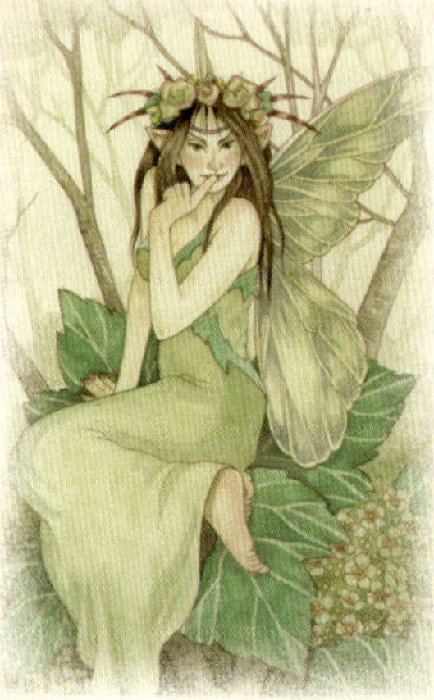

11 Add washes of olive green to the gown, raw umber to the skin, rose madder to the cheeks, lips, and ears, and alizarin crimson wash to the flower centers. Begin darkening the branches with raw umber washes.

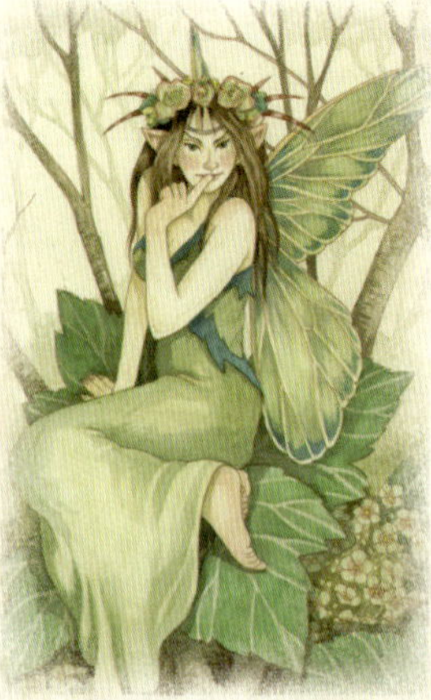

13 Now use a neutral wash of Payne's gray to add more shading and a sense of form and depth to the body, the folds of the gown, and some background areas.

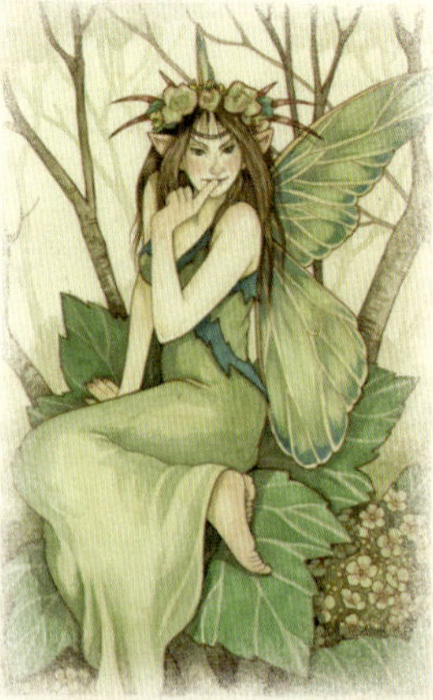

14 If you like crisp outlines, draw around the figure again with the sepia pen. Don't make the line too heavy; simply define the image a little to reinforce the shapes.

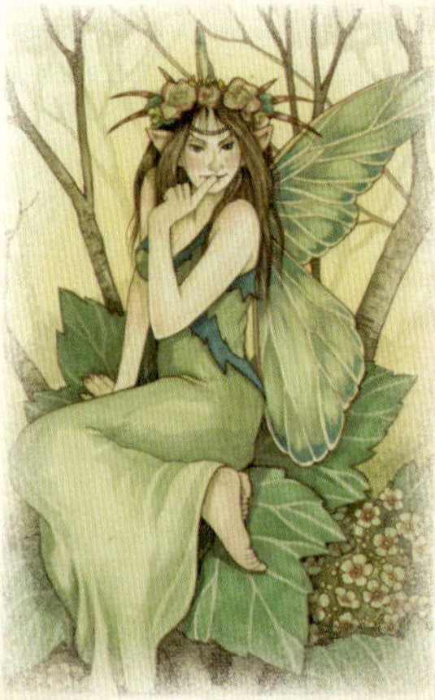

15 Use a chromium orange colored pencil to add a soft glow to the background behind the trees, blending the pencil strokes carefully with a tissue.

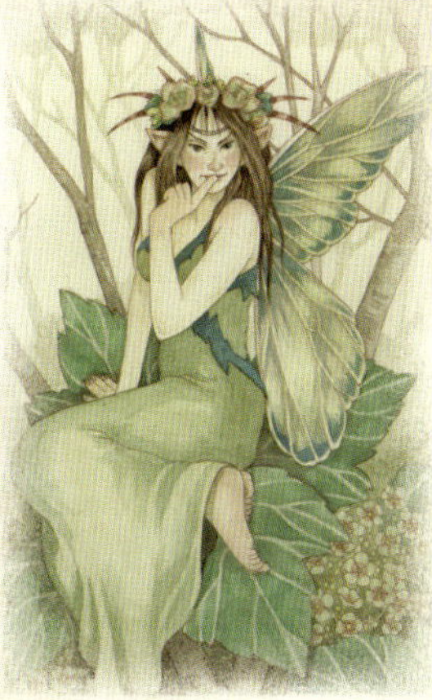

12 Use cobalt green to deepen the trimming on the gown and add detail to the wing pattern. Notice how these details begin to add more depth to the image.

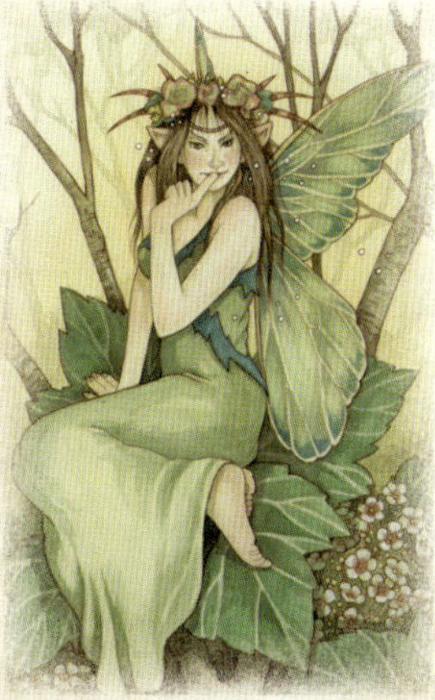

16 Add touches of white gouache to highlight the flower petals. Scatter further spots of white around the fairy's head to suggest pollen floating on the breeze.

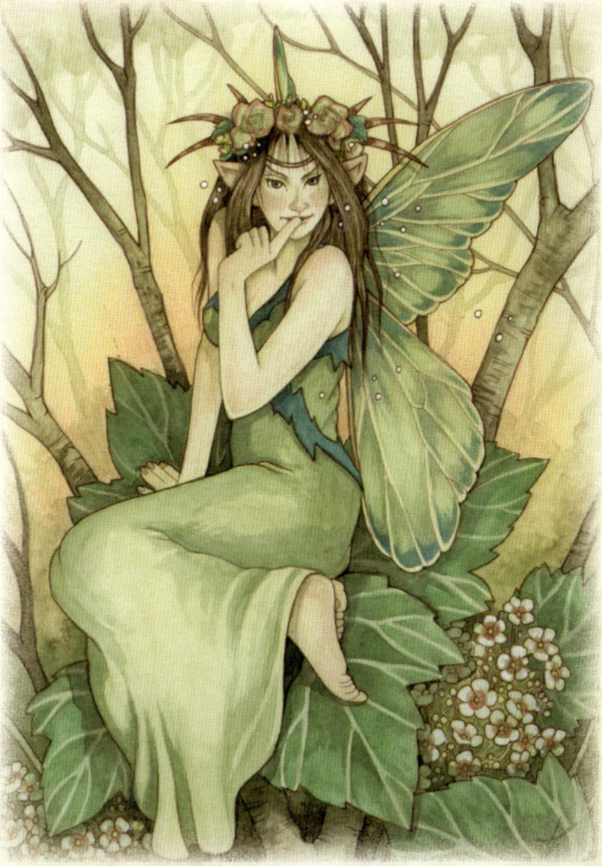

17 Finally, blend a little cadmium red colored pencil into the orange background area to add a warm sunset halo. Notice how this cleverly accentuates the complementary green of the fairy figure.

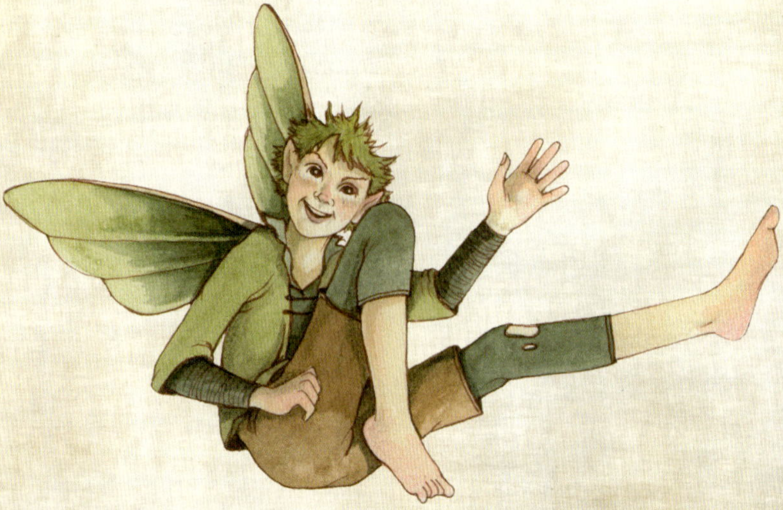

Part 3

Human and fairy anatomy

Fairies, even ugly twisted ones, are based on the human form, so you must first learn to understand and draw the human figure convincingly. This might seem a daunting task—the human body is often considered a difficult subject. However, with a keen eye and plenty of practice, your skill and confidence will grow. Use every opportunity to sketch adults and children from life or photographs. Once you've mastered this you can adapt and distort your figures as much as you like and they'll still look credible.

Figure construction basics

THE HUMAN FIGURE IS COMPLEX, BUT IT IS MADE EASIER WHEN IT IS VISUALIZED AS A SERIES OF SIMPLIFIED SHAPES THAT CAN BE EXAGGERATED TO ACCENTUATE FAIRY FEATURES.

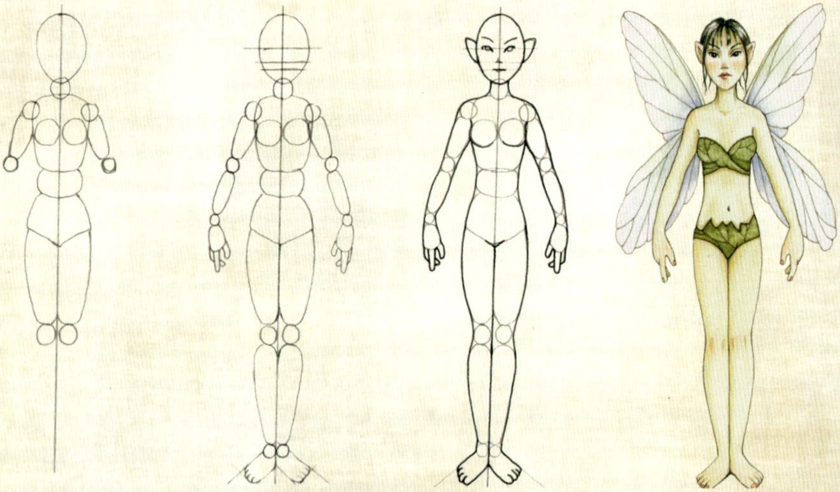

1 The human body is made up of circles, ovals, and rectangles. Plot the main anatomical features using the basic collection of shapes above.

2 Divide the face into segments as shown, and extend the arms and legs with further shapes. The fingers are simple sausage shapes, for example, and the lower legs are elongated ovals tapering in slightly toward the ankles.

3 Add facial features, then draw around the whole figure with smooth, flowing lines, tapering in and out slightly around the joints.

4 Finally, finish your fairy by adding wings, clothing, and other accessories in color. You can draw around the image with a pen adding details as you go, or trace the image and redraw it to create more fairy folk.

Template fairy figures

It is important to understand the anatomical structure of the fairy figure, even when it is hidden from view. Scan this page into your computer, print it out, and cut around the outline figures below. Then use them to style the costume design ideas in this book. Clothe the female figure in the dresses and robes on pages 76–77, and the male figure in the tunics and jackets on pages 78–79—or turn to selected pages in the directory for further costume ideas.

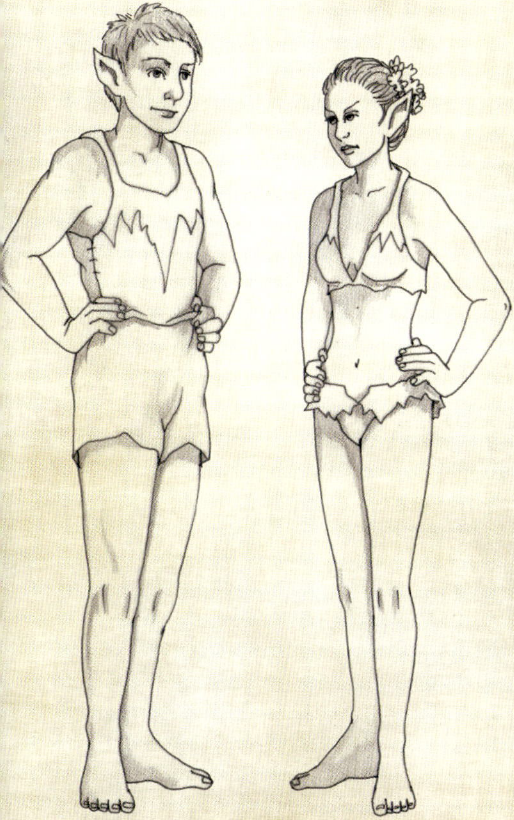

See also: Dresses and robes, page 76.

Differences between male and female figures

- Males and females share the same vertical proportional measurements, but the female form is narrower horizontally.

- The most significant anatomical difference between the sexes is the pelvis. In women, the pelvic bone is larger in relation to the rest of the skeleton. This results in wider hips and a more pronounced waist.

- Notice the relationship between the hips and shoulders. A vertical line drawn through the figure at the outer edge of the hips on male and female figures passes through the shoulder at different points. In the male, the shoulders are much wider, placed outside the line. Females have narrower shoulders and wider hips, placing the shoulders inside the line.

- To accentuate the feminine form, the artist may choose to further stylize the proportions. Lengthening the legs increases the figure's elegance. Narrowing the wrists, ankles, and waist exaggerates the curves of the hips, legs, and bosom; all of which may be deliberately drawn with a dramatic curve to push this impression further. This should always be performed with care, and with a sound knowledge of correct artistic proportion, in order to avoid an unrealistic or cartoon-like figure.

- It is important to recognize the distinction between realistic and artistic proportions. In reality, most human beings are between six and seven heads tall. These proportions look stunted and unexciting on the page. Artists generally accept a figure standing about eight heads tall as the standard. These idealized proportions are more attractive and dynamic on the page, and are ideal for fantasy artists.

Fairy poses

FAIRIES ASSUME AN INFINITE RANGE OF POSES AND THEIR CHARACTERISTIC STANCES REFLECT THEIR PERSONALITIES. YOU NEED FIRST TO UNDERSTAND HOW THE BODY WORKS.

Using a mannequin

Manipulate a mannequin into endless static and action poses to help you understand how the body moves and balances.

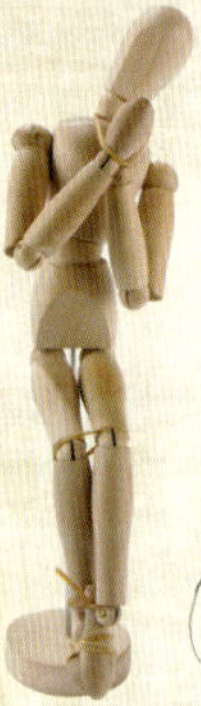

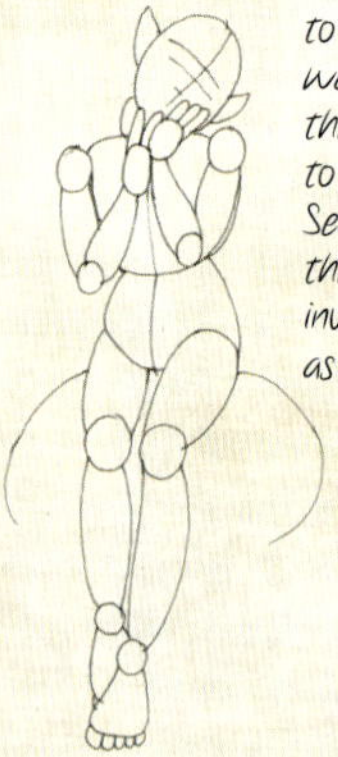

SEATED
This figure tilts over to one side from the waist. The head tilts in the opposite direction to maintain balance. Seated poses seen from the front always involve foreshortening, as in the thighs here.

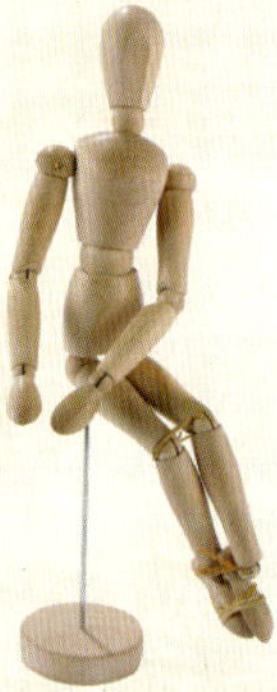

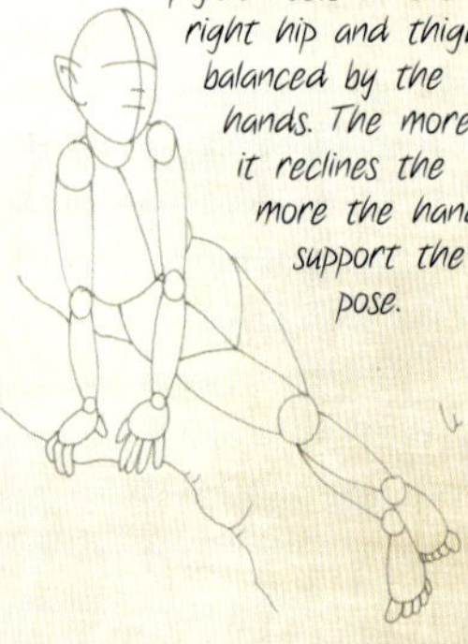

RECLINING
The weight of this figure rests on the right hip and thigh, balanced by the hands. The more it reclines the more the hands support the pose.

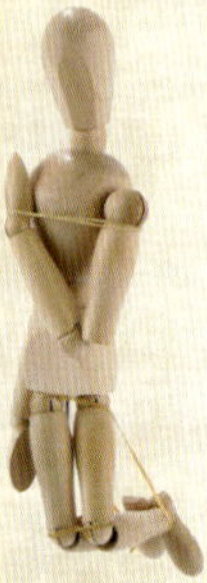

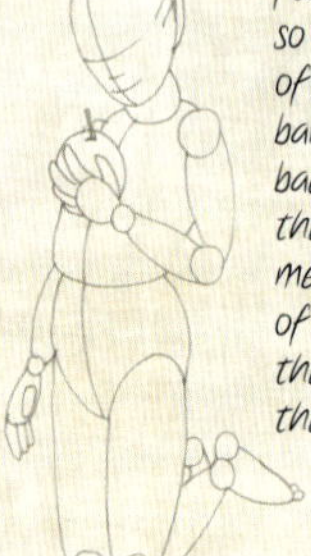

KNEELING
Knees aren't as good for balancing as feet, so kneeling figures often keep their balance by leaning back slightly from the waist. This means the center of gravity is above the mid-calf, not on the knees.

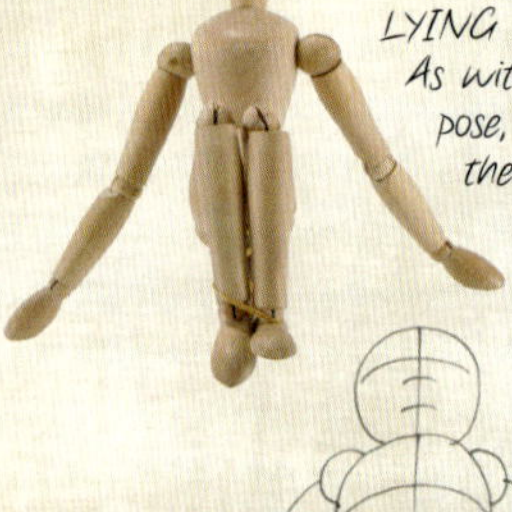

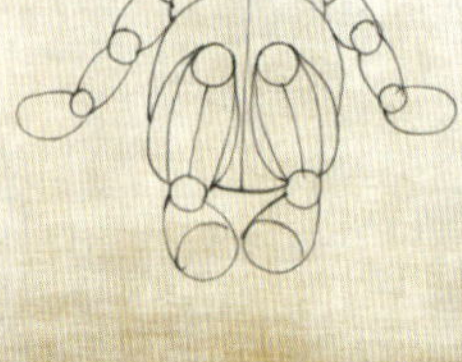

LYING DOWN
As with the simple seated pose, this pose is seen from the front and there is a good deal of foreshortening in body, legs, and arms.

FLYING POSES

The ability to fly is a fundamental fairy attribute and you'll want to show airborne fairies from different angles. It must look like a totally natural and plausible activity.

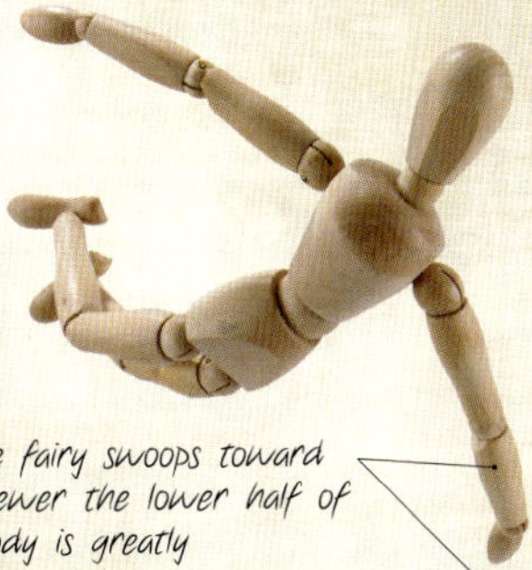

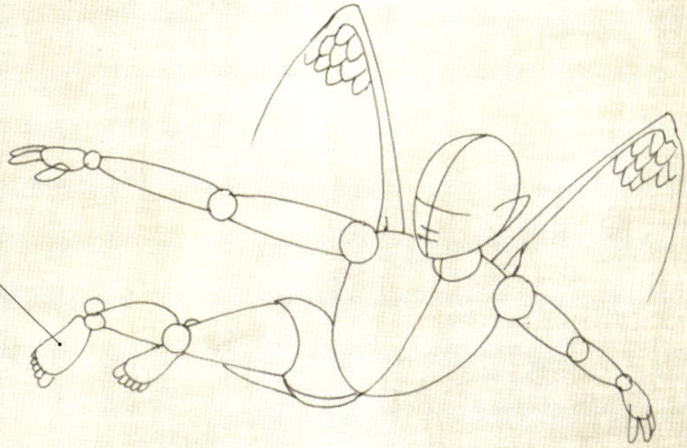

As the fairy swoops toward the viewer the lower half of the body is greatly foreshortened.

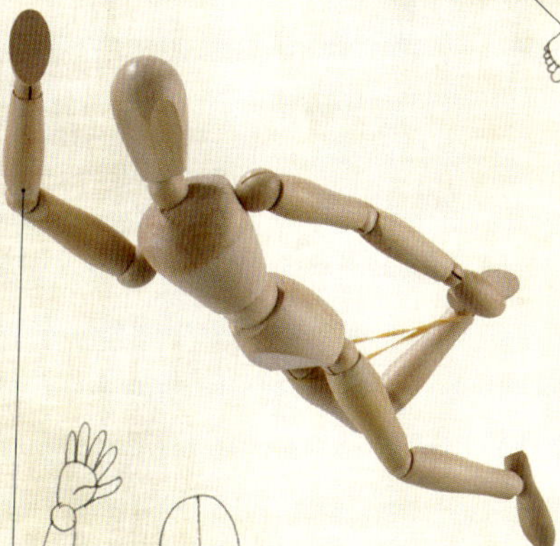

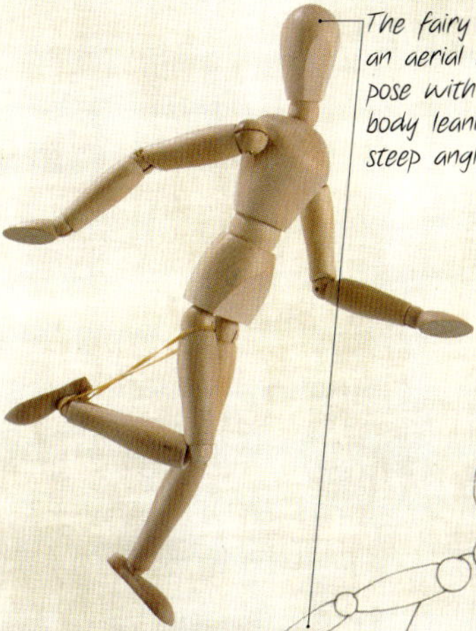

The fairy assumes an aerial walking pose with her body leaning at a steep angle.

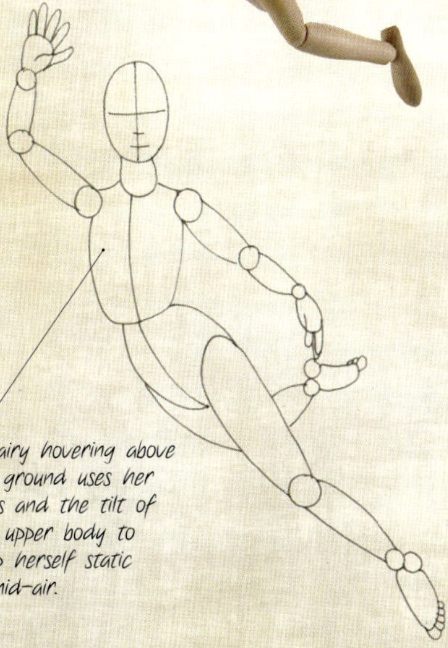

A fairy hovering above the ground uses her arms and the tilt of her upper body to keep herself static in mid-air.

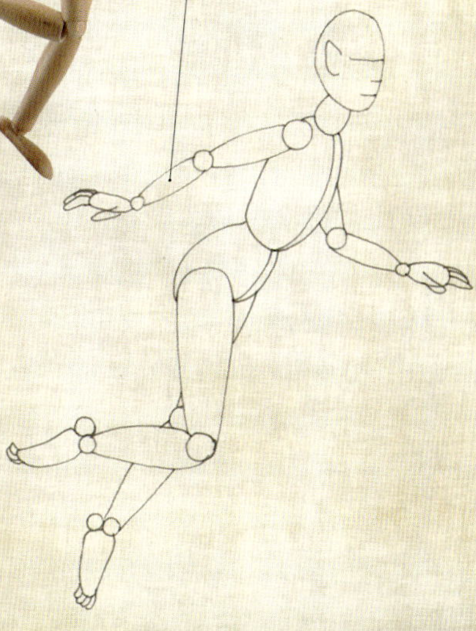

Adding character

Postures reflect character. Think of the difference between the dainty poses of a flower fairy and the twisted postures of a wicked Spriggan. As a fairy artist you are dealing with a fantasy world, so you can be extreme in your characterizations—tell your story with as much conviction as possible to convince and entertain your audience.

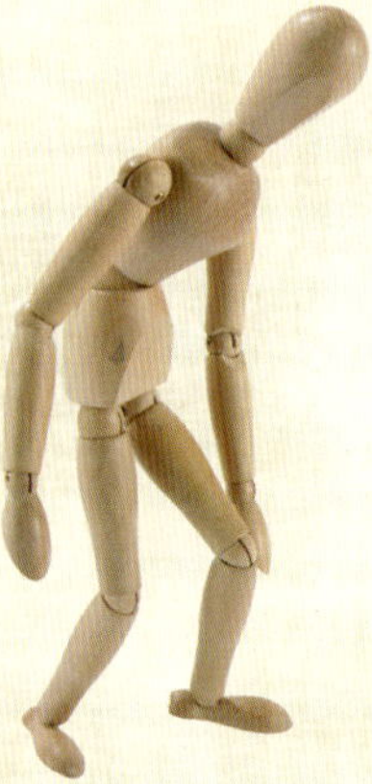

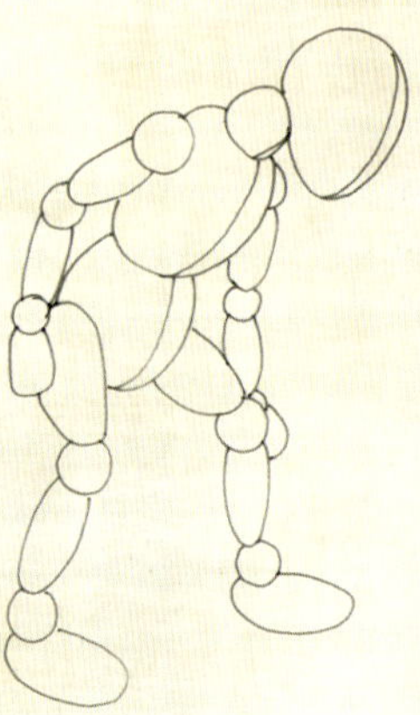

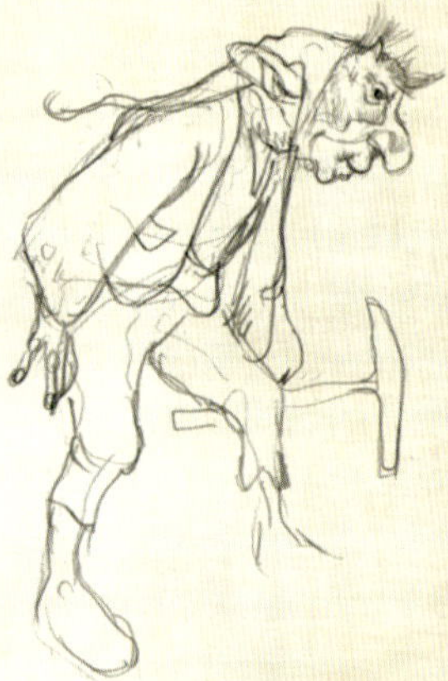

1 Use a mannequin to select and adjust a pose for your character. In this case it's the stooped, skulking stance of a malevolent creature up to no good.

2 Sketch out the character using just the basic underlying shapes. Refer to the mannequin for angles and balance and check that the pose conveys the nature of the personality.

3 Now "flesh out" the character, building details on the basic scaffolding. Add appropriate clothing and a suitably unpleasant face. At this stage you can adjust the pose to make it more expressive.

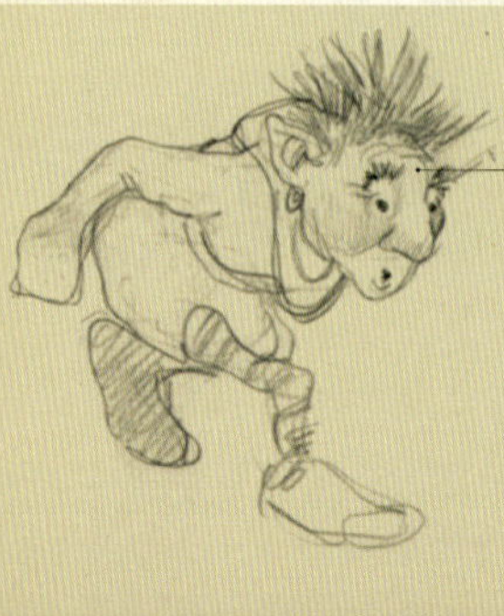

This variation develops the initial stooped, creeping pose further. Bending the figure over more creates a stronger sense of stealthy movement.

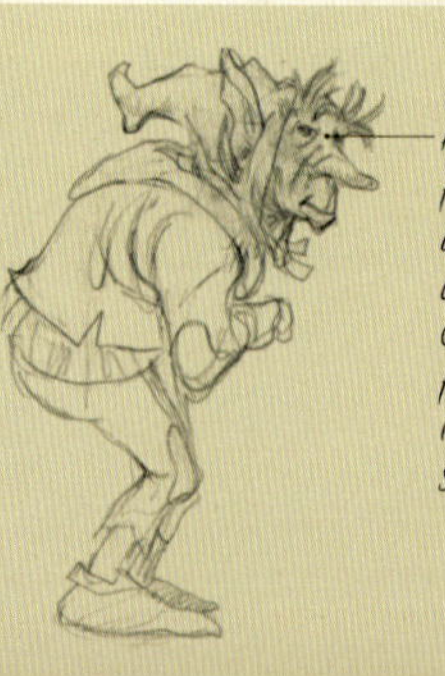

Here the pose is viewed from the side. This enables us to see him casting a sly glance over his shoulder. The face has developed into something scarily subhuman.

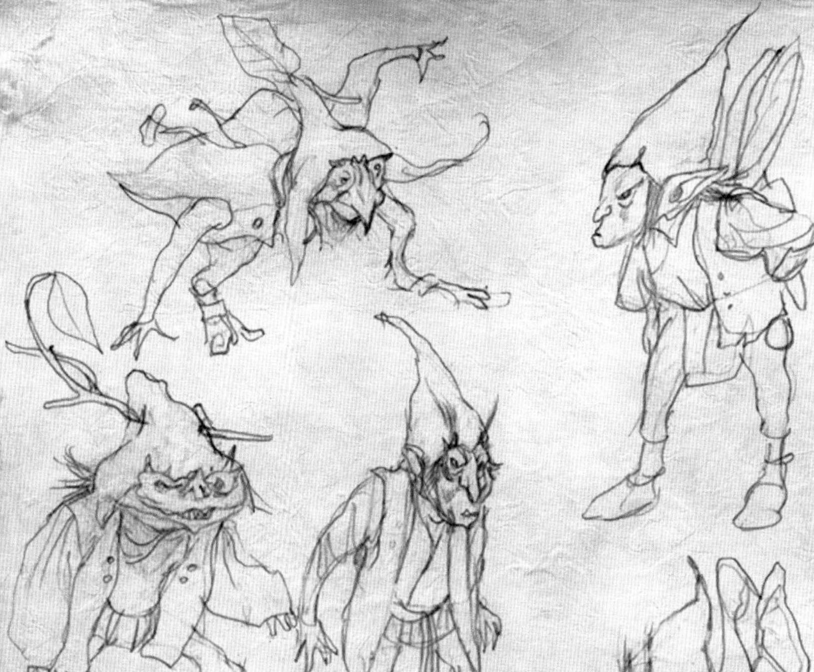

Keeping a character sheet

There are countless ways to depict every imaginary creature. Your initial ideas will change as you work into a character, and you need to record this thought process. Always keep your preparatory sketches—what you reject now may be just right for a later creation.

Constructing the head

A BASIC FORMAT FOR THE HUMAN HEAD WILL HELP YOU DRAW REALISTIC CHARACTERS. FACIAL FEATURES GENERALLY CONFORM TO A SIMPLE GRID, WHICH CAN BE ADAPTED EASILY.

Constructing the head: *front view*

1 Draw a circle with a line through the middle and two lines touching the outer edges. Extend it into an egg shape. Draw a small circle at the bottom of circle 1 for the nose, and a large one at the bottom of the egg shape for the chin. A horizontal line halfway between marks the mouth. Draw lines from the center of circle 1 for the brows.

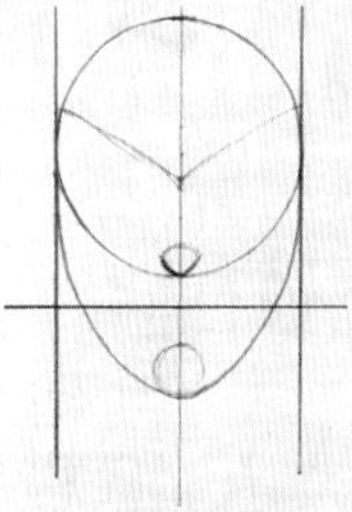

2 For the eyes, draw two small circles in the center of each half of the big circle. Draw oval shapes around them and define the eyebrows. Draw lips above and below the horizontal line, and make two small semicircles at each side of the nose for nostrils. Draw ovals for the ears, placing them level with the tip of the nose.

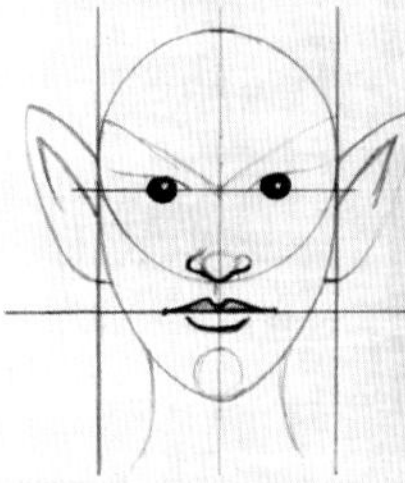

Constructing the head: *three-quarter view*

1 Draw a large teardrop. Add a crescent-shaped slice to give a center line to the face. Place a circle at the bottom for the chin, leave a space the same size as this circle, and mark a rectangle for the nose. A line halfway between chin and nose marks the mouth. Brow lines radiate from the center.

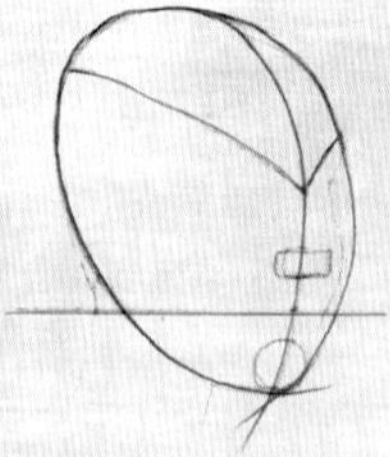

2 Draw features in the same way as for the front view. Note that the ear is more visible than in a front view, so be sure of its placement: the bottom should line up with the bottom of the nose; the top is level with the eye. The tip can protrude, as pointy ears are a prominent feature of fairies.

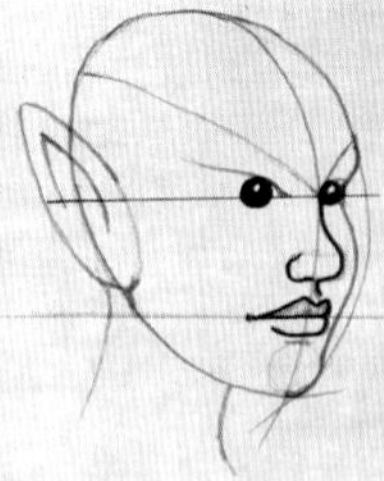

Female head

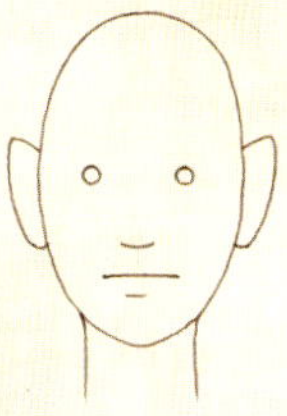

1 Set up the basic head shape and indicate the positions of the features. Female faces are generally softly rounded, with small chins.

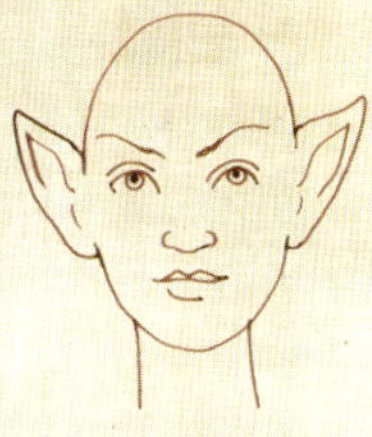

2 Extend and develop the ears. Add detail to the features, and introduce the facial expression at this stage.

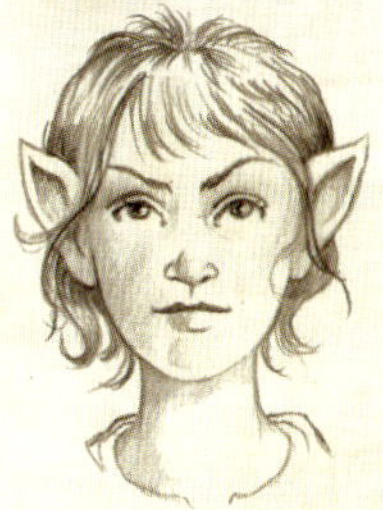

3 Add the hair. Note that it lies on top of the skull, not within the oval outline. Add shading to describe the volume and form of the facial features.

Male head

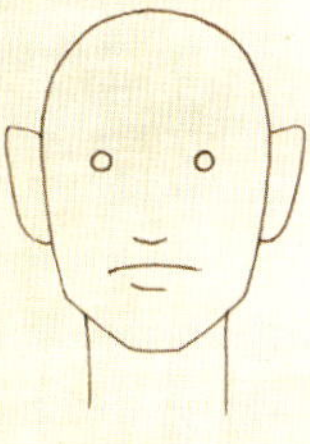

1 Set up the basic grid. Male heads, especially young ones, have broader faces with strong square chins.

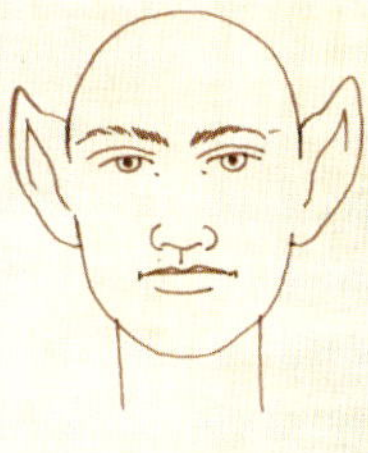

2 Create the fairy ears and add facial details. Note the features that express his gender: a broader nose, heavier eyebrows, thinner lips.

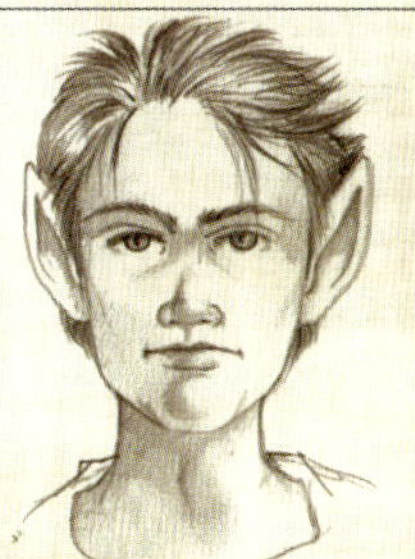

3 Develop the character-defining details, draw the hair, and shade the face to give three-dimensional form.

The head in rotation (three-quarter view)

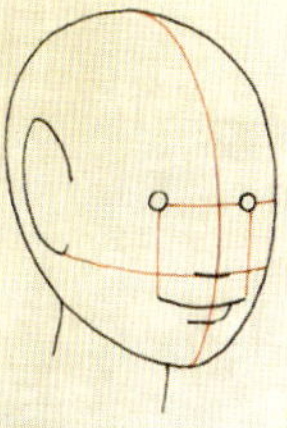

1 Use the same basic grid to construct the rotated head. Seen from this angle, the construction lines become contours that indicate the volume of the head.

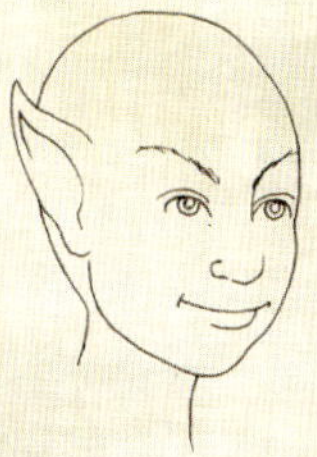

2 Add facial details. At this angle one ear is hidden, the shape of the nose is visible and partially obscures one eye, and perspective changes the shape of the mouth.

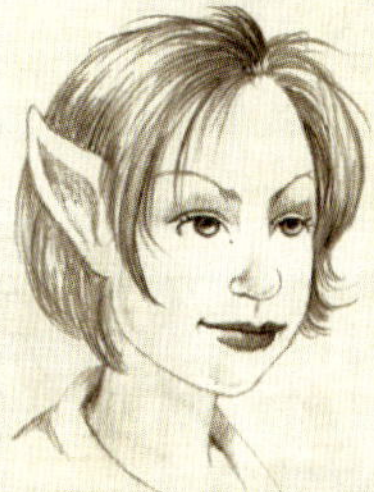

3 Refine the face, adding the hair. Make sure it sits on top of the rounded head. Notice that the nose creates an area of deeper shadow across the far eye.

Facial expressions

THE FACE IS THE MOST EXPRESSIVE PART OF THE HUMAN BODY, AND THE SUCCESS OF ANY CHARACTER IS MEASURED BY THE ARTIST'S VISUALIZATION OF THE HEAD AND FACE.

Creating character

A character may be beautiful, perfectly proportioned, adorned with fabulous accessories, and exquisitely rendered—but without expression she sits lifeless on the page. An effective expression shows your character's thoughts, reveals something of the figure's soul, and stirs the viewer's emotions. It breathes life into your figures.

Notice how the addition of a mouth and eyebrows transform a simple face in these basic line drawings. This is simple shorthand for facial expression, but it is often just as effective at communicating emotion as a realistic head. Develop your own line drawings before you fully render your fairy's facial features. Exaggerated expressions such as these are easily understood and this approach is often suitable in fairy art, which is a relatively playful genre. However, use extreme expression with caution; the more exaggerated the expression, the less subtle the emotion. This can give an unwanted comical result, or give the impression that the character is emotionally shallow.

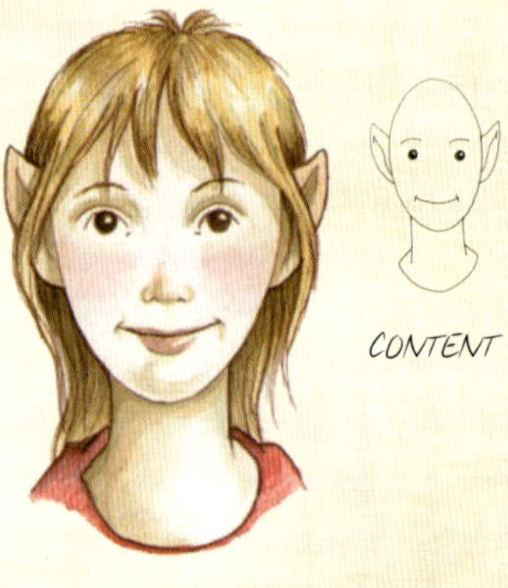

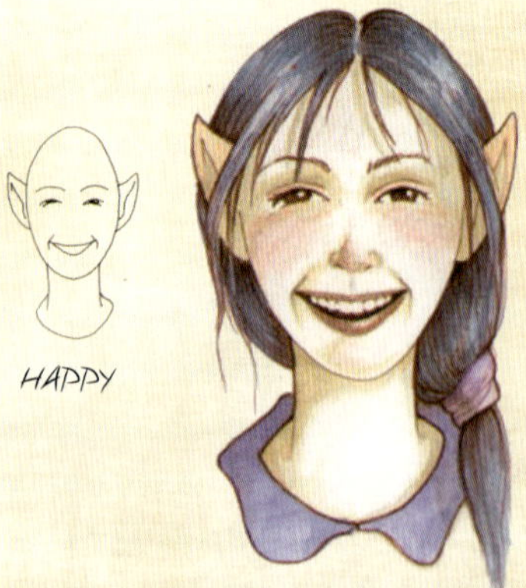

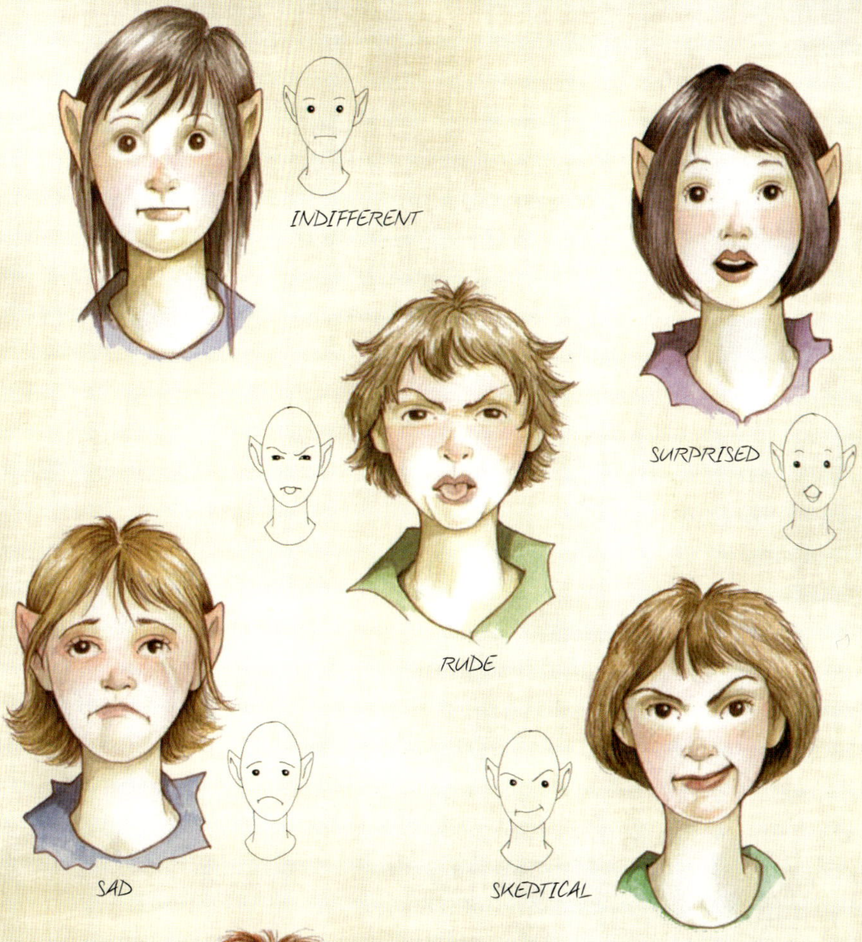

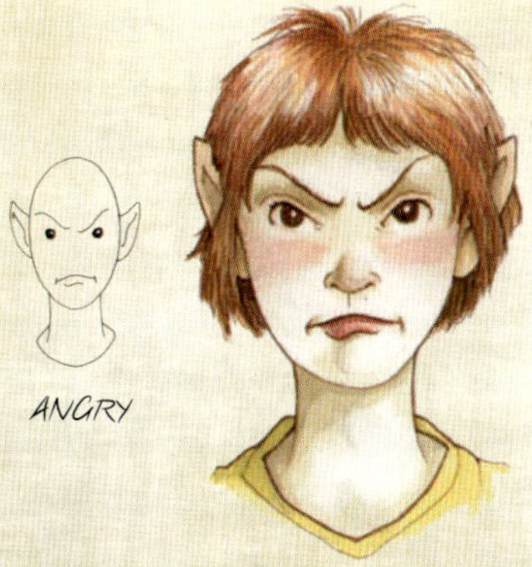

Practice expressions in front of a mirror

Watch how your face distorts, what muscles move, and how masses change, especially around the brow and cheeks. Observe the whole face, not just the brow and mouth, for subtle movements that can be used to add realism to expressions. Think in terms of the emotion you want to express, rather than the name of the expression—there is a distinct difference between a smiling face and a face displaying happiness.

Constructing hands and feet

HANDS AND FEET ARE CONSIDERED HARD TO DRAW AND ARE SOMETIMES LEFT AS GENERALIZED SHAPES. HOWEVER, THEY ARE EXPRESSIVE ANATOMICAL FEATURES.

Drawing simple feet Side view

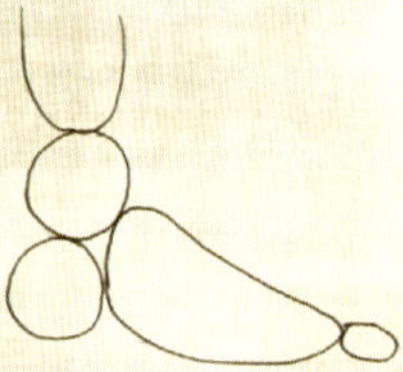

1 Feet are simple shapes. In profile, the heel and ankle are circles, the foot and toe modified ovals.

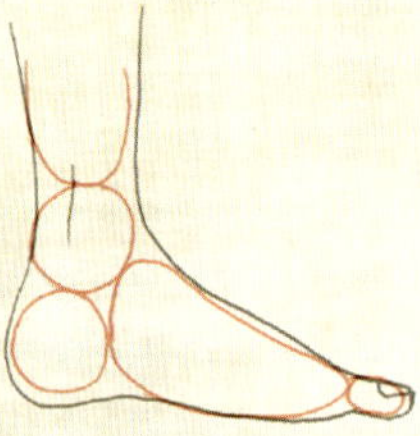

2 Draw an outline that skims around the basic underlying forms, rising at the arch. Add the nail of the big toe.

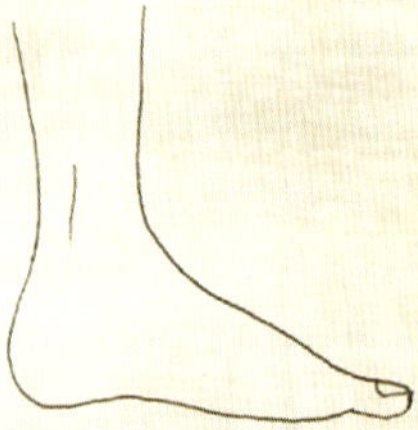

3 Erase the construction lines and you are left with a credible drawing of a solid, weight-bearing foot.

Drawing simple feet Three-quarter view

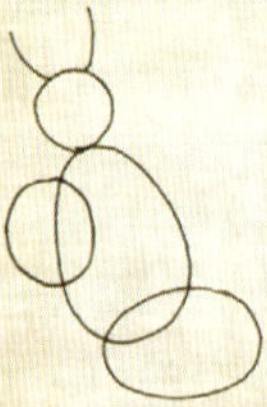

1 Start with the underlying shapes. From this view, the ovals and circles change their relationship with each other.

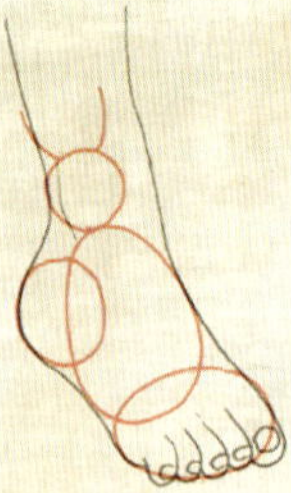

2 Draw the foot outline. At this angle, all the toes are visible and graduate in size to fill the large oval.

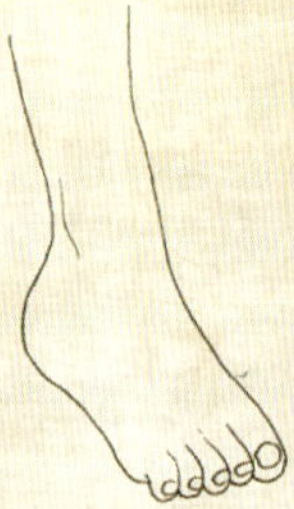

3 Erase the construction lines leaving the drawn foot.

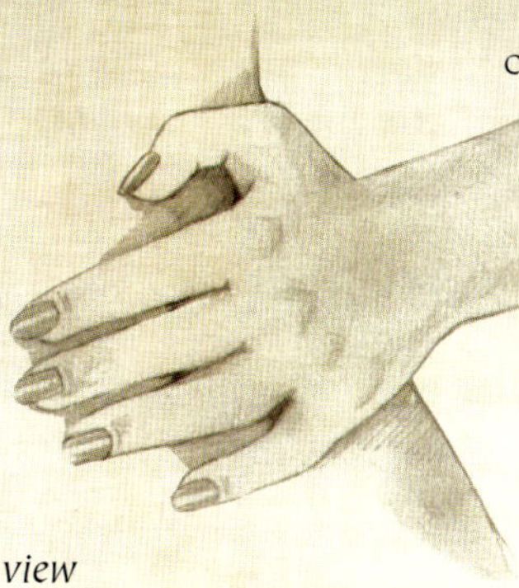

Drawing simple hands Front view

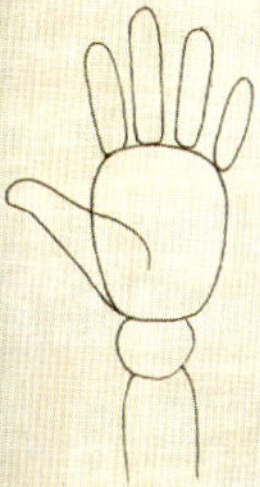

1 Visualize an outspread palm as a rounded rectangle, with a circle for the wrist joint. Add long sausage shapes for fingers and thumb.

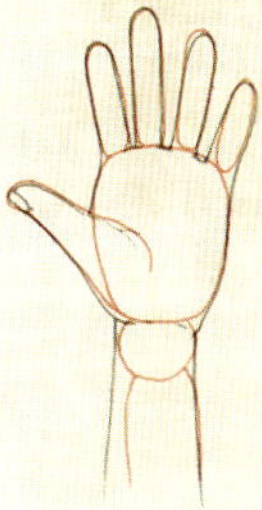

2 Draw the outline of the hand around the basic shapes. Add the nails if you are drawing the back of the hand, omitting them for a front view.

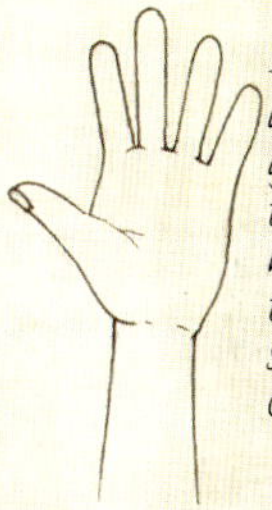

3 Now erase the structural underdrawing. If you are drawing the front of the hand, remember to indicate the swell at the base of the thumb.

Drawing hands in different positions

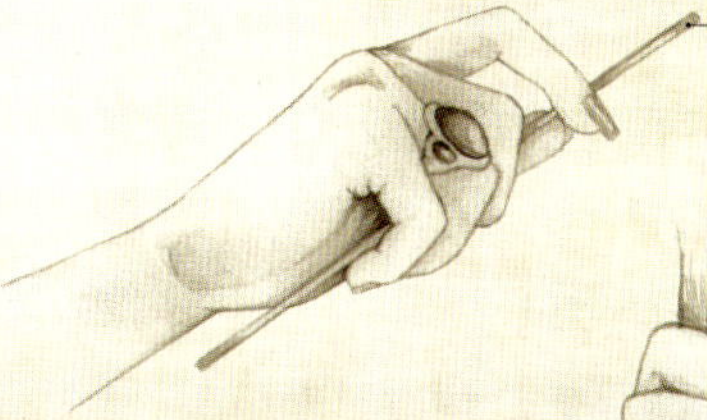

HOLDING A WAND
The three-dimensional sausage shapes that make up the fingers are divided into three jointed sections. Here, you can see how each finger bends to support the wand.

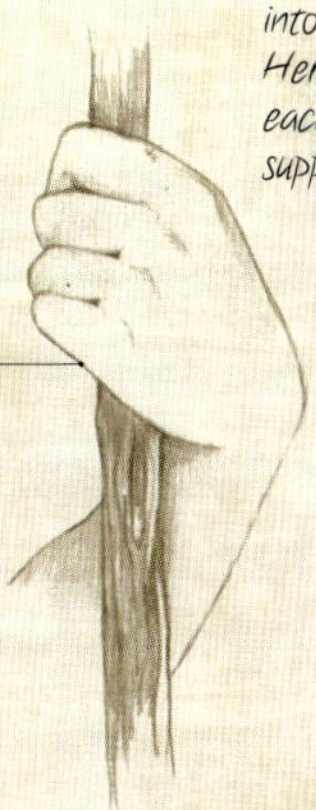

HOLDING A STAFF
The hand twists at the wrist and at the knuckles and only one section of the fingers is visible.

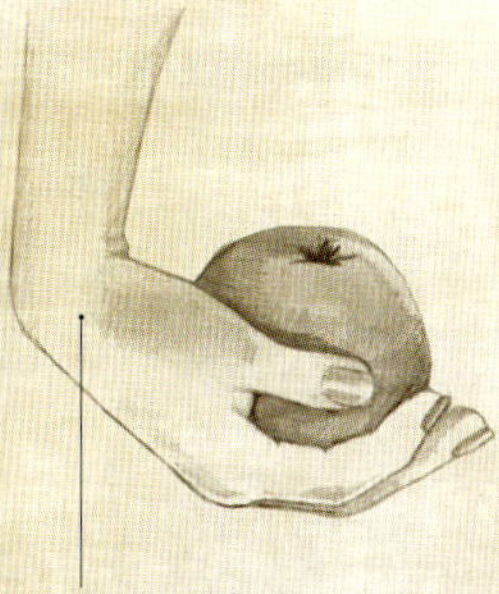

HOLDING AN APPLE
Draw the apple first so that you can curve the fingers around the sphere in a realistic way.

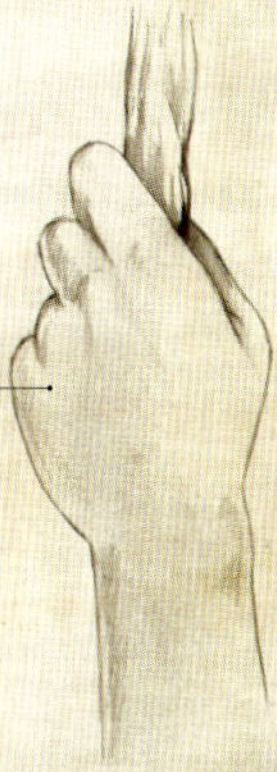

HOLDING A BRANCH
The fingers are only partially seen here, but the knuckles are visible and create a change of tone that describes the three-dimensional form.

Fairy wings

WINGS ARE AN ESSENTIAL ELEMENT OF FAIRY ANATOMY. IT IS THEIR WINGS THAT GIVE THESE DELICATE CREATURES THEIR ESSENTIAL "FAIRYNESS," AND SET THEM APART FROM THE MORTAL WORLD.

Drawing inspiration from nature

Natural history books have beautiful photographic studies of all kinds of flying creatures, as well as flowers and leaves. Use these as your starting point and adapt the shapes, patterns, and colors to suit your needs—your sketchbook is the place for visual notes.

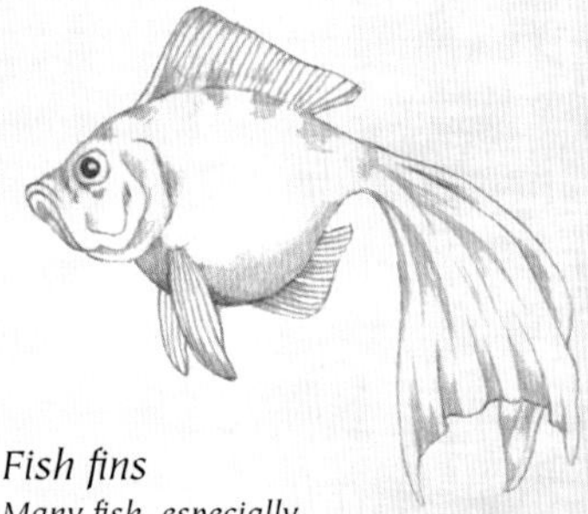

Fish fins

Many fish, especially goldfish and tropical species, have fins that are extravagantly shaped and vividly colored. Others have smaller, iridescent fins. All can provide inspiration for fairy wings.

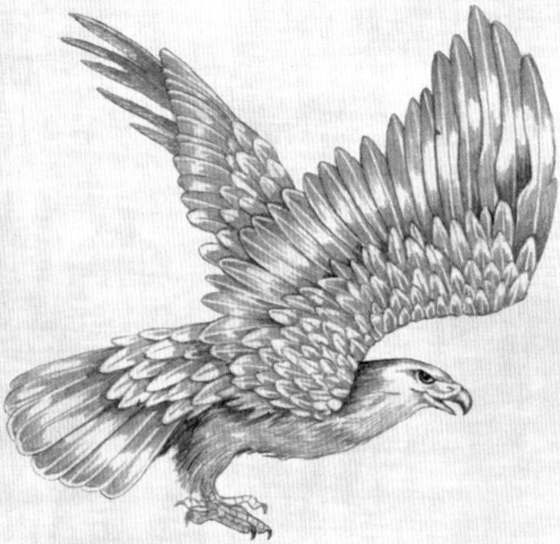

Bird wings

Consider your fairy's character—eagle wings give a sense of enormous strength and power. Smaller, more gentle birds, such as swans and doves, suggest elegant winter fairies and angelic creatures.

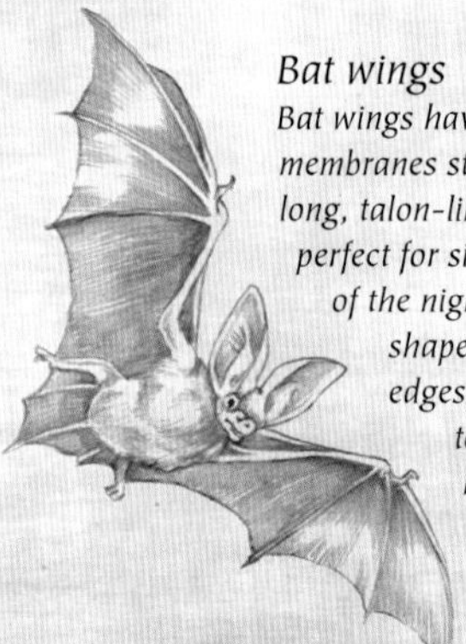

Bat wings

Bat wings have leathery membranes stretched between long, talon-like "fingers"—perfect for sinister, dark fairies of the night. Adapt the shape, create torn edges, and add talons to increase the horror element.

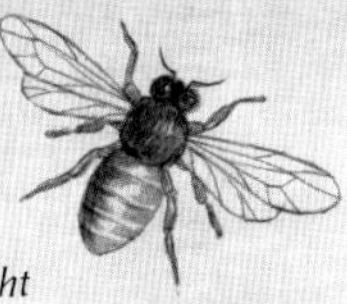

Winged insects

Bees and dragonflies have fragile, diaphanous wings for a fairy that's light as thistledown. Their shapes vary from small and rounded to long and slender.

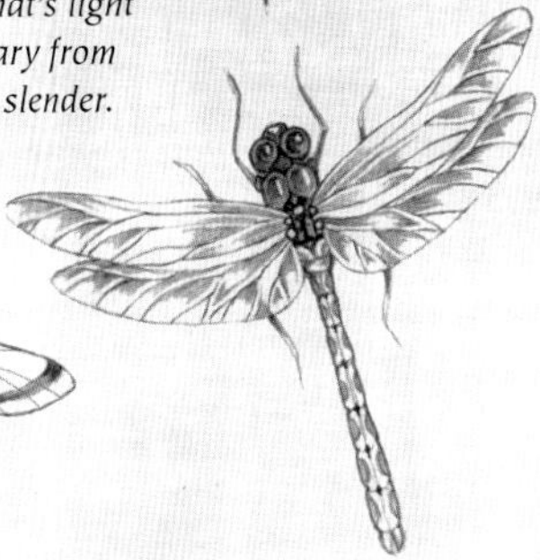

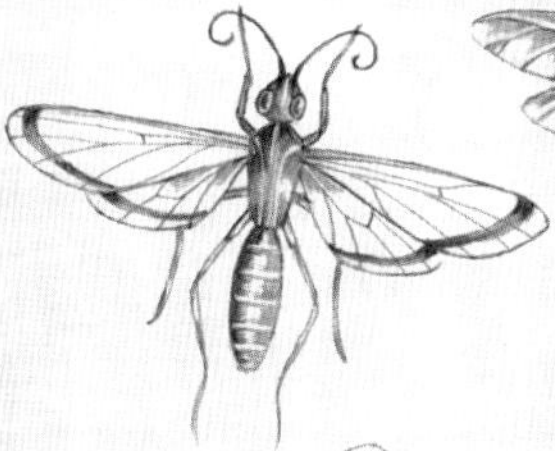

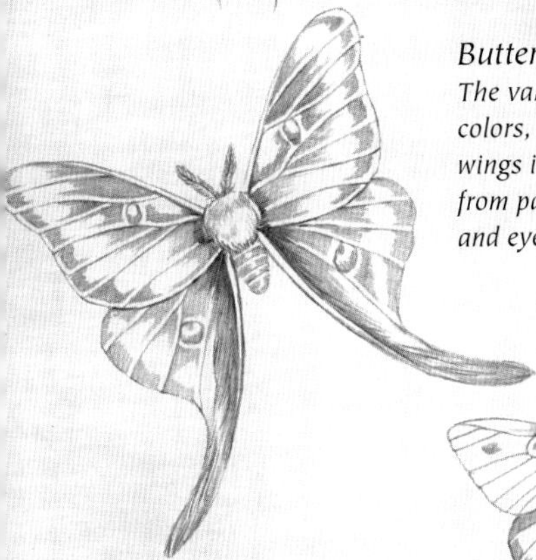

Butterflies and moths

The variety of sizes, shapes, colors, and patterns of butterfly wings is breathtaking, ranging from pale and delicate to bold and eye-catching.

Flowers and leaves

Leaf forms and petals make ideal wing designs for woodland sprites and flower fairies. Choose the right seasonal varieties and colors for the character.

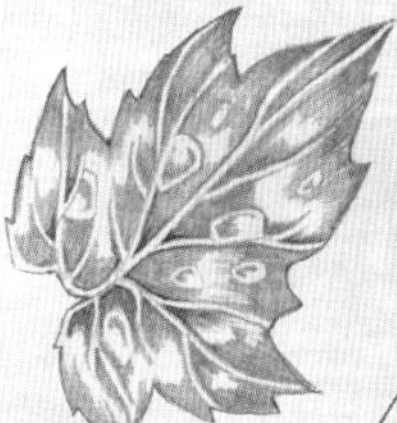

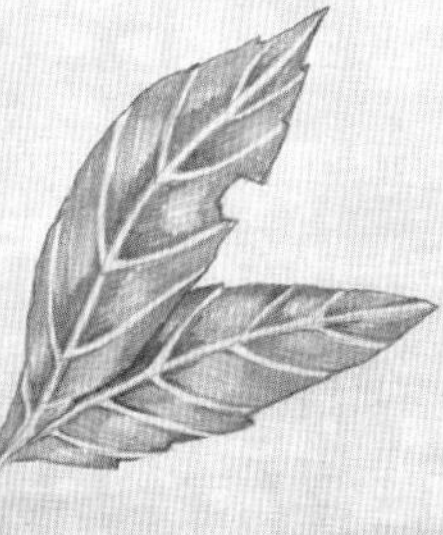

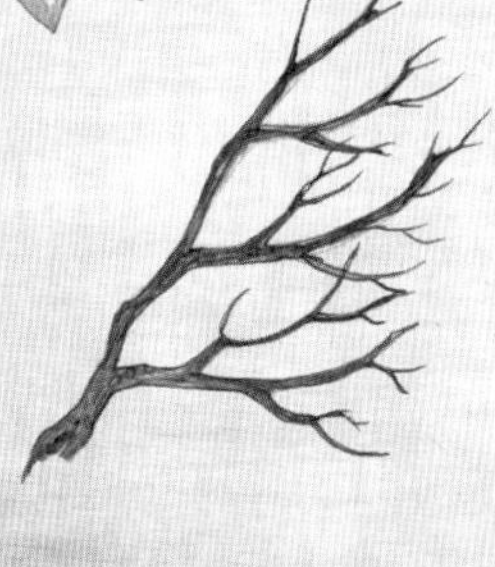

Wing templates

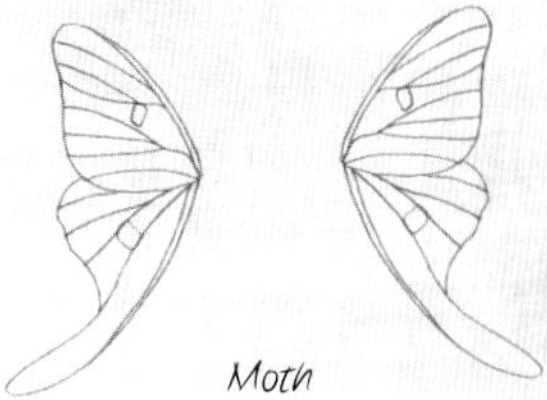

Moth

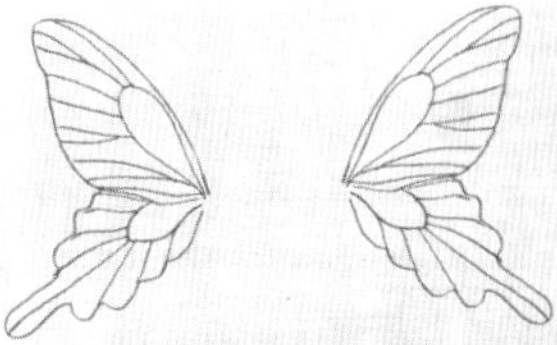

Butterfly

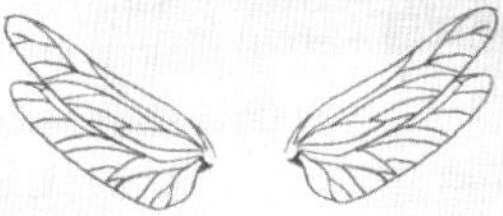

Dragonfly

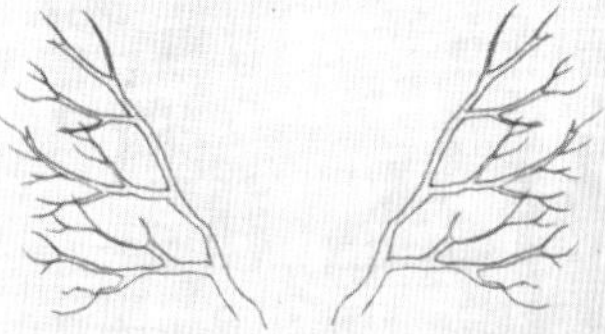

Twigs and branches

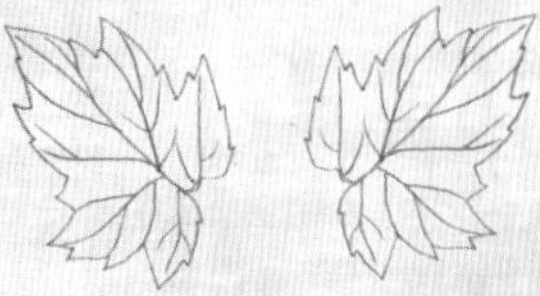

Leaves

Wing patterns

Source wing patterns from moths, butterflies, insects, leaves, and flowers. Render them with bright gouache or acrylics for vivid patterns; colored ink washes for silky translucence; or pale watercolor washes for gossamer effects. First explore your ideas with detailed pencil studies.

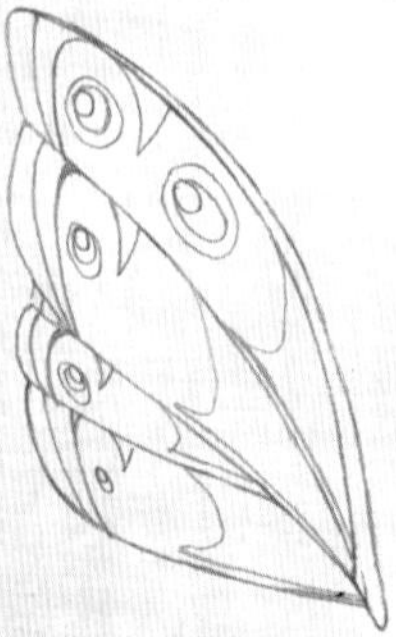

1 Draw the overall shape of the wings lightly, indicating the division between the large upper and smaller lower wings. With soft pencil marks, begin to delineate the most boldly patterned areas.

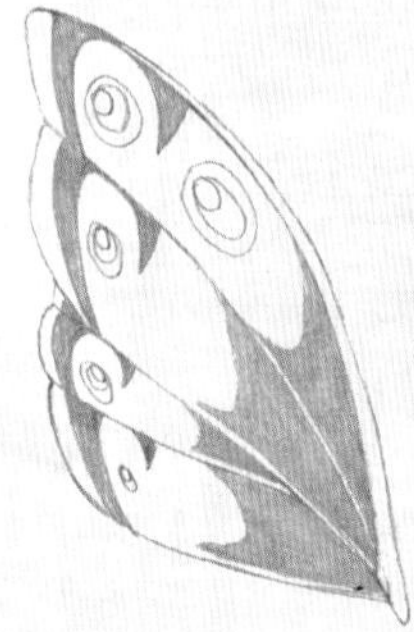

2 Shade in the midtones of the pattern, leaving the lightest areas white. Note that for this study tone is used to indicate depth of color, not to depict areas of shadow.

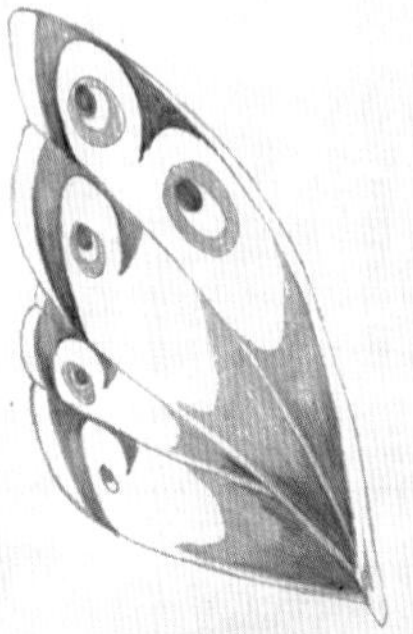

3 Add the darkest tones with heavier pencil marks. This wing pattern resembles that of a peacock butterfly, only with several "eyes." The high tonal values create a bold design.

Pattern variations

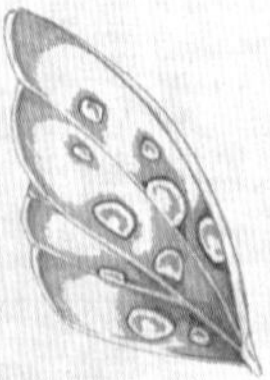

CIRCLES
Mossy growths on tree bark or underwater bubbles blown by a fish might inspire a design like this.

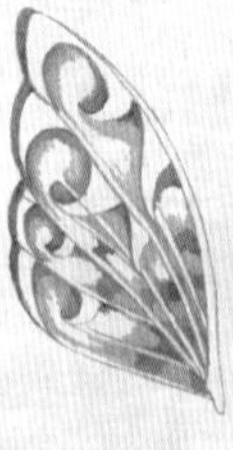

SPIRALS
This design might be an adapted fabric design.

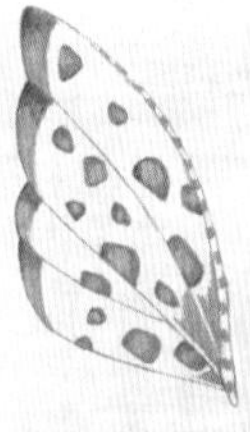

SPOTS
Using the markings of a wild animal will suggest to your audience that your fairy shares some of the animal's characteristics.

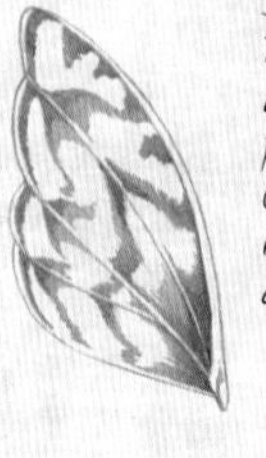

STRIPES
This zebra-inspired design might be painted in bright or subdued colors instead of black and white.

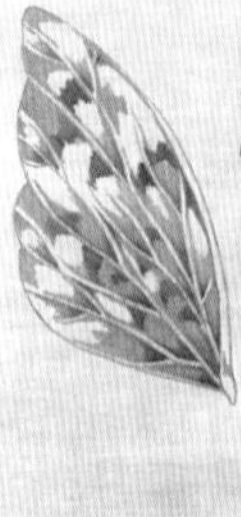

MOTTLED
Plumage patterns are a good source of ideas for fairy wings.

Wing positioning

Fairy wings are not merely ornamental. They must look capable of lifting the fairy into the air, so their positioning is crucial. Placing them on the mobile shoulder blades means they will move whenever the arms are raised, and thus the idea of flight becomes more credible.

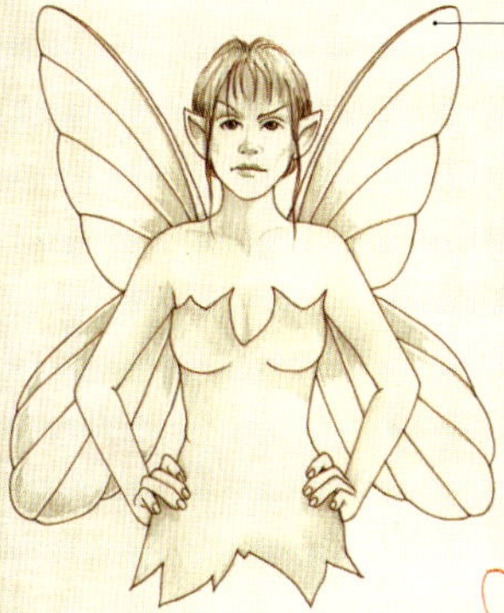

FRONT VIEW
Seen from the front, the outer edges of the wing pairs are equally visible, while the tapering inner corners disappear behind the shoulders to the points of attachment.

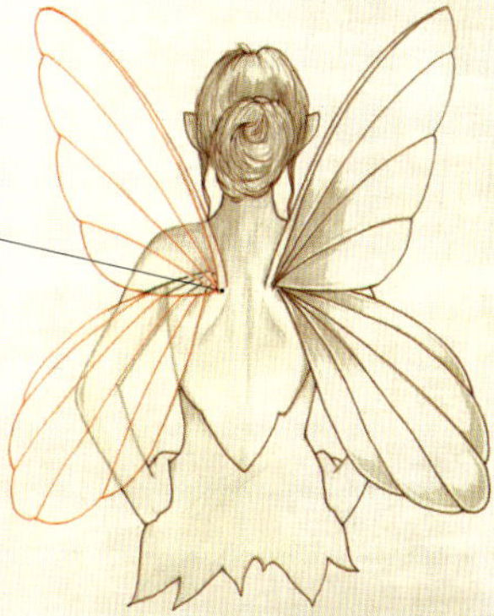

BACK VIEW
A back view shows exactly where the wings are attached to the inner edges of the shoulder blades. Every movement of the arms and shoulders will make them move.

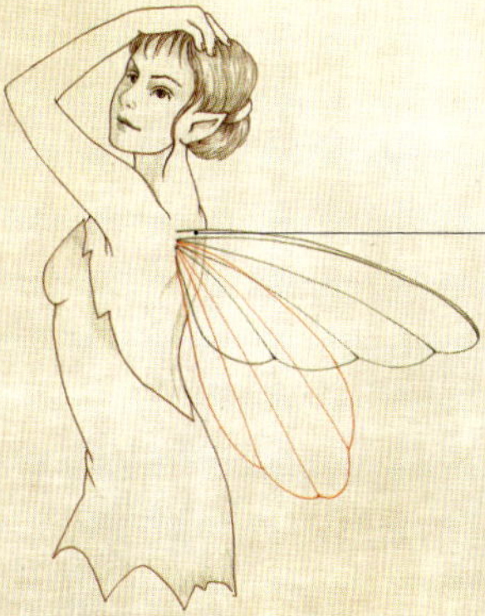

SIDE VIEW
Here the wings are folded down in rest, and the point of attachment is visible. The far wings are obscured from this viewpoint. The wing pairs would lift and separate when in flight.

Wing templates

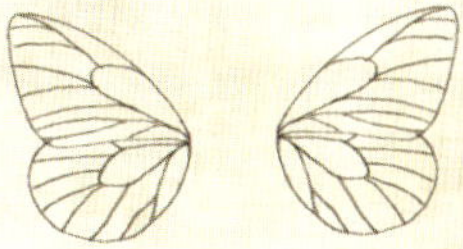

Small butterfly

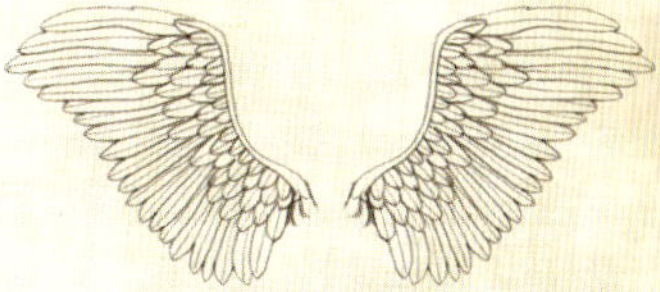

Bird

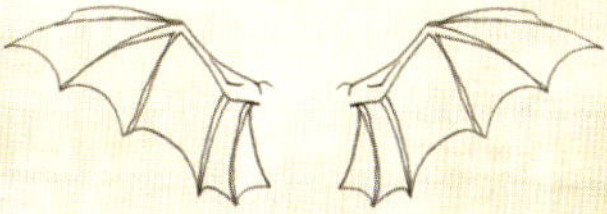

Bat

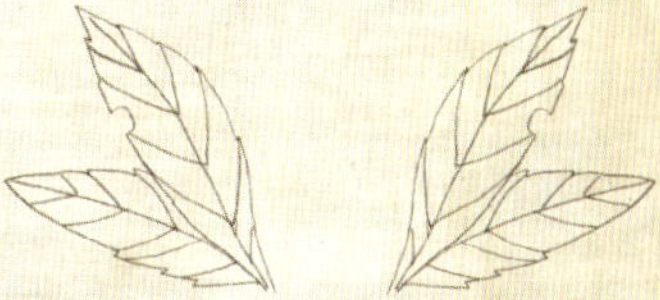

Leaves

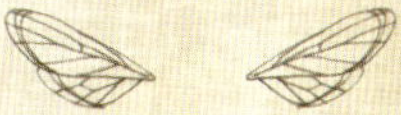

Moth

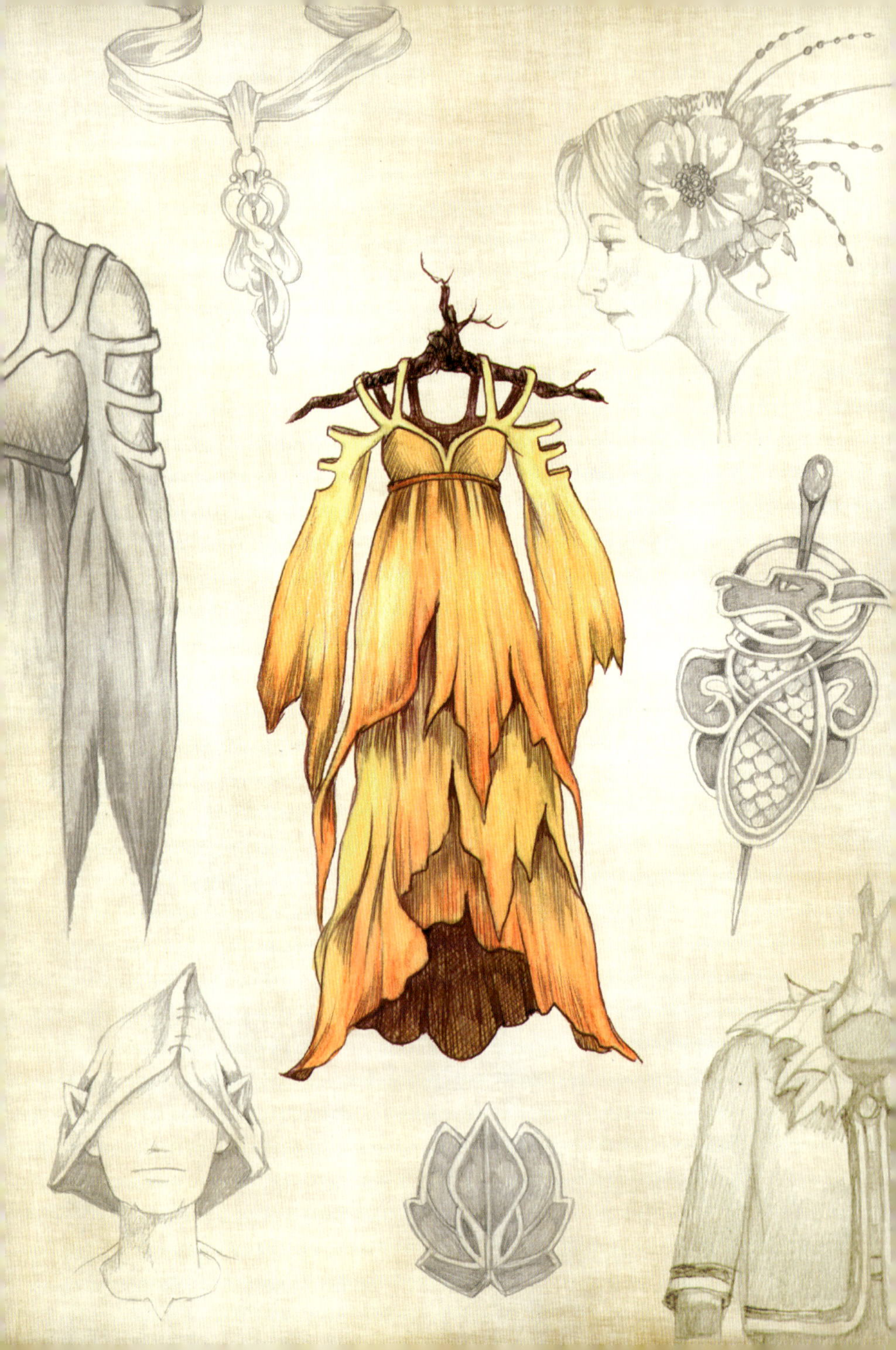

Part 4

Costumes and accessories

Fairy costume is as diverse as the characters themselves. For some, a flutter of diaphanous fabric suffices; others require elaborate outfits; and yet others wear homespun. You can adapt human garments, flowers, or leaves for fairy clothing, get ideas from Victorian and Medieval eras, or create original designs. In addition, magic wands, crystal balls, and Celtic jewelry are just some of the accessories essential to building fairy character.

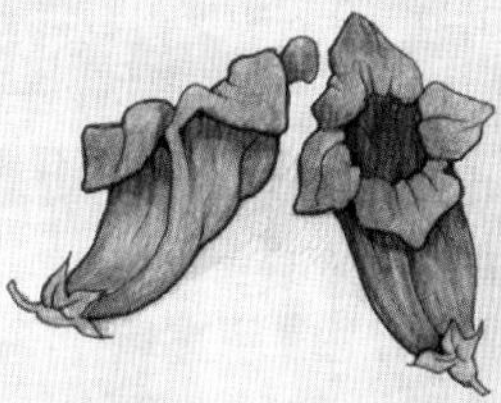

Dresses and robes

FINE CHIFFON, DELICATE SILK, RICH SATIN, OR VELVET; FAIRY DRESSES CAN BE PALE AND ETHEREAL OR VIBRANTLY COLORED, MODERN OR VINTAGE, COSTLY OR HOMESPUN.

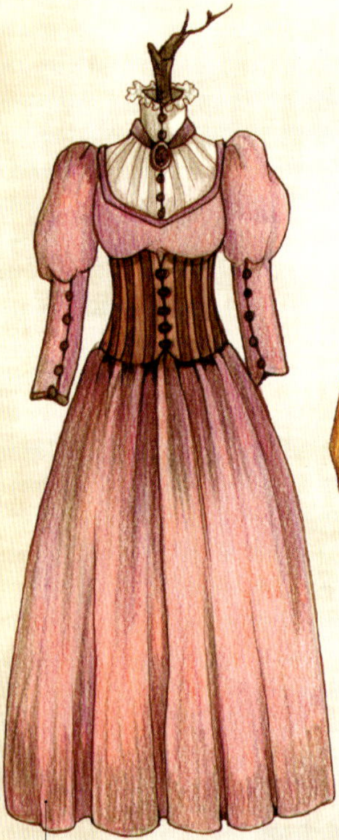

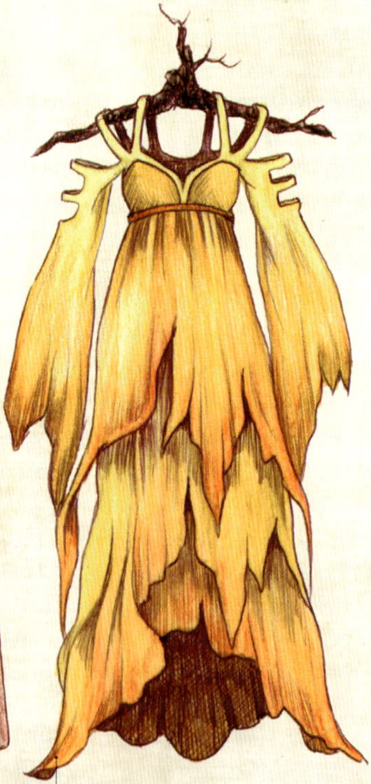

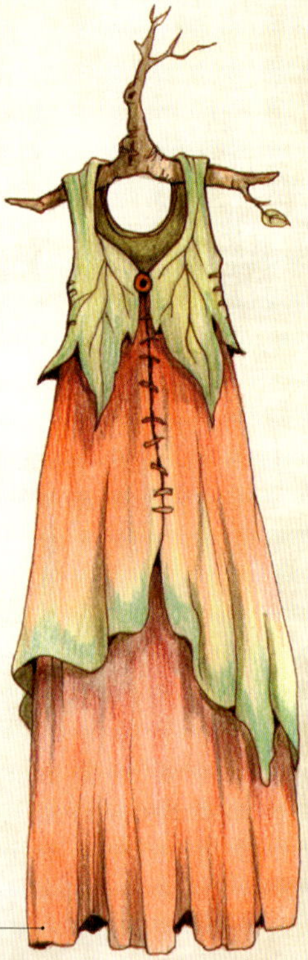

SUGGESTING FOLDS
Clothes drape according to the fabric. Heavy cloth forms stiff creases, lighter fabrics create soft folds. Depict these with carefully placed tonal gradations, using dark tones for the deep "valleys," and the lightest shades for the top of the folds.

DEPICTING SILKY FABRICS
Silk and satin reflect light from their smooth surfaces, creating large areas of bright highlight. Imitating this effect will suggest the quality of the fabric. Here, the highlights are almost white, suggesting a very reflective fabric.

USING COLOR
You can use color to create eye-catching contrasts that draw attention to your character. Here the bright floral combination of complementary red and green react with each other to create a vibrant effect. Harmonious color pairings have a quieter effect.

See also: The template fairy figure on page 59.

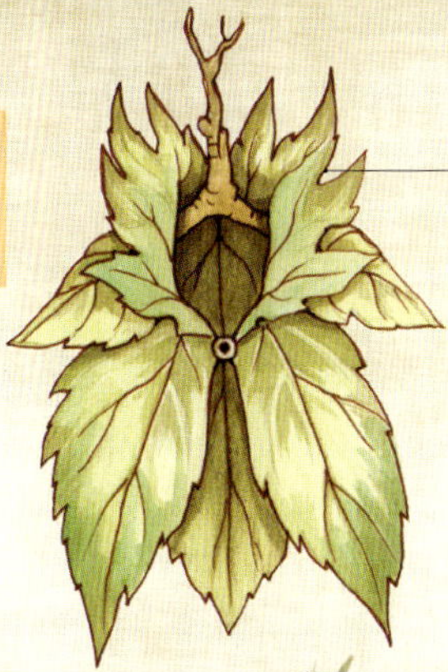

USING NATURE
Fairies are creatures of nature, and their costumes can reflect this. Leaves of all shapes, sizes, and colors are easily adapted to create garments. Here, spring leaves are fashioned into a jacket but they could equally well make a skirt.

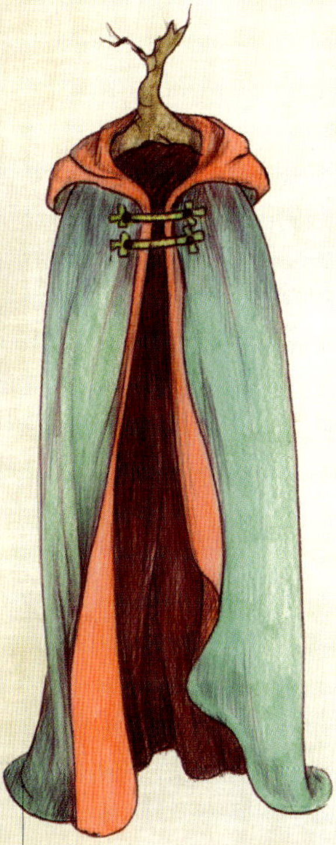

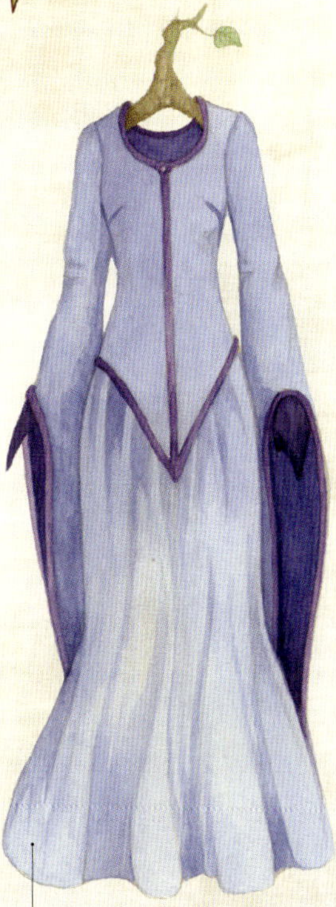

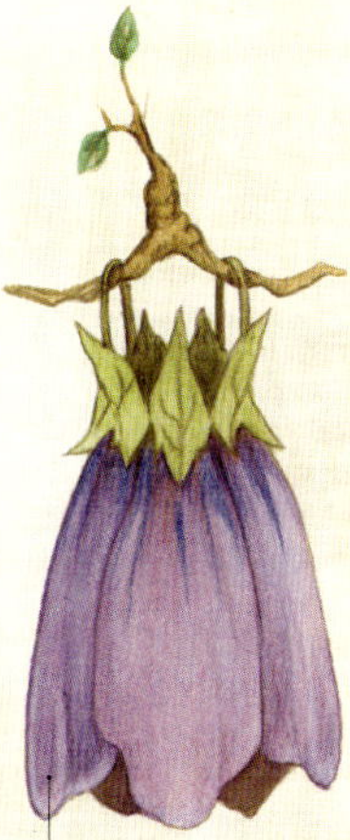

CREATING CONCEPTS
Flower fairies are an example of a total concept. Their host flowers define their identity, personality, and dress code. Garments are created, as here, from the natural forms they protect. With creative thought, this approach works for most fairy characters.

SUGGESTING HEAVY FABRICS
Heavy fabrics create large folds, and hang straighter than lightweight alternatives. Here there are no sharp creases. Instead softly rounded folds indicate the quality of velvet. Notice that the fabric hangs heavily and "pools" softly where it touches the floor.

CHOOSING SHAPE
The cut and shape of a gown reflect the character of the fairy. This fitted bodice, flowing skirt, and medieval-style sleeves suggest elegance and sophistication.
A cinched waist, full skirt, and strappy bodice would create a more frivolous image.

Tunics, jackets, pants

MALE FAIRIES NEED WARDROBES AS VARIED AS THOSE OF THEIR FEMALE COUNTERPARTS. EACH CHARACTER HAS HIS OWN DRESS CODE ACCORDING TO HIS NATURE AND ACTIVITY.

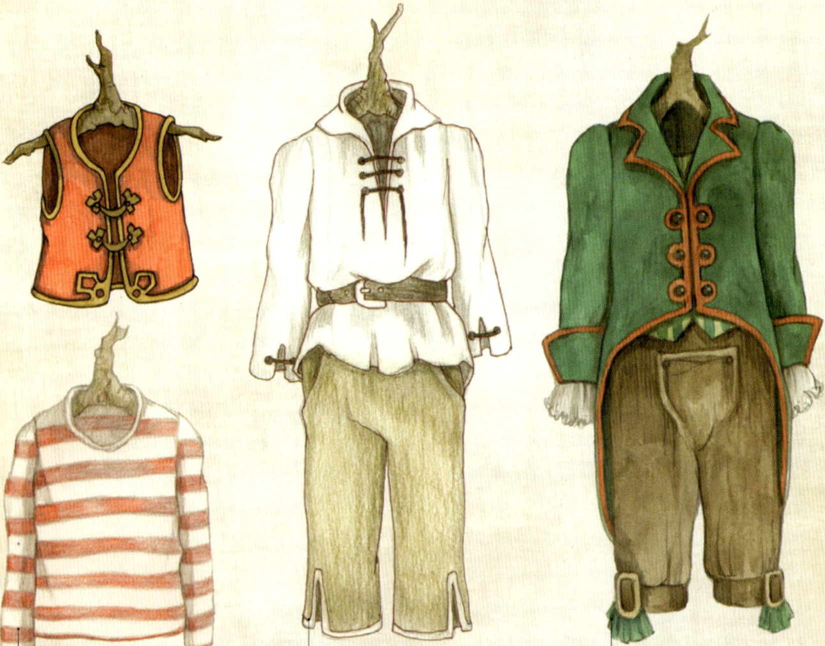

CHARACTER AND STYLE
Use telling costume styles and details to reflect and express character. A smart gold-trimmed vest, for instance, could belong to a dapper little Gnome, while a striped shirt suggests an altogether more laid-back and mischievous Pixie character.

SHAPE AND FIT
Loosely-belted shirts and knee breeches are standard wear for many male fairies. These garments are infinitely adaptable in fit, fabric, and color and have a rugged masculinity suitable for characters as diverse as the Fairy King or the smallest Gnome.

COLOR CHOICES
Here the shirt and breeches combination is smartened up with a stylish jacket. The vibrant color choice of emerald with complementary scarlet trim creates instant visual focus and a sense of richness, suggesting a more dapper and flamboyant character.

See also: The template fairy figure on page 59.

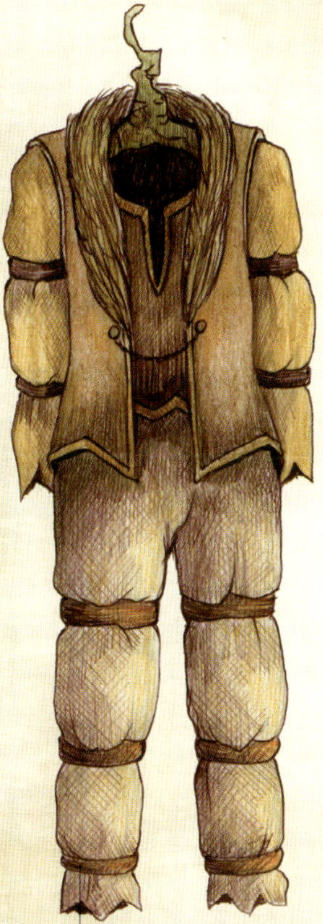

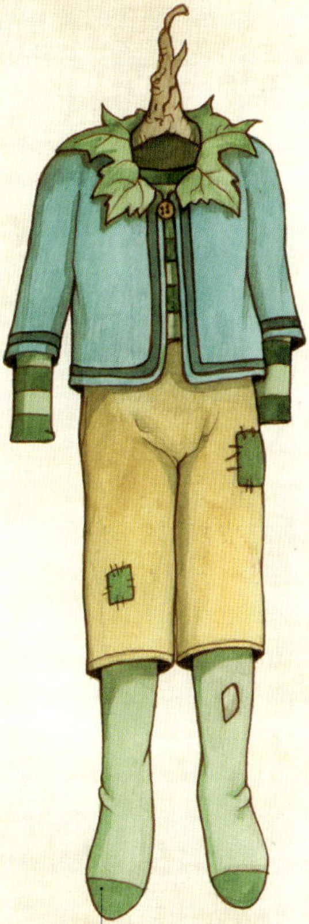

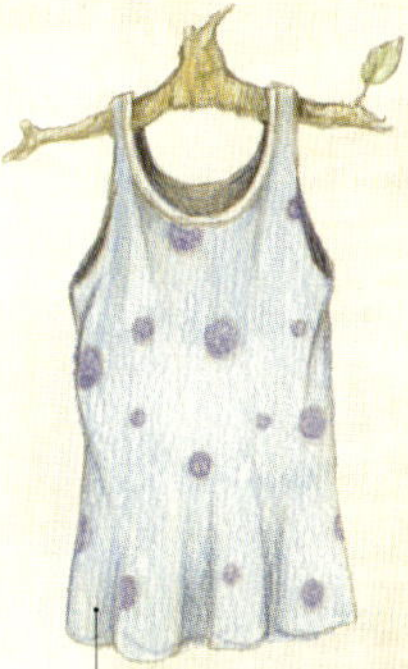

REFLECTING HABITAT
Fairies who live in dark, cold places need different costume considerations to those who live in warmth and sunshine. A wispy singlet like this would be insufficient for a chilly habitat but might suit a water sprite or a summer flower guardian.

SUGGESTING HOMESPUN
Many characters wear humble homespun garments. These have a rougher texture and duller color than costly fabrics. Here a monochrome palette implies natural dyes and creates a muted image, while cross-hatching and shading suggest the coarse texture.

DEVELOPING CONCEPTS
Use information about environment and function to develop a character concept and create a costume theme. This outfit, for example, suits a tree fairy. The palette of green, yellow, and blue has a fresh, outdoor feel, and leaf trims represent the tree he protects.

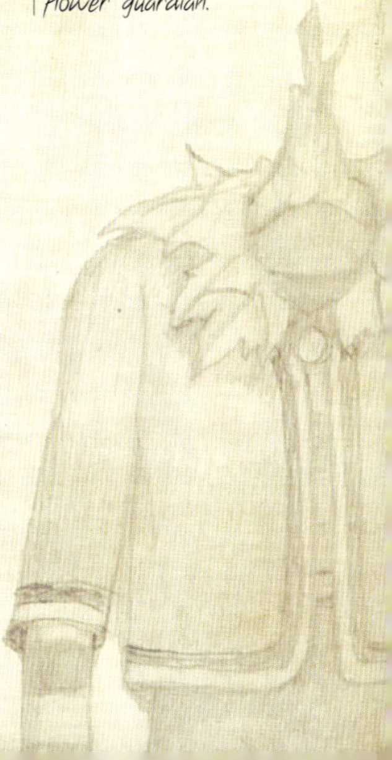

Fairy accessories

WHILE MANY FAIRIES GO BAREFOOT, OTHERS REQUIRE FOOTWEAR TO SUIT THEIR CHARACTER, OCCUPATION, AND HABITAT. MANY ALSO NEED PROPS. YOU MAY SPOT THE WANDS, STAFFS, CRYSTAL BALLS, AND OTHER PARAPHERNALIA SHOWN HERE LATER IN THE BOOK, ADORNING VARIOUS FAIRY CHARACTERS.

Fairy paraphernalia

1 *Jeweled silver dagger*
2 *Magic staff with crystal*
3 *Magic wand*
4 *Bowl*
5 *Magic staff with bird skull*
6 *Glass decanter for magic ink*
7 *Jeweled silver chalice*
8 *Pan pipe*
9 *Book of ancient spells*
10 *Tobacco pouch and clay pipe*
11 *Crystal ball for divination*
12 *Velvet pouch for fairy dust*

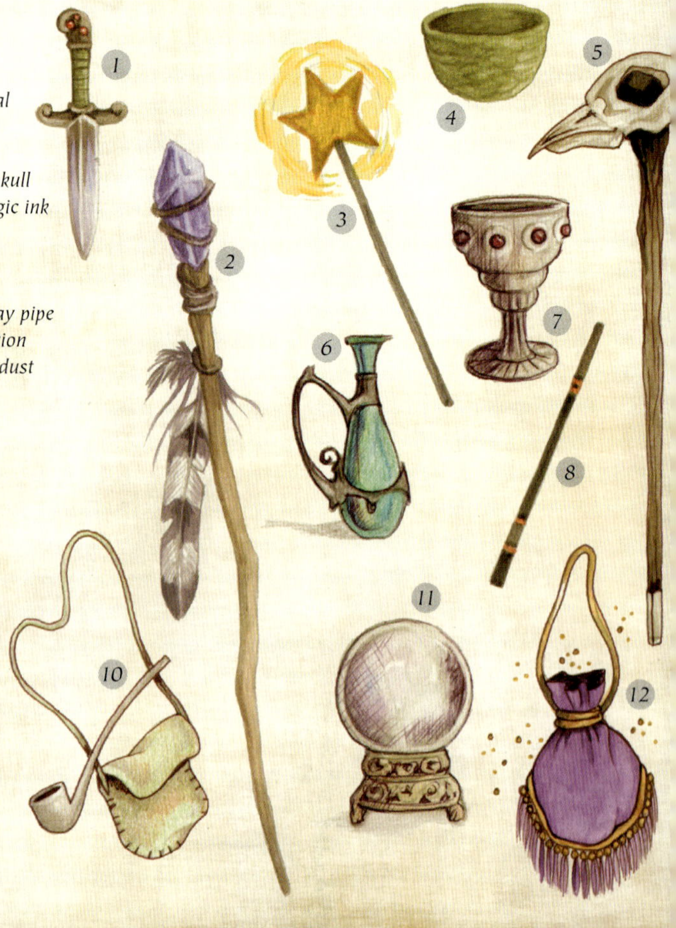

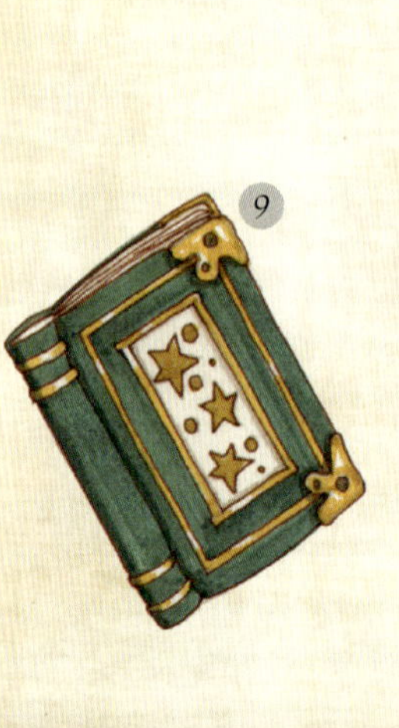

Shoe selector

1 *Buckled shoes*
2 *Satin dancing shoes*
3 *Victorian lace-up boots*
4 *Embroidered satin slippers*
5 *Green leaf slippers*
6 *Red patent shoes*
7 *Flower slippers*
8 *Female buckled shoe*
9 *Stout leather boots*
10 *Pixie boots with bells*
11 *Striped stockings*
12 *Forget-me-not slippers*
13 *Buckled biker boots*
14 *Spare pixie boots*

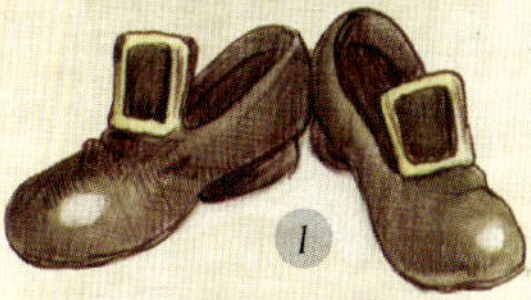
1

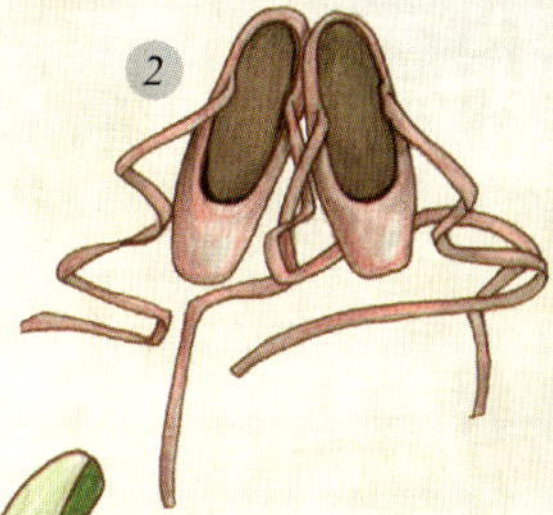
2

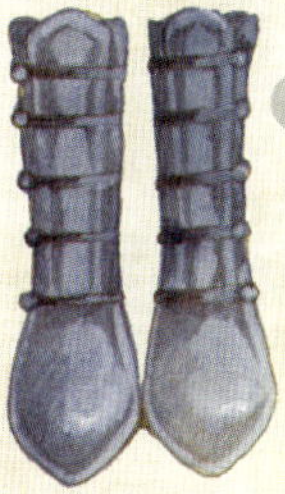
3

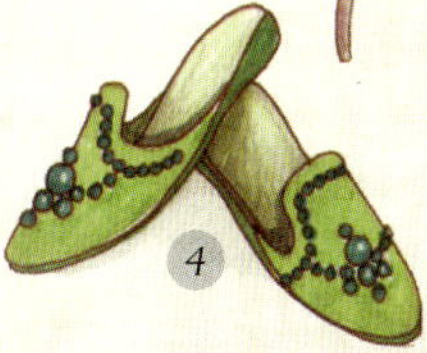
4

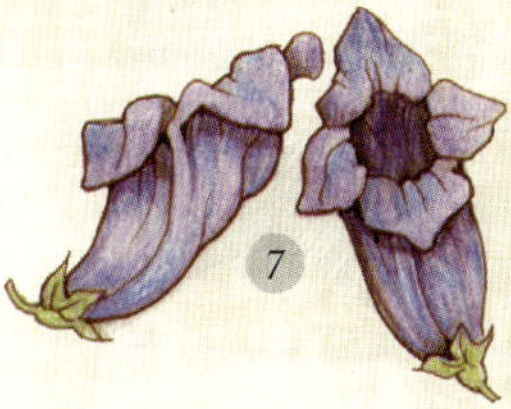
7

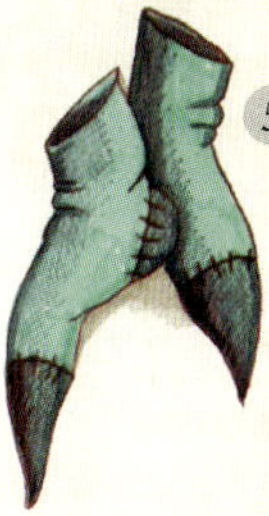
5

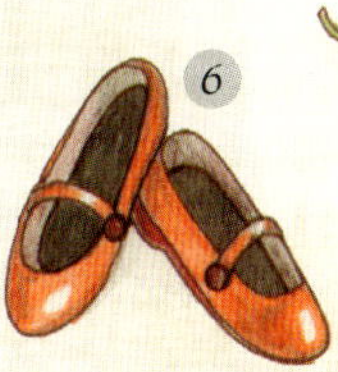
6

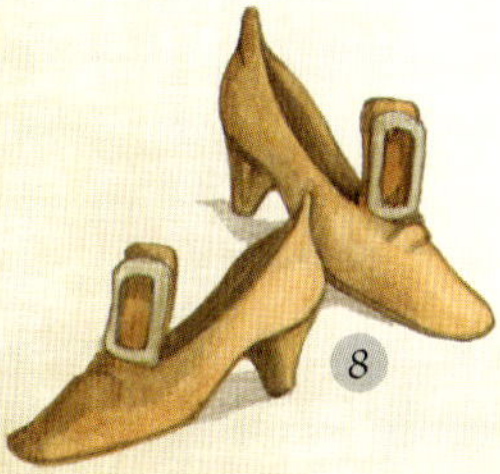
8

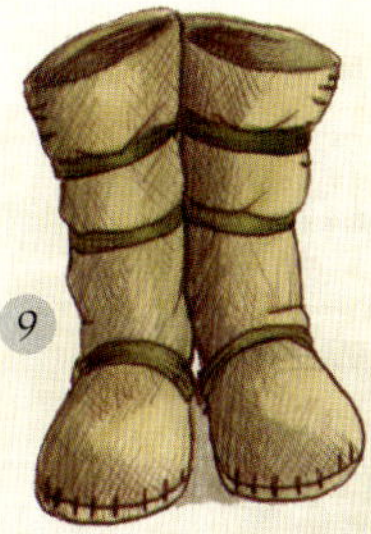
9

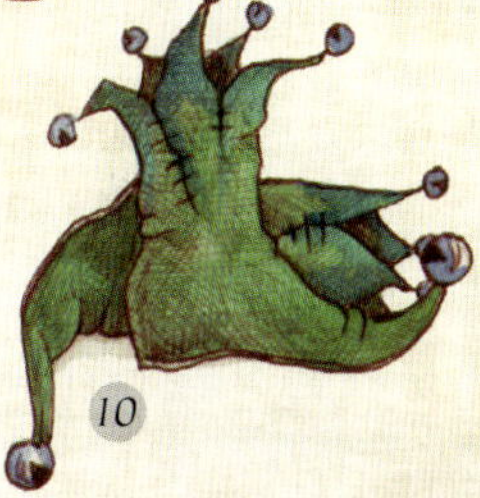
10

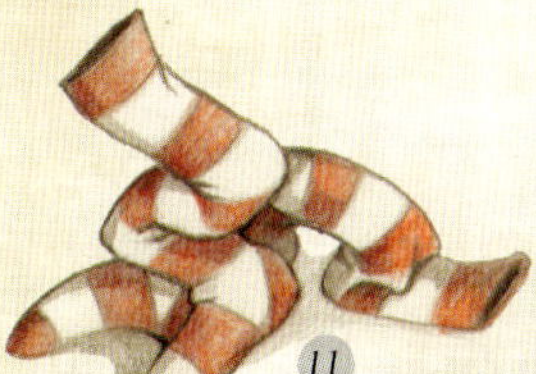
11

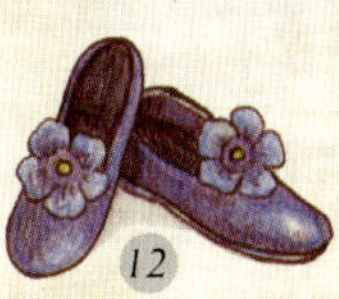
12

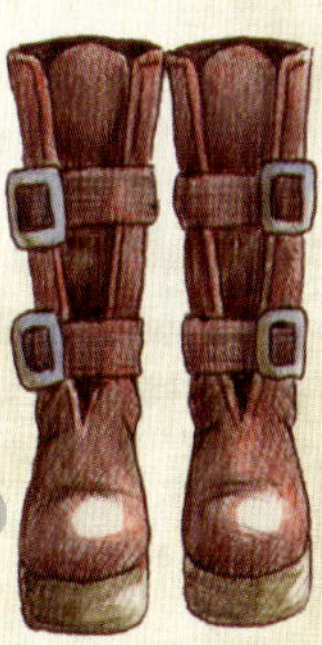
13

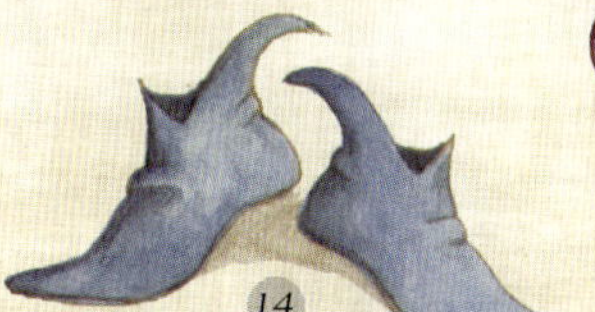
14

Hair and headwear

THE CHOICE OF HAIRSTYLE IS FUNDAMENTAL TO THE NATURE OF YOUR FAIRY. COLLECT AND SKETCH HUMAN HAIRSTYLES, BOTH MODERN AND HISTORICAL, TO ADAPT FOR YOUR FAIRY NEEDS.

Typical fairy hairstyles

Female fairy hair can be long and romantic or short and modern, curly or straight, loose or braided. Male fairies can have similarly varied hairstyles according to their character, and they too, like many human males, can wear their hair tied back.

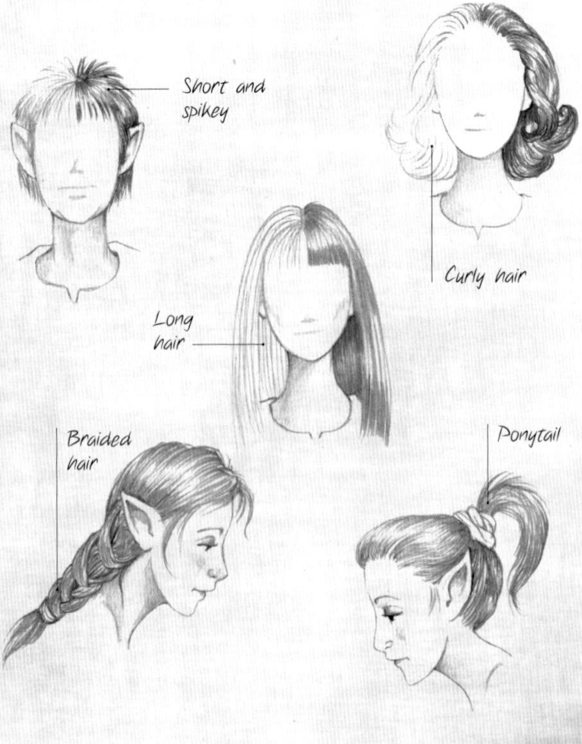

Creating hair textures

Graphite pencil is an ideal medium for creating hair textures. Working from light to dark, you can deepen the tone and texture in gradual stages. Use an HB pencil, which creates soft light tones and fine details. With increased pressure and overlaid marks it builds up darker tones to add depth.

1 Start lightly, mapping out the overall shape of the hairstyle.

2 Use soft broken marks to add pale tones, leaving some areas white for highlights.

3 Increase the pressure on the pencil to add successive layers of tone, using open marks to build up texture and depth.

4 Leave light areas for highlights, or lift these out with a kneadable putty eraser.

Hats and headdresses

A single flower or garland of blooms, leaves, or berries provides instant clues to the nature and habitat of the fairy. Feathers and beads intertwined in the hair suit older and more sophisticated characters.

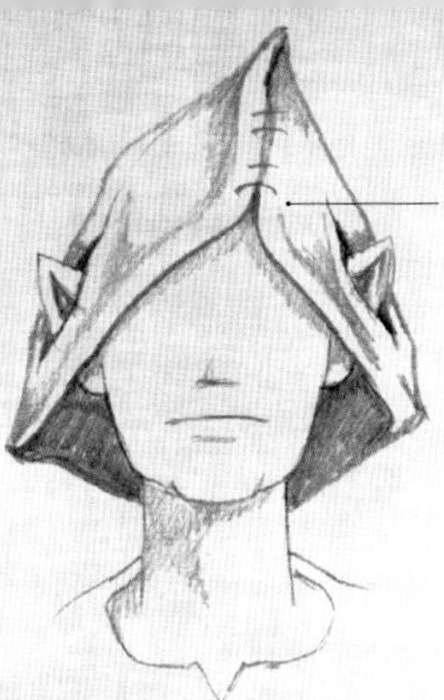

SIMPLE STITCHED HAT
Leaves, petals, or scraps of fabric can be fashioned into caps and hats with just a few fairy stitches. The pencil shading suggests a smooth surface such as a piece of material or even paper.

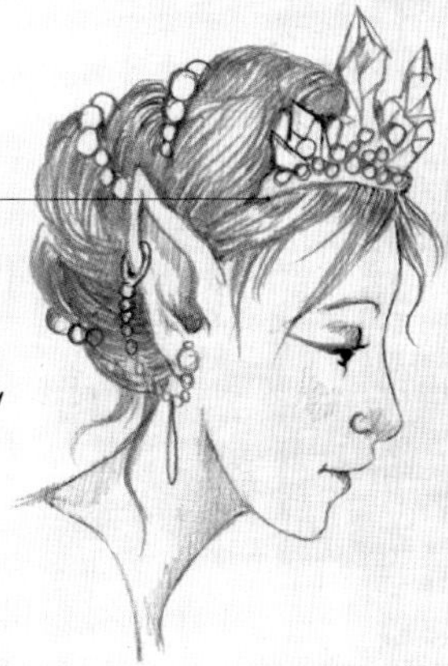

JEWELED TIARA
Dark hair tones create an eye-catching contrast with the white of the hair ornament. These high tonal values create the illusion that the jewels and pearls are glittering and lustrous.

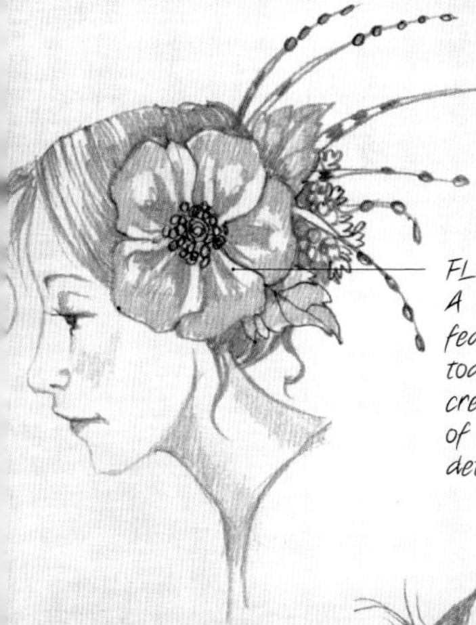

FLOWER AND FEATHERS
A large bloom teamed with feathers creates what is known today as a "fascinator." Graphite creates both the generalized tones of the hair contrast and the fine details of hair adornment.

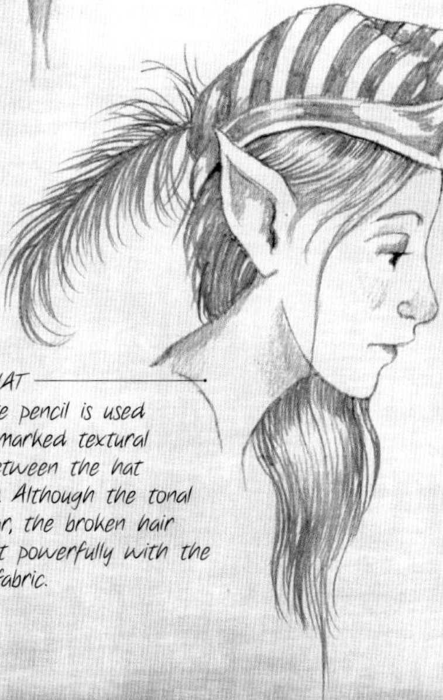

PLUMED HAT
Here graphite pencil is used to create a marked textural difference between the hat and the hair. Although the tonal value is similar, the broken hair tones contrast powerfully with the smooth hat fabric.

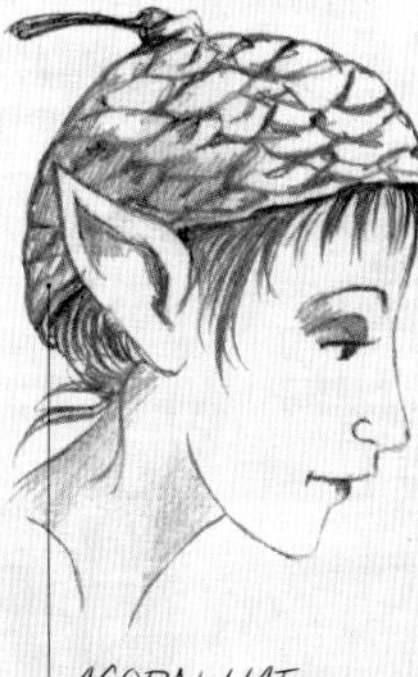

ACORN HAT
An upturned acorn cup creates an instant ready-to-wear hat. Notice how the pencil is used in different ways to describe every texture, from smooth skin and soft hair to rough acorn cup.

Fairy silver

FAIRY SILVER IS STEEPED IN MAGIC AND SYMBOLISM AND MANY FAIRIES ARE DEPICTED WEARING INTRICATE ITEMS OF SILVER JEWELRY THAT ADD TO THEIR AURA OF MYSTERY AND ENCHANTMENT. RINGS, NECKLACES, BROOCHES, PENDANTS, AND BRACELETS ARE OFTEN INLAID WITH CRYSTALS AND JEWELS, AND DISPLAY ANCIENT ESOTERIC RUNES AND CELTIC SYMBOLS.

Ear jewelry

There's plenty of inspiration for fairy ear decorations amongst the wealth of innovative designs on today's fashion scene.

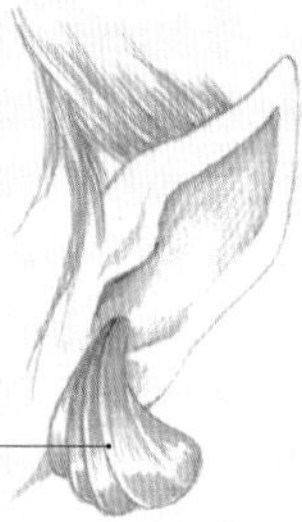

SHELL EARRING
A bold earring with an organic feel that imitates natural seashell forms.

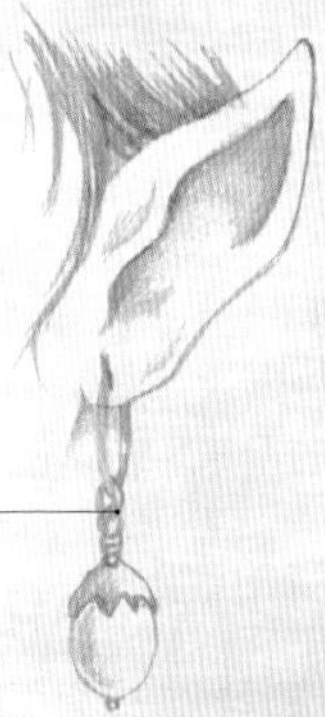

TRADITIONAL PENDANT EARRING
This simple pendant teardrop earring conveys traditional understated elegance and sophistication.

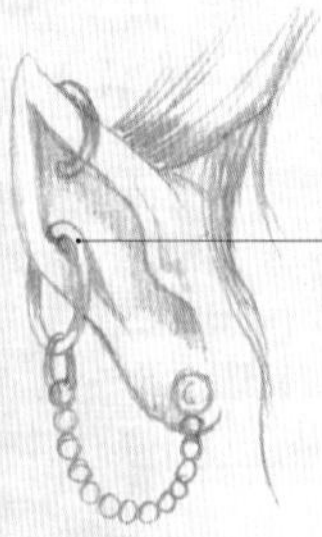

COMBINATION EAR DECORATION
A plain stud combined with a chain and ring is a young and pretty fashion.

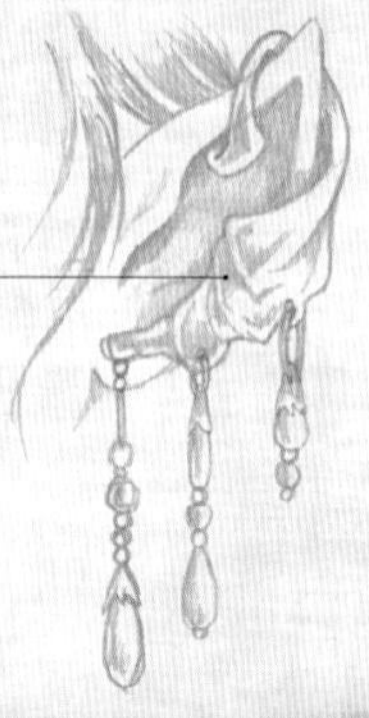

EAR CUFF
Elaborate ear cuffs combine current fashion with traditional pendant elements.

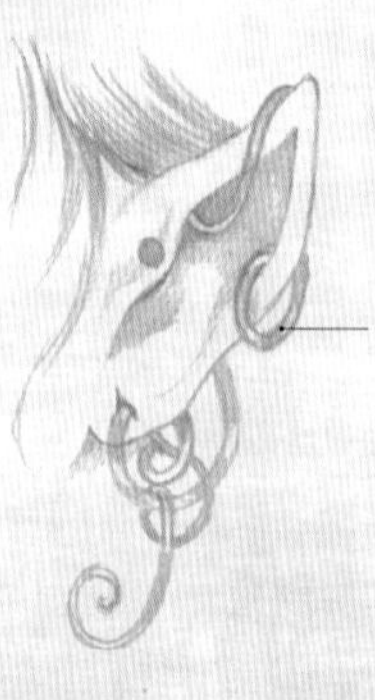

MULTIPLE EARRINGS
Multiple piercing is perfect for a Gothic Fairy with modern Goth fashion tastes and attitude.

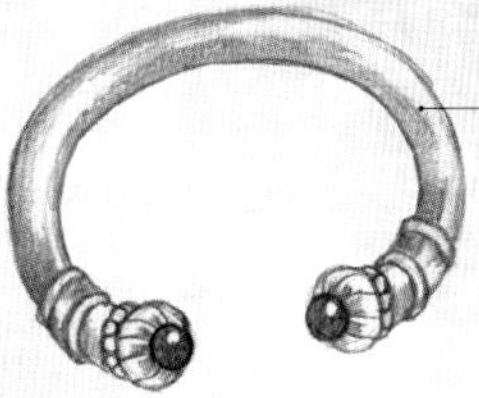

JEWELED BANGLE
Heavy bangle inset with jewels.

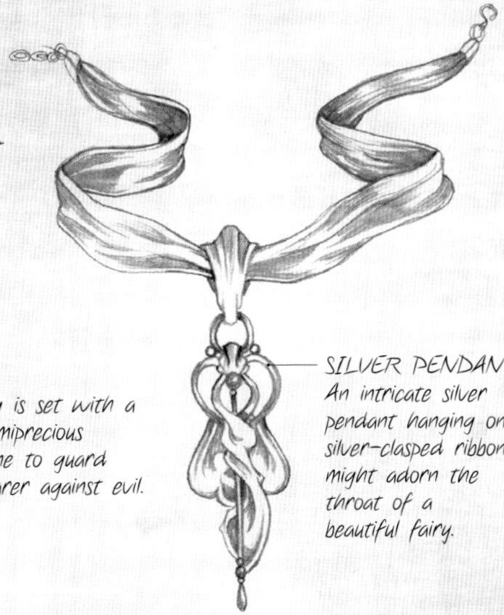

SILVER PENDANT
An intricate silver pendant hanging on a silver-clasped ribbon might adorn the throat of a beautiful fairy.

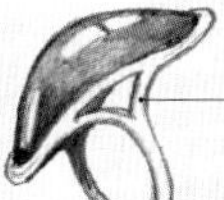

RING
This ring is set with a large semiprecious moonstone to guard the wearer against evil.

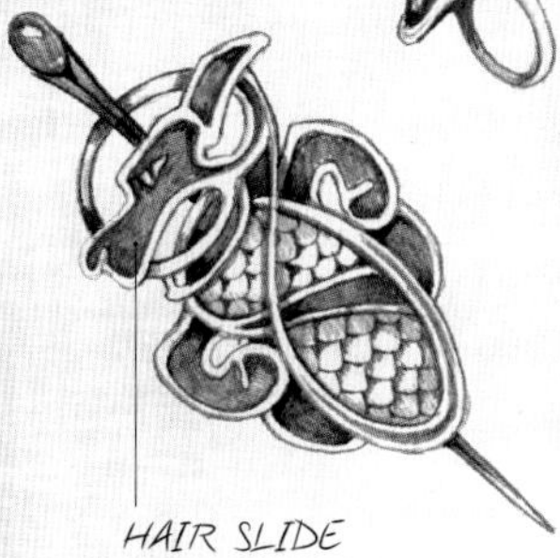

HAIR SLIDE
Elaborate hair decorations incorporate filigree work in a swirling Celtic-style design.

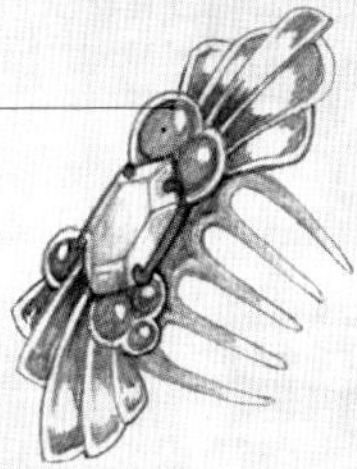

HAIR COMB
Hair decorations are high on the list of must-have fairy accessories, and a jewel-encrusted silver comb is a simple way to secure flowing tresses.

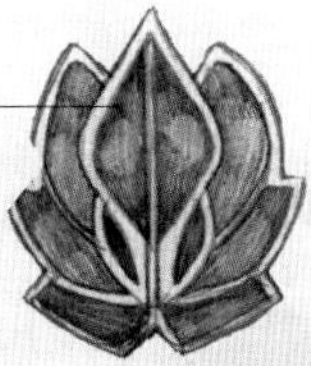

SILVER BROOCH
Brooch fashioned in the form of a symbolic leaf design, suitable perhaps for the Guardian Fairy with her deep connection to nature.

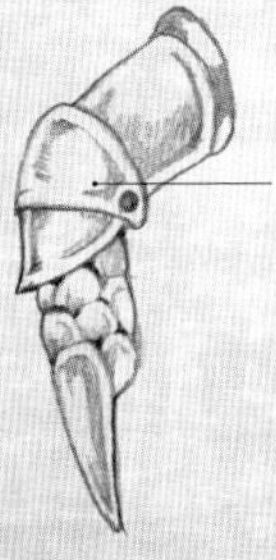

FINGER GUARD
Sinister jointed finger cuff with an overtly aggressive air; this would suit the challenging nature of a modern Gothic Fairy.

Pencil techniques

A study of silver jewelry must convey both the design of the piece and the metal from which it is made. Graphite pencil is perfect for this purpose. An HB pencil creates soft, even tones for the smooth surface, and crisp lines and deeper tones to delineate design details. Highlights are key to suggesting silver's unique shine. These can be reserved as paper white, or lifted out later with a kneadable eraser shaped into a point.

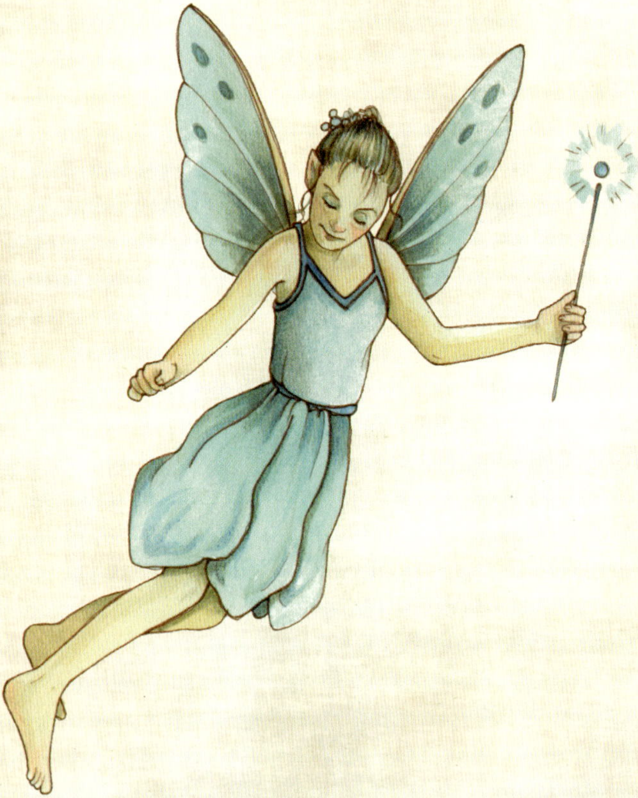

Part 5

Character directory

From Flower Fairies to Garden Gnomes, via Sylphs, Dryads, Boogies, Spriggans, and many more, this is your chance to create convincing fairy characters from all over fairyland. Recreate the paintings using the skills you learned in Parts 1–4, or develop your own fairy character using some of the ideas presented in this chapter.

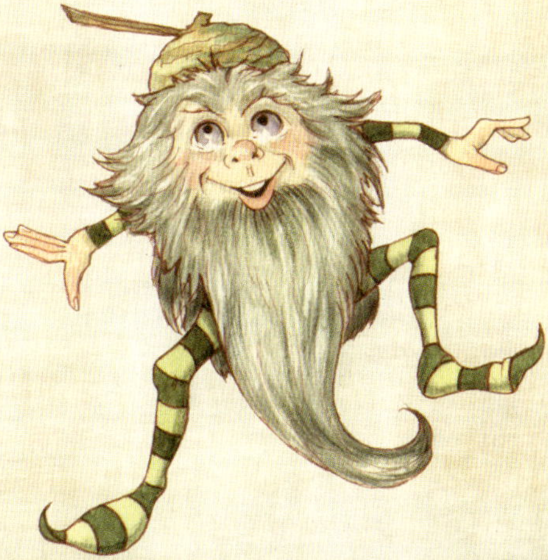

Rose Fairy

ROSES ARE AMONG THE PRETTIEST AND MOST FRAGRANT OF ALL GARDEN FLOWERS, AND THE FAIRY WHO PROTECTS THEM FROM HARM IS AS SWEET AND APPEALING AS THE BLOOMS THEMSELVES.

Character and appearance

The Rose Fairy epitomizes all that her flower stands for: youth, innocence, and purity. The rose is known as "The Queen of the Flowers" because of the essential oils that can be extracted from its flower, which calm grief and anger and soothe the skin. The Rose Fairy is said to gather the purest morning dew to create intoxicating rose-scented perfume for her Fairy Queen.

In this painting, she is depicted in a kneeling position, balancing lightly on a leaf to collect the delicate water drops. Translucent watercolors give the image a light and feminine touch, the delicate pinks contrasting subtly with a neutral, soft gray background.

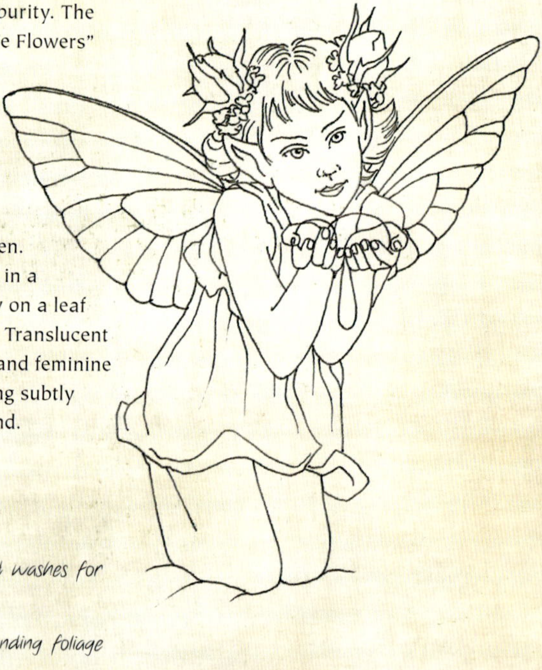

MAIN COLOR PALETTE

- *Rose madder: use in layered washes for gown and wings*
- *Sap green: leaves and surrounding foliage*
- *Cobalt green: leaves and surrounding foliage, trims, and headdress*
- *Olive green: leaves and surrounding foliage*
- *Raw umber: light wash used for skin; darker wash for hair*

Copy it!

Copy or trace the drawing or scan it into your computer. Then color it.

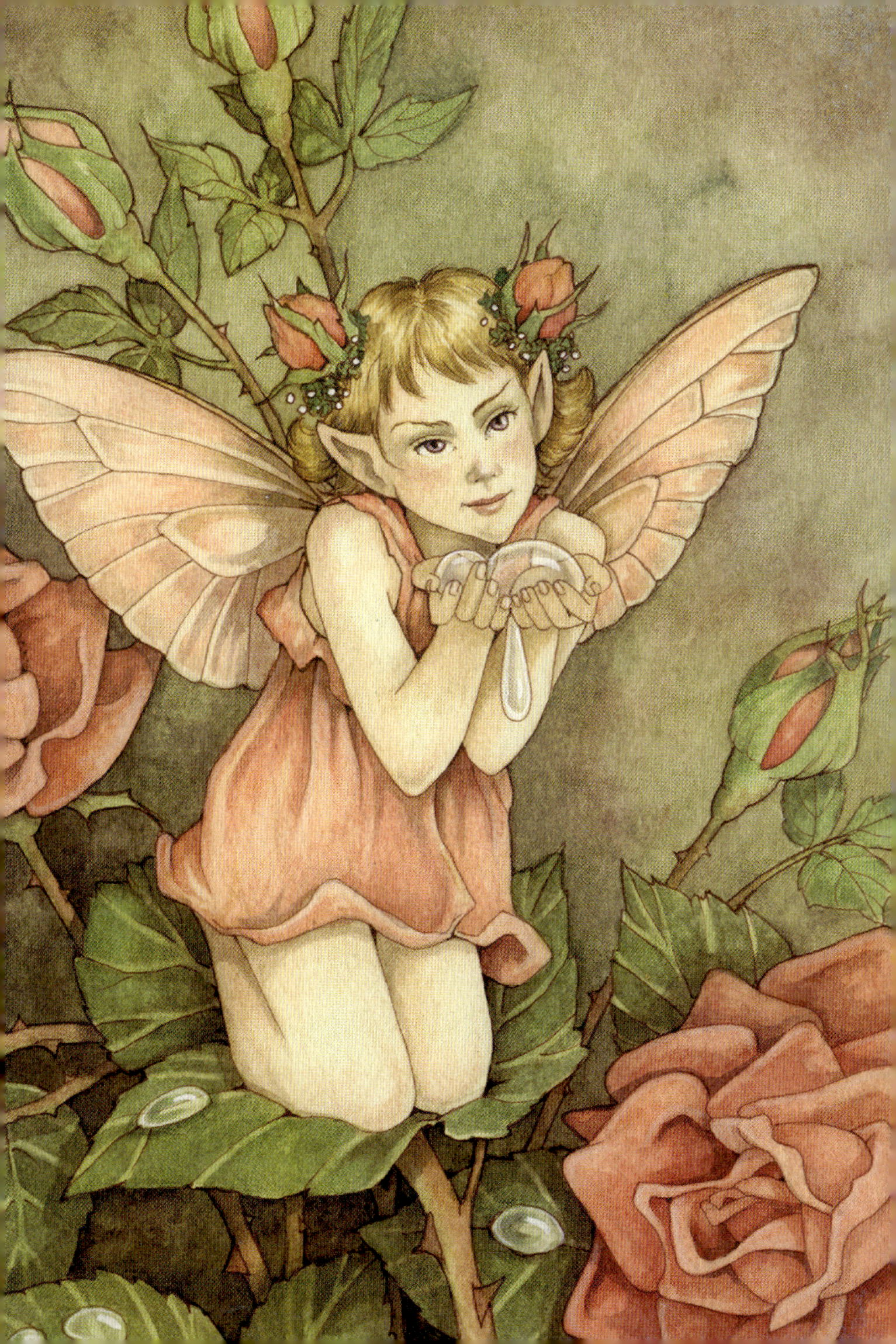

Constructing the figure

The kneeling figure of the Rose Fairy is poised with her weight forward on her knees (she is not sitting back on her heels as you may have at first suspected). In order to get this delicate balance right, look beneath the garments to the underlying shapes that form the basic structure. For example, in the finished image the foot is hidden by the dress, but you need to understand its shape and volume so that the skirt sits convincingly over it.

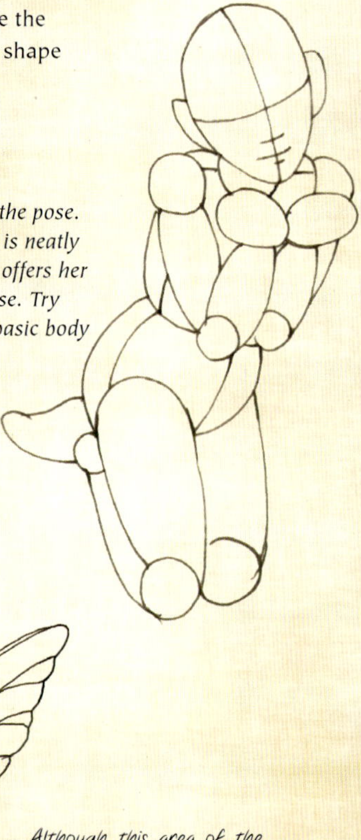

Note the angles of the body that characterize the pose. The figure leans forward from the hips, which is neatly counterbalanced by the tilt of the head as she offers her precious dewdrops, making this a dynamic pose. Try posing a mannequin to help you block in the basic body shapes necessary to this simplified anatomy.

Now you can add superficial (or "visible") anatomical detail, clothe the body, and add the wings.

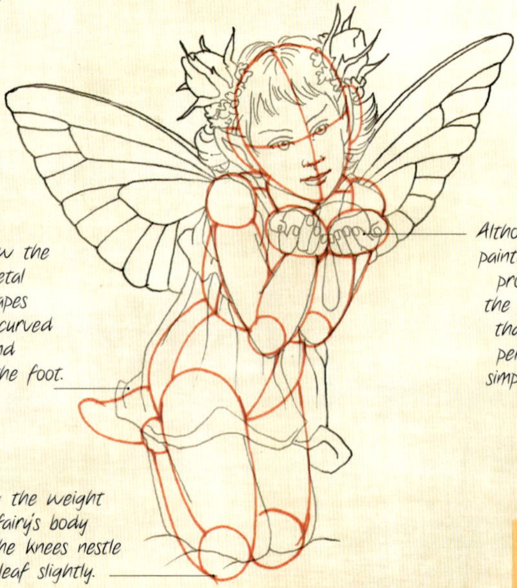

See also: Figure construction basics, page 58.

Costume and accessories

The Rose Fairy looks every bit as pretty as her flower. Both petals and buds create enchanting dresses, hair clips, and slippers with little need for adaptation. The waxy, curved petals sit naturally around the body—even the curl at the edge of the full-blown petals offers an attractive ready-made design detail, adding movement and flair.

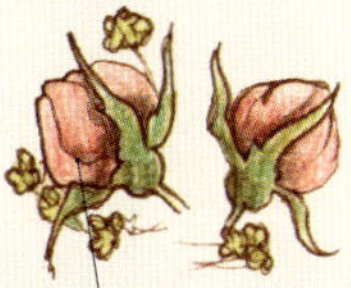

Small buds make perfect hair decorations for a little girl fairy and add flower power to dainty slippers (below).

A delicate dress teams overlapping curling rose petals (for the skirt) with a floaty petal bodice. Green sepals emphasize the waist.

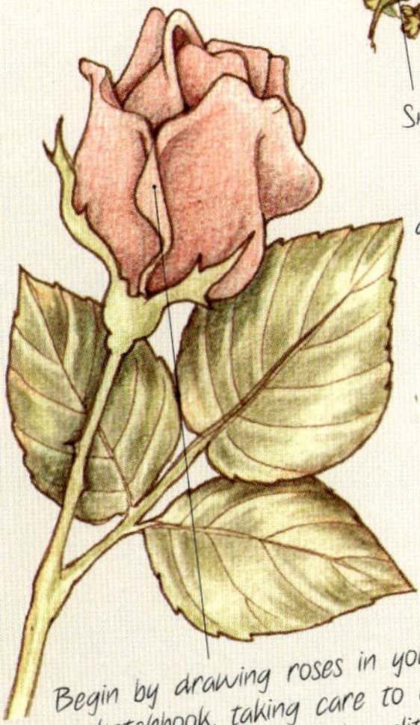

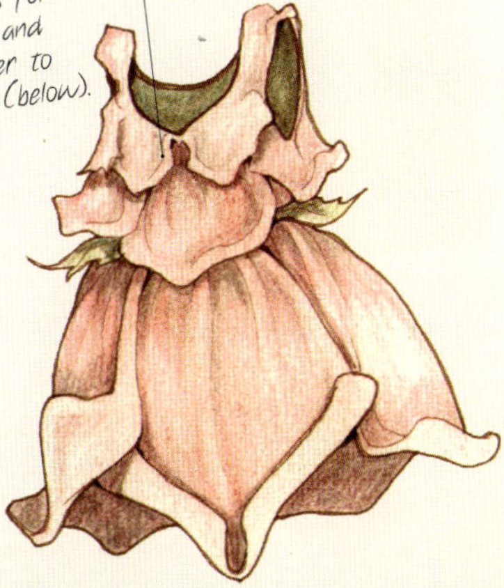

Begin by drawing roses in your sketchbook, taking care to understand their shape, textural quality, and how they react to light. Observe, for example, how the edges of the petals curl outward; a detail that works well in the fairy gown on the right.

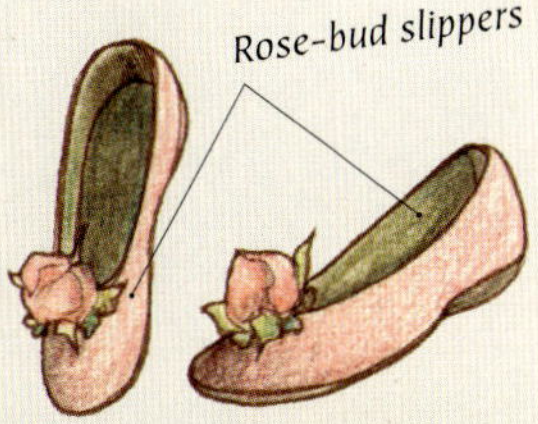

Rose-bud slippers

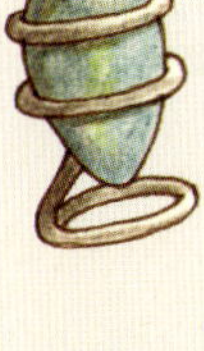

Every Rose Fairy needs a perfume bottle (made from fairy glass) in which to store her delicious fragrance. Render in green and gold watercolor to complement the softer pinks.

Garden flower garments

Garden flower fairies make full use of their chosen flowers to create their delightful costumes and accessories. Flowers are easily adapted to create pretty garments. Botanical books, garden catalogs, and your own garden will provide plenty of inspiration for flower fairy fashions.

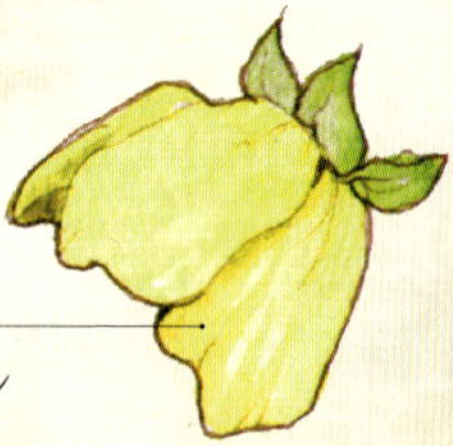

PRET-A-PORTER SKIRT
For a tiny fairy, a glossy yellow upturned buttercup makes a beautiful skirt with a green sepal feature at the waist.

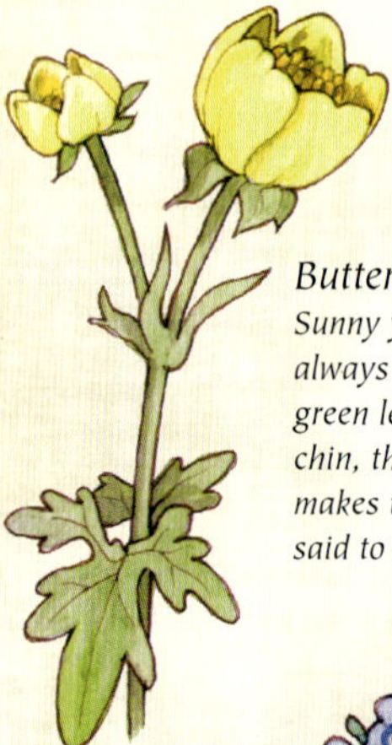

Buttercup

Sunny yellow buttercups are always eye-catching amongst green leaves. Held under the chin, the color is so vibrant it makes the skin glow yellow—said to indicate a love of butter!

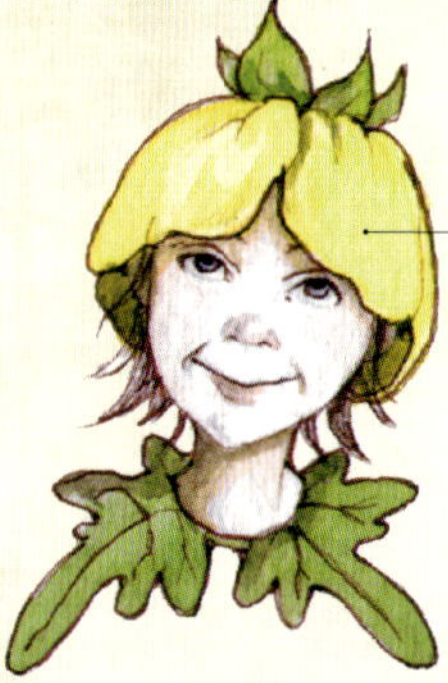

INSTANT HAT
The same upside-down buttercup makes a perfect, snug-fitting cap to keep off the summer rain, while two leaves create a pretty collar.

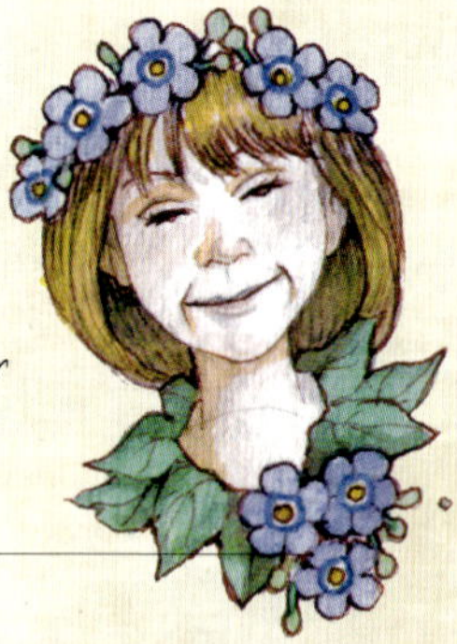

Tiny forget-me-not blooms are perfect for adding eye-catching costume details, like this pretty collar fashioned from flowers and leaves.

Forget-me-not

Dainty, jewel-like forget-me-not flowers have a special shade of blue all of their own. With their bright yellow centers, they make the prettiest accessories for garden flower fairies.

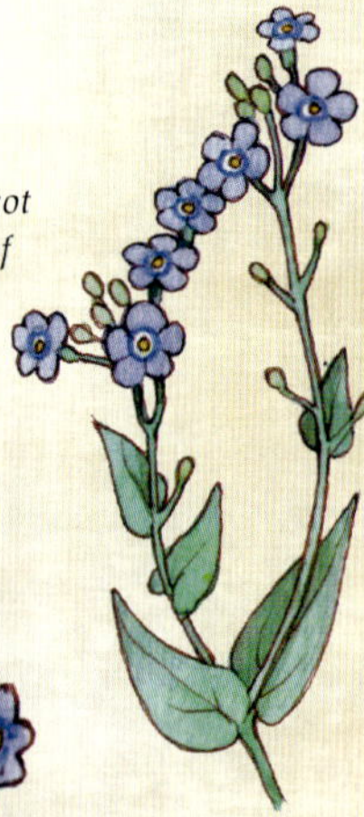

CROWNING GLORY
Fairies are resourceful and use whatever is on hand. Here, a spray of forget-me-nots is woven into an enchanting coronet.

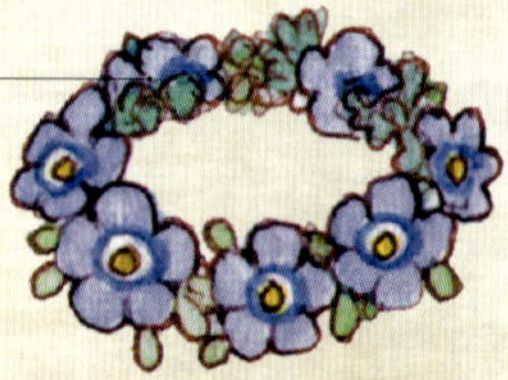

See also: Dresses and robes, page 76.

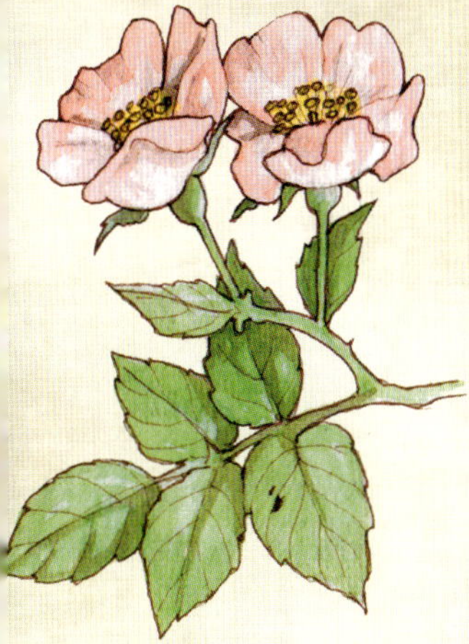

Wild dog rose

In shades from pink to white, dainty dog roses—less showy than their cultivated garden cousins—decorate the hedgerows throughout the summer. Their fairy, like her flower, is modest, simple, and charming.

SWEET SIMPLICITY
A few petals are all it takes to make a little fairy dress that's delicate and pretty. Leaves and stamens provide waist focus.

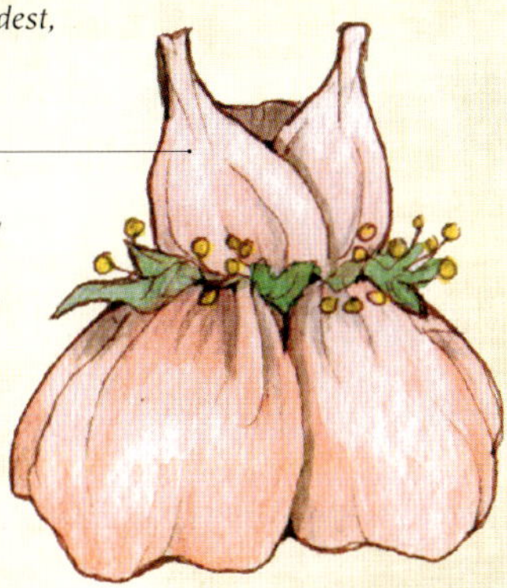

A simple cap for a demure Dog Rose Fairy uses small petals sewn to a little coronet of stamens and sepals.

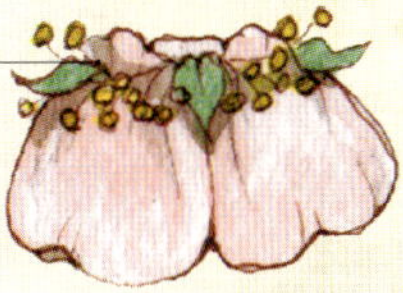

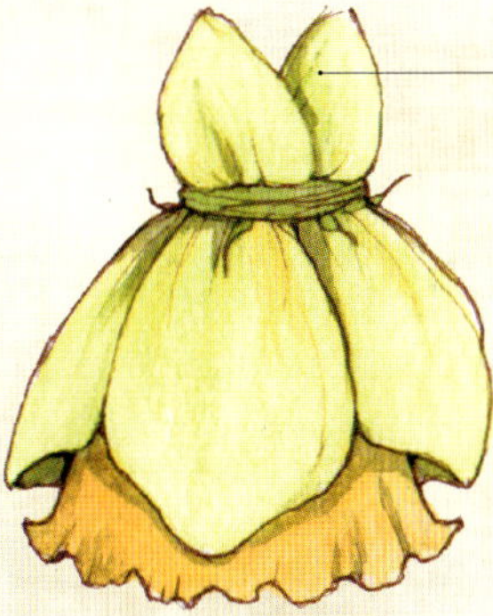

SIMPLE DAY DRESS
The daffodil flowerhead needs only to be cinched at the waist with grasses to make a simple fairy frock.

Daffodil

The sunny daffodil is the herald of spring, promising warmth and new growth after the long, dark winter. The bold flower adapts beautifully to make real "statement" garments.

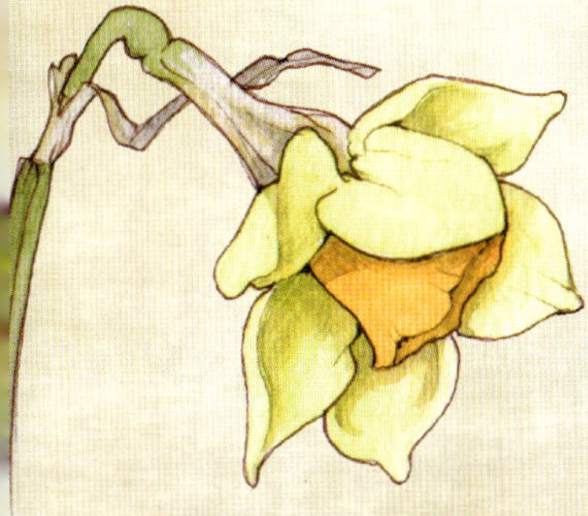

FAIRY GLAMOR
With corset-style bodice and flouncy layered skirt, this dress makes full use of all elements of the daffodil flower to create an elegant formal design.

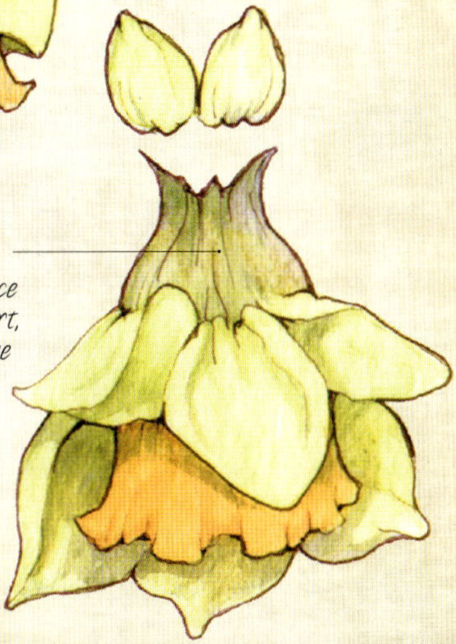

Poppy Fairy

HEDGEROWS, FLOWER MEADOWS, AND CORN FIELDS ARE HOME TO MYRIAD COLORFUL FLOWER FAIRIES WHO PROTECT AND NURTURE THE BRIGHT, WILD FLOWERS IN THEIR CARE.

Character and appearance

The wild flowers that spangle the countryside with bright spots of blue, red, yellow, and white all have their own fairy custodians to guard them. Poppy Fairies are kindly, generous, and sweet-natured creatures who are friendly and protective toward their fellow field-dwellers. They are often depicted with harvest mice, voles, frogs, and other small creatures that share their habitat.

The cadmium red used in this painting makes this gentle, childlike Poppy Fairy a colorful member of her fairy tribe. Her brilliant red costume creates a vibrant picture, especially when set against the complementary greens of the poppy leaves. Like other field-dwellers such as the tiny harvest mouse, she is definitely a fairy worth looking out for on a summer day.

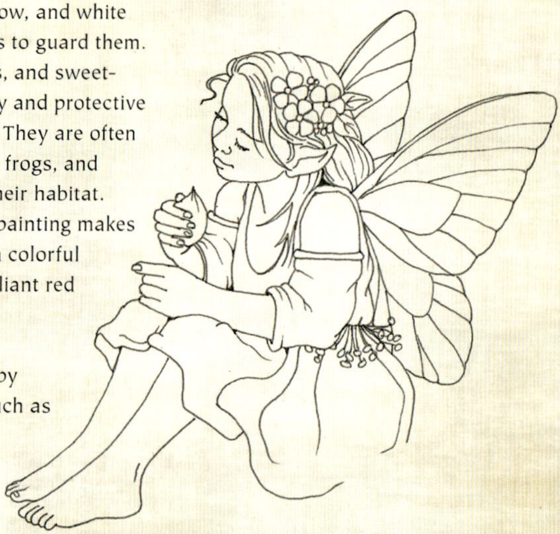

MAIN COLOR PALETTE

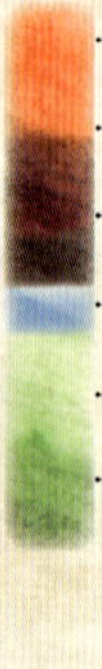

- Cadmium red: build up color gradually on dress
- Permanent magenta: poppy stamens and wing tips
- Lamp black: hair and shadows
- Cerulean blue: forget-me-not flowers
- Sap green: leaves and foliage
- Olive green: darkens the poppy leaves
- Raw umber (not shown): wash for the skin

Copy it!

Copy or trace the drawing or scan it into your computer. Then color it.

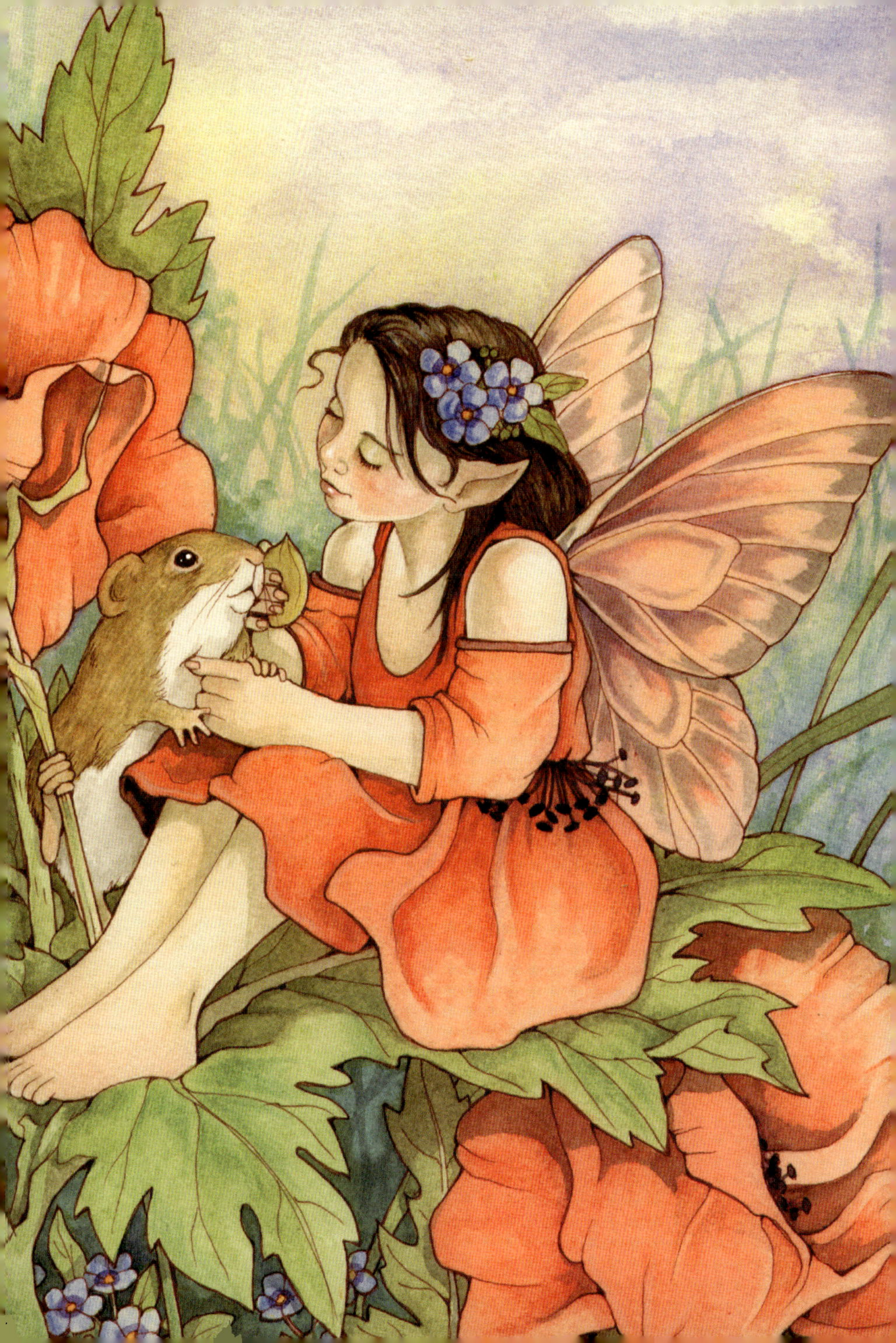

Constructing the figure

When drawing seated figures, note how the weight is supported and how the body is balanced. Never try to guess what's going on beneath the clothes—they only hang the way they do because of what lies beneath them. The easiest way to approach even complex poses is to break the figure down into its basic underlying shapes first.

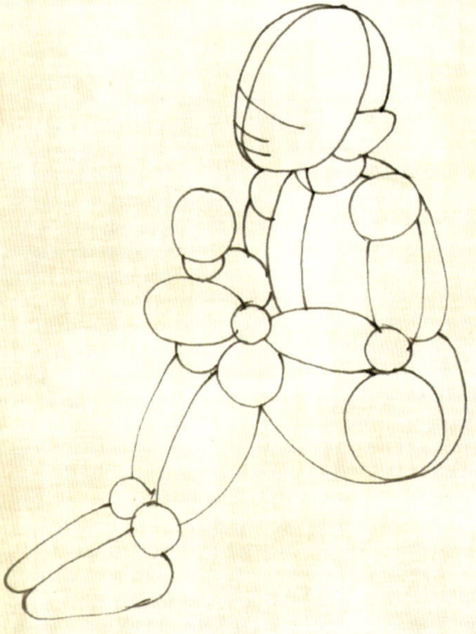

Block in the basic shapes, indicating the articulation points with circles. Check that the figure looks solid and balanced, and make sure the tilt of the head is correct—draw the center line of the face, neck, and torso to get the angles right.

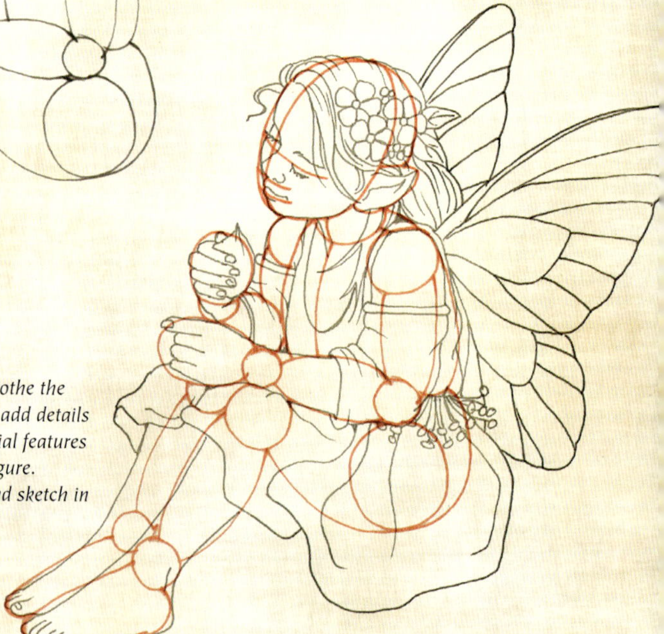

Once the pose is firmly constructed, you can clothe the body convincingly and add details such as fingers and facial features to create the finished figure. Finally, add the hair and sketch in the wings.

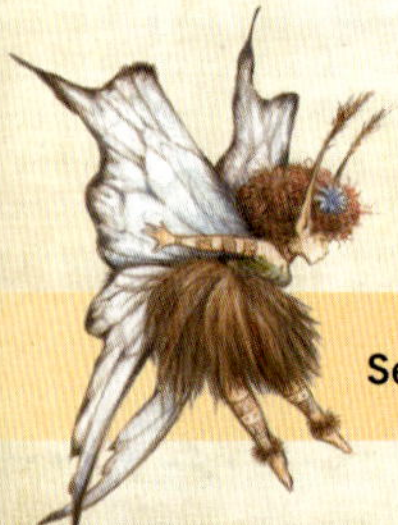

See also: Figure construction basics, page 58.

Costume and accessory variations

As with all flower fairies, the Poppy Fairy uses aspects from her own flower to make her dresses and accessories. The flamboyant field poppy lends itself perfectly to all kinds of pretty skirts and tops. Although silky and fragile, the brilliant red petals will create an eye-catching contrast to the greens and browns of the fields and hedgerows.

Many flowers make colorful contrasting accessories. Always make sure you choose seasonal flowers appropriate for your fairy. Here, jewel-like, blue forget-me-nots that bloom in summer make an enchanting headdress. Try snowdrops or crocus tips for winter and spring fairies.

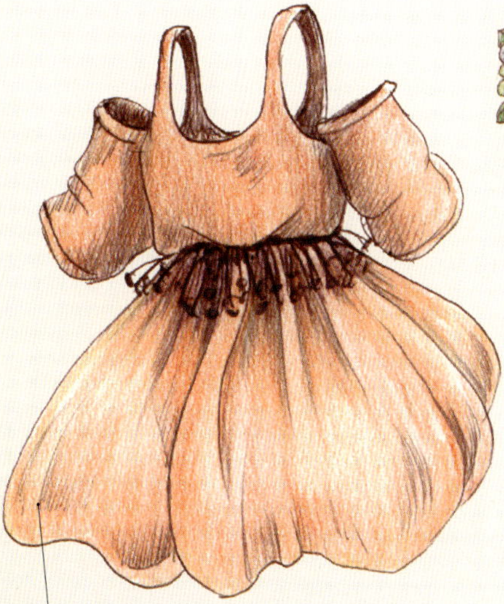

The glossy black stamens of the poppy flower create a clever waist detail to trim the petal dress.

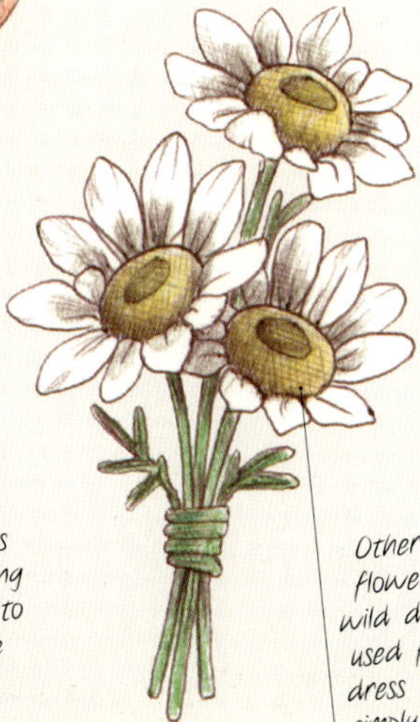

Other field flowers, such as wild daisies, can be used for hair and dress decorations, or simply as bouquets.

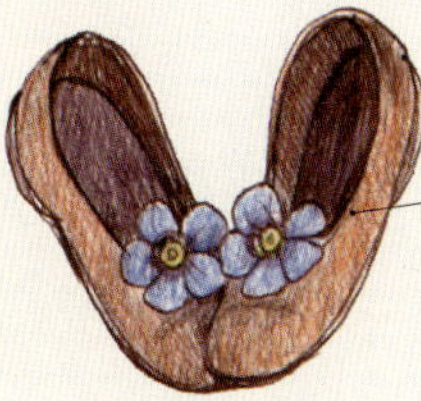

Red poppy petals make enchanting scarlet slippers to trim with little forget-me-not flowers.

Drawing the head and facial features

The Poppy Fairy's pose is led by the angle of her head as she gazes at her field mouse friend. It is slightly tilted and seen in a three-quarter view. To draw a successful head and face at this angle, you need to look carefully and draw what you see, not what you know.

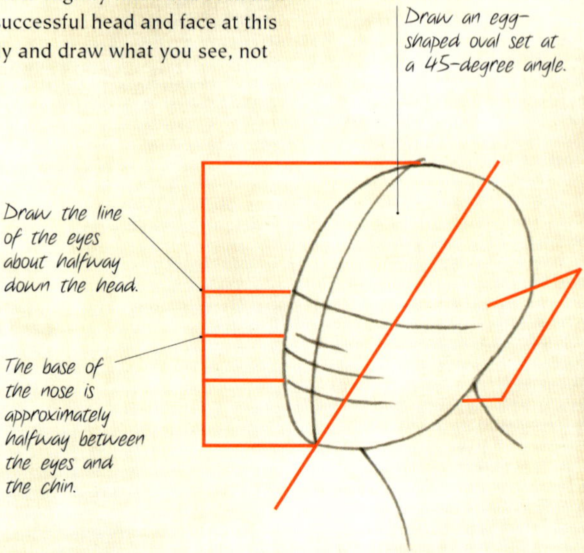

1 Draw the basic underlying egg-shaped oval of the head tilted at a 45-degree angle. Draw in the center line of the face and mark the position of the features as shown.

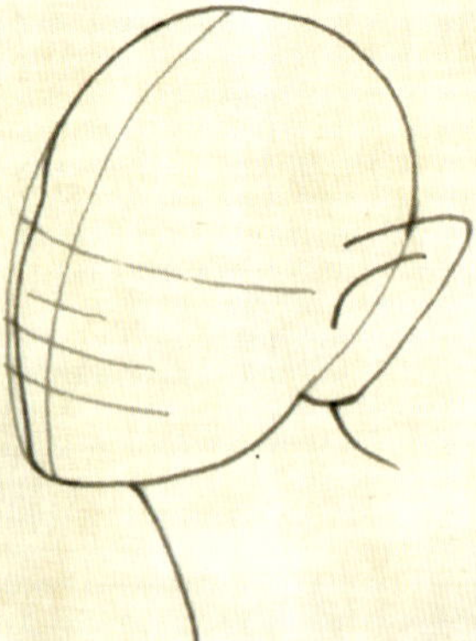

2 Refine the basic underlying form by adding the inward curve of the eye socket with the swell of the cheekbone below, and round off the ear shape.

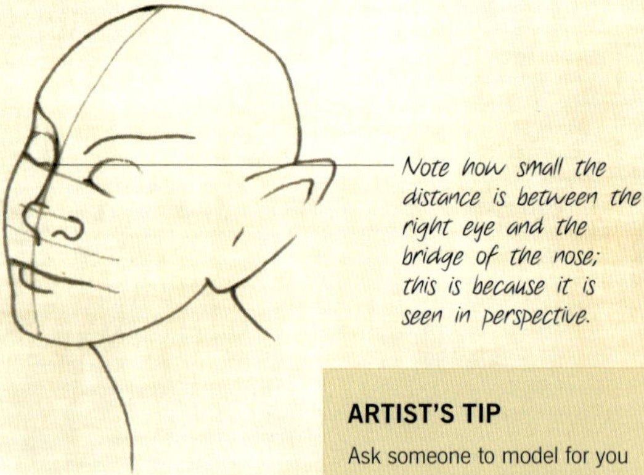

3 Define the features. Add the line of the nose and the one visible nostril. Indicate the lips with simple curved lines.

ARTIST'S TIP

Ask someone to model for you and use your sketchbook to draw heads from all angles. Practice makes perfect—the more you draw, the more you will see and understand how the forms change their appearance when tilted in different directions.

See also: Constructing the head, page 64.

4 Add graphite pencil shading to round out the eyelids and hint at the shape of the cheekbones and chin. Add the top lip—at this angle only one half is in full view.

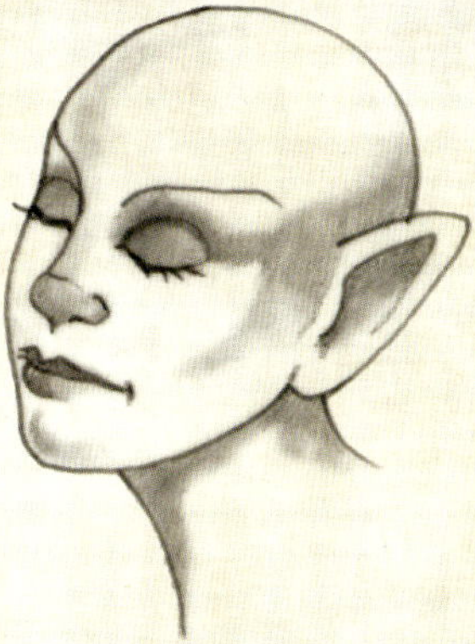

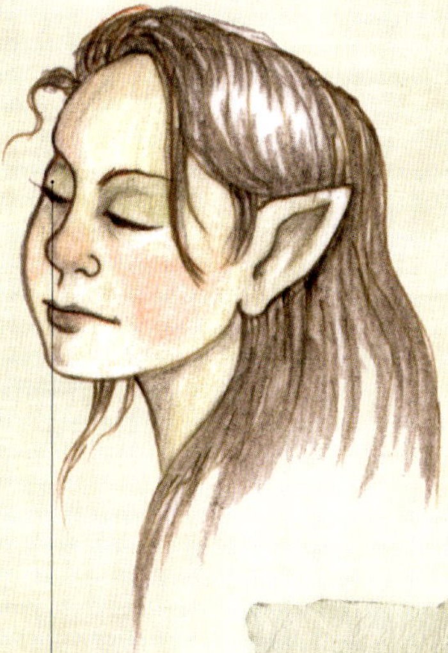

Add only light shadow to the eyelids.

5 Now add color to render the character fully. For a very young fairy, make the cheeks rounded with no visible cheekbones, and keep the top lip thin.

Adult variation

Adapt the same template to create an older fairy. Lengthen the head and reduce the childish fullness of the cheek. Shade the cheekbones and eye sockets to add sharper definition, and to create fuller lips.

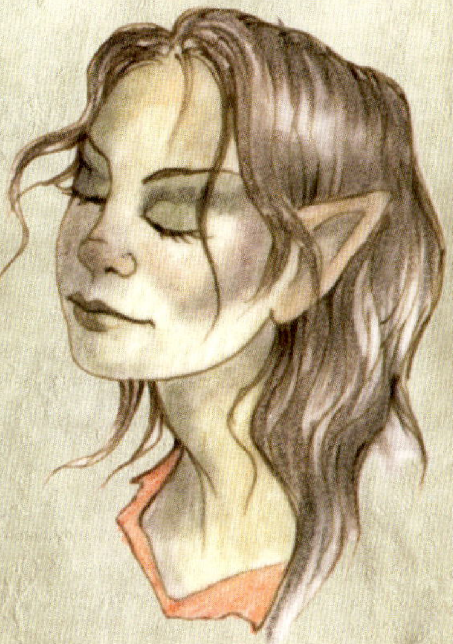

Violet Fairy

WOODLANDS AND FORESTS ARE FULL OF DELICATE, SHADE-LOVING PLANTS, EACH ONE WATCHED OVER BY ITS OWN ENCHANTING FAIRY THAT REFLECTS THE NATURE OF THE FLOWER IT REPRESENTS.

Character and appearance

Woodland fairies have sweet, generous natures and are usually depicted as babies to reflect their natural innocence. However, their actual age is unknown, and they are much wiser than their appearance suggests. Like the flowers they represent, they flourish in semi-shaded areas, and are thought of as modest, well-meaning, and gentle.

The Violet Fairy's pose, body proportions, and features are very different from those of her older counterparts, and you will want to nail this anatomical detail in the pencil underdrawing first, before you color it with varying purple watercolor washes. When the wash is dry, add highlights to clothing, eyes, and flowers with opaque white gouache.

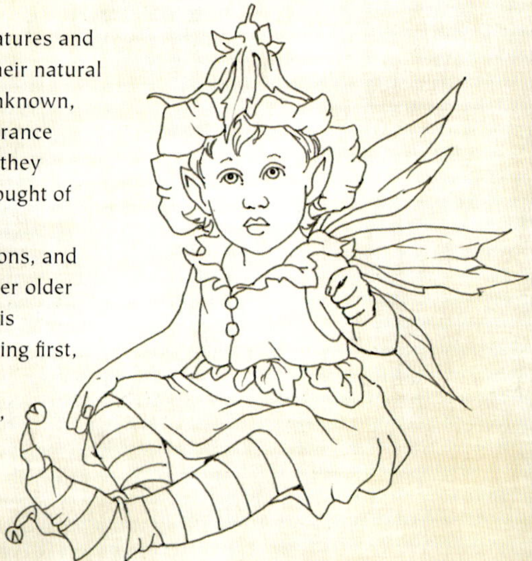

MAIN COLOR PALETTE

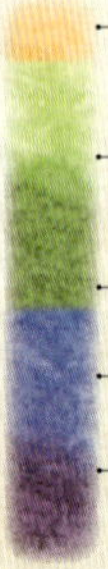

- Raw umber: light wash for skin tone; dark wash for hair
- Sap green: base color for leaves and foliage
- Olive green: creates depth in leaves
- Ultramarine: base wash for dress and hat
- Mauve: apply as weak wash to wings and cheeks; darker wash for stockings and eyes

Copy it!

Copy or trace the drawing or scan it into your computer. Then color it.

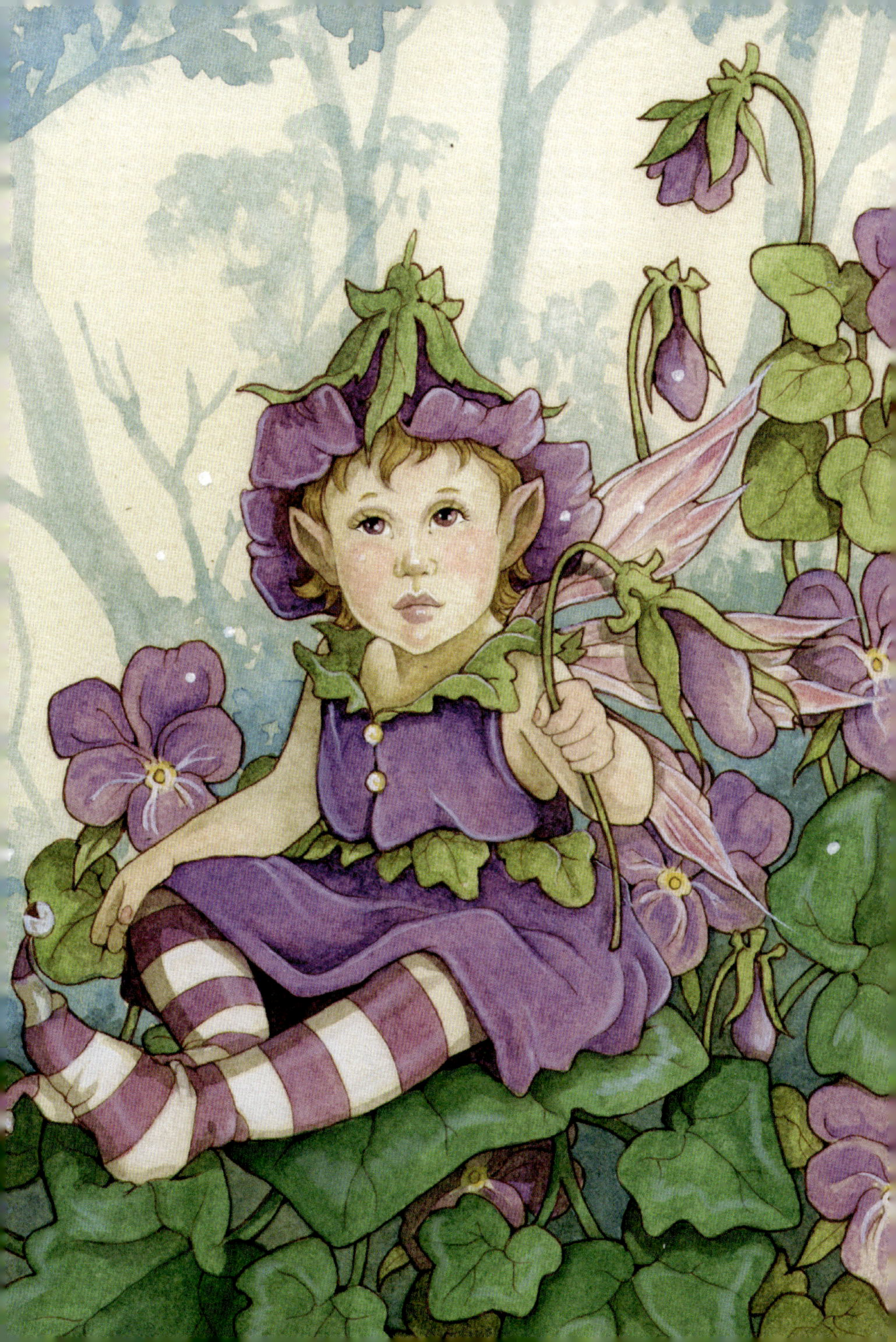

Constructing the figure

See also: Figure construction basics, page 58.

You will need to understand the proportions of a baby's body if you want to create a convincing drawing. Looking for the simple shapes beneath the form helps to construct the figure. Follow the guidelines here, and use your sketchbook to make studies of babies and children—either from magazines, books, or from life—that you can refer to later.

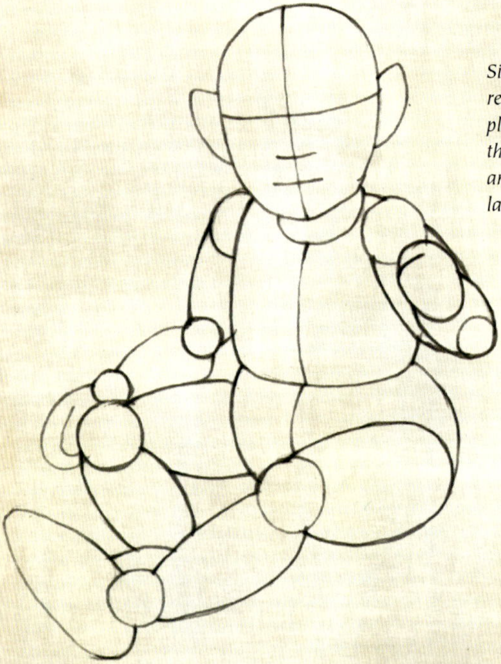

Simplify the baby's body by representing it as a collection of plump, softly rounded shapes. Note that there are no sharp angles anywhere and that the head is large in proportion to the body.

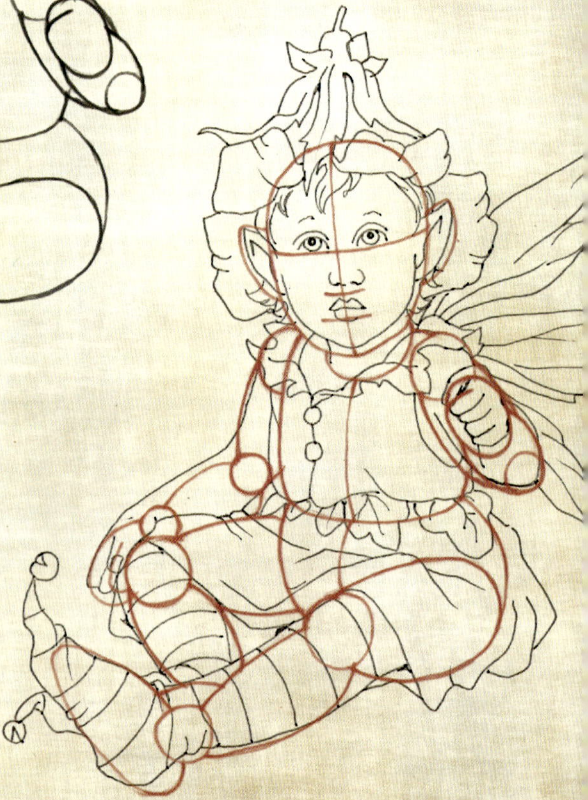

Once you have the pose and the proportions right, you can "flesh out" the baby's figure with more detail and add clothes that cover the anatomical shape structures.

Constructing the arms

Like the rest of the body, a baby's limbs should be rounded and the joints not sharply defined. They can be represented by a series of simple shapes.

1 *Indicate the points of articulation at shoulder, elbow, and wrist with three circles descending in size. Link the circles with curved lines for the arm and forearm.*

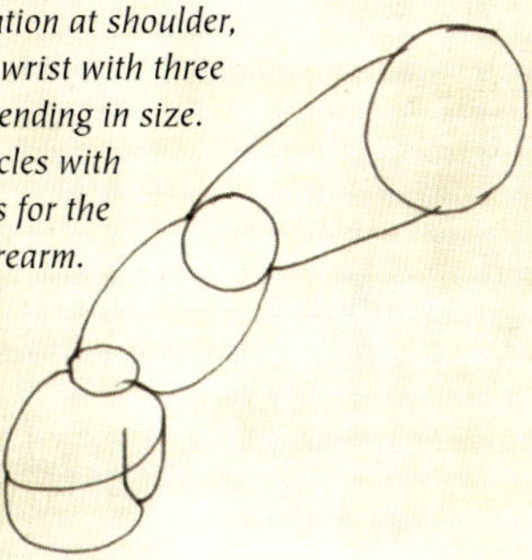

2 *Draw in the shape of the arm more accurately, building on the underlying basic shapes.*

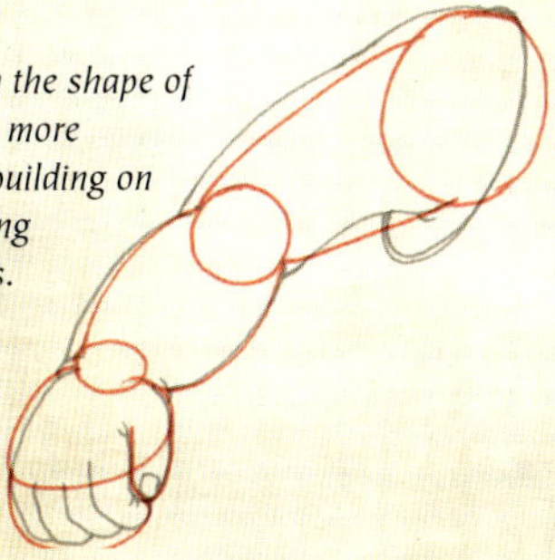

3 *In the finished drawing, the elbow and wrist are indicated with slight indentations in the curve of the arm. Notice the telling chubby "bracelet" at the wrist.*

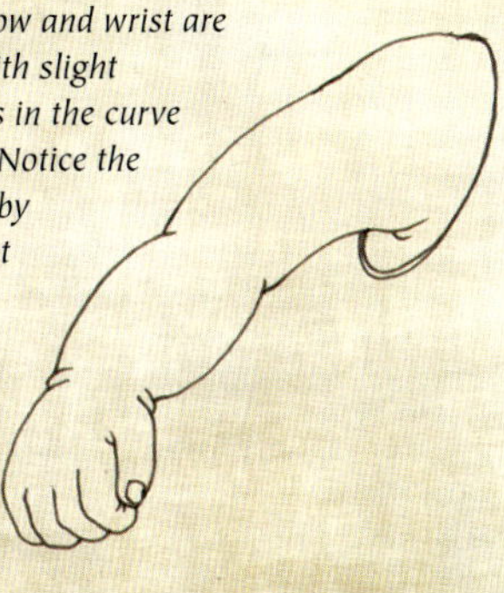

Constructing the hands

Hands can be daunting to draw, but the same basic shape technique will help you get them right. Remember, babies' fingers are short and the palms rounded.

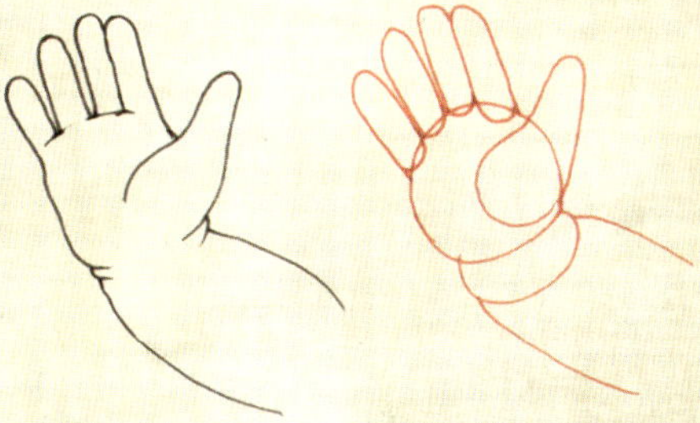

Palm up

In the palm up position, represent the fingers and thumb as short, fat sausages, and the palm as a circle. Then draw the hand more accurately, building on the basic shapes. Note the wrinkles at the wrist.

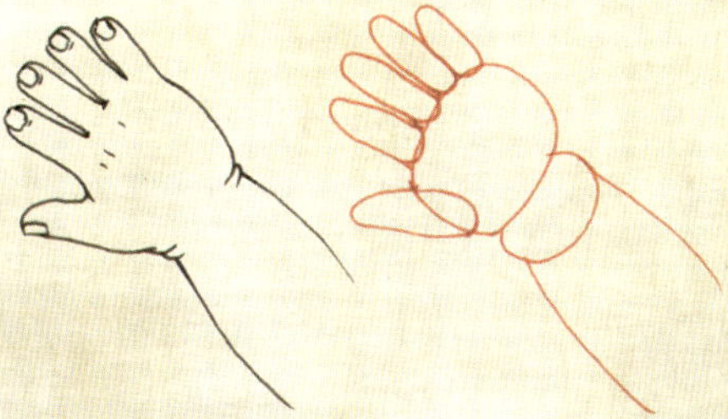

Palm down

Seen from above, the baby's hand can be represented in the same way with simple rounded shapes. The knuckles are visible only as dimples in the flesh and the wrist is defined by a chubby "fold."

Drawing baby faces: front view

Beware of making child fairies look like miniature adults. Babies and young children have rounded faces, plump cheeks, button noses, and large eyes set wide apart. While each fairy is unique, the simple formula below will help you draw convincing child characters.

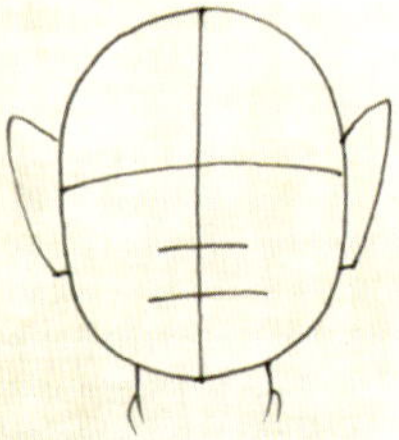

1 A baby's face is a slightly elongated circle with the features clustered in the lower two-thirds of the shape as shown, leaving a characteristic high-domed forehead.

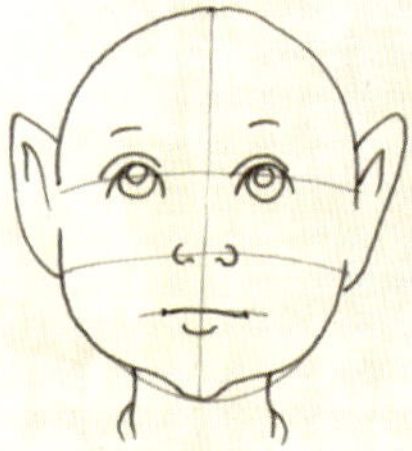

2 Shape the cheeks and chin and add the features. The eyes are large, round, and evenly spaced. Define the snub nose with simple curved shapes. Add a sensitive line where the lips meet and a small curve for the bottom lip.

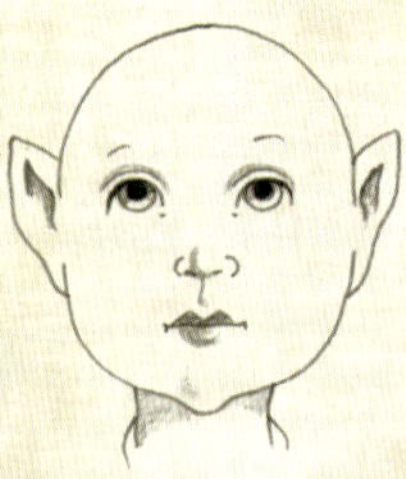

3 Add shading to the eyes, nose, and mouth to describe their shape and volume. Now that the features are more defined, you will see the character is developing.

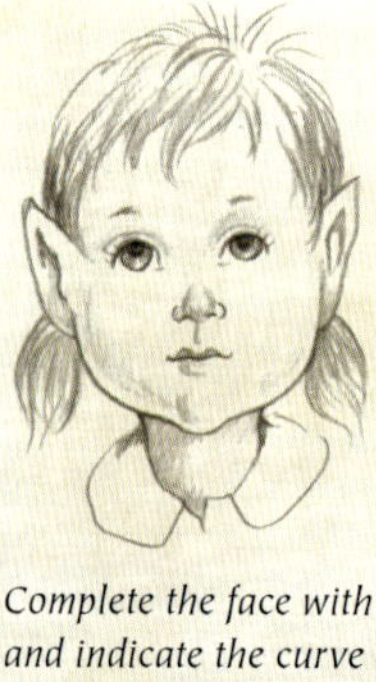

4 Complete the face with hair and indicate the curve of the cheek with shading. Adapt this basic toddler face by drawing shorter hair and adding a cap for a boy, or by adding curls for a girl.

Profile variation

If you are nervous about drawing faces, try a different approach. Here, the head is seen in profile with no visible facial features.

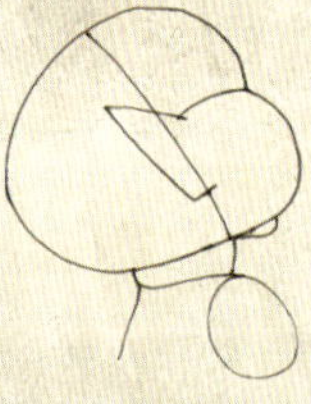

1 Draw a rounded heart set at an angle. Indicate the ear and add a small semicircle underneath for the chin.

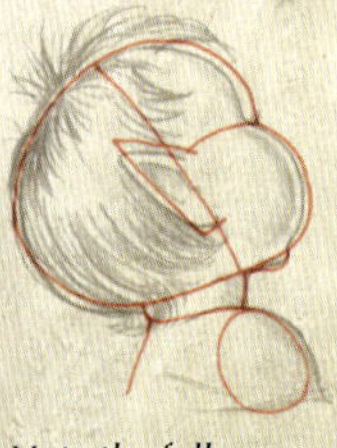

2 Note the full curve of the back of the head—don't flatten it. Begin to add detail with white pencil.

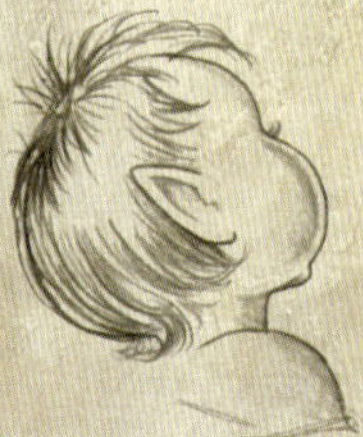

3 Add texture to the hair, neck, and chest. Notice the tiny neck supporting the large head. Add eyelashes at the top of the cheek.

Clothes and accessories

The Sweet Violet Fairy blends perfectly with her surroundings in clothes made from the flower she represents. Copy these ideas, or create your own unique designs. Study wild flower books for inspiration and use your sketchbook to make studies of sweet violet plants before you adapt the flowers, buds, and leaves to make garments and accessories.

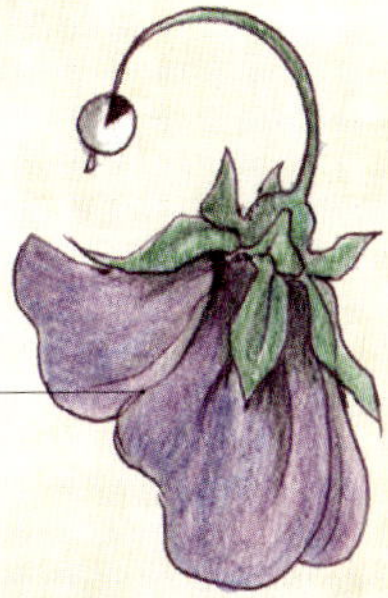

A sweet violet flower is a perfect ready-to-wear cap. Top it with a tiny silver bell that will tinkle every time the fairy moves her head.

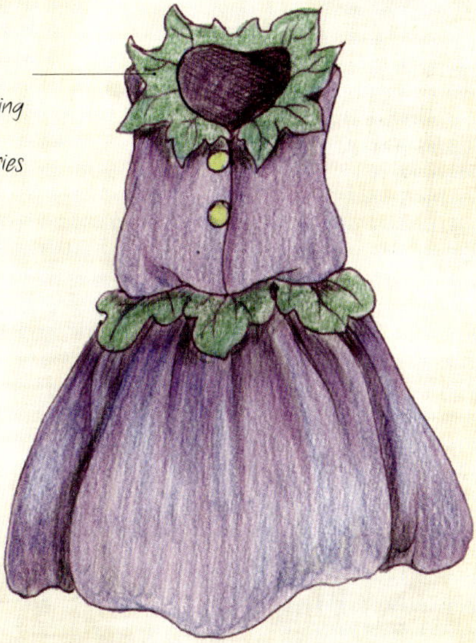

In order to blend into her woodland home, the Violet Fairy makes her clothing from the petals of the flower after which she is named. These little fairies are gifted from an early age and are able to fashion clothing with ease.

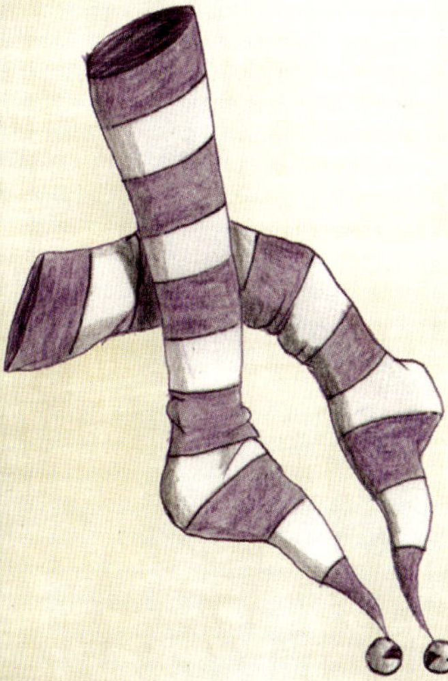

The woodland flower fairies are very partial to dancing and feasting, and many of them choose to wear small silver bells on their clothing. These bells are not only wonderful to dance with, but they can also act as a warning alarm to other woodland creatures should the need arise.

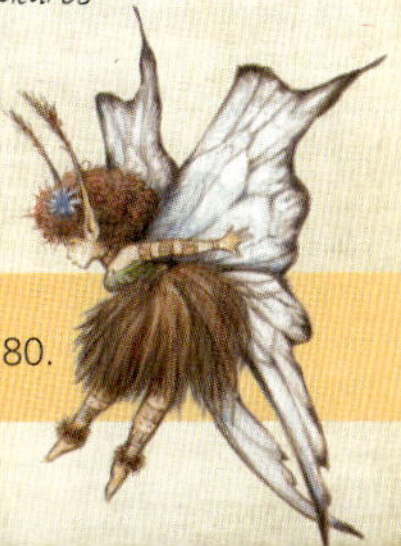

See also: Fairy accessories, page 80.

Dryad

DRYADS ARE THE FAIRIES OF THE TREES; ALWAYS FEMALE, BEAUTIFUL, AND UTTERLY IRRESISTIBLE TO MORTAL MAN—ONE GLIMPSE AND HE FALLS HOPELESSLY IN LOVE.

Character and appearance

Shy, illusive, and alluring, Dryads have the physical attributes of the female form, with long, slender limbs and a curvaceous body. But they also adopt treelike aspects that give them a mysterious, otherworldly quality. Their skin becomes bark-like or mossy, and leaves or branches grow from their bodies to camouflage them from prying human eyes. They hide until the full moon tempts them out to dance and play.

Unlike Dryads, a Hamadryad (shown here) cannot separate from her tree; if the tree is cut down, she dies. In this painting, black ballpoint pen creates a dark underdrawing with cross-hatched shading that expresses the atmosphere of a secluded wood. Delicate, almost monochromatic watercolor washes add to the sense of mystery.

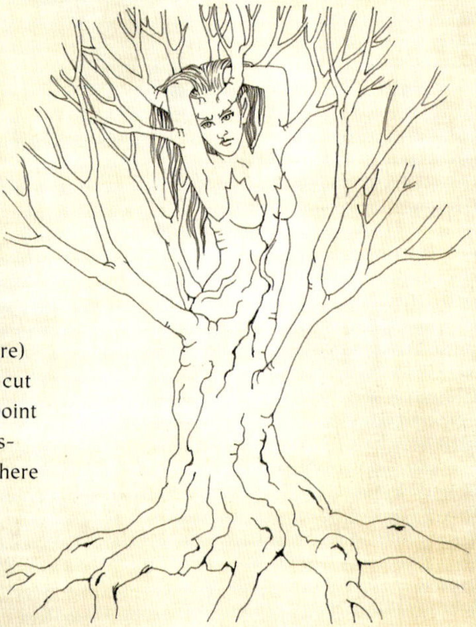

MAIN COLOR PALETTE

Raw umber: main base coat for tree and figure

Sepia: overpainting on the tree trunk and hair

Dark olive green: leaves

Light olive green: wash applied to the skin tones

Rose madder (not shown): use sparingly for blush on cheeks and lips

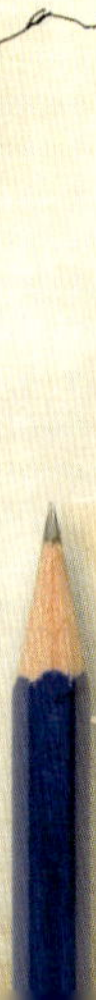

Copy it!

Copy or trace the drawing or scan it into your computer. Then color it.

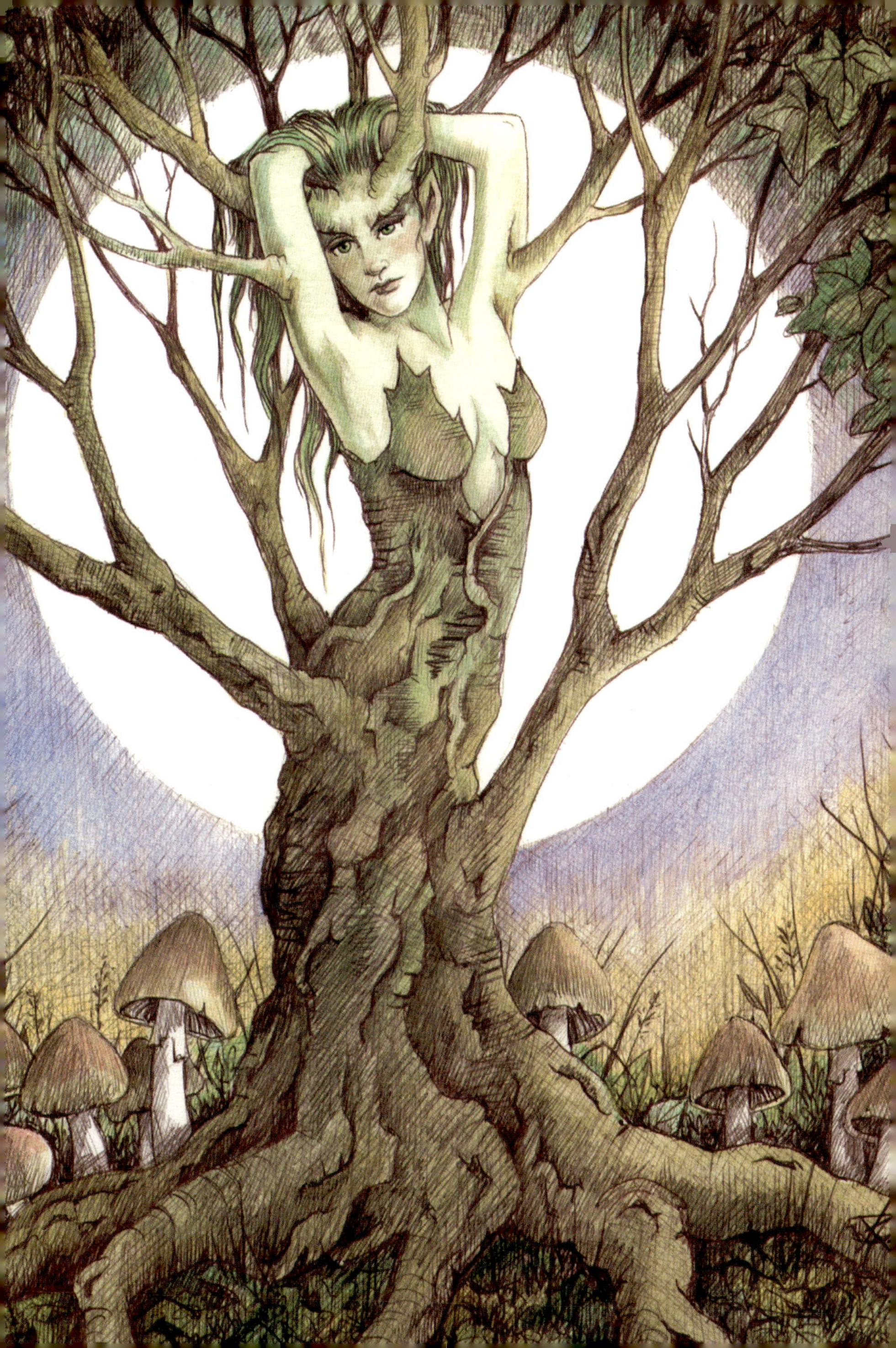

Hairstyles and headdresses

Let your imagination run wild when designing your Dryad's hairstyle or headdress. Remember that every detail conveys information about the character. Twigs and foliage create all sorts of curled and twisted hair forms for a Dryad, while a Hamadryad may have branches growing directly from her head. Such disturbing elements will be tempered by her graceful figure and obvious femininity.

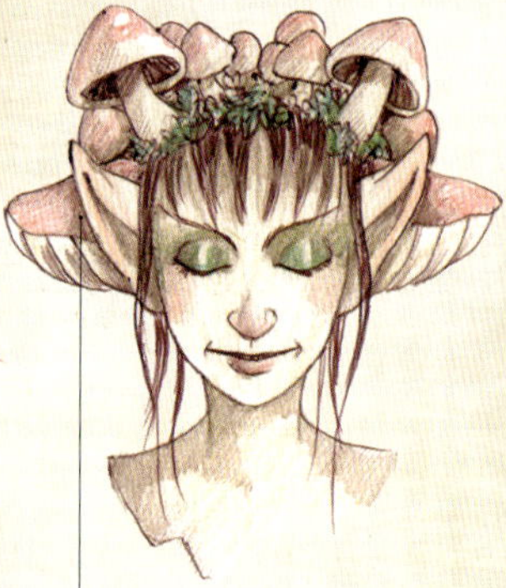

TOADSTOOL HEADDRESS
Many types of colorful and interestingly shaped fungi flourish in damp woods and on trees themselves. Here, a Dryad adorns her hair with a selection of toadstools and mushrooms.

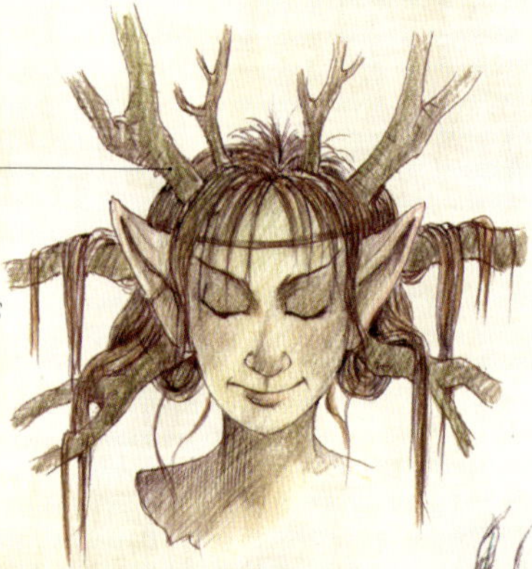

HAIR EXTENSIONS
This fairy is changing into a Hamadryad and becoming part of her tree. Branches and twigs grow from her head, and her draped hair resembles the moss-covered limbs of ancient trees.

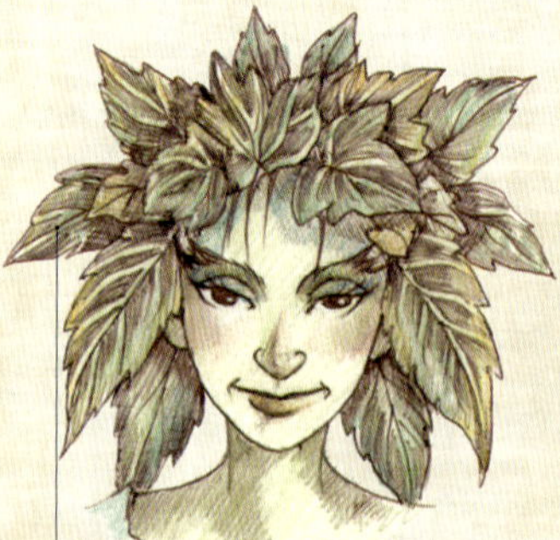

LEAF WIG
Many fairies use leaves to create headdresses. Here, a Dryad covers her head in a glorious and flamboyant crown of leaves that will help to hide her from prying eyes.

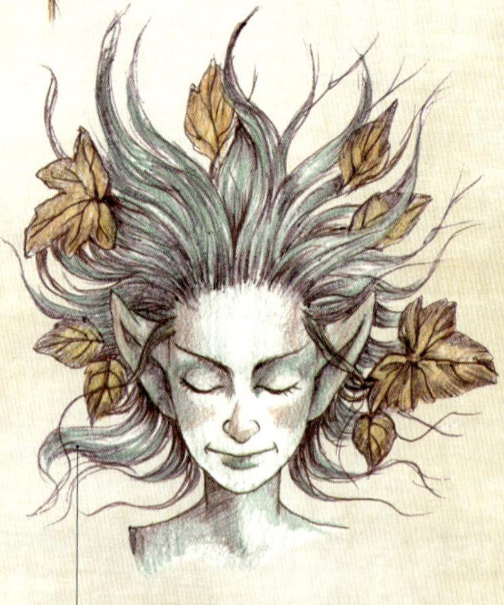

THE WINDSWEPT LOOK
The breeze separates the hair of this Dryad into windswept, branch-like locks. A scattering of fall leaves among the tendrils further develops the treelike character of the fairy.

Physical characteristics

Overlay human characteristics with exaggerated fairy features to create a credible character. Let your ideas loose, but remember to harness them to real life, or your fairy won't evoke the reaction you want. Be selective, edit, and adapt these ideas to suit your designs.

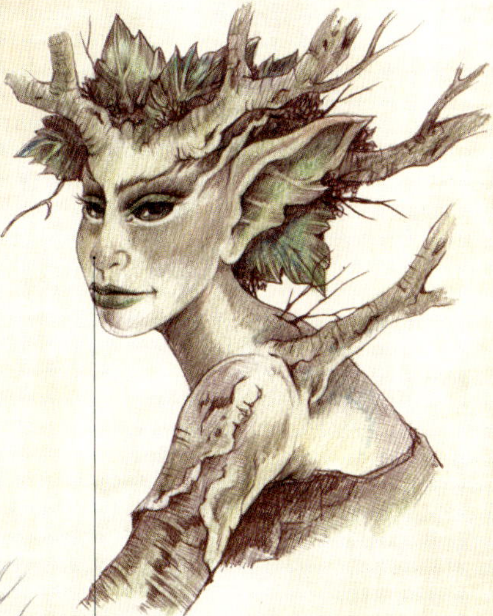

BRINGING THE FORM TO LIFE
Distort your fairy's human features to create a subtly disturbing creature. Here, branches grow from the Dryad's body and head (the branch on her shoulder might be fashioned into a wing for example). With shading and texture, her skin resembles bark, the ear is leaflike, and leaves and moss cover her head.

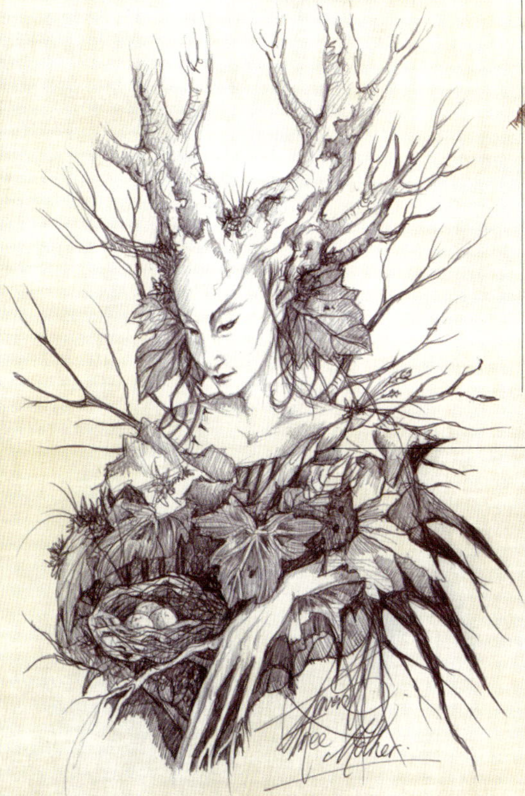

ROOTING HER IN REALITY
While the face remains human, this fairy's head and body are part of the tree's structure, her hands are long and twiglike, and she even shelters a bird's nest among her leaves. This graphite drawing reveals a creature that is totally integrated with her tree, but she remains remarkably lifelike.

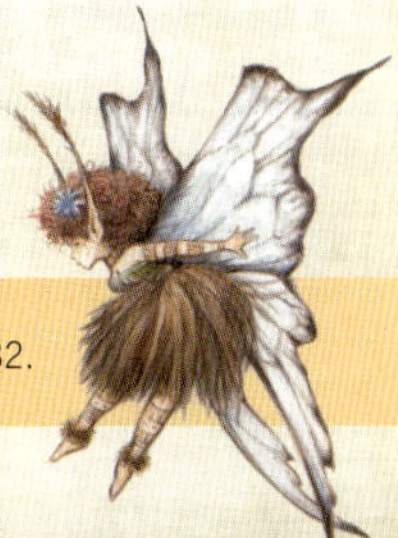

See also: Hair and headwear, page 82.

Variations on skin texture

Dryads blend with their chosen tree, merging chameleon-like with the branches and foliage to hide whenever they choose. They therefore require outer coverings that imitate the colors and textures of the forests and woods that are their natural habitat. To maintain their alien quality, avoid clothing that is overtly human in style. Instead, look at bark, foliage, woodland creatures, and insects for inspiration.

See also: Dresses and robes, page 76.

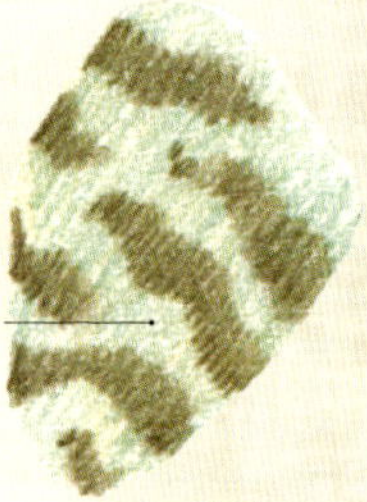

ANIMAL MARKINGS
Animal skins are often marked to provide camouflage, a useful means of disguise.

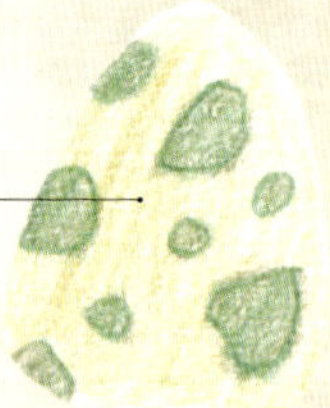

MOSSY GROWTH
Green spots such as these suggest mossy patches on old bark.

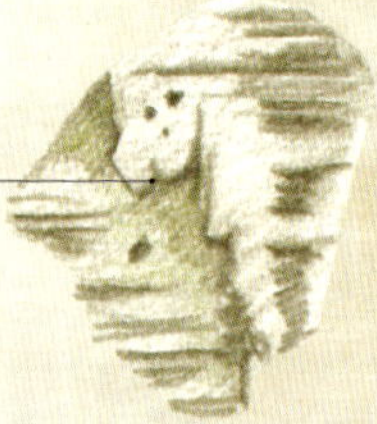

BARK TEXTURES
Horizontal shading marks create effective bark surfaces, rough or smooth.

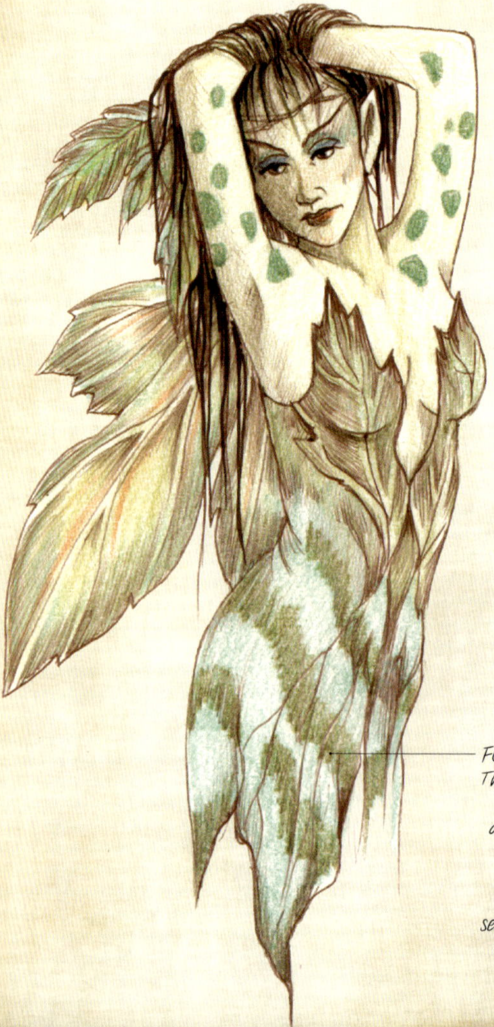

FULL FOREST OUTFIT
This creature's pose echoes the graceful, curving shapes of surrounding trees, and enhances her alluring beauty. Clad in leaflike shapes, she would effectively melt into her surroundings and be hard to spot. Even her wings are large leaves, and her trailing hair and mottled skin further serve to disguise her.

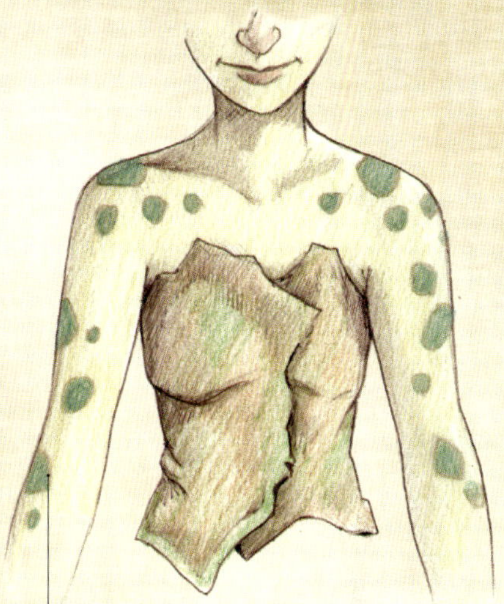

LICHEN PATCHES
Diagonal shading suggests a wrap-style bodice of thin, smooth bark, while the skin has green patches reminiscent of moss and lichen patches that develop on ancient trees.

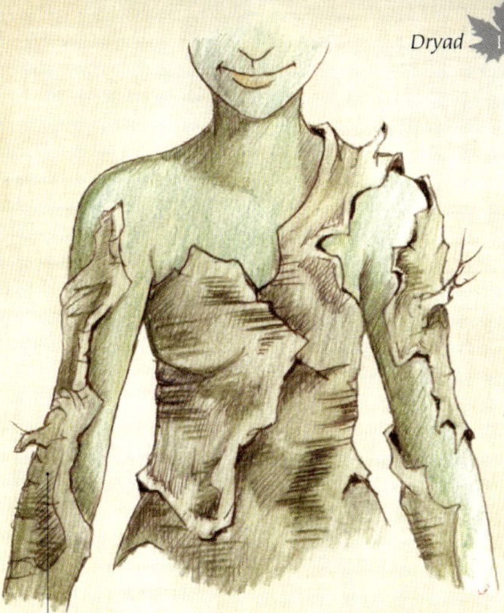

SILVER BIRCH
Here, the skin is smooth and green like young wood. The bark that wraps the torso and arms is rendered with horizontal shading to imitate the appearance of silver birch bark.

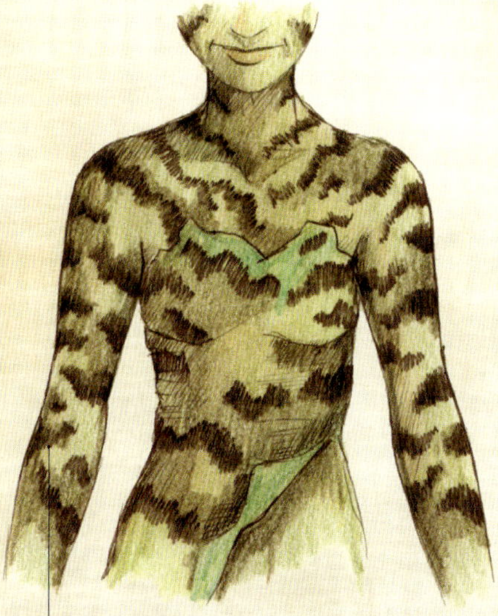

CAMOUFLAGE
Horizontal stripes, almost like animal skin, merge into the bodice and provide perfect camouflage among the trees of the forest.

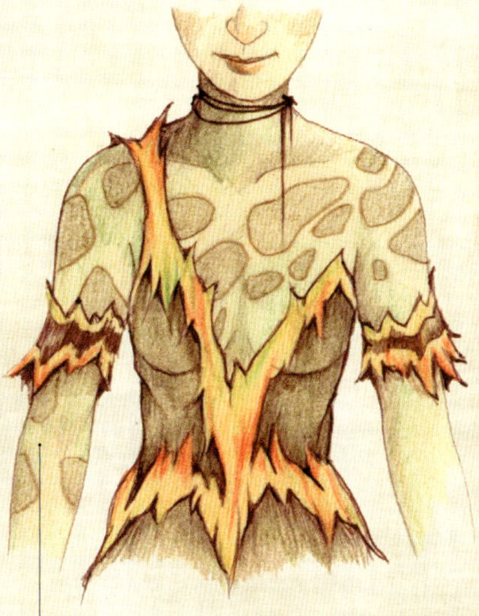

COLORS OF FALL
This covering suggests the rich and fiery colors of fall leaves, while the mottled skin resembles animal markings.

Puck

PUCK, ALSO KNOWN AS ROBIN GOODFELLOW, IS A MISCHIEVOUS NATURE SPRITE WITH MAGICAL POWERS, AS LIKELY TO CAUSE MAYHEM AS HE IS TO DO GOOD DEEDS.

Character and appearance

Although fundamentally well meaning and loyal, Puck also has a darker side. He is a troublesome prankster, associated with things that go bump in the night, and the perpetrator of many a rascally trick. Among other literary incarnations he is probably best known as the loyal servant of Oberon, King of the Fairies in Shakespeare's *A Midsummer Night's Dream*. Puck tries to be helpful, but instead causes untold mischief when the play's central love triangles fall comically out of shape.

Robin Goodfellow is often seen as a Pan-like creature of the forest. In this image, Puck has obvious animal attributes, with protruding horns and facial features that are not quite human. He is painted with watercolor over a line drawing. A pale background wash and faint, silhouetted trees suggest distance.

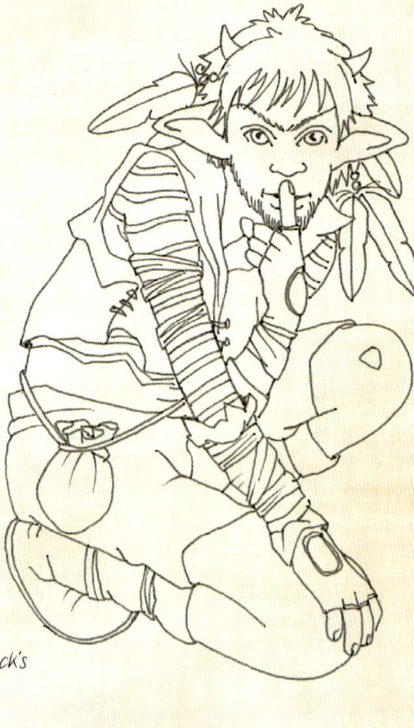

MAIN COLOR PALETTE

- Raw umber: light wash applied for skin
- Yellow ocher: mix with raw umber for Puck's boots and outfit
- Olive green: sleeves and stockings
- Alizarin crimson: stripes on sleeves and pouch; paler wash used for blush on cheeks
- Burnt sienna: mix with alizarin crimson for lower sleeves; mix with lamp black (not shown) for hair

Lamp black (not shown): gloves, feathers

Copy it!

Copy or trace the drawing or scan it into your computer. Then color it.

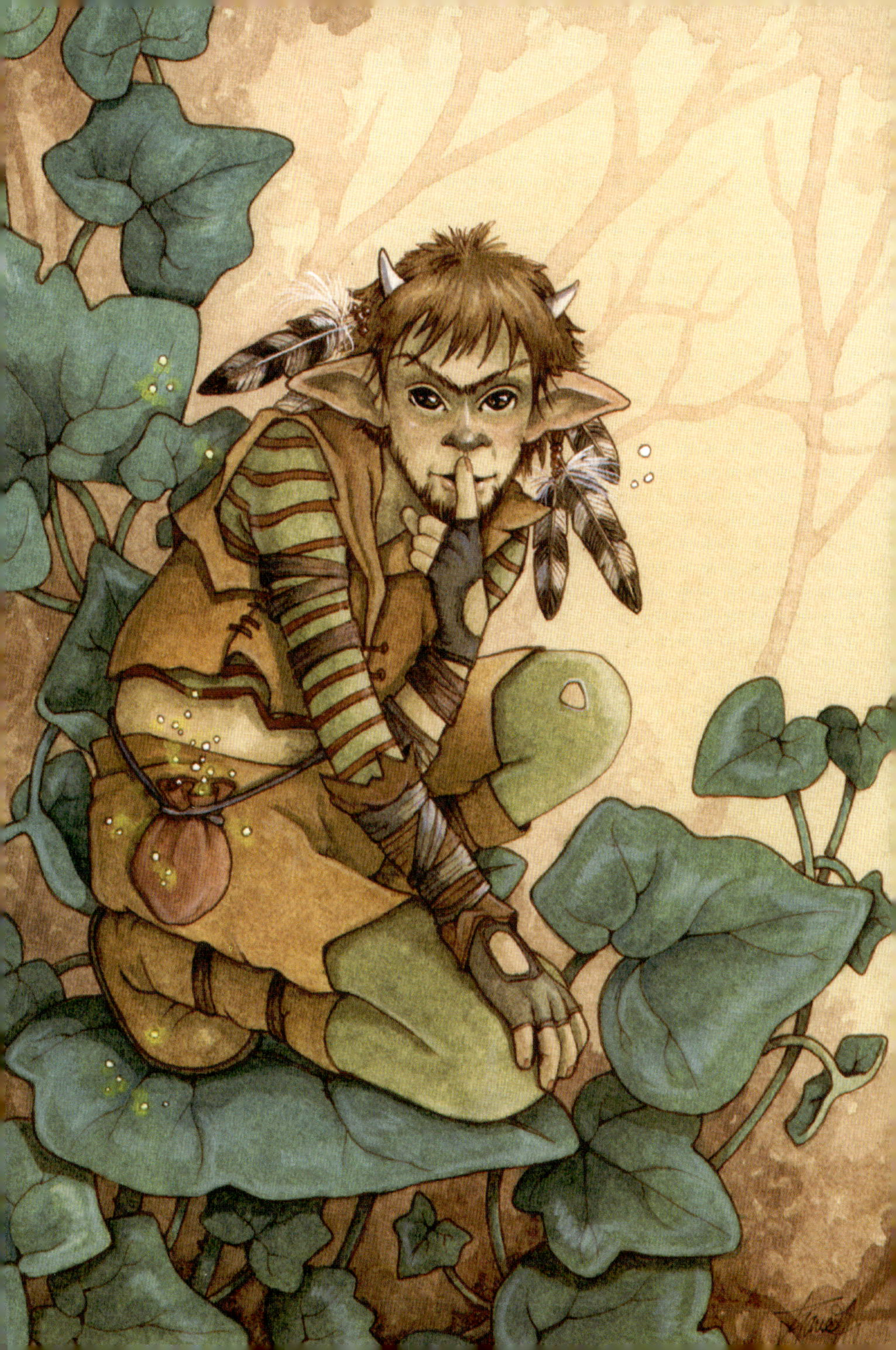

Constructing the figure

Trace the line drawing of Puck if you wish to recreate the painting, or perhaps you might want to use this simple constructed figure as a guide. You can see here how the series of round and oval shapes make up the body; then, by drawing around the outer edges, the figure appears. Make up your own poses and figures using this method.

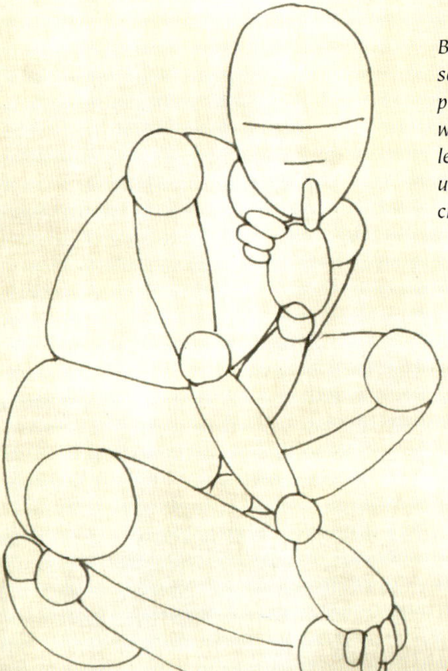

Breaking the figure down into basic shapes gives a solid foundation on which to construct a credible pose. Here Puck's crouching figure places the weight on the right knee and foot, stabilized by the left leg and hidden foot. Drawing the basic underlying shapes makes this clear and helps to create a lightly balanced but stable pose.

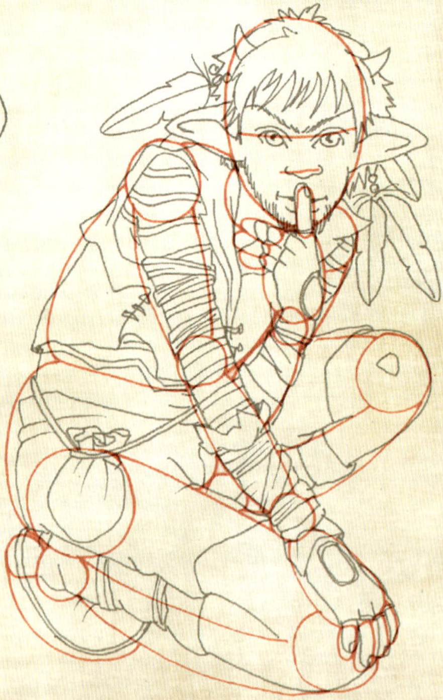

Build your detailed line drawing onto the basic underlying structure, checking that the balance is right.

See also: Figure construction basics, page 58.

Varying your body language

It is vital to consider the personality of your characters when creating and posing your figures. Well known as a very impudent character, Puck has a reputation to live up to. You might visualize him as a naughty imp, poised for mischievous action, or pausing to consider how to sort out the problems he has caused. Here are some typical poses that would express the rascally nature of this character.

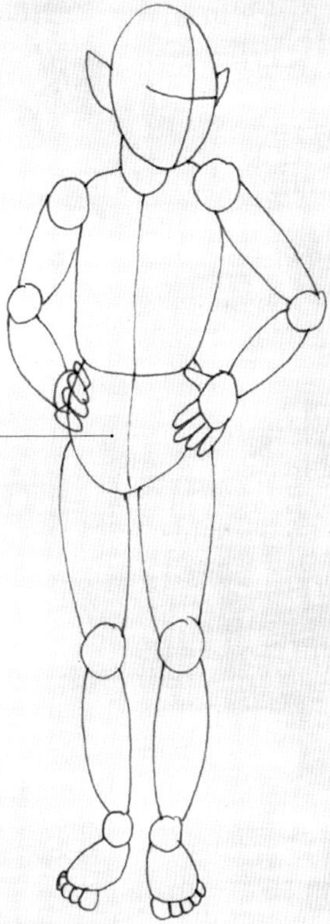

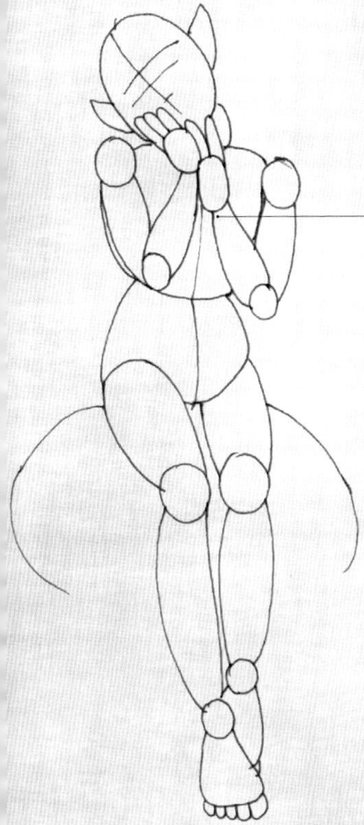

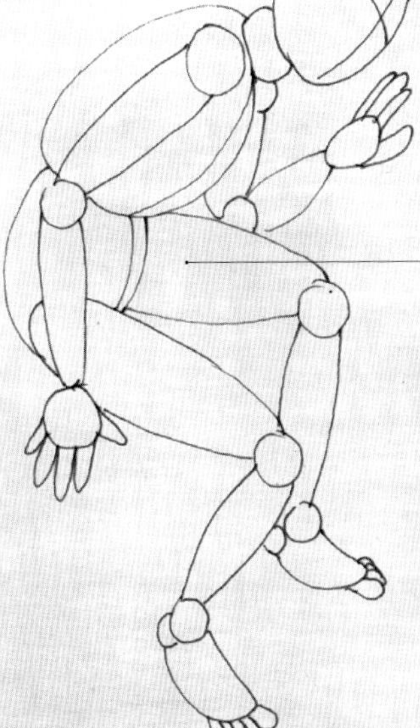

Accentuating features

Puck is an untamed spirit of nature who has grown to resemble the creatures around him until he is part animal and part fairy. He is often portrayed with small Pan-like horns and even cloven hooves. Unlike the devil, who is also classically portrayed as a hybrid, Puck is not a malevolent creature. The following ideas are just a start, but you should gather ideas, information, and inspiration from books or nature and use your imagination.

See also: Constructing the head, page 64.

Ear variations

These ears are naked, but they can be covered with fur if that suits your character better.

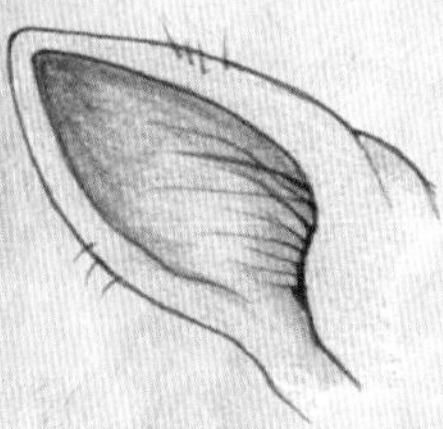

Pointed cat-like ears indicate an intelligent, independent creature always on the alert.

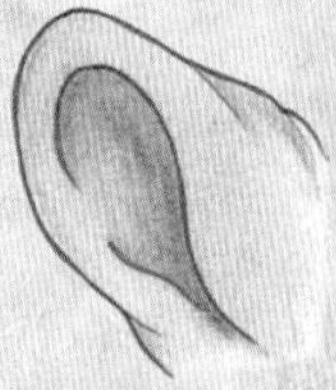

Little mouse ears suggest a bright and inquisitive creature, always exploring and never still.

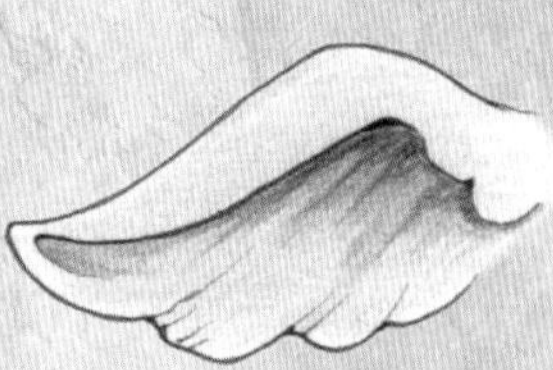

Dog's ears suggest a softer, more affectionate and communicative character.

Eyes variations

Eyes are the most expressive feature of the face. Choose the right animal eyes and your character will speak volumes.

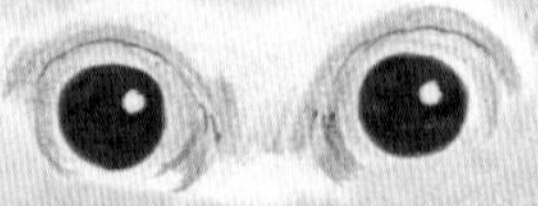

Round beady eyes suggest a cute, mouselike character, all wide-eyed innocence.

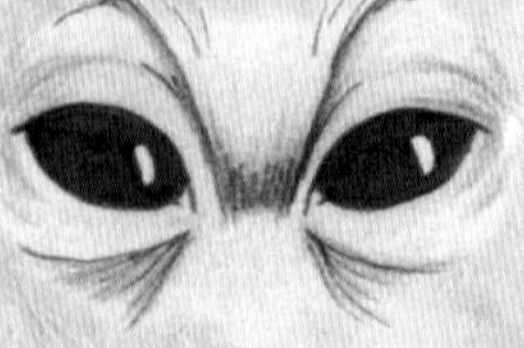

Monkey eyes are strange and discomforting, almost human and yet not quite.

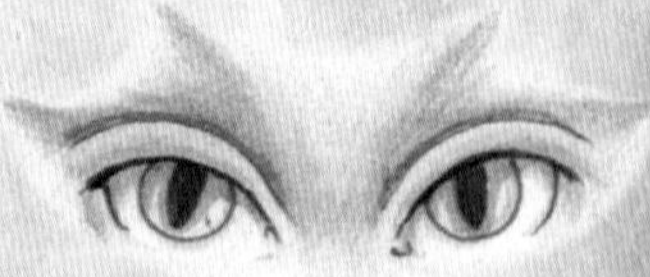

Wild cat eyes are challenging and rather alarming, warning of danger if their owner is angry.

Nose variations

Even human noses have great character. Try some animal ones for added character value.

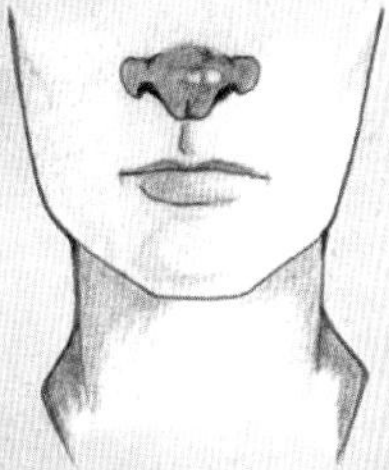

A doglike nose suggests loyalty and a gentle spirit.

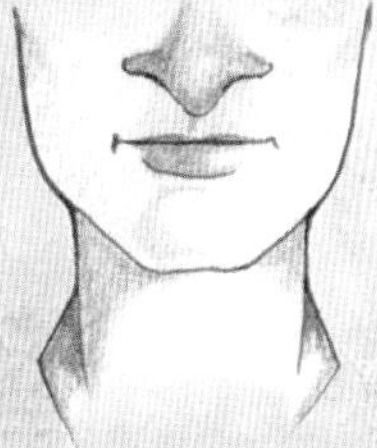

A pointed beak-like nose suggests a sharper character.

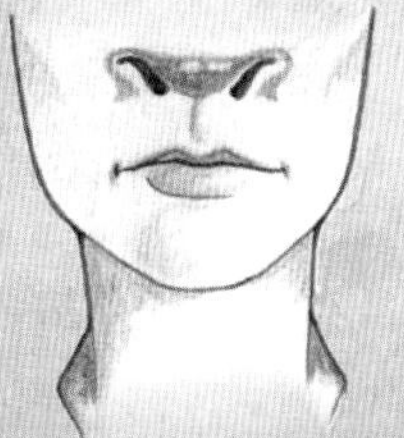

A stag or deer nose could indicate a proud, aloof nature or a gentle, compliant one, depending on how you develop your fairy character.

Horn variations

Horns come in all shapes and sizes—choose ones that suit but don't overwhelm your character.

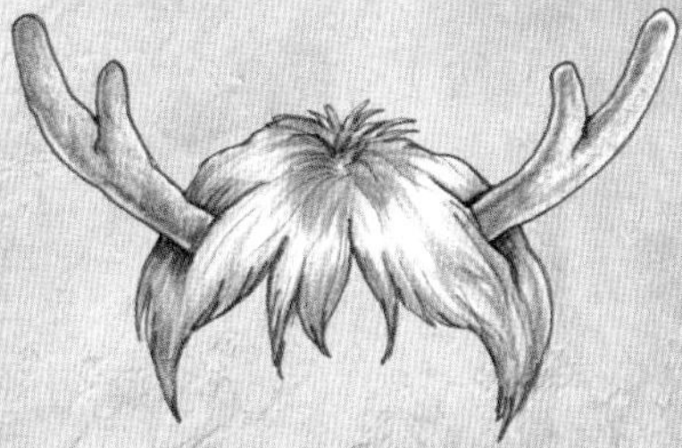

Deer antlers are huge and impressive in fully grown males. These, however, are the velvet-covered horns of a young male, and are perfect for Puck.

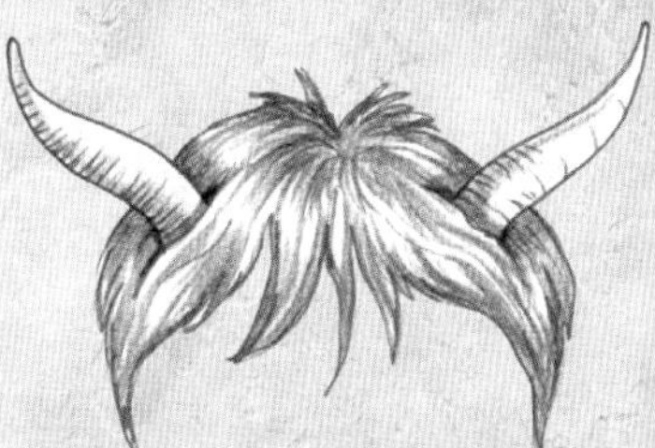

Antelope horns are slender and unobtrusive, and make a non-aggressive statement for a Puck character.

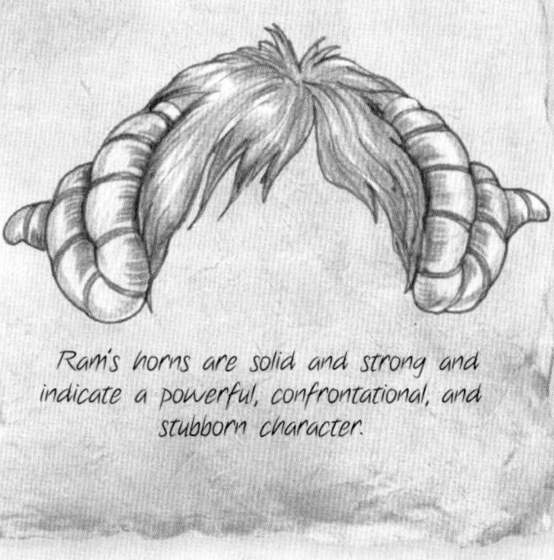

Ram's horns are solid and strong and indicate a powerful, confrontational, and stubborn character.

Gnome

ACCORDING TO LEGEND, GNOMES ARE EARTH ELEMENTALS AND HOMELY CREATURES WITH A WEALTH OF PRACTICAL WISDOM AND KNOWLEDGE THAT THEY LIKE TO PUT TO GOOD USE.

Character and appearance

The archetypal Garden Gnome is a popular figure interested in all things horticultural. However, Gnomes are an ancient race with plenty of other interests, such as inventing and tinkering with machinery. They are generally thought of as a peace-loving band, preferring to live underground and given more to hard work than creating mischief.

Benevolent, kindly, and often jolly, Gnomes are usually depicted as old and gnarled as befits their ancient lineage. Each has his own character and occupation and you should reflect this in your drawings. Many, like this individual, have rosy cheeks and twinkling eyes and are happy just to sit back and reflect on life. He is drawn with a ballpoint pen, including the areas of cross-hatched shading, then tinted with watercolor washes for a strong, earthy image.

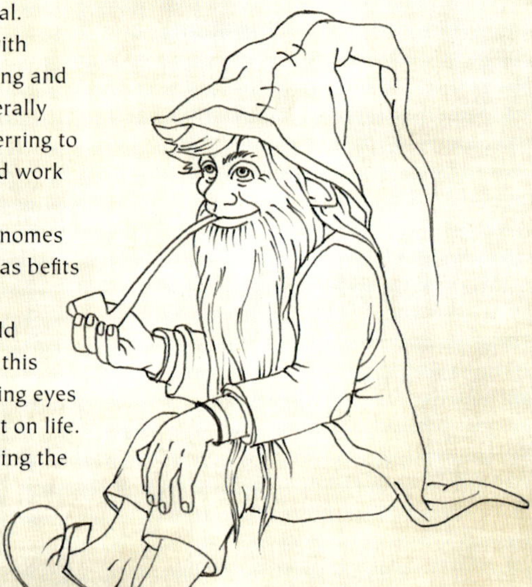

MAIN COLOR PALETTE

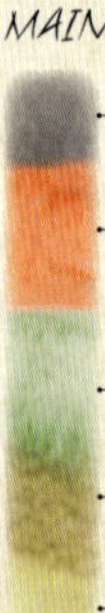

Payne's gray: beard and boots

Cadmium red: cap and sleeves; a light wash is used for the cheeks and nose

Cobalt green: jacket and stockings

Raw umber: skin tones, pipe, and trousers

Olive green: background wash and foliage

Black ballpoint pen (not shown)

Copy it!

Copy or trace the drawing or scan it into your computer. Then color it.

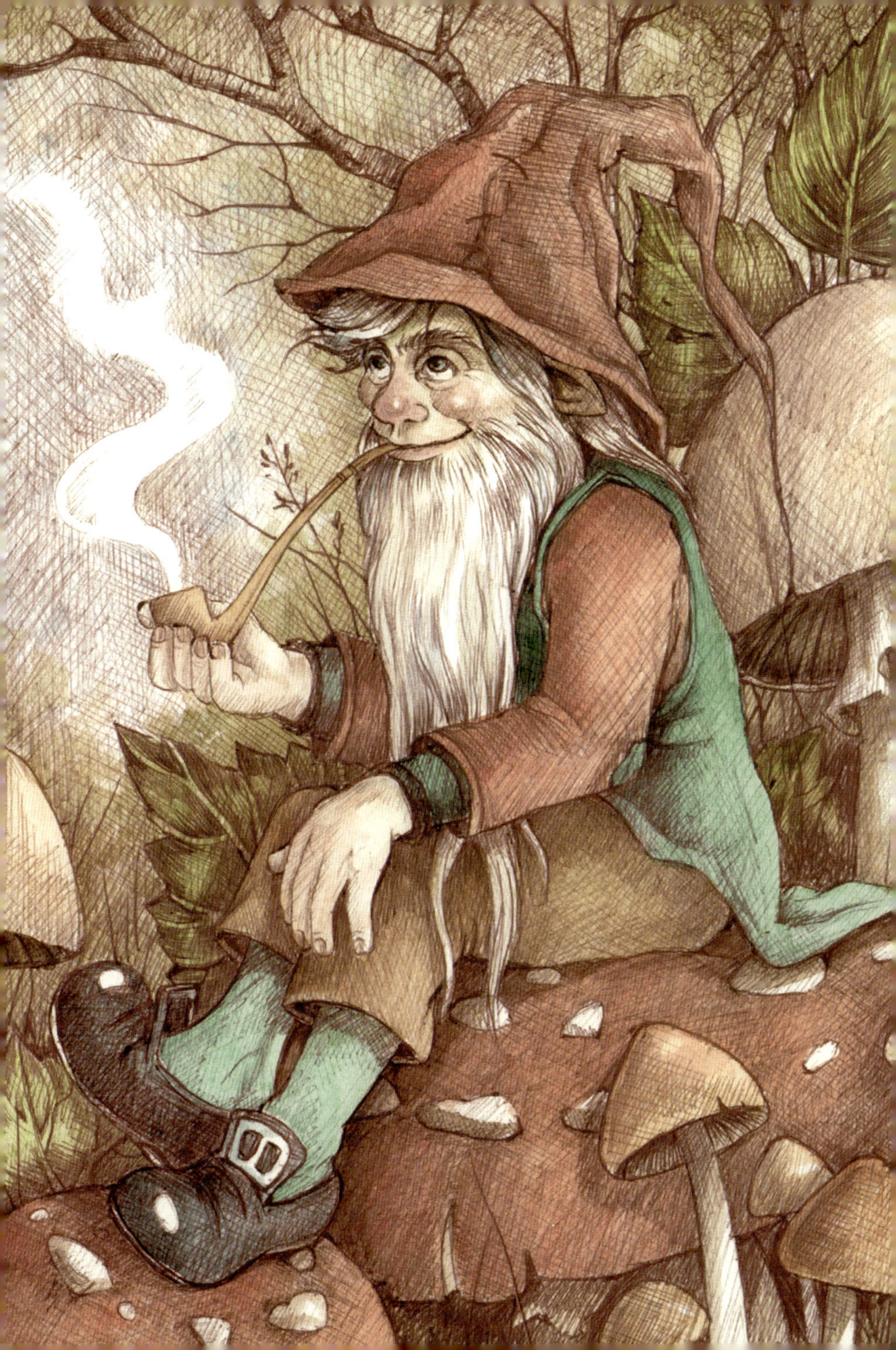

Costume and accessories

The clothes that Gnomes wear are serviceable to reflect the needs of their busy working lives. Jackets can have plenty of pockets for tools, while footwear is usually stout and durable though always well polished. Their advanced years mean that they often wear spectacles. These give you a unique styling opportunity as you can vary the style according to your character—half-moon specs or "pince nez" perhaps, or even a monocle or magnifying glass.

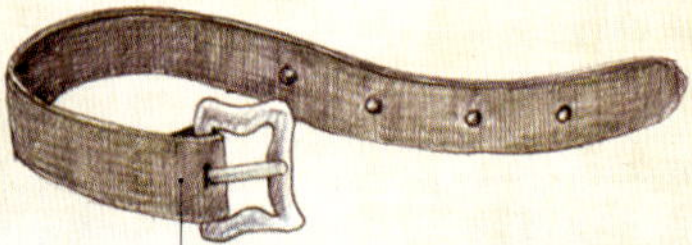

A strong belt is a must for buckling a jacket or holding up a pair of trousers.

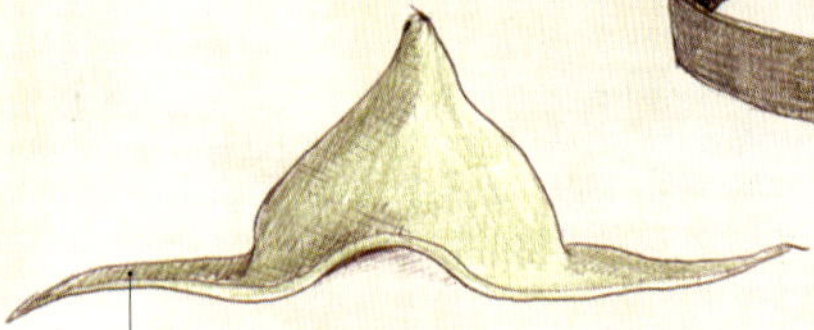

A durable hat with a wide brim might be made from soft leather.

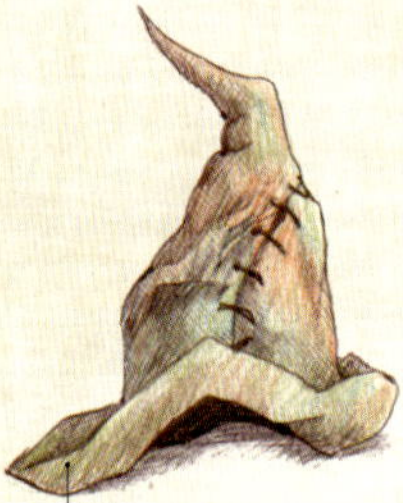

Draw a large, curled leaf with stitches down the center to make a typical pointed hat.

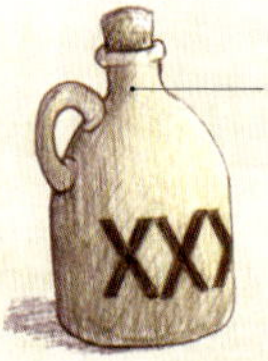

A rum pot holds elderberry wine, the Gnome's favorite drink.

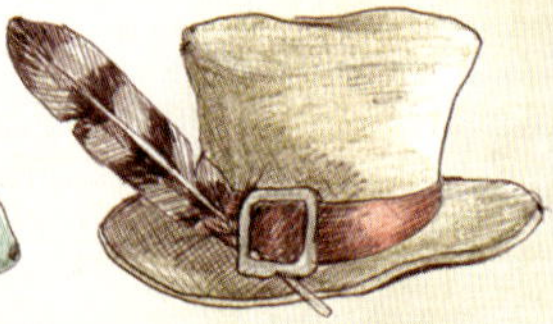

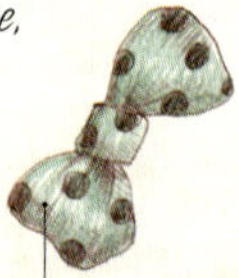

Gnomes are not averse to dressing up. How about a smart leather hat trimmed with a feather? Or a natty spotted bow tie for special occasions?

Spectacles are a telling accessory. Vary the style to suit your character.

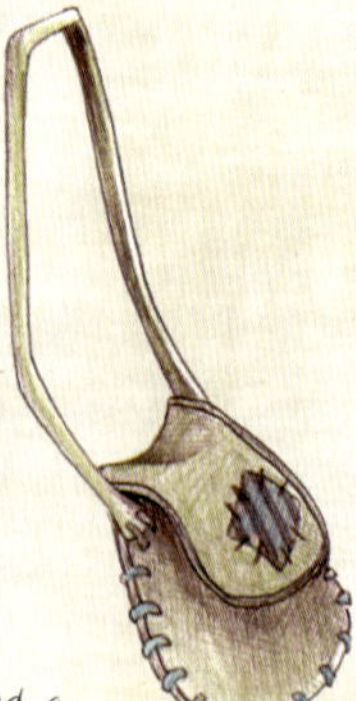

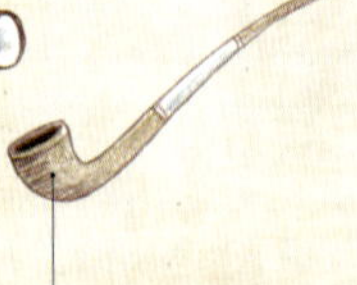

Your Gnome will need a tobacco pouch for his hedgerow tobacco mix and a clay pipe in which to smoke it.

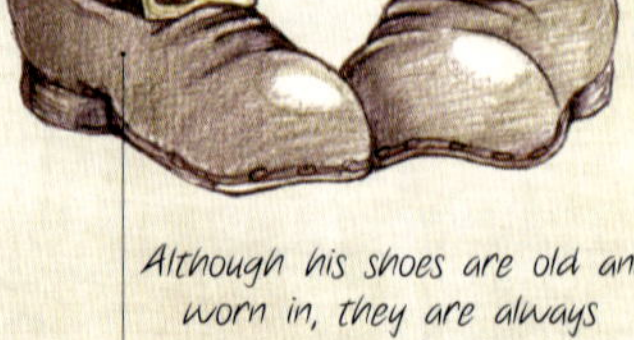

Although his shoes are old and worn in, they are always polished to a bright shine.

Creating character: hat variations

Gnomes are usually depicted as happy bearded characters. However, each is a unique individual with his own character, and his headgear can often give important clues as to his mood, personality, and occupation. Consider this important element of your design carefully.

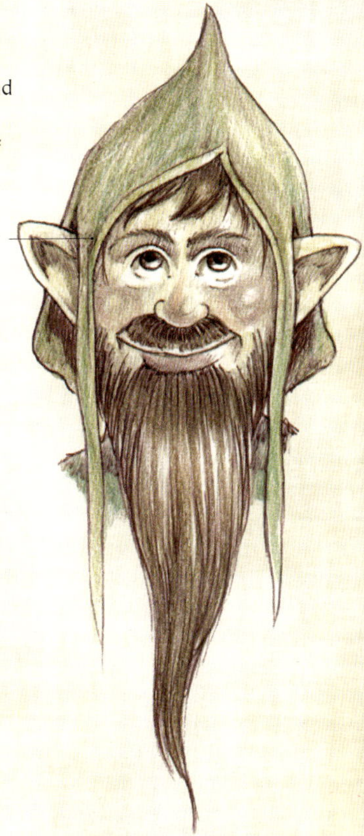

WEATHERPROOF HAT
This Gnome has dark hair and a long, thin beard. His hat has a more peasant-like appearance and might be a working hat.

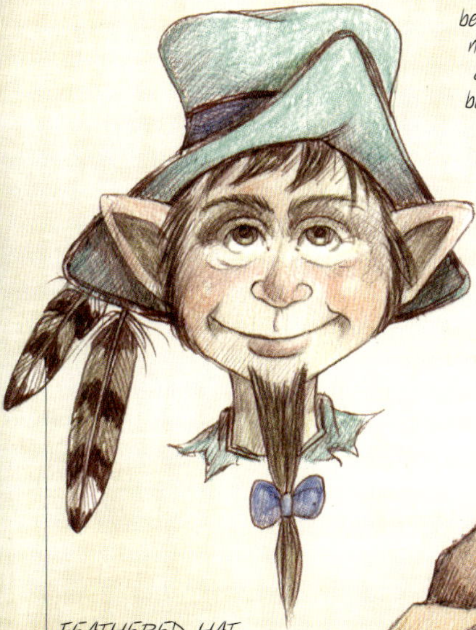

FEATHERED HAT
This Gnome has a more affluent air. He has a jaunty hat trimmed with feathers and his long, thin goatee beard is neatly tied with a ribbon bow.

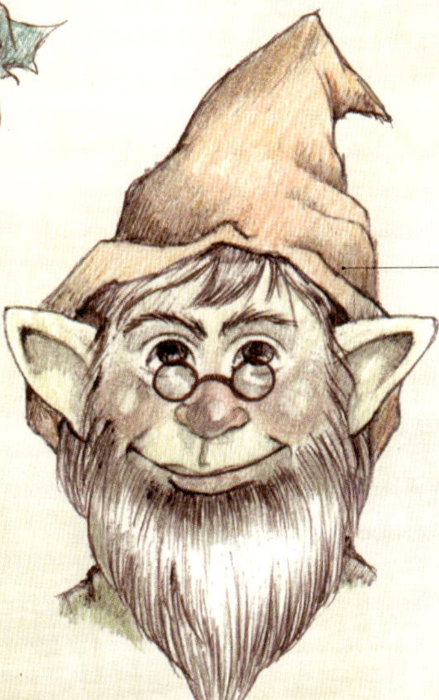

WIZARD-STYLE HAT
This is a commonly accepted stereotypical representation of a Gnome. He has a benign, smiley face with plump, rosy cheeks, a red nose supporting round glasses, a pointed hat, and, of course, a bushy white beard.

See also: Hair and headwear, page 82.

Creating character

Gnomes are jovial and kindly, and this needs to be immediately apparent in your rendering of these peaceful little folk. As always, facial features and expressions are key to character.

See also: Facial expressions, page 66.

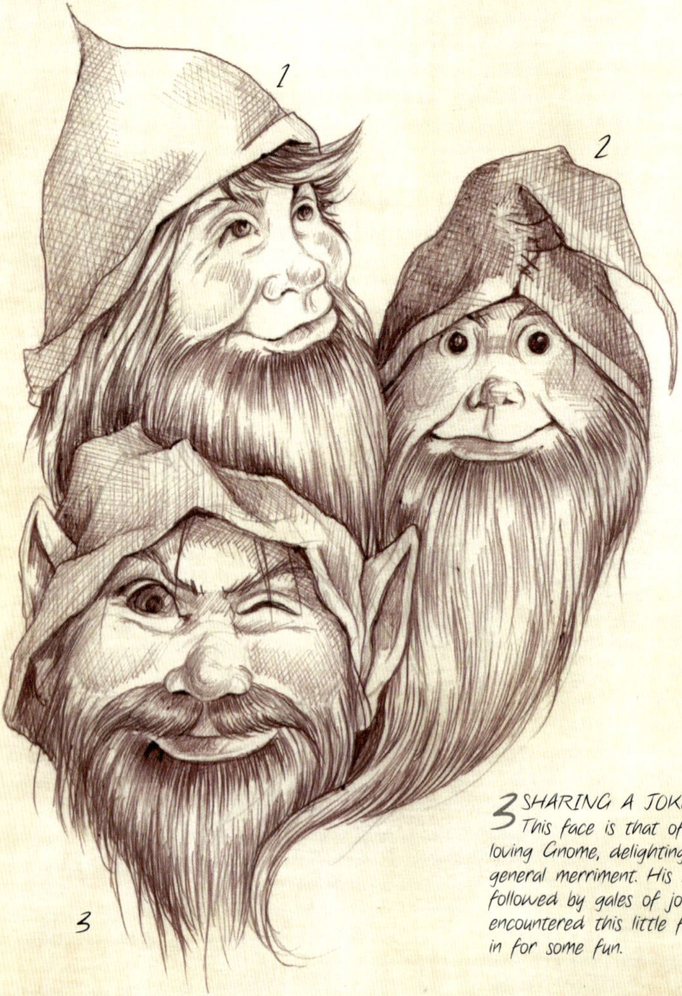

1 THE ARCHETYPAL GNOME
With round apple cheeks, twinkling eyes, and a friendly smile, this diminutive chap epitomizes the universally popular notion of a Gnome. He looks honest and trustworthy, kind and warm, happy and friendly, and is a hard-working and conscientious guardian of earth's treasures.

2 A SIMPLE AND OPEN CHARACTER
The wide-eyed gaze of this Gnome suggests an openness and innocence. There's nothing malevolent about him. Gnomes are practical and resourceful, and this Gnome has stitched his hat from a scrap of fabric. His long beard indicates his considerable age, and with age comes wisdom.

3 SHARING A JOKE
This face is that of an unmistakably fun-loving Gnome, delighting in a little joking and general merriment. His huge wink might be followed by gales of jovial chuckles. If you encountered this little fellow, you'd definitely be in for some fun.

Mood swinging

Facial expressions are vital for portraying character and mood. Here, the same features are simply rearranged to create two very different emotions.

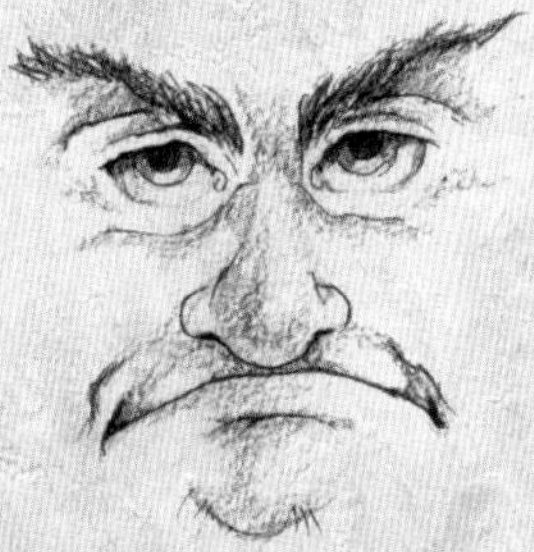

GRUMPY GNOME
For a grumpy face, the eyebrows draw sharply down toward the bridge of the nose, furrowing the brow. The eyes droop at the sides, the lips are clenched, and the mouth is turned firmly downward.

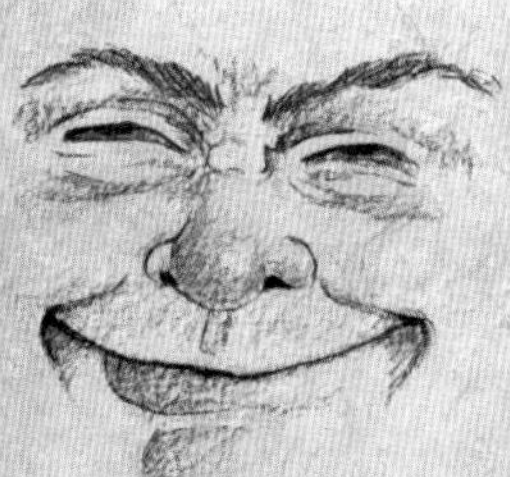

HAPPY GNOME
In total contrast, a happy face is created with lifted eyebrows and eyes that narrow to slits as the broadly grinning mouth lifts the cheeks upward, deepening the indentations at each side.

Posing your Gnomes

Gnomes are perceived as short, rather rotund creatures, with stocky legs and large heads. They like to work and play, and simply relax while the world goes by. The character of your Gnome will dictate his activity and suggest suitable poses. Always start with the simple shapes, remembering the distinctive Gnome proportions. Then flesh out your character with detail.

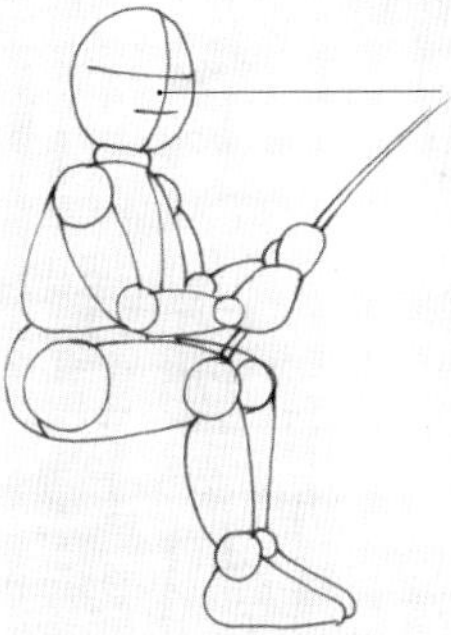

FISHING
Many Garden Gnomes are shown fishing in ponds. Alternatively, omit the fishing rod and give him a clay pipe to smoke instead.

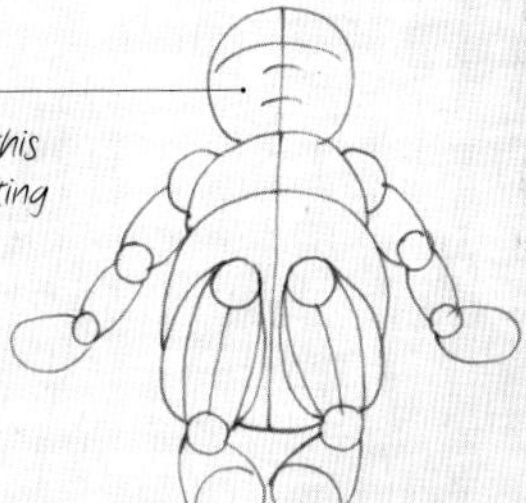

RECLINING
The picture of relaxation, this figure lies on his back, resting his weight on his arms. His round tummy is clearly visible in all its well-fed glory.

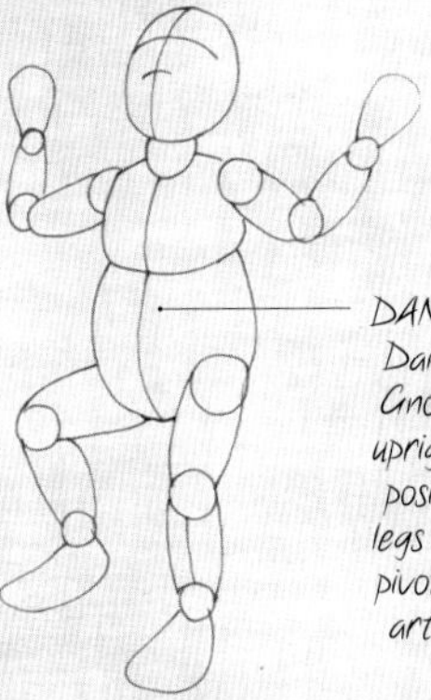

DANCING
Dancing is a favorite Gnome pastime. Vary this upright pose by positioning the arms and legs in different ways, pivoting the limbs at the articulation points.

Jack Frost

TYPICAL OF THE SPRITE FAIRY RACE TO WHICH HE BELONGS, JACK FROST IS A MISCHIEVOUS CREATURE MUCH GIVEN TO TROUBLEMAKING, WHO LIVES MUCH OF THE YEAR IN LONELY ISOLATION.

Character and appearance

While not evil, Jack Frost is a somewhat malevolent creature. He is sneaky, naughty, and sly, and delights in the power he holds to freeze everything he touches. He also, of course, paints intricate and beautiful patterns on window panes and decorates the leaves and grass with magical ice crystals. He has an important role to play as the herald of winter—when Jack Frost visits, nature takes cover until spring.

Here, Jack Frost is poised to embark on some winter mischief. He's covered with sharp icicle spears, while warm brown leaves emphasize the blue-gray chilliness of the figure. Opaque white gouache is used over dry watercolor washes to create the spiky frost formations all over the image.

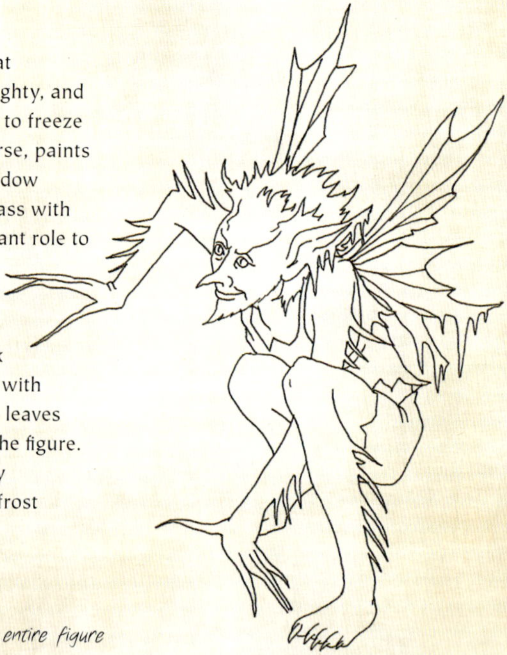

MAIN COLOR PALETTE

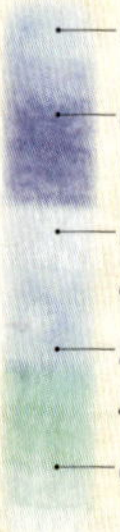

- Cerulean blue: light wash over the entire figure
- Ultramarine: use very sparingly to add depth to the clothing, hair, and eyes
- Cobalt blue: light wash over the clothing, hair, and wings
- Neutral gray: highlight and add definition to the shaded areas of the figure
- Cobalt green: light wash on the skin and wings
- Opaque white gouache: apply thickly to create spiky frost effects

Copy it!

Copy or trace the drawing or scan it into your computer. Then color it.

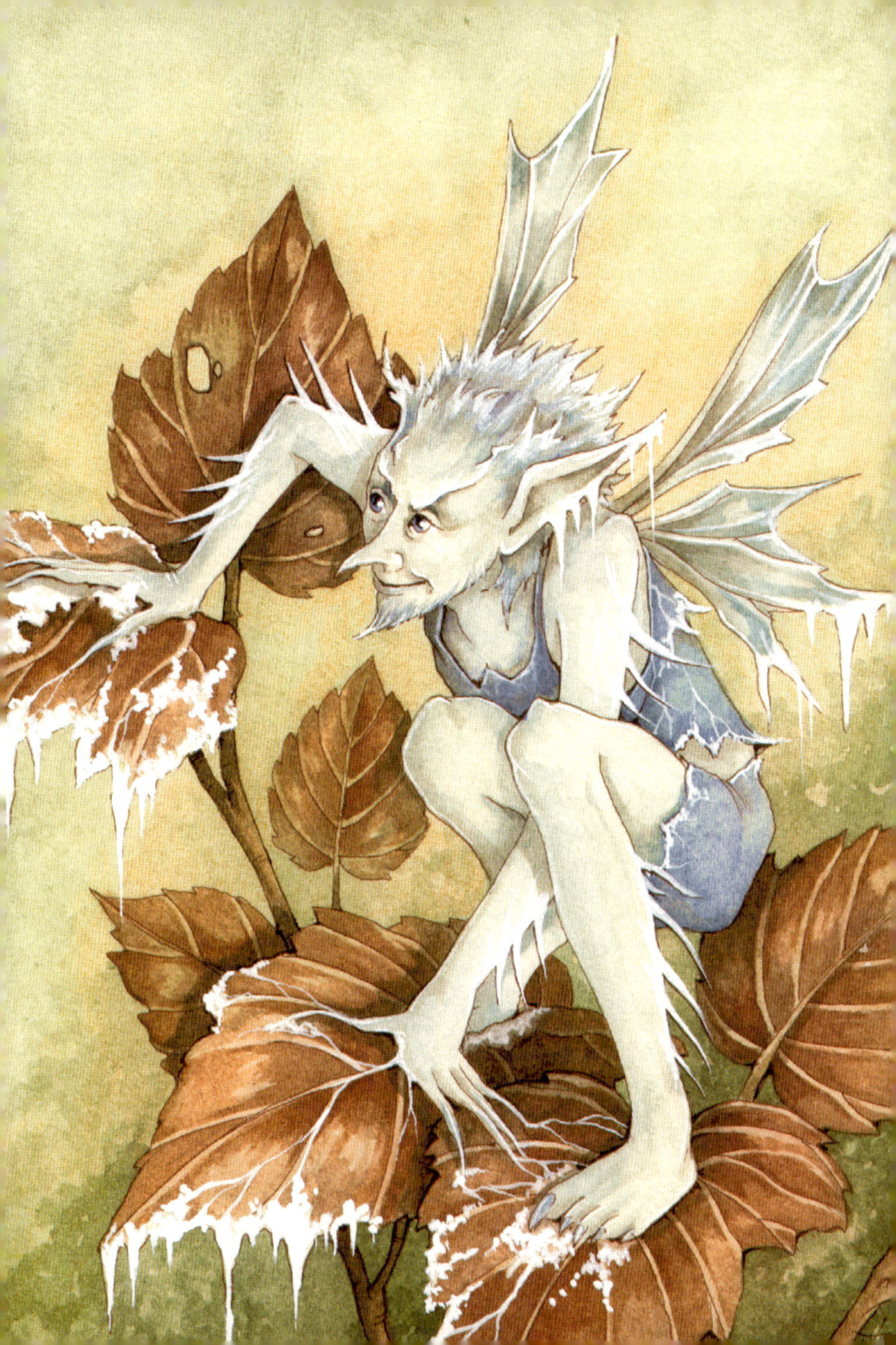

Constructing the figure

Jack Frost is a cold, sly character and his physical appearance should support this. To make his figure and posture as angular as possible, you should pay special attention to details such as the ears, hands, and feet, extending them into exaggerated points as the following sequences illustrate.

Constructing the ears

Everything about Jack Frost is elongated and sharply pointed, including his ears. The "frozen look" is accentuated here with hanging icicles.

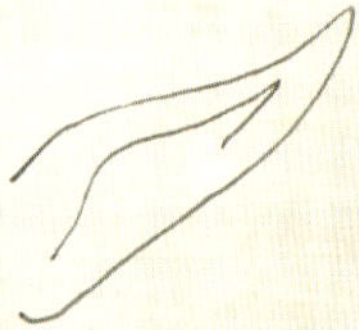

1 First draw the basic ear shape.

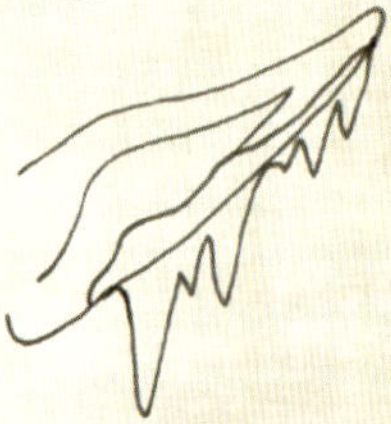

2 Using a zigzag pattern, freely sketch in a row of icicles hanging from the lower ear.

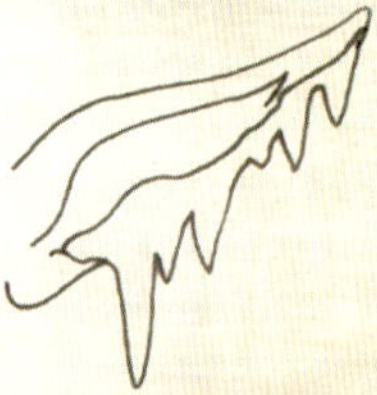

3 Erase the lower edge of the ear, leaving only the icicles. If this is too tricky, it is possible to hide the line later by painting the ice using opaque gouache.

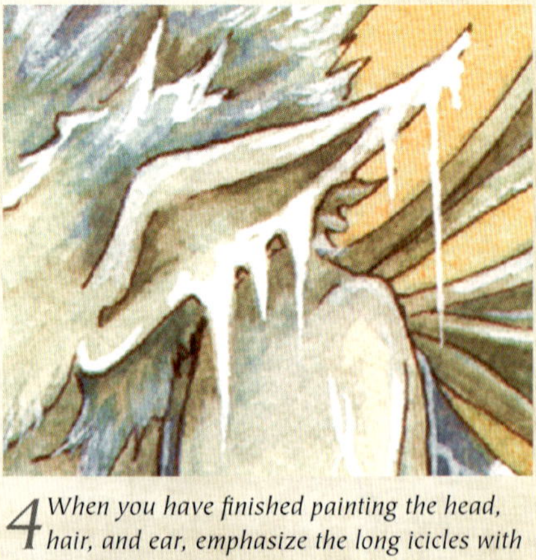

4 When you have finished painting the head, hair, and ear, emphasize the long icicles with a layer of white gouache, painted directly on top of the dry watercolor wash.

See also: Constructing hands and feet, page 68.

Constructing the hands

Jack's hands are characterized by long, pointed fingers and elongated, icy fingernails. Although unnaturally exaggerated, they must be credible, so construct them as for normal hands using simple shapes first.

1 Represent the hand with a simple oval, the wrist with a circle, and the fingers with five curved and pointed digits.

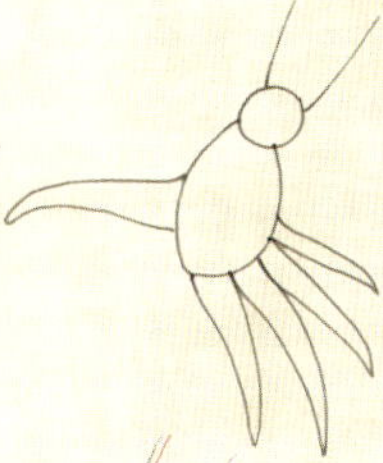

2 Draw the hand more accurately, including the very long nails.

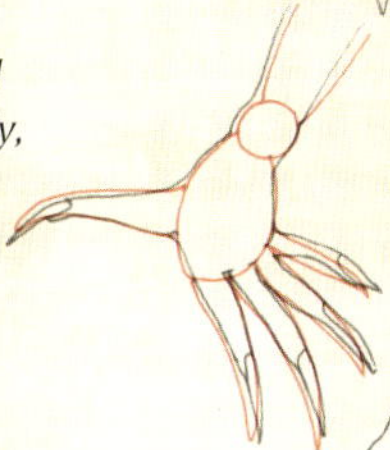

3 Erase the underlying structural shapes carefully, leaving an outline drawing of the hand.

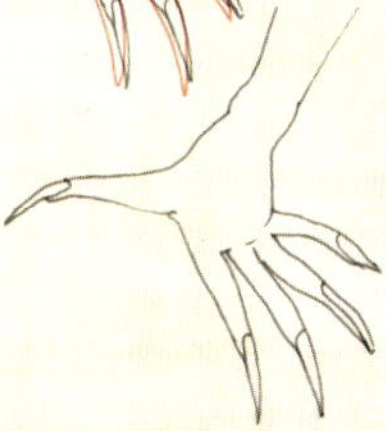

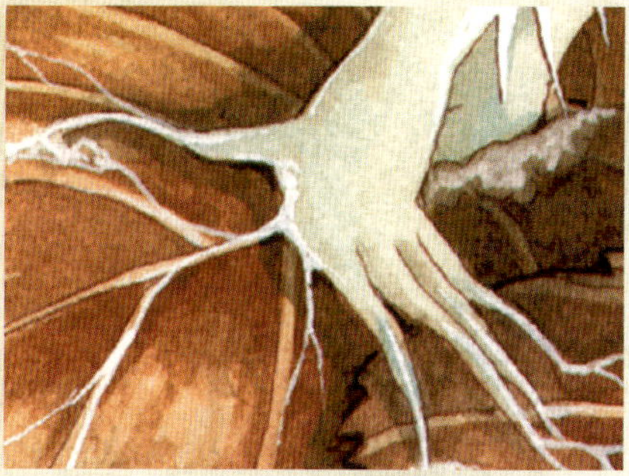

4 Paint the hand with watercolor and then white gouache. Extend the nails further, as if the ice is dripping from them and freezing the leaves.

Constructing the feet

Like the hands, the feet are clawlike, sharp, and icy, as befits Jack's character. They are loosely based on human feet, so start with simple shapes to make them convincing.

1 Start with a basic oval. Add five pointed digits of graduating size, the largest on the inside edge of the foot for the big toe.

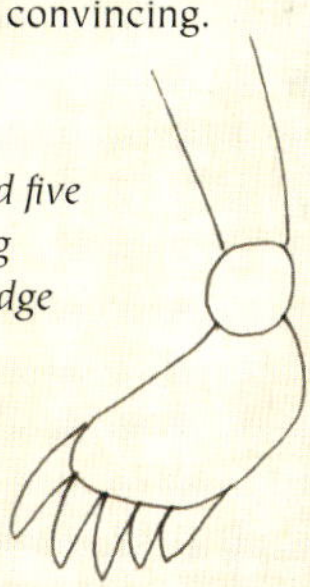

2 Flesh out the simple shapes into a realistic foot, and sketch in the long nails.

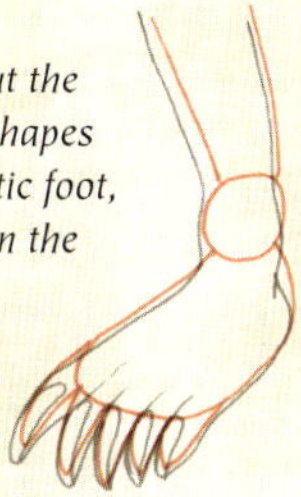

3 Carefully erase the construction lines, leaving an accurate outline drawing.

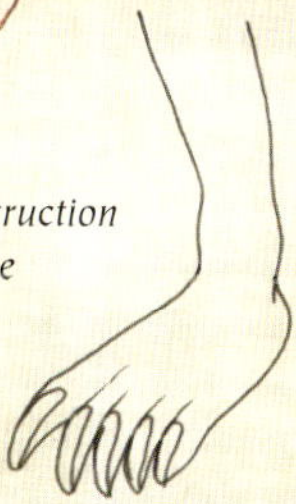

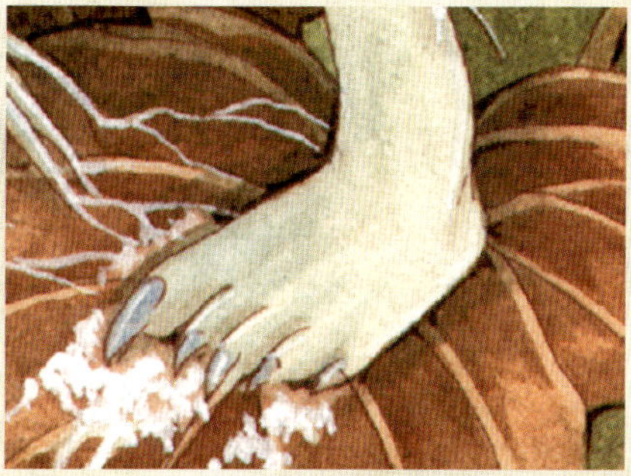

4 Paint the foot in the same cold shades. Use white gouache to add highlights on the icy nails and a sprinkling of frost where the foot rests on the leaf.

Ice and snow effects

A chilly atmosphere is often created by the use of cool, icy colors, but it can also be suggested with the help of white gouache.

Rendering ice

1 *Draw a simple leaf shape. This leaf is based on beech leaves that turn a deep orange color in fall.*

2 *Paint the leaf with a watercolor wash of raw sienna, adding highlights to suggest the arch and curl of the form.*

3 *Create the frost patterns once the wash has dried. Apply spots of opaque white gouache to the leaf edge and veins. When this dries, apply more raw sienna to make them stand out.*

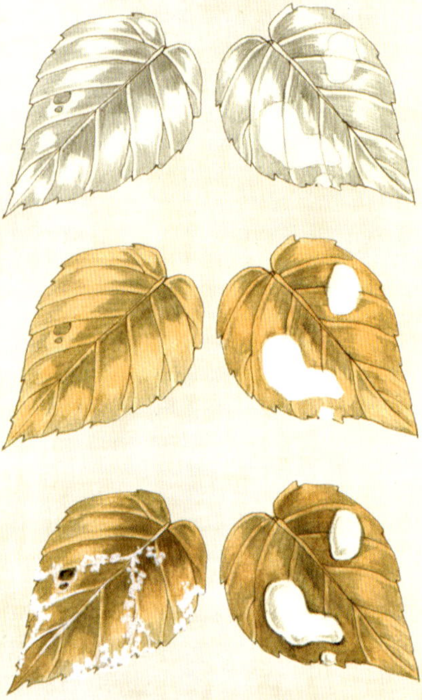

Rendering snow

1 *Draw out a few snow shapes on the surface of the leaf—these are only guidelines and will be removed later.*

2 *Paint the leaf with a wash of raw sienna. Leave the snow shapes white, removing the pencil outlines after the wash has dried.*

3 *Add shading to the white areas to "raise" the snow from the leaf surface. Darken the leaf with another raw sienna wash.*

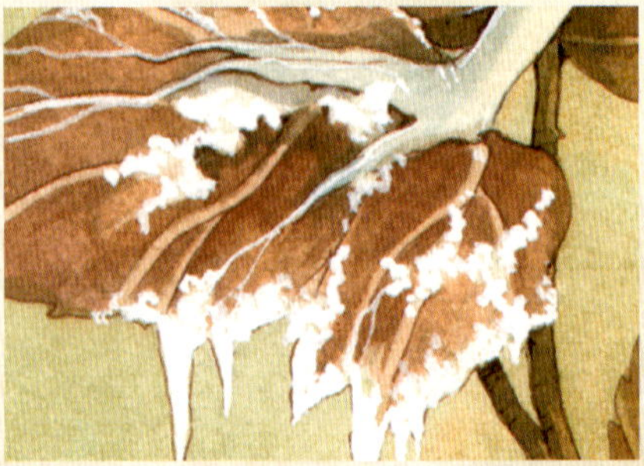

Gouache effects
This is a close-up of one of the leaves from the painting of Jack Frost. You can see how the gouache was used to make the frost effects and icicles dripping down the leaf edge.

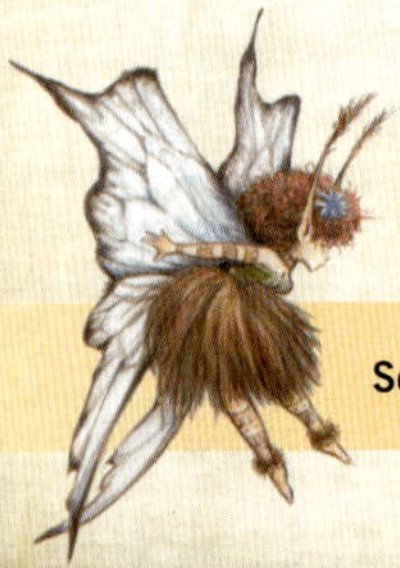

See also: Basic watercolor techniques, page 50.

Creating snowy landscapes

Using very limited materials, it is still possible to produce effective results. Here are two methods that use soft colored pencils to create a cold, wintery effect on cream/taupe pastel paper.

1 With a sepia pencil draw a series of overlapping diagonal lines, giving the effect of hills receding into the distance. Add shading where they dip down behind each other in successive layers.

2 Cover the tops of the hills with a layer of white pencil. Work with medium pressure so that the paper texture shows through to add surface interest to the snow.

3 Gently blend the white areas with a soft tissue to give the smooth appearance of fresh snow. Lightly apply cobalt blue and cadmium yellow to the sky and blend.

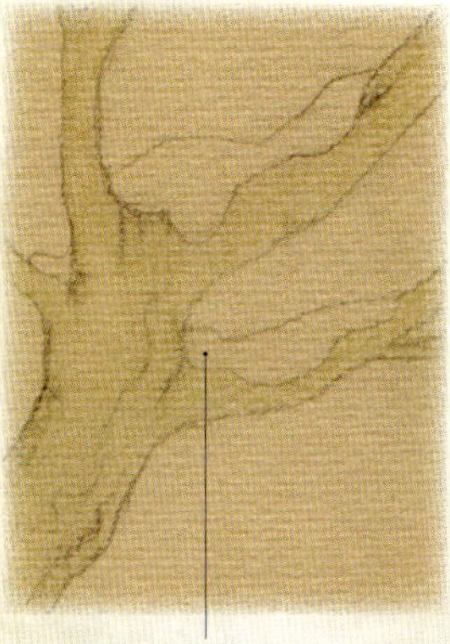

1 Use a sepia pencil to sketch a tree. Mark where the snow might gather on the branches. Color the trunk with raw umber, adding stronger shading to give form to the tree.

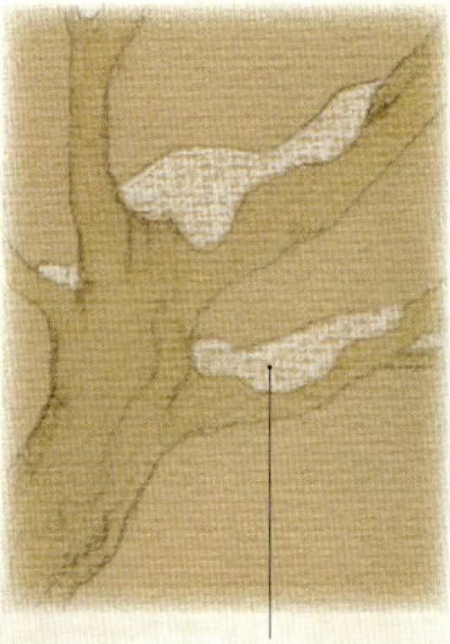

2 Apply white pencil heavily to the snow-covered areas, and gently blend the snow with a cotton ball or soft tissue.

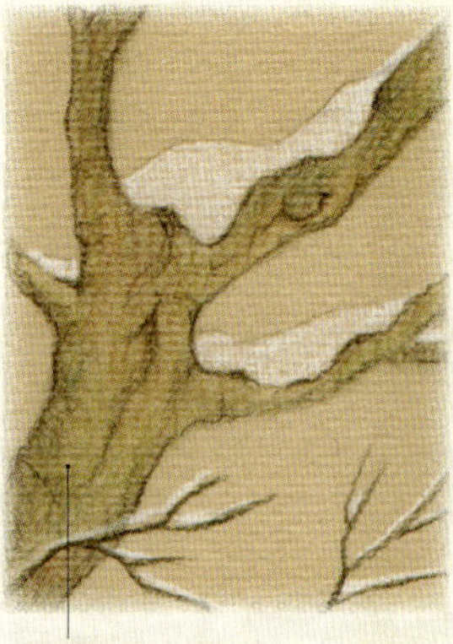

3 Add tonal depth to the tree with a sepia pencil. With firmer pressure and the same pencil, draw some smaller branches and add a little snow.

Spriggan

SPRIGGANS, UNLIKE THEIR DISTANT COUSINS THE PISKIES, ARE NOT LIGHT-HEARTED AND MISCHIEVOUS. THEY ARE DARK FAIRIES WITH MALICE AND THIEVERY IN THEIR HEARTS.

Character and appearance

Spriggans do not like humans and will torment them with their malevolence and trickery whenever they can. They gather in lonely places like abandoned houses and ruins, sometimes guarding treasure. Their pernicious deeds include stealing children and leaving changelings, blighting crops, and causing sudden illness. They are small, twisted creatures that resemble grotesque old men. But they are also shape-shifters and can bloat their bodies to gigantic proportions.

Some firsthand accounts suggest that Spriggans are a tiny species of the evil "Red Cap" fairy tribe. Another tells of Spriggans wearing green vests and describes them dancing with bizarrely grotesque and distorted movements, as pictured here.

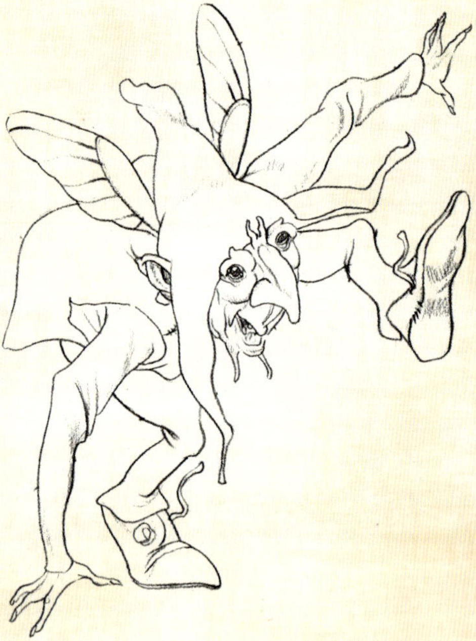

MAIN COLOR PALETTE

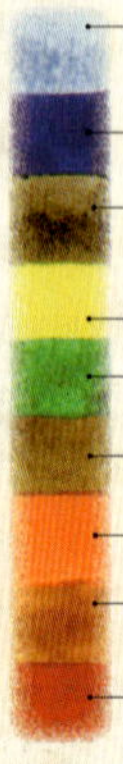

- Cerulean blue: washes for background, skin, clothes, and wings
- Ultramarine blue: vest washes, facial details, wings
- Van Dyke brown: background washes, facial details
- Cadmium yellow: skin tones, clothes, and boots
- Hooker's green: background washes, vest
- Burnt sienna: background washes
- Cadmium scarlet: skin tones, clothes, and wings
- Bronze yellow: clothes, shoes
- Alizarin crimson: hat

Copy it!

Copy or trace the drawing or scan it into your computer. Then color it.

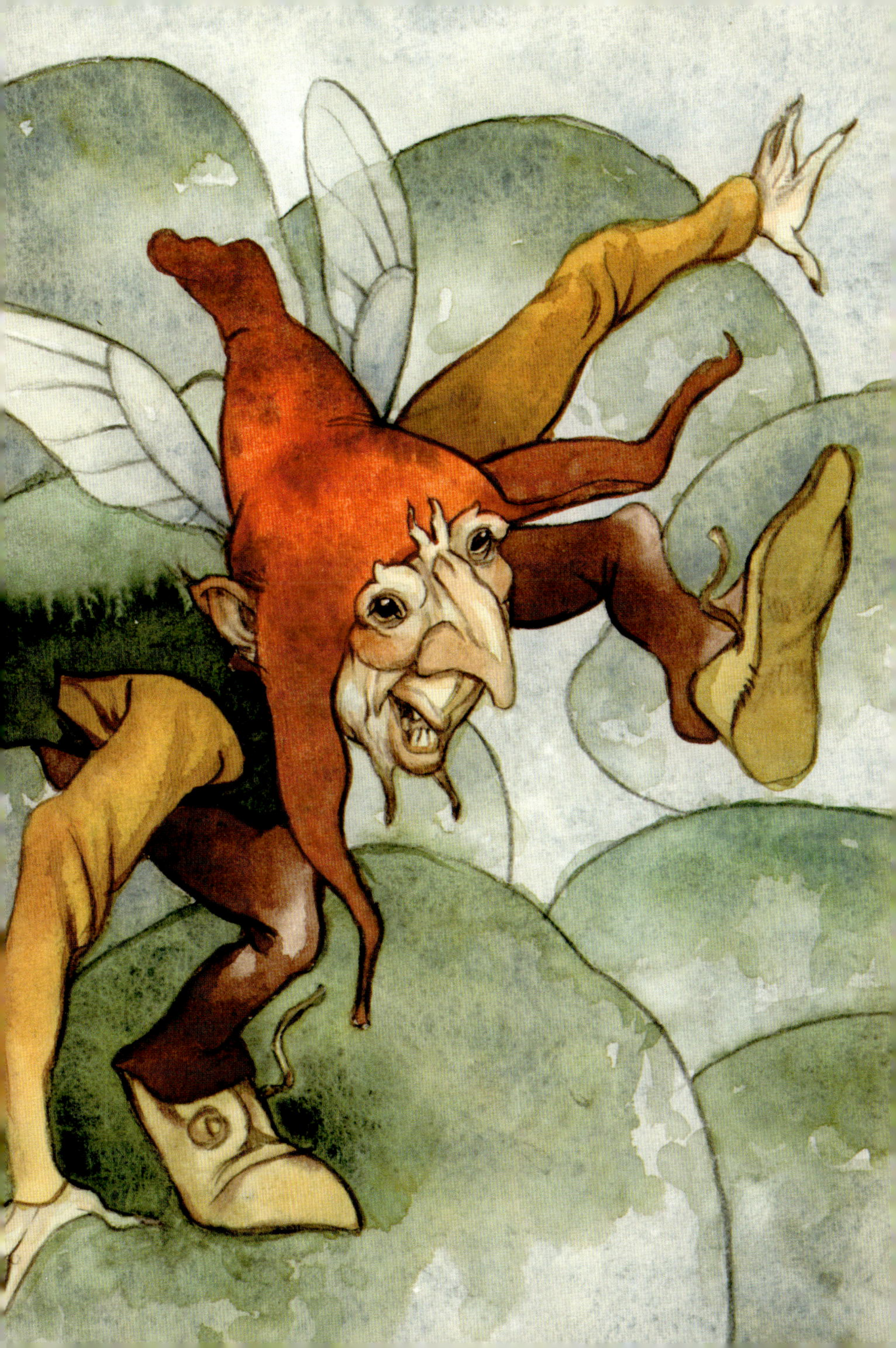

Facial expressions

The face and head is the first part of a character that a viewer reacts to, so explore different ways to visualize the individual. Facial structure and expression are vital in the descriptive process. Each Spriggan shown here combines different elements to capture the fairy's dark persona—and mixing animal and human features give a creature another subtle and disturbing dimension.

TWISTED OLD MAN

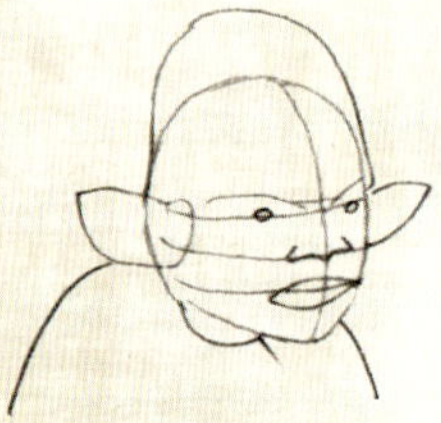

1 Start with a basic sphere and divide it in half in both directions. Divide the lower half of the face roughly into thirds. Indicate the cylindrical neck and add the curve of the shoulders. Building on the basic shape, imagine the features in their simplest form.

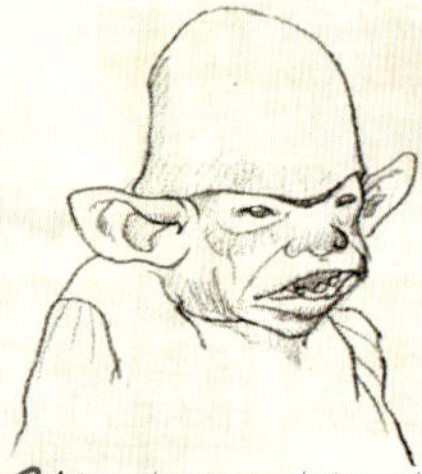

2 Now begin to bring the character to life. Add detail to the ears, eyes, and mouth and note the lines that indicate the sagging cheeks and jaw line. Shade to give shape and form to the face; indicate the hunched shoulders.

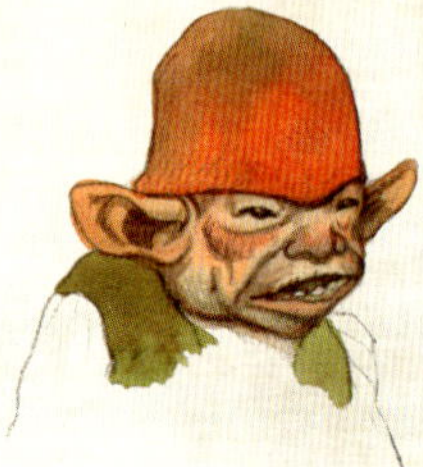

3 Add color to complete the character. Flushed cheeks and a red nose give an unnaturally florid, bad-tempered appearance. Dark animal eyes and a mouthful of pointed teeth highlight the dangerous disposition of this character.

SINISTER SPRIGGAN

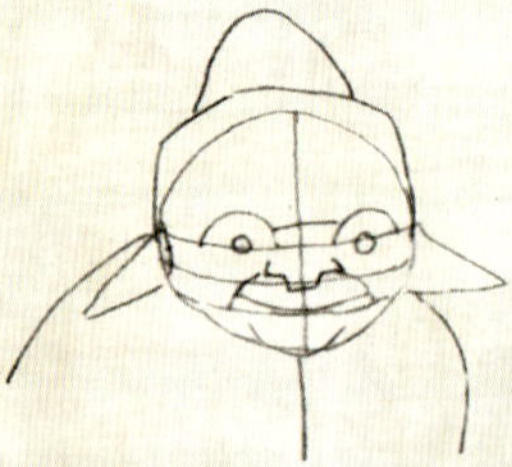

1 This straight-on view portrays a squat head shape based on a circle. Divide the basic shape as before and plot the position of the eyes, nose, mouth, and ears.

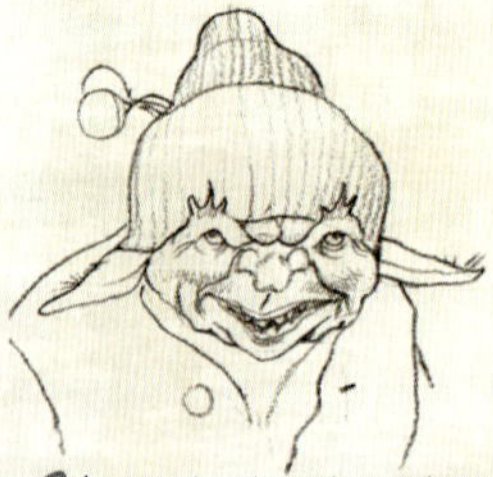

2 Now develop the evil character. Focus on the twisted mouth full of nasty teeth. The eyes are deep set and wide spaced to lend a demented air, and the eyebrows are bulges of skin. Add shading to show the sagging skin folds.

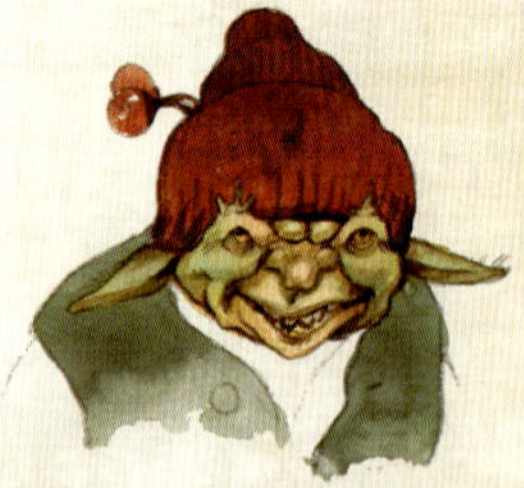

3 Add a green tinge to the skin for an evil reptilian feel. Create yellow teeth in the twisted, sneering mouth and highlight the anger lines bulging between the brows. All these amplify the creature's maniacal appearance.

Facial detail

However distorted the facial features, you need to start with a solid underdrawing for a credible result.

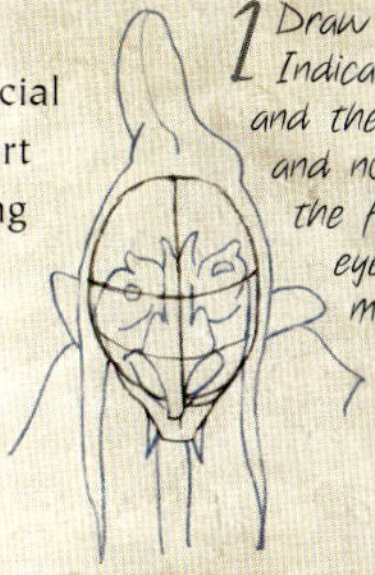

1 Draw a basic oval. Indicate the center line and the positions of eyes and nose. Manipulate the features; the eyes and ears might be asymmetrical, for example.

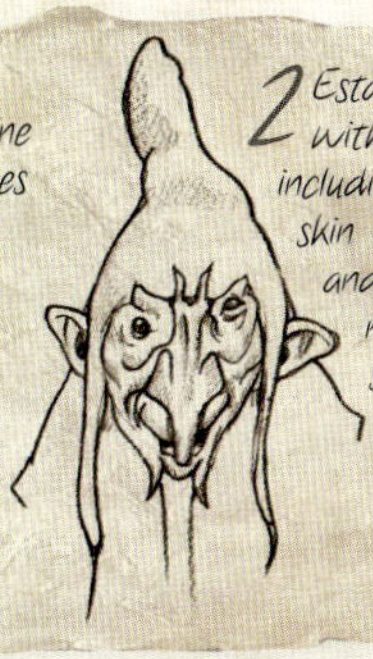

2 Establish the features with a strong line, including the folds of skin below the eyes and each side of the nose. Add a little shading to make the face look three-dimensional.

TOAD FACE

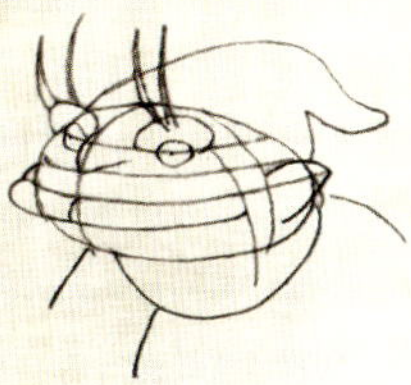

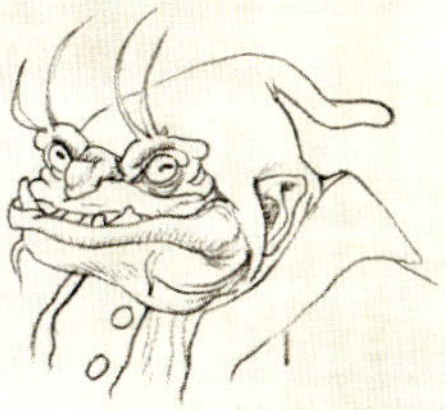

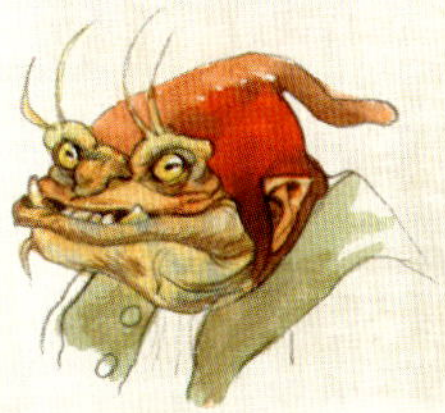

1 This grotesque face combines an old man with a toad. Sketch in the flattened oval of the head and indicate the eye, nose, and mouth lines and the fat, short neck.

2 Now go all out for the toad features. Add detail to the bulbous eyes buried in flesh and the wide, leering mouth with its evil fangs. Add shading to the fleshy bulges.

3 Add a green tinge to the skin to emphasize the toady nature of this character's face. He's creepy but a bit whimsical, too. Deliberately offset the eyes to generate a mentally unbalanced appearance.

POINTED HAT

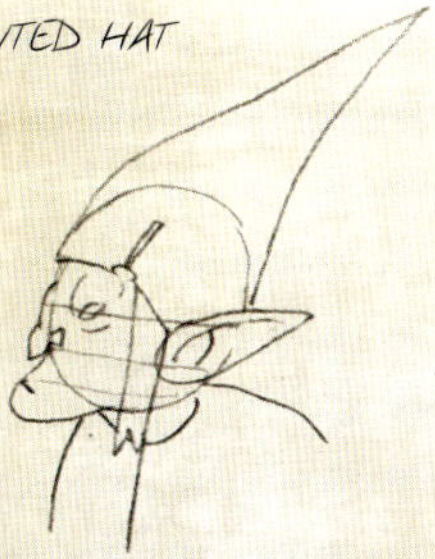

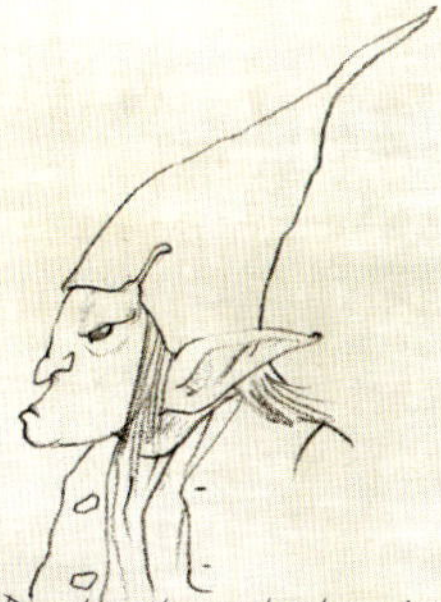

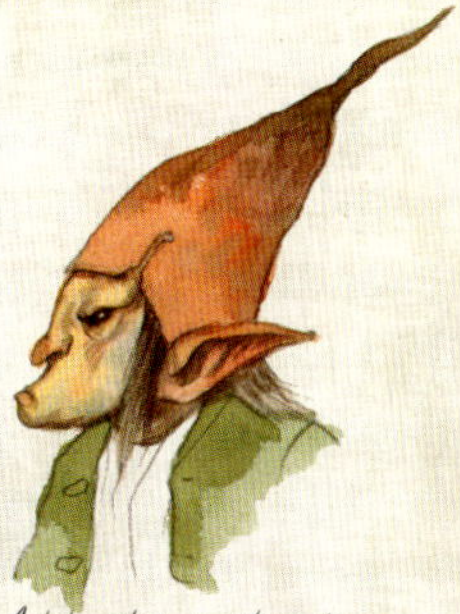

1 An elongated jaw and tilted eye gives this face its disturbing aspect. Start with the basic head shape, then extend the jaw. Draw the down-pointing nose, elongate the hat, and echo the shape with long, pointed ears.

2 Develop the underslung jaw with its bad-tempered mouth, draw in the feral, slanting eyeball, and add straggly wisps of hair. Add minimal shading to describe the sunken cheek.

3 Add color washes to complete the otherworld quality of the character. He has an undoubtedly evil disposition and would be dangerous to meet. A small, snail-like antenna adds to the feeling of general nastiness.

Alternative poses

For a successfully resolved character, try different poses to see which best personifies the creature's traits. To be believable, every figure needs a solid underlying structure that acts as a scaffold for the final character. Start with the basic forms, and then refine these at each stage of the work. Draw the first simple shapes lightly so they disappear beneath the final drawing.

STANDING SPRIGGAN

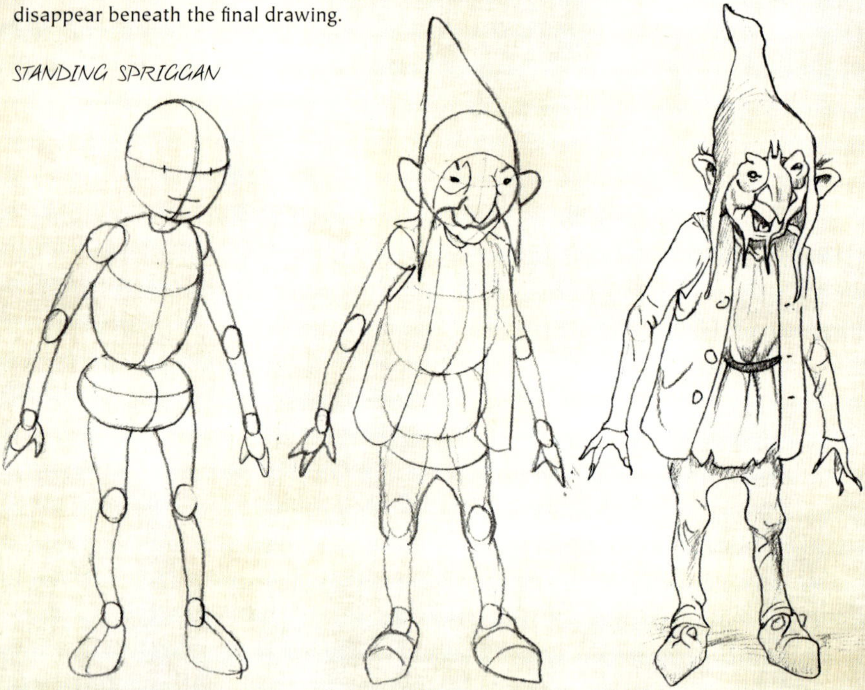

1 Plot the basic underlying forms, adding the articulation points. Note that the weight is evenly distributed on both feet.

2 Add the clothing, keeping things simple at first and making sure it drapes convincingly over the basic structural shapes. Begin to indicate the facial features with simple lines and add the long pointed hat.

3 Now refine the face, resolving the features for an exact character description. Add clothing details to describe the soft fabric folds, using shading for a three-dimensional feel.

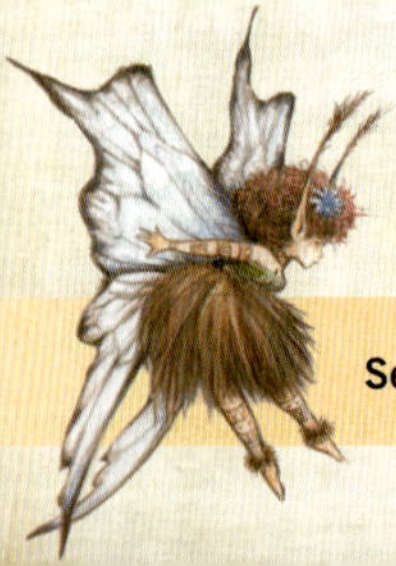

See also: Fairy poses, page 60.

CREEPY STALKING POSE

1 The crouching figure of the stealthy Spriggan is easy to achieve with simple shapes first. Notice how the torso doubles over and the hip oval is tipped under. Legs and arms are folded into exaggerated zigzags for the creeping action.

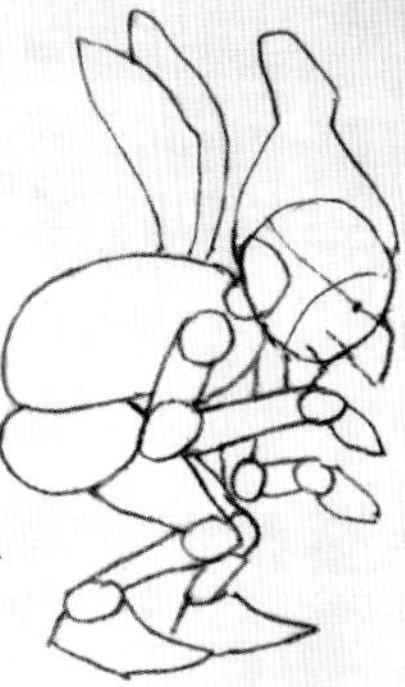

2 With the solid underdrawing, the clothes sit correctly on the body without masking the action. From this side view, the far arm and leg are copies of the front ones, but at a slightly different angle. The far arm drops lower for a natural twist of the shoulders.

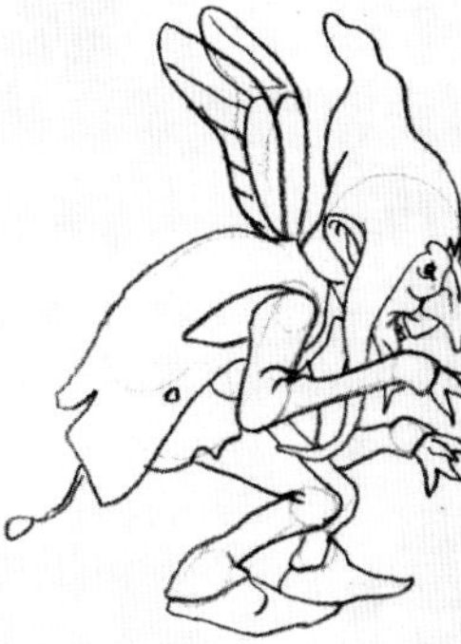

DYNAMIC SPRINGING POSE

1 Dynamic action poses can be hard to visualize, as foreshortening and perspective come into play. An artist's mannequin helps to make sense of the pose. Here, the underlying forms are still the same, but seen from this different angle they appear altered..

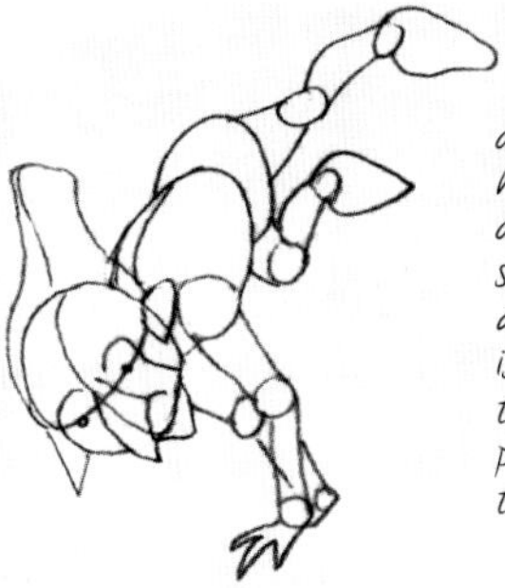

2 The figure springs in the air and lands on his hands. The active arms and legs are seen in perspective. By drawing exactly what is visible they appear to recede, giving a powerful sense of the thrusting movement.

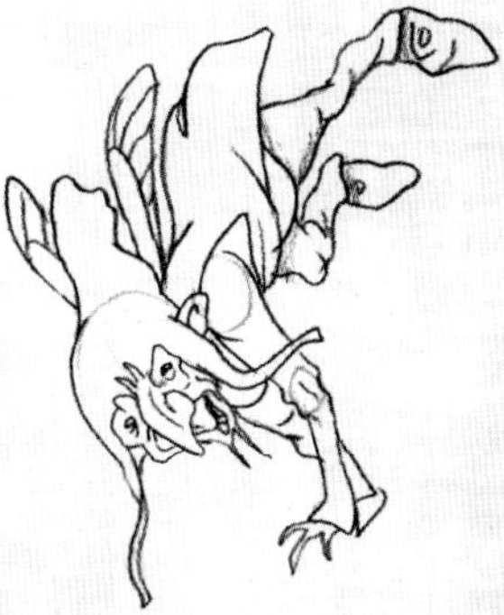

TWISTING THREE-QUARTER VIEW

1 Here, the stooped figure is seen from a three-quarter angle with the head almost straight on. Basic shapes help to get the twisting pose to look believable. The hunched figure looks slightly deformed and awkward, which helps to convey the wily, groveling character.

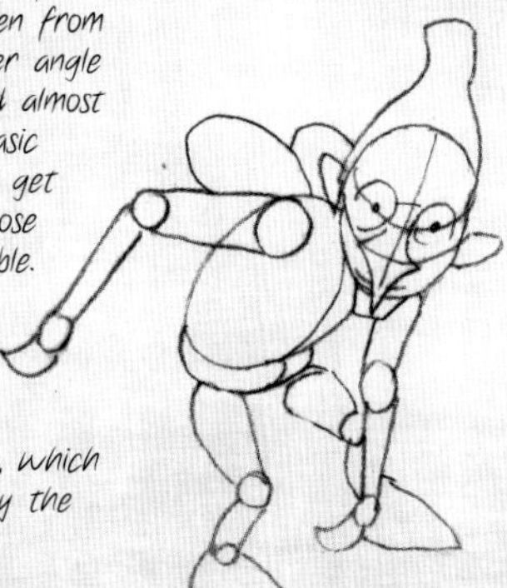

2 With the twist of the shoulders, one arm almost drags on the ground, adding to the demented look. The front view enables the nasty nature of the Spriggan to be displayed in the facial expression.

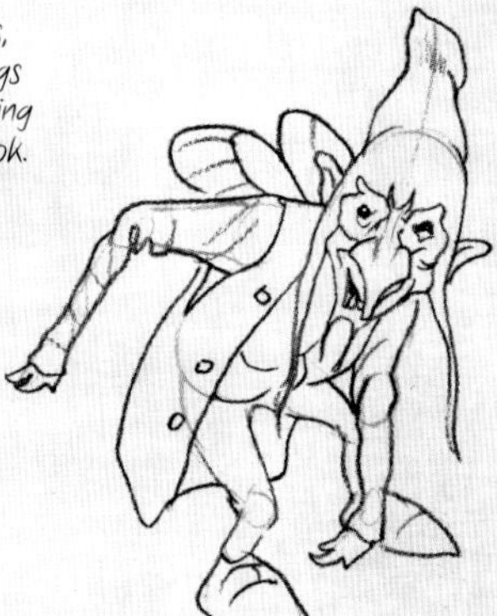

Spriggan: from sketch to finished painting

See also: Rendering, page 52.

Every detail of this image conveys the malicious Spriggan nature. The grotesquely twisted figure fills the picture area with a sense of frenetic action. His crazed, angular forms and wicked grin contrast with the gentle curving rhythms of the mossy rocks, while the green background throws out the complementary reds and browns of the manic figure.

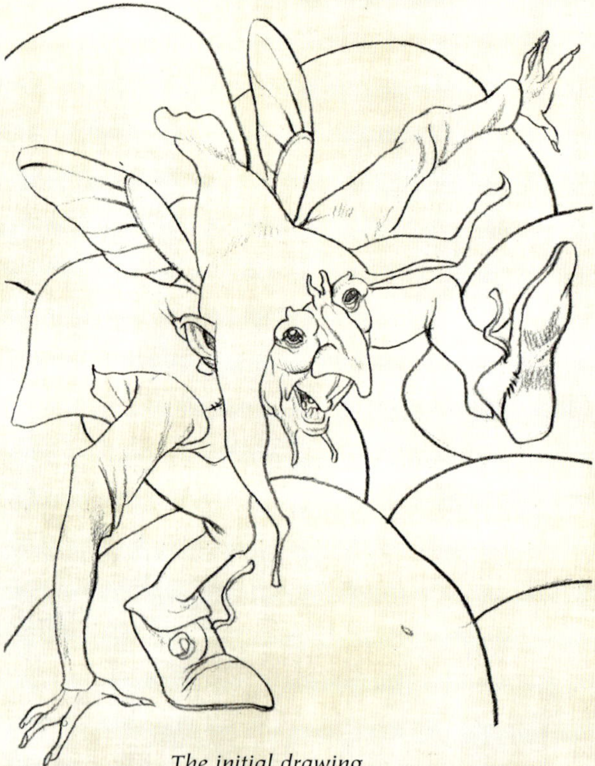

The initial drawing

- *Lightly sketch in the figure and the background with a graphite pencil, remembering the underlying forms.*
- *At this stage you can adjust things until both composition and pose work.*
- *With the pencil foundations in place, firm up the lines with a black colored pencil, adding clothing and facial details.*
- *When the drawing is complete, erase the sketched pencil lines.*

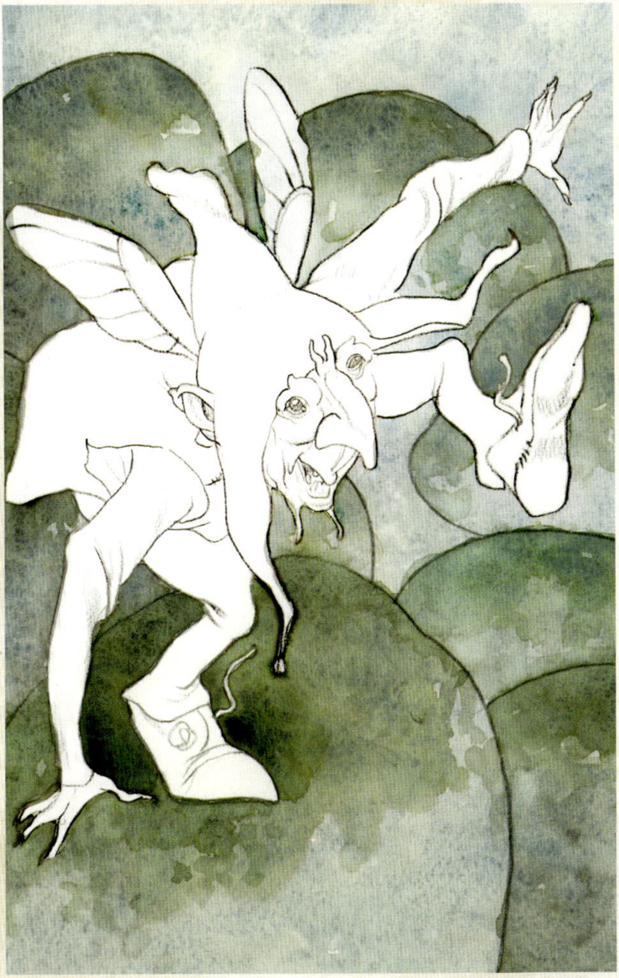

Artist's tip

Cerulean blue is an interesting color to work with. When diluted alone or with other colors, the blue pigment mixes unevenly and creates interesting mottled textures. This effect is exploited here as a shorthand way to suggest the mossy rocks.

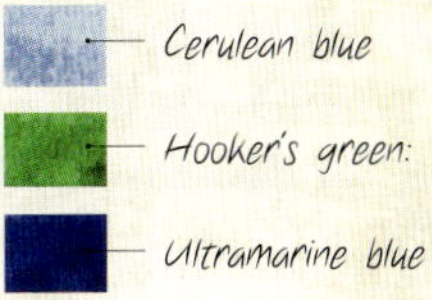

Laying in the background

- *Run a thin mix of cerulean blue and Van Dyke brown over the entire background with a no.8 brush.*
- *Lay darker mixes into the wet paint to create the rocks.*
- *While still wet, apply a mix of Hooker's green, burnt sienna, and cerulean blue to the mossy areas on the rocks.*
- *Note the darker shadow area beneath the figure.*

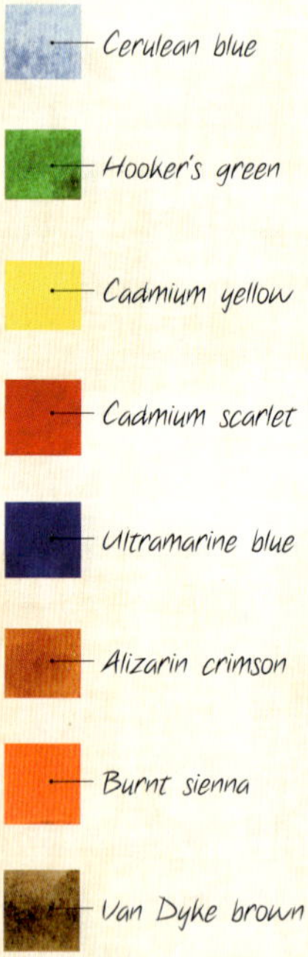

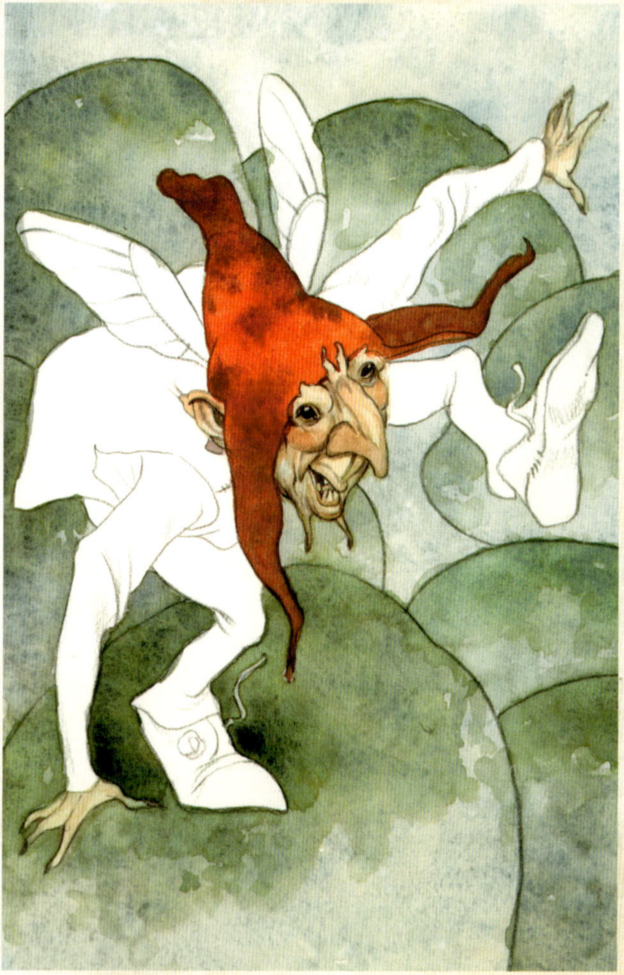

Adding skin tones and hat

- *Paint the face with cadmium yellow warmed with cadmium scarlet.*
- *While wet, add a cerulean blue and cadmium red wash to jaw and eye sockets, and scarlet to cheeks and ears.*
- *When dry, paint the hat with a cadmium scarlet, alizarin crimson, and cadmium yellow mix, adding cerulean blue for darker areas.*
- *Define the facial lines with a Van Dyke brown, alizarin, and ultramarine mix applied with a fine brush.*

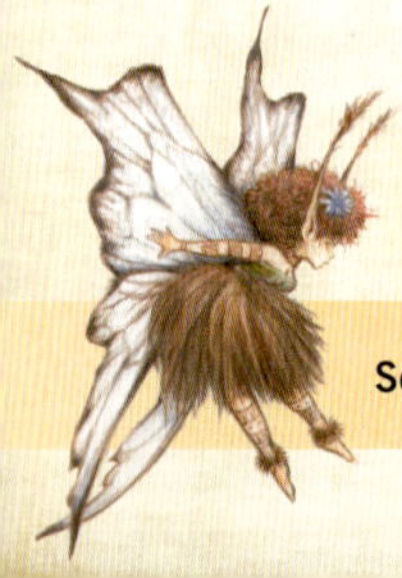

See also: Basic watercolor techniques, page 50.

See also: Finished Spriggan image, page 131.

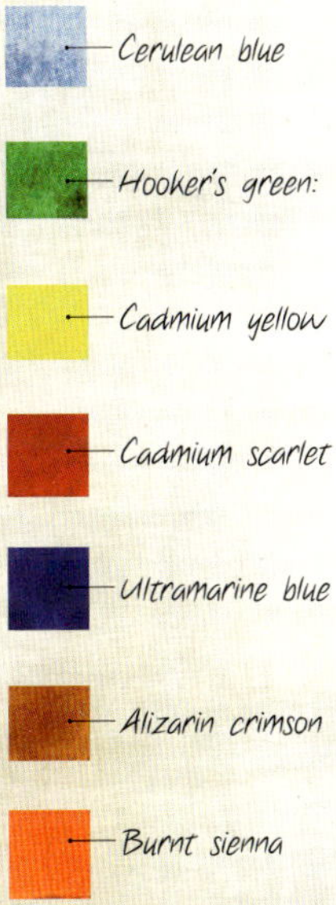

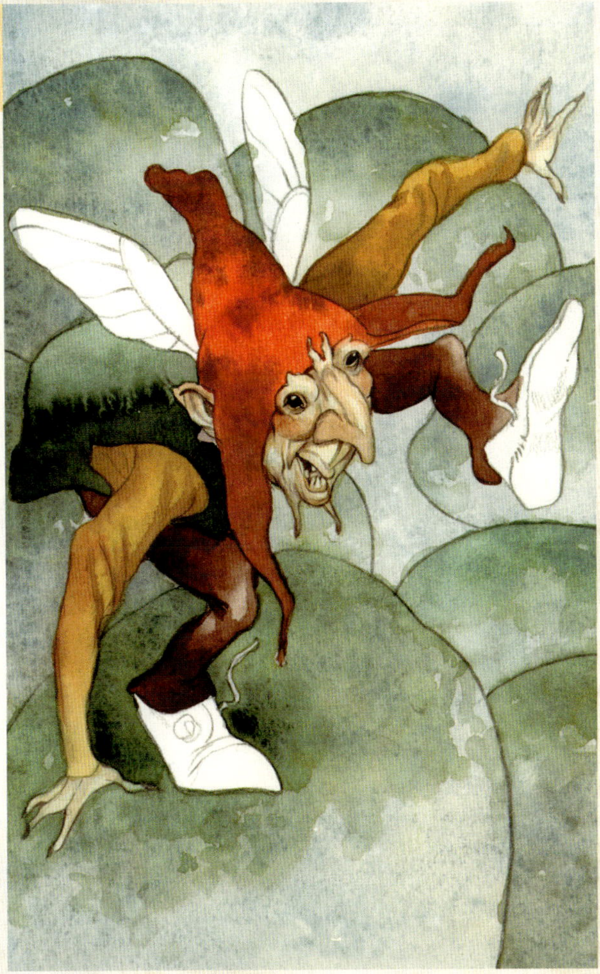

Add clothing to finish the work

- *Paint the vest with a thin cadmium scarlet, Hooker's green, and ultramarine wash, darkening the wash for the shadow area.*
- *Mix cadmium yellow, cadmium scarlet, and cerulean blue for the shirt and boots, adding ultramarine to the mix for the shadows.*
- *Wash the wings with cerulean blue touched with cadmium scarlet, and add the lines with ultramarine and Hooker's green.*
- *Develop some of the original line work with a mix of alizarin crimson, burnt sienna, and ultramarine applied with a fine brush.*

Fairy Queen

THE BEAUTIFUL, DEMURE, AND PROUD FAIRY QUEEN IS SET APART FROM OTHER FAIRY FOLK BY HER REGAL STATUS AND IS DEEPLY RESPECTED BY ALL AROUND HER.

Character and appearance

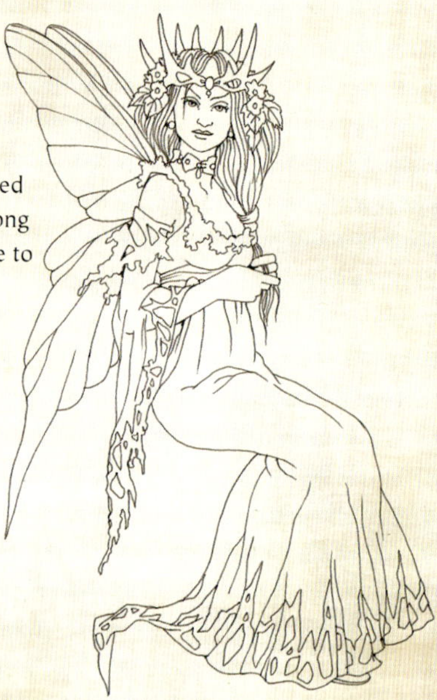

In traditional folklore, the Queen of the Fairies has no name. In *A Midsummer Night's Dream*, however, Shakespeare created Titania. She has become the archetypal Fairy Queen, and many artists have created breathtaking images of her. The Fairy Queen has strong connections to land and sea and watches over nature to ensure the safety of all her subjects.

Compassion and matchless beauty are the Fairy Queen's most important attributes. She is modest, serene, graceful, and elegant, and, as shown, wears gowns of the finest gossamer silk and decorates her hair with natural ornaments. This image is painted with translucent watercolors on hot pressed (smooth) paper to create suitably delicate washes of ethereal color.

MAIN COLOR PALETTE

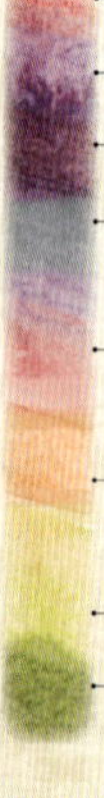

- Rose madder: wash for blush and lips
- Blue violet: very pale wash used on the wings and gown
- Mauve: trims on gown and flowers in hair
- Payne's gray: pale wash applied to gown, wings, and crown
- Quindacrone violet: light wash applied to wing tips and gown
- Burnt sienna: pale wash applied to skin; darker wash used for hair
- Yellow-green: wash applied to leaves and foliage
- Olive green: used to create darker areas of greenery
- White gouache (not shown): gown trims, wing tips, flowers

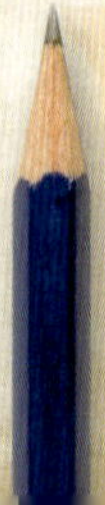

Copy it!

Copy or trace the drawing or scan it into your computer. Then color it.

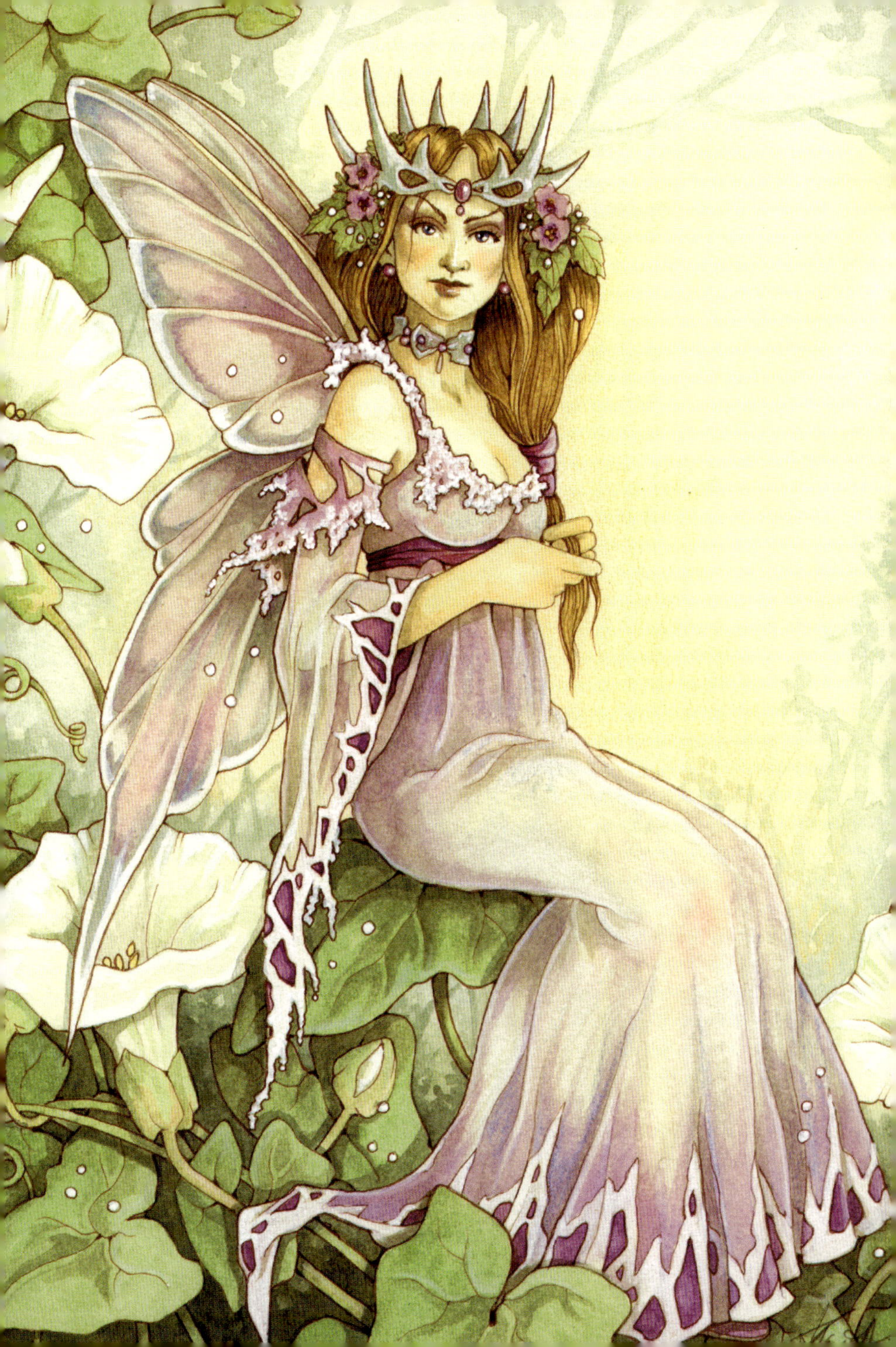

Gown and robe variations

The Fairy Queen wears garments of the finest silk and delicate cobwebs that create a sense of enchantment. Choose soft or vibrant colors to harmonize with the setting in which you paint her, and visualize robes that both suit her personality and royal status and befit the occasion. Below are some ideas, but you can dress your Fairy Queen in your own unique designs—look at evening gowns in fashion magazines for inspiration.

See also: The template fairy figure on page 59.

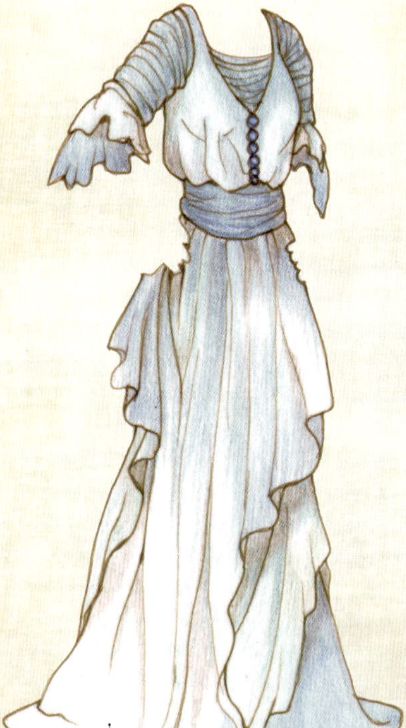

EVERYDAY WEAR
Delicate shades of blue create a gossamer whisper of a dress for everyday wear. The softly draped skirt has an asymmetrical hemline, and a wide sash defines the waist.

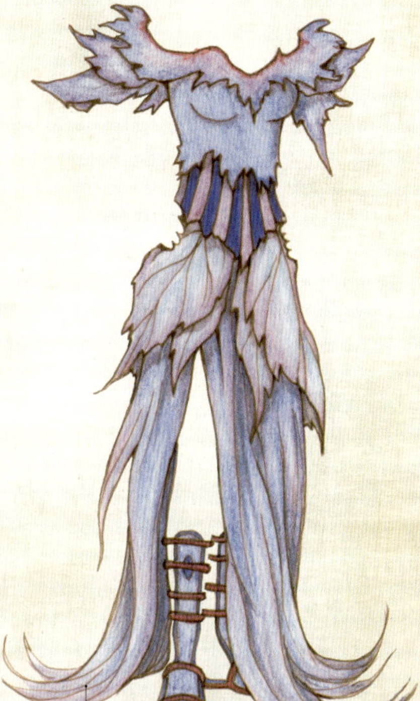

BOHEMIAN BODICE
For a relaxed and bohemian look, stronger blues and lilacs create an off-the-shoulder gown decorated with leaves and feathers and featuring a striped, corset-style bodice. The split skirt reveals Romanesque sandals.

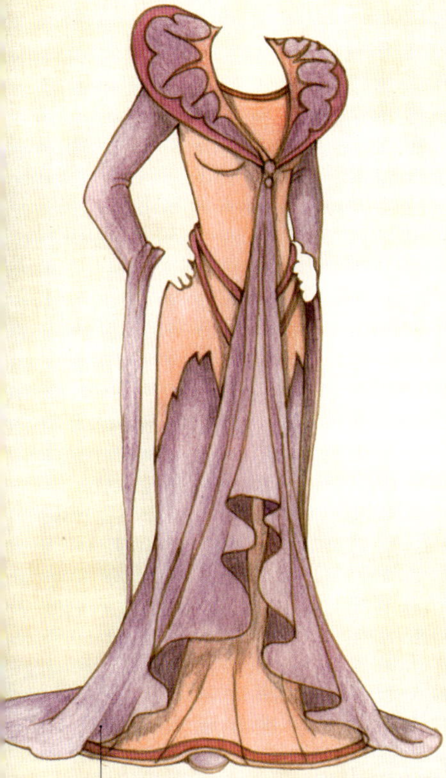

CEREMONIAL GARB

Rich purple and red create a more formal gown for ceremonial occasions. The graceful, slim-fitting style, with its stand-up collar and elegantly draped sleeves and front, creates a regal, Medieval look.

Creating a balanced pose

A seated figure must look balanced and stable. Starting with the underlying structure will help to create a convincing pose. Practice by copying the figure below, constructed with a combination of basic three-dimensional shapes. Then try adapting it, still using the basic underlying forms, to change the nature of the character—an upward tilt of the head, different hand positions, or changing the angle of one leg will convey a very different Fairy Queen.

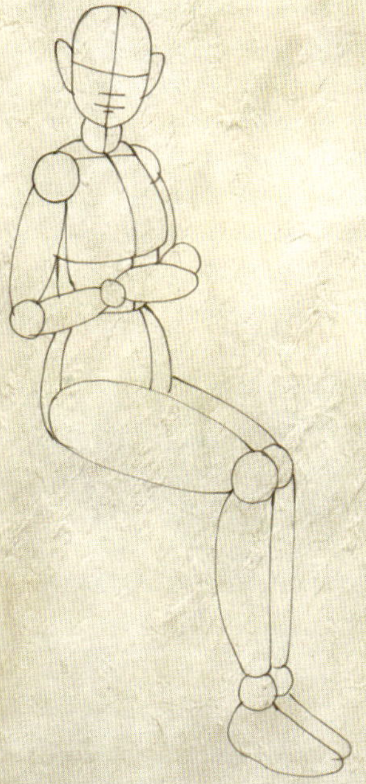

Note the angle of the head, and the position of the hands, knees, and feet. These telling details convey exactly the demure and modest pose that reflects the character of the Fairy Queen perfectly.

Crowns and headdresses

It's easy to imagine that a Fairy Queen would have all kinds of headdresses and hair decorations to add the crowning glory to her regal attire. Her garments range from informal to ceremonial, and each outfit requires its own complementary adornment. Colorful leaves, flowers, and berries, as well as feathers, butterfly wings, dew drops, jewels, and crystals offer endless options for beautiful headdresses and reflect her intimate connection with nature. Here are some ideas to kick-start your creativity.

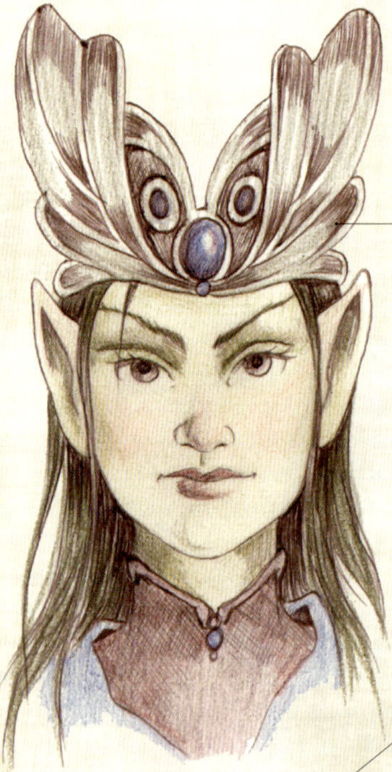

SILVER CROWN
Closed moth wings are the inspiration behind this headdress. Made from fairy silver and jewels, the design creates a majestic crown for ceremonial occasions.

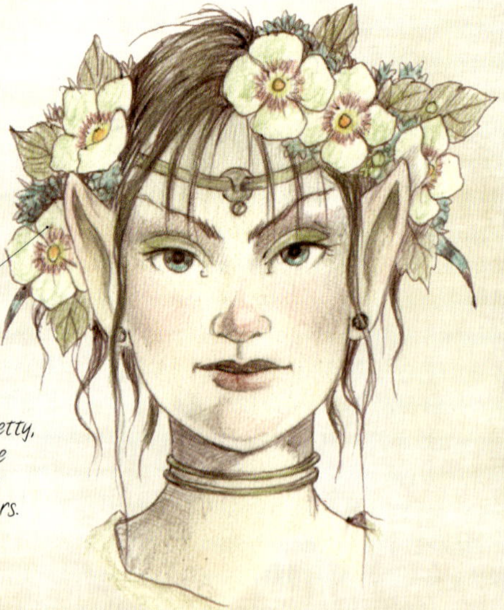

FLORAL HEADDRESS
A favorite choice of the Fairy Queen, these can be simple, delicate, and pretty, as shown. Alternatively, create a more glamorous and eye-catching look with vibrantly colored flowers and feathers.

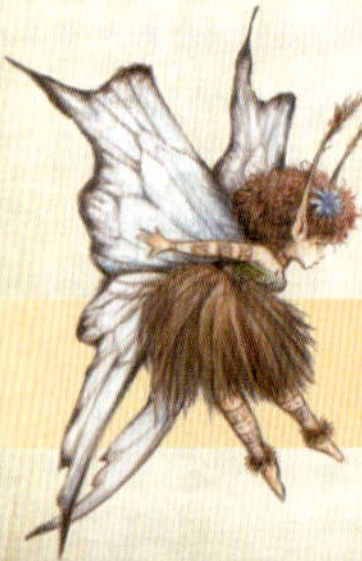

See also: Hair and headwear, page 82.

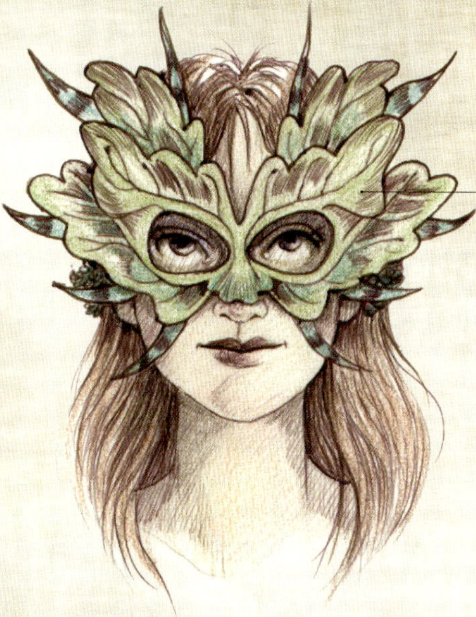

LEAFY HEAD MASK
Masks create an air of magic, mystery, and allure. This simple mask of leaves, perfect for a masquerade ball, could be decorated with silver and crystals for added enchantment.

CRYSTAL CROWN
A luxuriant cluster of magnificent sapphire crystals creates a rich sense of majesty for the Fairy Queen. The crown is studded with precious jewels and pendant gemstones to complete the effect.

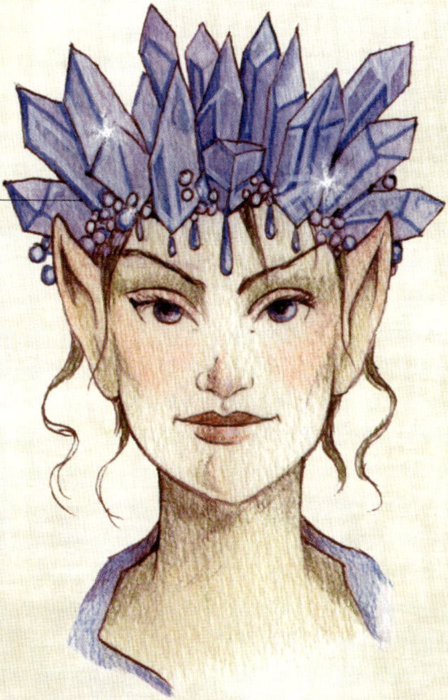

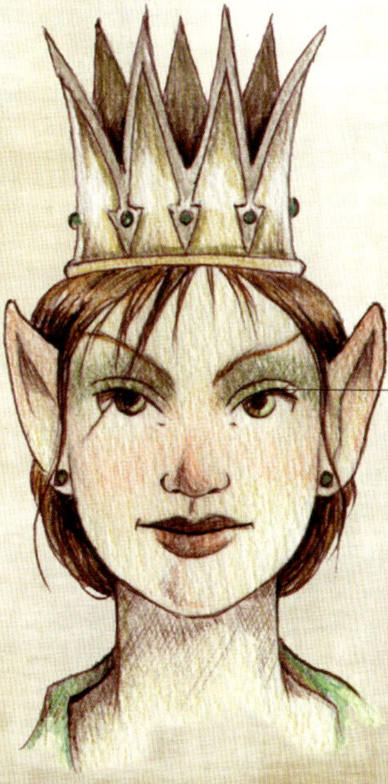

FAIRY SILVER CORONET
A dainty, jewel-studded coronet of gleaming silver is shaped in typical fairy crown fashion. Wearing this headdress, as all the others, the Fairy Queen would move gracefully with head held high.

Fairy King

THE UNEQUIVOCALLY MASCULINE KING OF THE FAIRIES IS UNDOUBTEDLY THE MOST IMPORTANT AND IMPRESSIVE OF THE MALE CHARACTERS IN FAIRYLAND.

Character and appearance

The Fairy King is strong, powerful, courageous, and opinionated. He is argumentative, but he is nevertheless fair and just. He is overlord of the woodlands and master of the elements—indeed, as Oberon in *A Midsummer Night's Dream*, the force of his quarrel with Titania calls forth storms.

This image of the Fairy King shows a self-confident, virile male. The leaves and antlers that adorn his head represent his strength and dominion over the forest; a dowsing pendulum indicates his magical powers over the elements; and stone and wood emphasize the forcefulness of the character. Black ballpoint pen creates a dark and vigorous underdrawing with cross-hatched shading to add form. Thin watercolor washes add depth to the image.

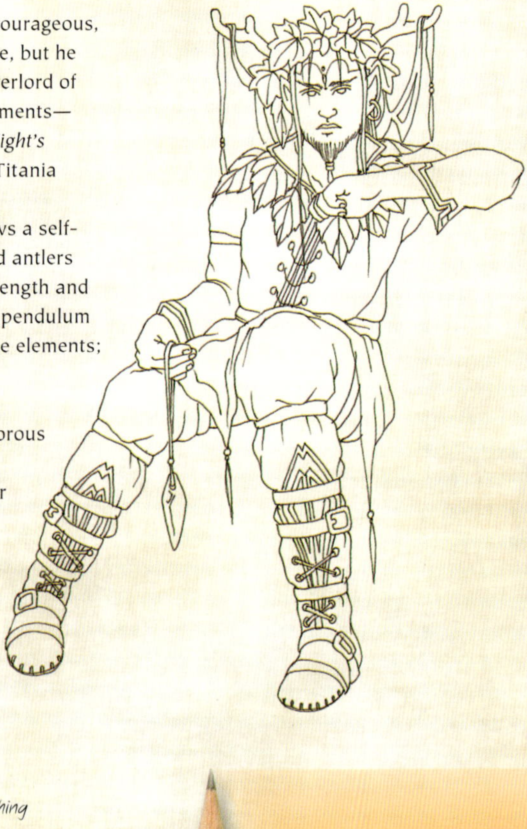

MAIN COLOR PALETTE

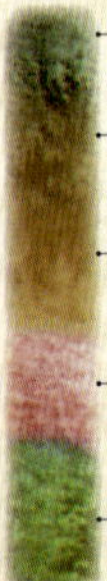

Copy it!

Copy or trace the drawing or scan it into your computer. Then color it.

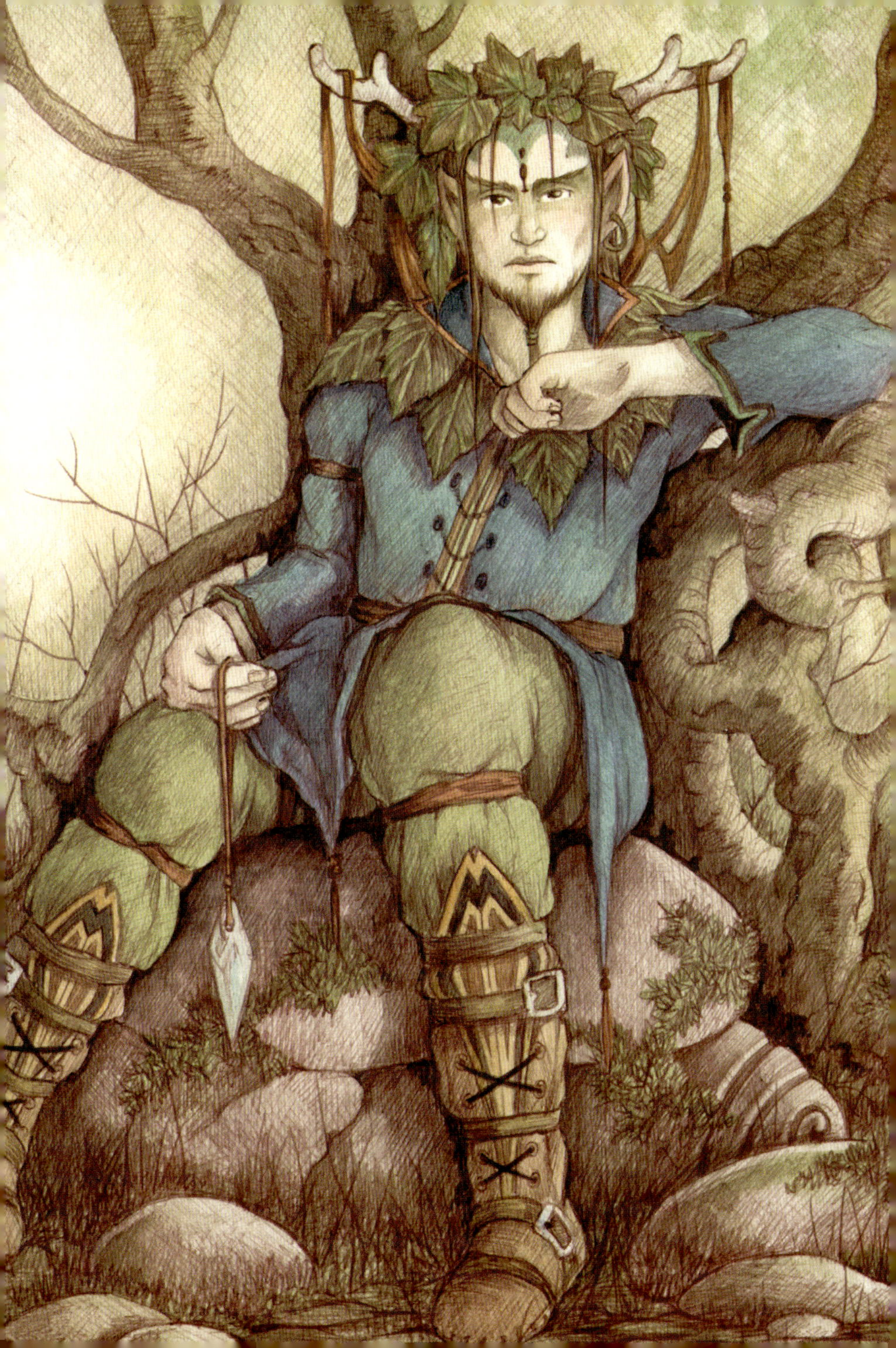

Constructing the figure

The Fairy King's seated figure leans to one side with his weight off-center. This dictates how the body is supported and balanced. When you approach this slightly complicated pose, don't make assumptions. Tackle the basic underlying structure first, plotting the positions of the head, torso, and limbs with simple geometric shapes. An artist's mannequin is a useful aid to unlocking complicated poses such as this.

See also: Figure construction basics, page 58.

As you can see from this constructional drawing, the weight is all on the Fairy King's left-hand side; the right leg and arm take no strain at all.

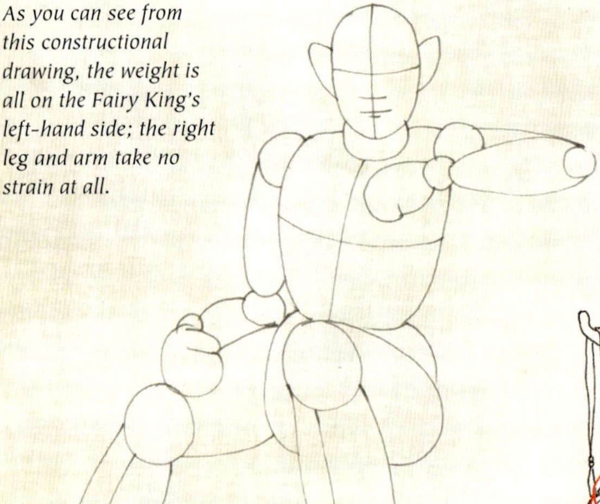

Note the powerful, balancing position of his left leg. Seen straight on, the thigh is foreshortened. Pay attention to the tilt of the shoulders as the left arm is raised to help support the leaning pose.

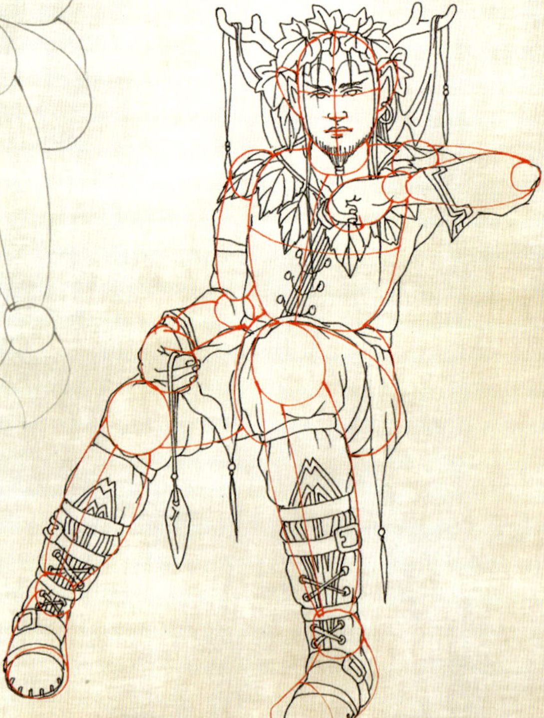

Alternative poses

The Fairy King is slim, with the typical broad shoulders and long muscular legs of a fit, young male. These two poses indicate the basic structure—once you've mastered this, you can position him to create your own poses.

Standard pose

Standing square on to the viewer, the weight is well balanced and evenly distributed from head to toe. Note the broad shoulders and slim hips of the male figure.

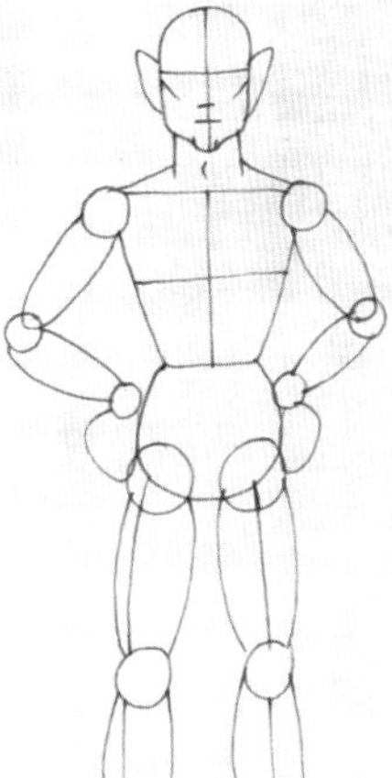

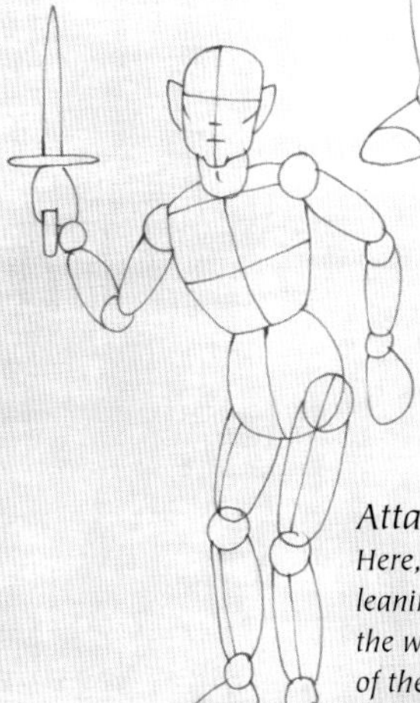

Attacking pose

Here, the figure is leaning forward from the waist. Notice the tilt of the shoulders and the compensating opposite tilt of the head. The backward arm helps to balance the forward motion of the figure.

Constructing the head

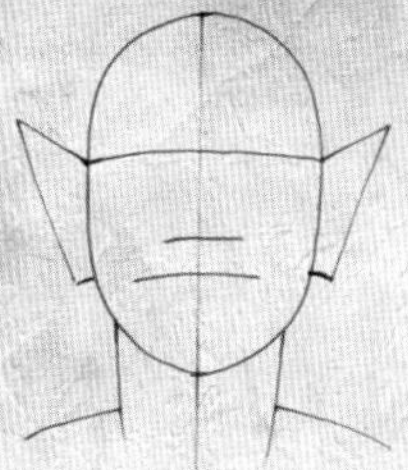

1 The Fairy King's face is rectangular with a squared chin. Plot the basic broad oval shape and indicate the positions of the eyes, nose, mouth, and ears. The neck is almost the same width as the face.

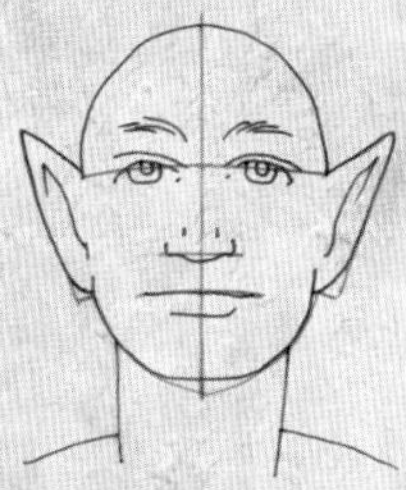

2 Begin to form the features. The eyes look straight ahead with an almost arrogant gaze, the nose is broad and strong, and the mouth is wide. Square off the chin to give a strong jawline.

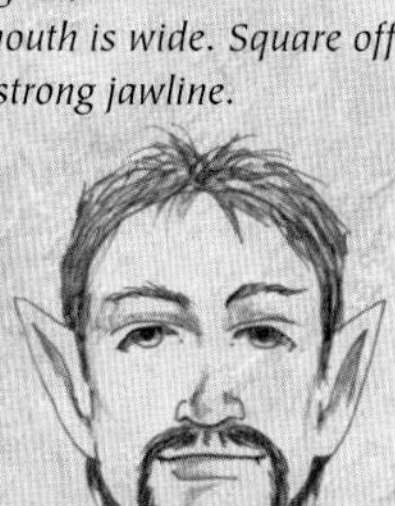

3 Shading gives three-dimensional form to the face and features. The addition of hair and beard and a hint at an Adam's apple give additional masculinity and character to the finished drawing.

Crowns and headdresses

Like all monarchs, the Fairy King needs dramatic headgear to indicate his importance, but this doesn't necessarily mean a golden, jewel-encrusted crown. Antlers are the epitome of masculinity in the animal kingdom and, teamed with leaves, they make excellent regal headdresses and masks for ceremonial occasions. Fairy silver and ram's horns have similar magisterial impact, while a simple crown of leaves indicates royalty.

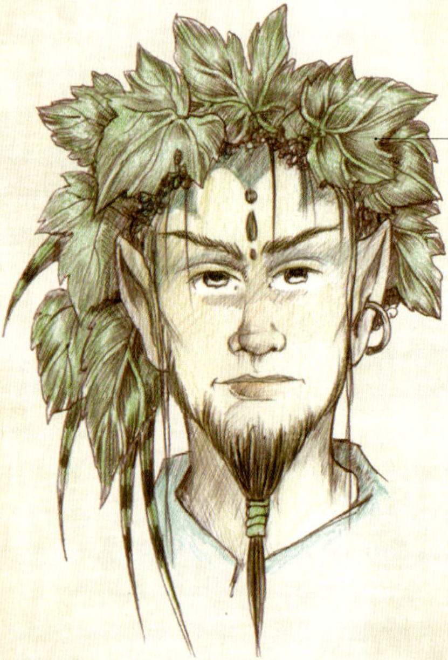

WREATH HEADDRESS
This luxuriant headdress of leaves and slender feathers is fit for Oberon himself. Sacred markings adorn his forehead and a fairy silver ring pierces his ear. His beard is bound with grasses.

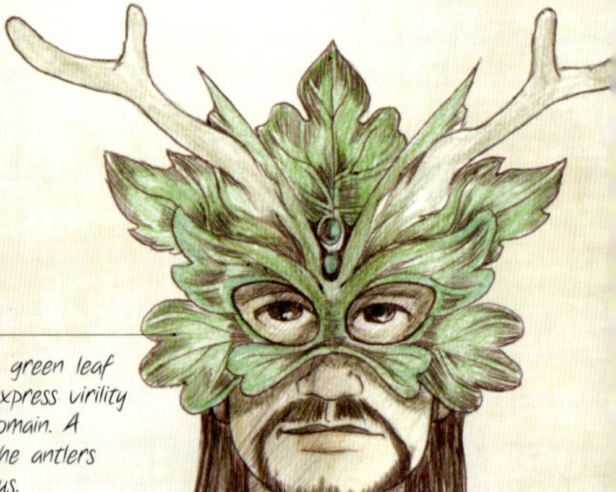

LEAFY MASK
A pagan Fairy King wears a green leaf mask with deer antlers to express virility and power over his forest domain. A green jewel nestles where the antlers meet, a symbol of regal status.

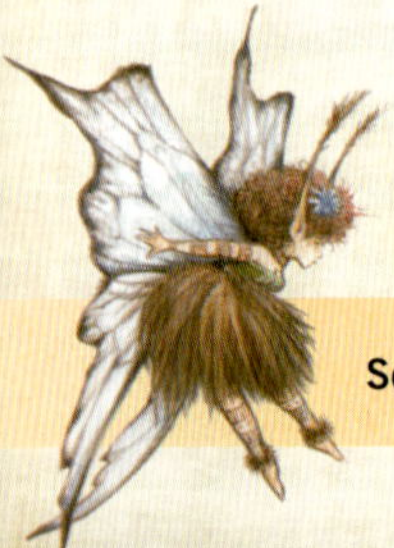

See also: Hair and headwear, page 82.

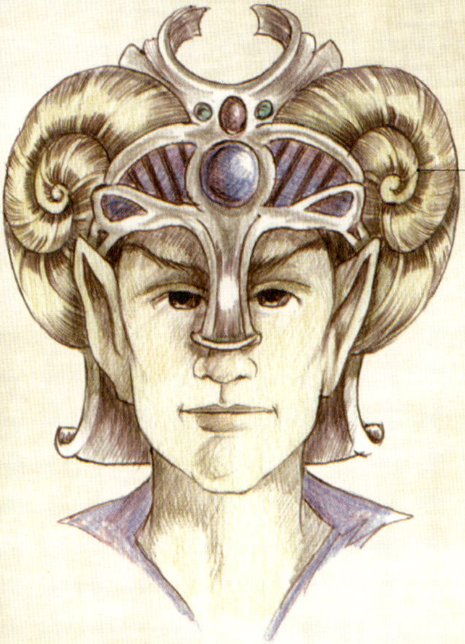

RAM'S HORN HELMET

Warrior dress is sometimes appropriate for ceremonial purposes. This fairy version of a battle helmet uses ram's horns to indicate strength and determination, while fairy silver and huge jewels denote royalty.

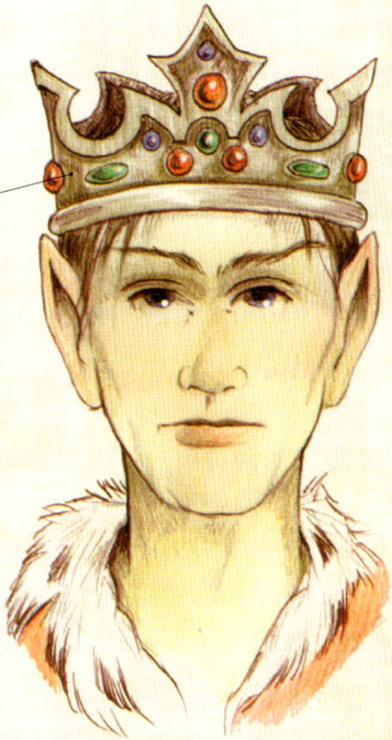

JEWELED CROWN

A costly jeweled crown is suitably regal attire, instantly signifying the pre-eminence of the Fairy King at formal occasions and ceremonies. Note the ermine collar, another unmistakable statement of royalty.

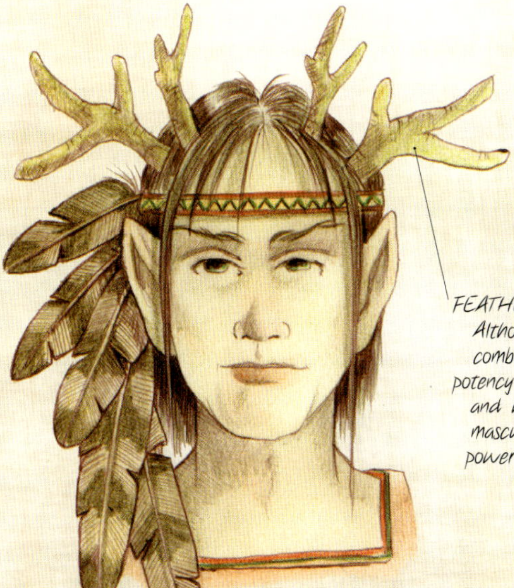

FEATHER HEADDRESS

Although less formal, this headdress combines natural elements to express the potency of the King of the Fairies. Antlers and horns are a potent symbol of masculinity, while wing feathers denote power over the air.

Guardian

GUARDIAN FAIRIES ARE ONE OF THE MOST SENSITIVE AND ETHEREAL OF ALL FAIRY TRIBES, AND ARE DEEPLY RESPECTED FOR THEIR INNATE WISDOM AND INTIMATE UNDERSTANDING OF NATURE.

Character and appearance

Guardian Fairies possess the knowledge and wisdom of the ancient Greek oracles. Their understanding of nature and magic and their ability to foresee the future set them apart from other fairies. They rarely share their secrets for fear that they might be misused. Mystical, clever, and elegant, they are often shown reading ancient texts inaccessible to others, and are the true guardians of nature.

To express her oneness with nature, this fairy wears a gown of natural fabrics rendered with opaque acrylics in the rich colors of her woodland habitat. Her wings are leaf-shaped, while berries, foliage, and feathers decorate her hair.

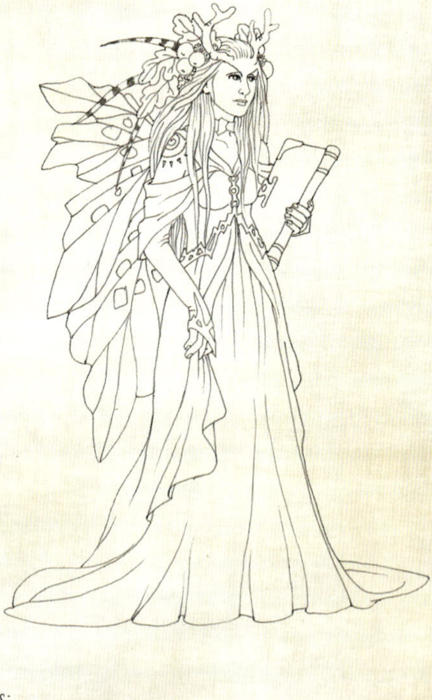

MAIN COLOR PALETTE

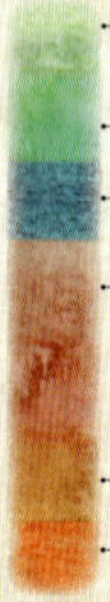

- Sap green: bodice, sleeves, leaves, and wings
- Hooker's green: over-gown and shawl
- Payne's gray: book, antlers, and tattoo
- Alizarin crimson: gown, wings, blush, and lips; used in heavier washes on berries, bodice trims, and headdress
- Raw umber: wings and skin
- Burnt sienna: used in deeper washes for auburn hair

Copy it!

Copy or trace the drawing or scan it into your computer. Then color it.

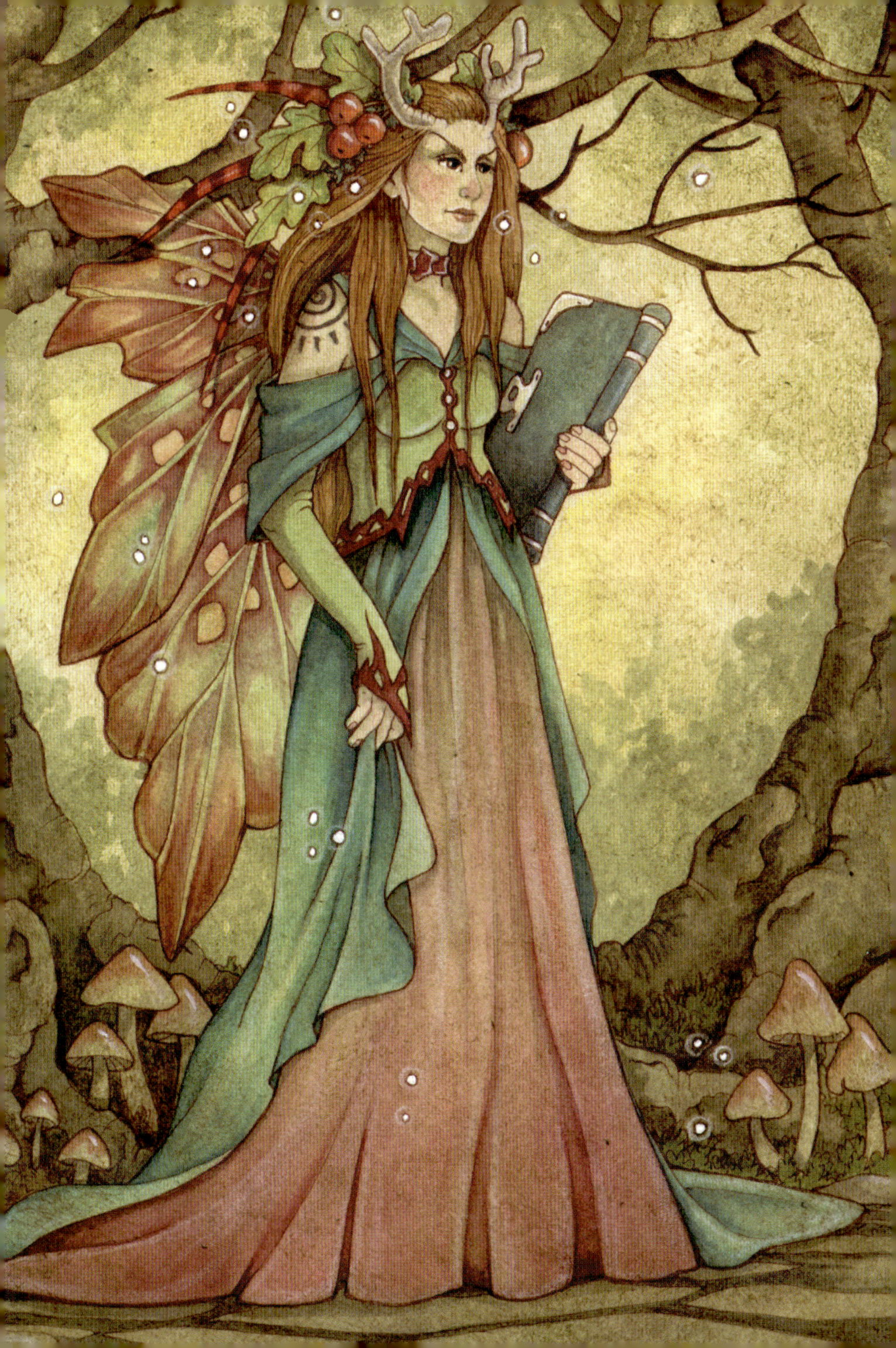

Headdress variations

Just as the Guardian Fairy's clothes are fashioned from natural materials, so her headdresses and accessories are created entirely from a mixture of objects that nature provides. Berries, feathers, and crystals all play a part in her rituals, so use these to create characteristic adornments, together with leaves and grasses of all kinds.

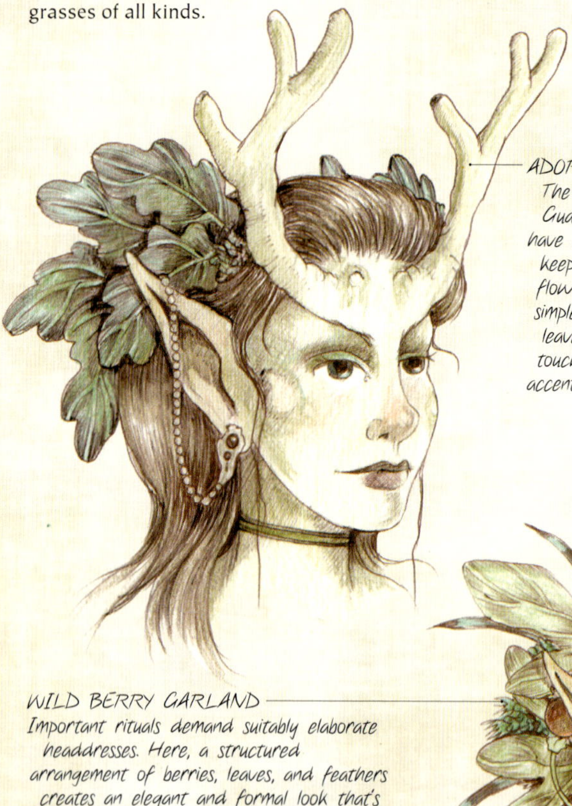

ADORNING ANTLERS
The most nature-loving Guardian Fairies sometimes have antlers. In this instance, keep the hair long and flowing and add only the simplest of accessories: a few leaves and an understated touch of fairy silver to accentuate the pointed ear.

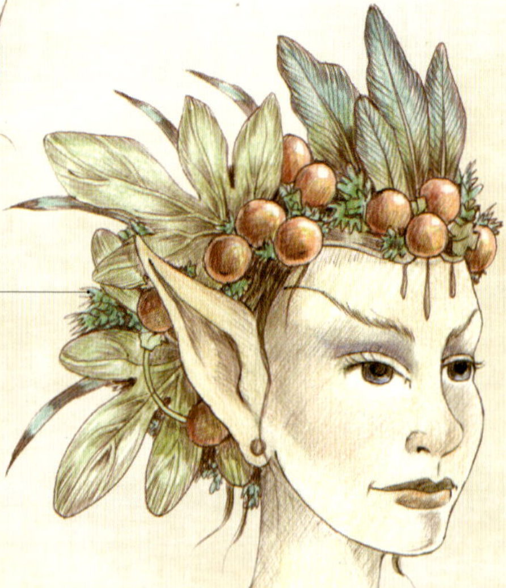

WILD BERRY GARLAND
Important rituals demand suitably elaborate headdresses. Here, a structured arrangement of berries, leaves, and feathers creates an elegant and formal look that's nevertheless taken straight from nature. Look for other suitable leaves and berries for alternative shapes and color schemes.

See also: Hair and headwear, page 82.

ROSE CLIP

A single wild rose positioned off-center on the top of the Guardian's head forms a simple but elegant hair clip that associates the character with her wild, woodland habitat. Fashion a similar design with the wild flower of your choice, spending plenty of time sketching from life first, before adding color.

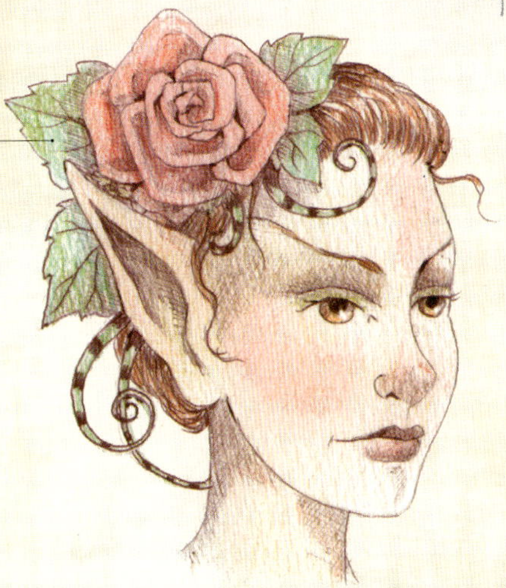

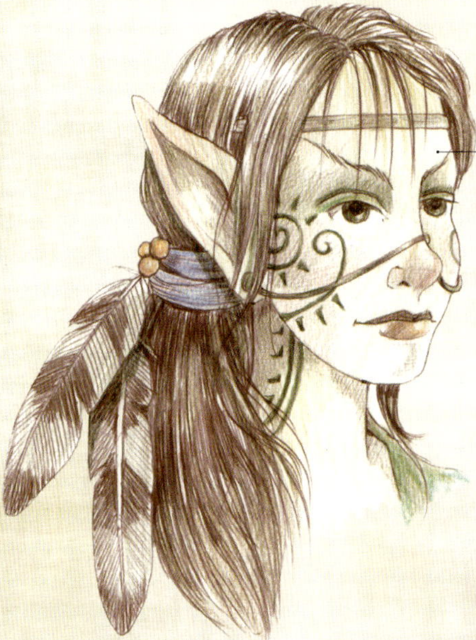

FEATHERS AND FACIAL MARKINGS

In true nature-spirit tradition, this variation teams a simple ponytail tied with grasses, a few berries, and feathers, with a silver band that sits across the forehead. Sometimes Guardian Fairies are shown with tattoos. These are not merely decorative but denote traditional, symbolic meanings that hint at a backstory steeped in ritual.

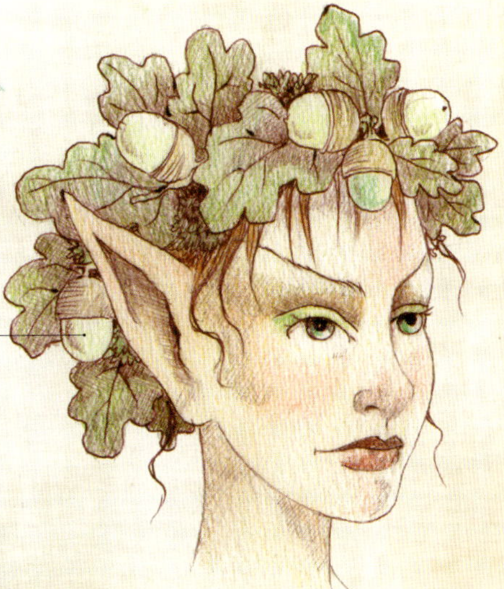

CROWN OF ACORNS

Traditionally, oak trees symbolize ancient wisdom, an attribute best associated with the Guardian Fairy. Here, the browns and greens of the leaves and acorns bring out the green in the fairy's eyes, which are accentuated further by a thin wash of green paint, applied to each eyelid for a touch of fairy eyeshadow.

Costume variations

The ethereal Guardian Fairy wears only entirely natural clothing fashioned from leaves and lustrous silks in the colors of the forest. Her bohemian style reflects her intimate connection with nature, and her clothes range from elegant, ceremonial gowns to casual, informal garments. Look at the structure of different leaves, and make straightforward sketches from life before you shape them into garments.

See also: The template fairy figure on page 59.

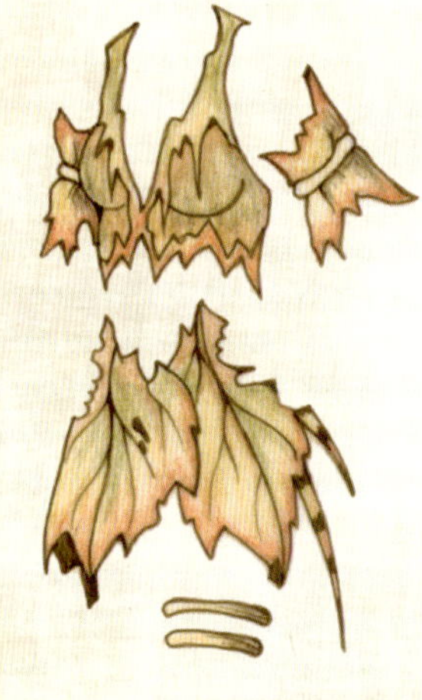

SHORT AND SKIMPY

Here, fall leaves are easily transformed into a casual outfit with a short skirt and cropped bodice. Matching armbands and boots complete a carefree look that blends with the forest surroundings.

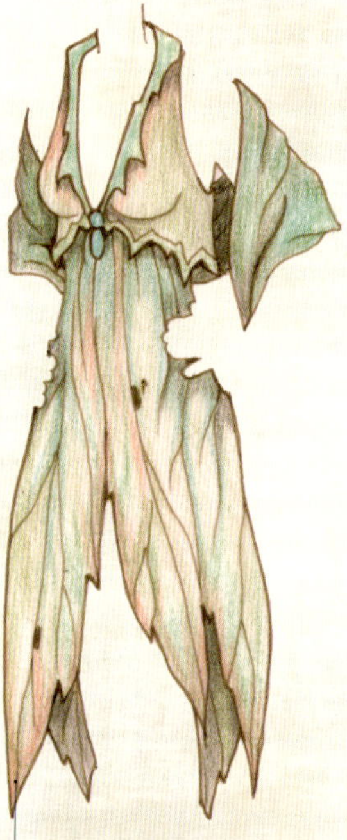

COOL AND CASUAL

Versatile leaves of different shapes can create a variety of informal garments. The dress is longer than the previous variation, but a split skirt for easy forest walking and a matching shawl provide protection from the elements.

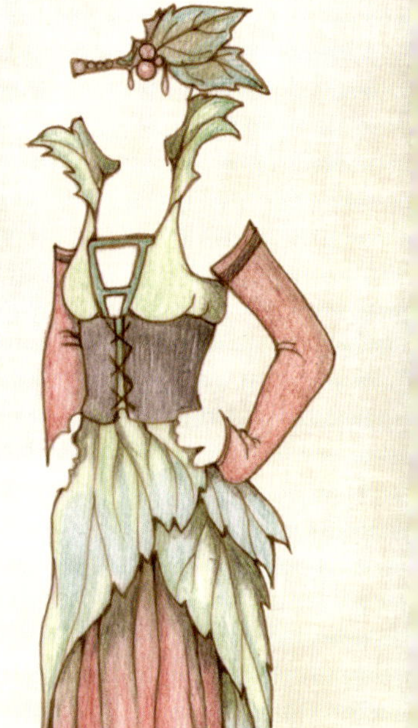

DINNER DRESS

Fresh green leaves team with a bodice made from bark over a full-length silk gown to make a graceful ceremonial outfit. The red of the gown could echo the red berries used in the headdress on page 154.

WORKING WITH PATTERN

Use your artist's licence to adapt the colors of leaves and add patterns that might hint at texture. Here, stripes in subtle natural colors have been applied discreetly to the outside edges of a basic leaf shape; this suggests that the wings are opaque. Careful pattern work, rendered in selected areas only, can show how an implied texture responds to light. Perfect for those ephemeral fairy wings!

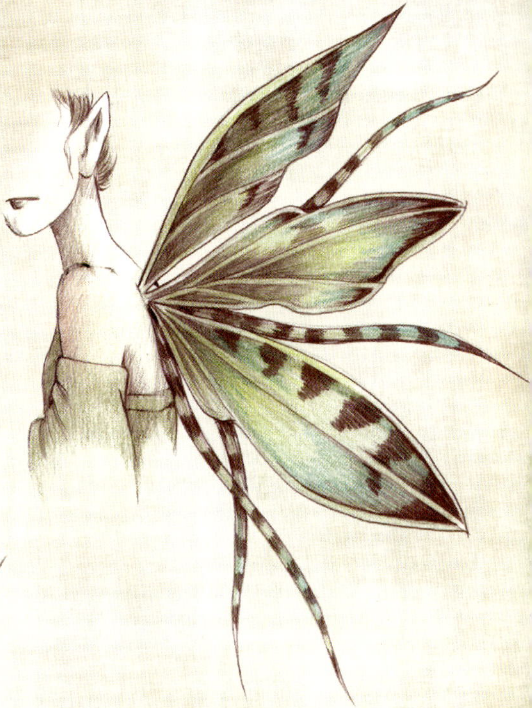

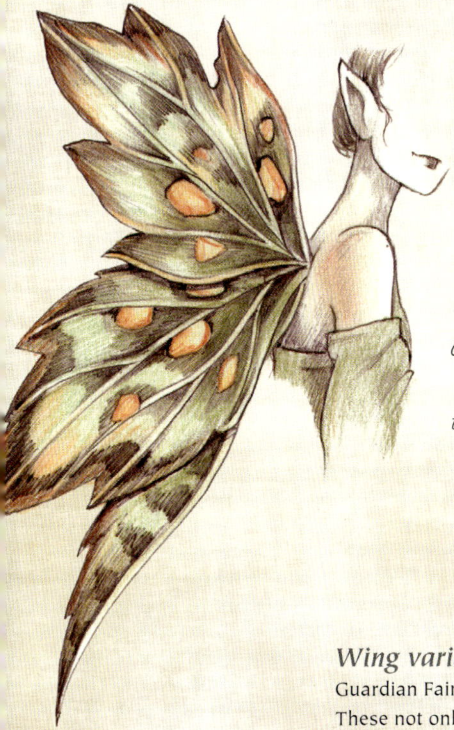

CHOOSING COLORS

The glowing colors of fall are represented here with the addition of tiny orange fungi that grow on the surface of many woodland leaves. Although orange and green are not strictly opposite each other on the color wheel, they are complementary colors that enhance each other's brightness, creating a dynamic effect.

Wing variations

Guardian Fairies have wings that are based on leaf shapes. These not only reflect their love of all things natural, but also enable them to blend with their forest surroundings and remain hidden from view. To create your own original wing designs, make a variety of leaf studies in your sketchbook and try adapting them into wings of varying shapes and proportions.

Fairy Godmother

IN TRADITIONAL FAIRY TALES, THIS BENEVOLENT CHARACTER APPEARS AT THE MOST DESPERATE OF TIMES, AND WHEN MAGIC HELP IS NEEDED MOST SHE ALWAYS SAVES THE DAY.

Character and appearance

The Fairy Godmother is kind, generous, and happy. Almost akin to a guardian angel, she is one of the most benign characters in fairyland. She has many guises but is often portrayed as a mature, maternal, and caring soul, although she can also be represented as a younger governess or nanny watching over her charges. She delights in using her magic powers to deflect evil and make dreams come true—everyone knows the story of Cinderella and the results of the Fairy Godmother's interventions.

This Fairy Godmother is portrayed as a native wise-woman, with butterfly wings and feather-adorned hair. Rich, bright watercolors create a cheerful image, while opaque white gouache stars, outlined in sepia ink, add sparkling impact to her cloak.

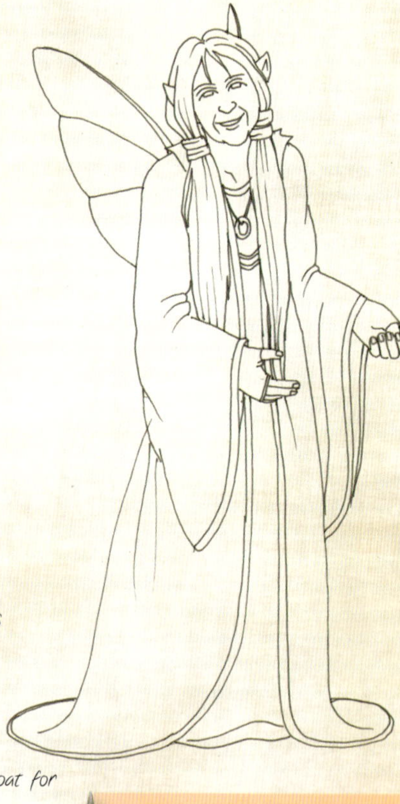

MAIN COLOR PALETTE

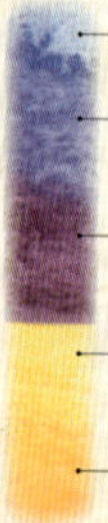

- Cobalt blue: pale washes on gown and wings
- Ultramarine: for cloak, hair ties, and wings
- Violet: for gown edges
- Cadmium yellow: for wand and as a base coat for the pumpkins
- Cadmium orange: overpainted washes on pumpkins

Rose madder (not shown): thin washes for skin

White gouache and sepia ink (not shown): stars

Copy it!

Copy or trace the drawing or scan it into your computer. Then color it.

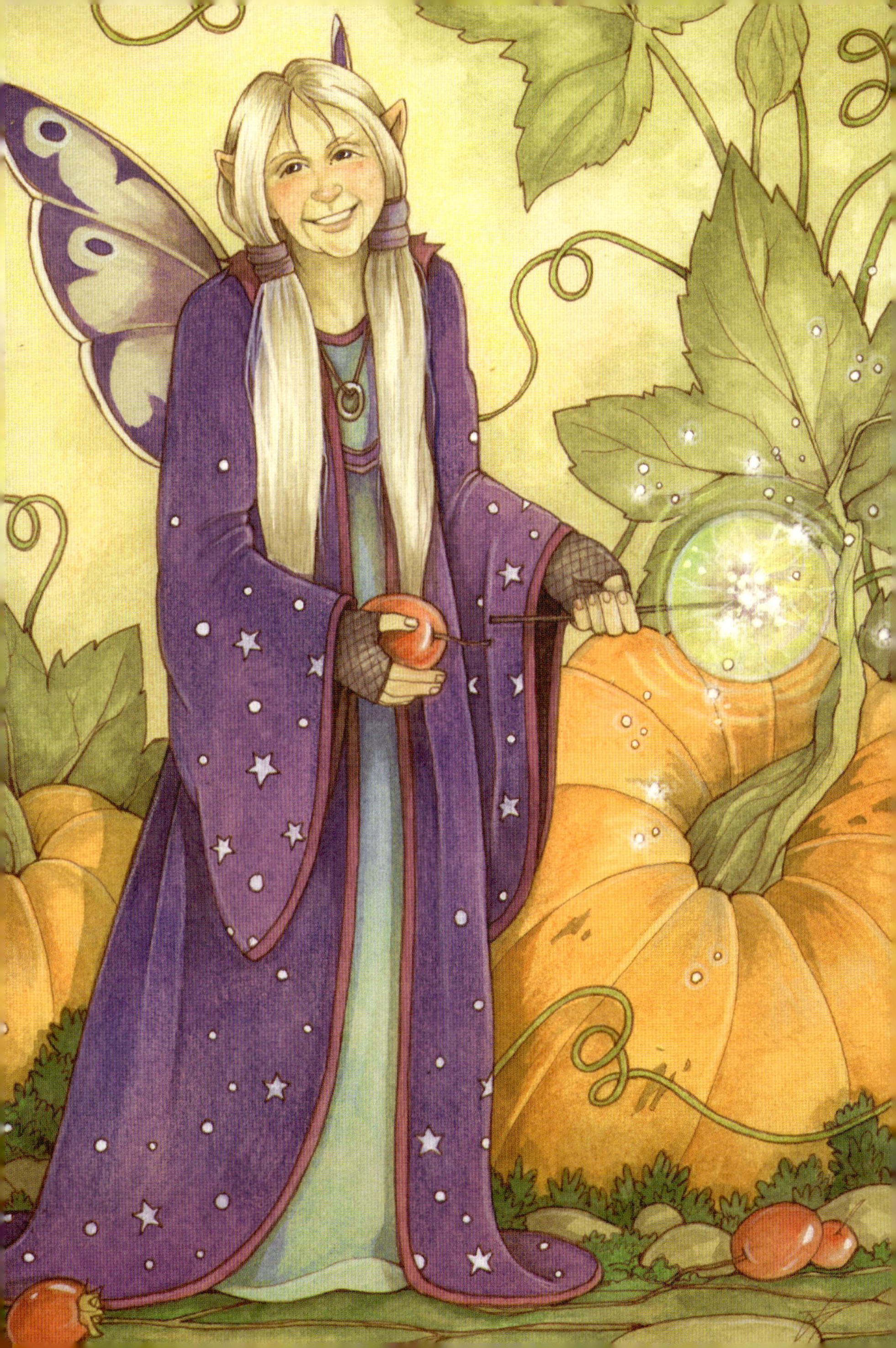

Constructing the figure

Here, the figure is seen front-view in a relaxed standing pose. Her weight is evenly distributed and her open arms and outspread hands, together with the gentle tilt of her head, create an open, warm, and giving character. Start with the underlying basic forms, even if they will be hidden by long robes, to create a credible pose.

See also: Figure construction basics, page 58.

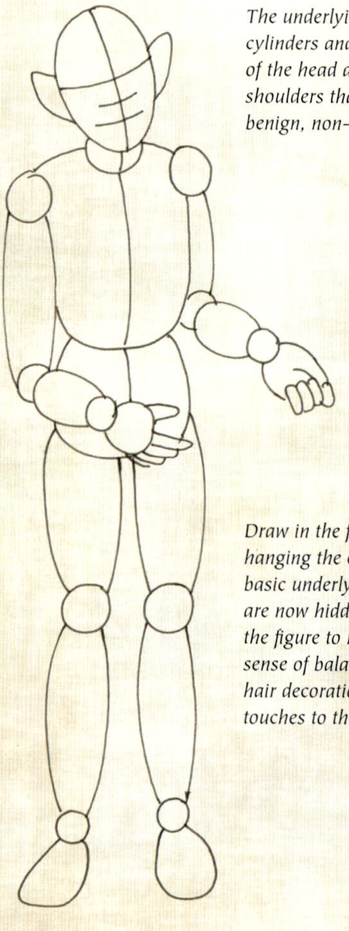

The underlying shapes are modified cylinders and spheres. Note the tilt of the head and the slight turn of the shoulders that give the pose a benign, non-threatening feel.

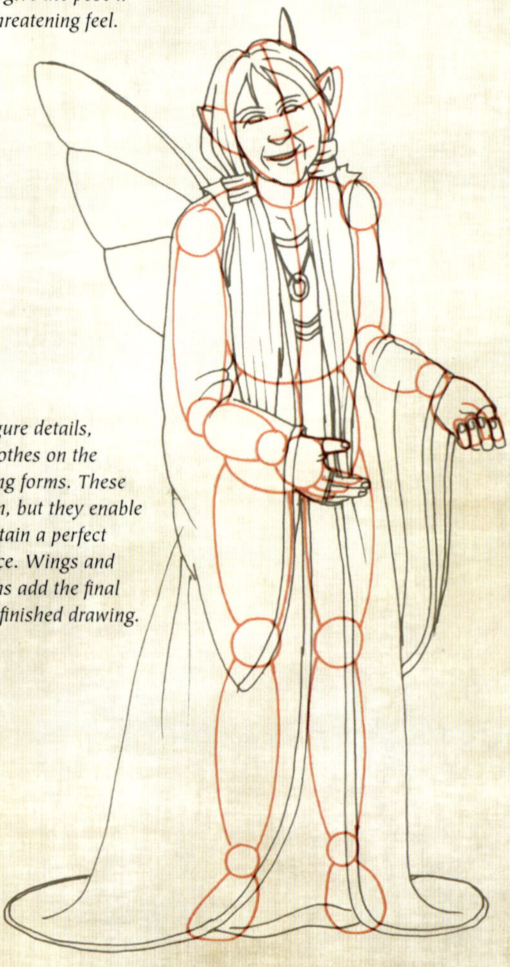

Draw in the figure details, hanging the clothes on the basic underlying forms. These are now hidden, but they enable the figure to retain a perfect sense of balance. Wings and hair decorations add the final touches to the finished drawing.

Creating the character

While often represented as a gentle and smiling old lady, a Fairy Godmother can adopt many aspects—a nursemaid from a bygone era, a wise woman close to nature, or a glamorous, younger governess.

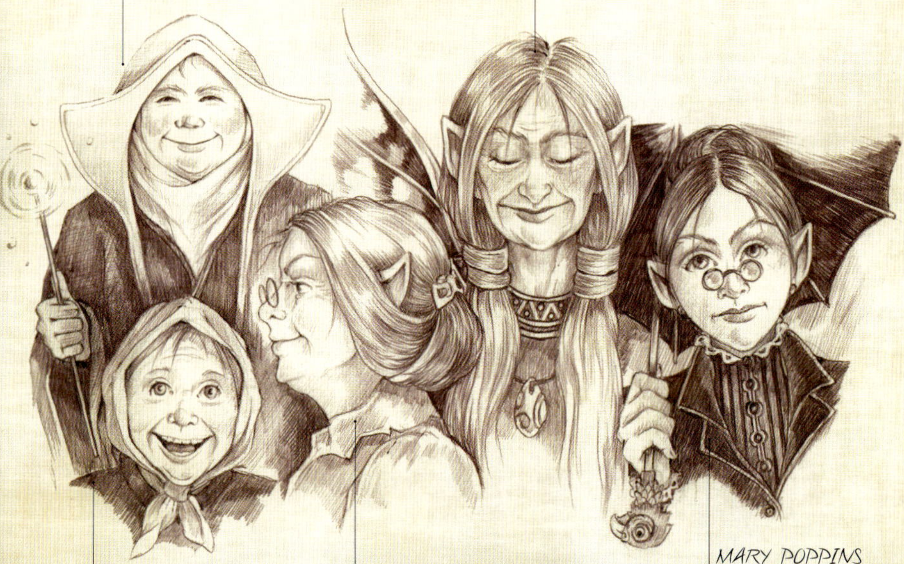

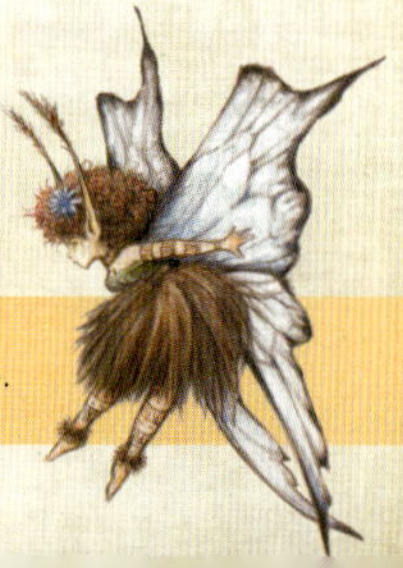

See also: Facial expressions, page 66.

Making your fairy smile

Godmothers are warm-hearted and compassionate, renowned for smiling faces that reflect their benign nature. A smile lifts and changes a face; the broader the smile, the more things change. Smile at yourself in the mirror and you will see how. Record the differences and incorporate them into your designs.

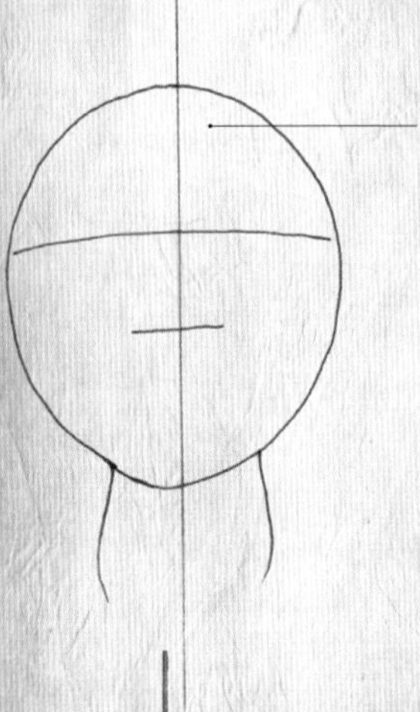

1 A smile widens the face, so start with a basic head shape that's rounder than usual. Draw in the center line lightly and indicate the position of eyes and nose.

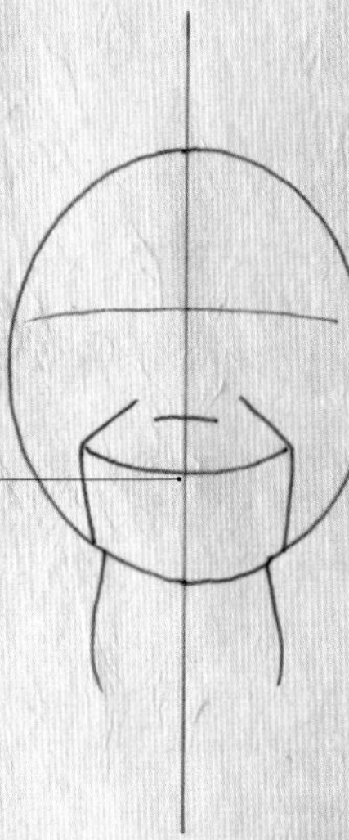

2 Indicate the curve of the smiling mouth and the lines running from nose to chin on either side that the expression creates.

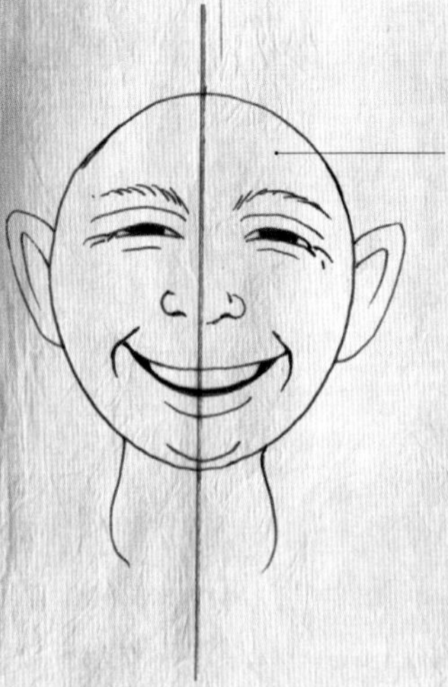

3 The smile pushes the cheeks upward, causing the eyes to narrow into curved arcs. Indicate the teeth and add the bottom lip and an extra line for the chin.

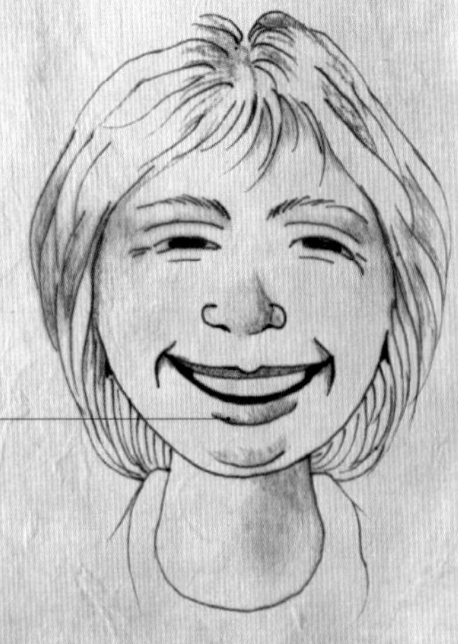

4 Now add the finishing touches with shading to describe the forms of the face. Add the hair to complete the happy, smiling character.

Drawing teeth

Teeth can be difficult to draw, but follow this advice for a simple way to make a toothy smile more realistic.

Don't draw straight lines between the teeth. This creates an ugly and unrealistic flat piano key effect.

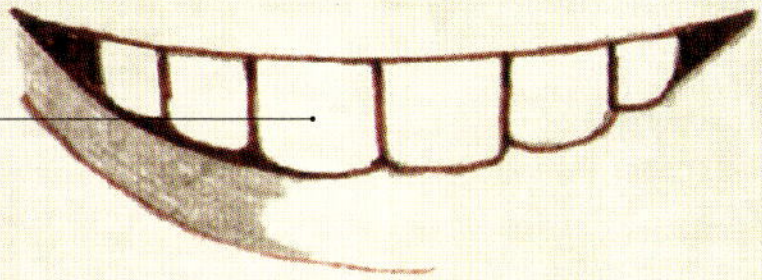

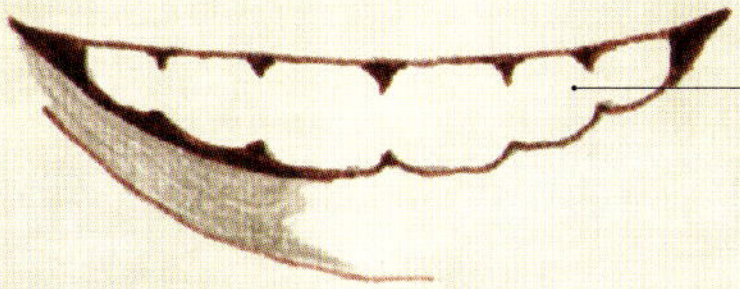

Instead, draw in just the v-shaped gaps at the top and bottom of the teeth. This creates a more natural and attractive smiling mouth and makes the teeth look rounded.

Smile variations

Smiles vary from a gentle curve of closed lips to a broad, open-mouthed grin showing top and bottom teeth. Each expression creates its own mood for the character. Try these:

A gentle smile with mouth closed stretches and changes the lips, creating dimples at the corners of the mouth and lifting the cheeks just a little.

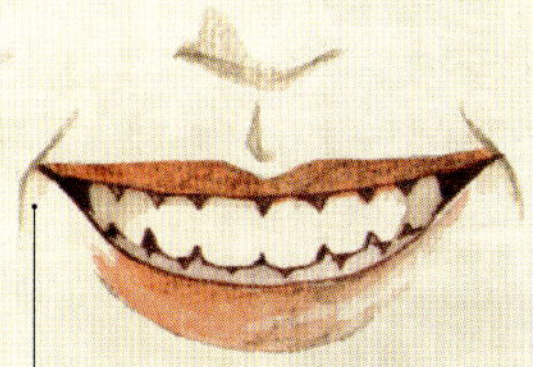

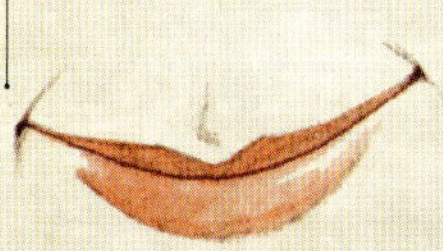

A broad smile reveals the top teeth but not the bottom set. It deepens the dimples at the corners of the mouth, lifts the cheeks, and narrows the eyes.

A wide-mouthed smile exposes both rows of teeth and the tongue and totally changes the face. Hint at the shape of the bottom teeth as described above.

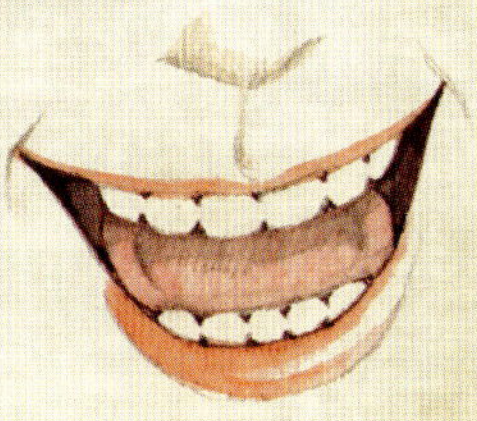

Sylph

GENTLE, DELICATE, AND TRANSLUCENT, SYLPHS ARE ELEMENTAL FAIRIES OF THE AIR WHO CONTROL THE WIND AND WEATHER AND RARELY SET FOOT ON THE GROUND.

Character and appearance

Sylphs are ethereal creatures, graceful and light as a soft breeze. They are rarely seen and can make themselves completely invisible or turn into birds at will. Their wings are sometimes similar to butterflies', but more often they have the white, downy feathers of birds such as swans or doves. Their clothes are always simple, gossamer-fine whispers of cloth that add no weight as they float on air.

Any image of a Sylph needs a light and sensitive touch to convey the delicacy of the character. Here, a limited palette of pale watercolor washes successfully combines with softly blended colored pencils to create a gentle, weightless feel for this elemental creature. Note that the lower part of her gown and legs are merely hinted at, giving the illusion of lighter-than-air invisibility.

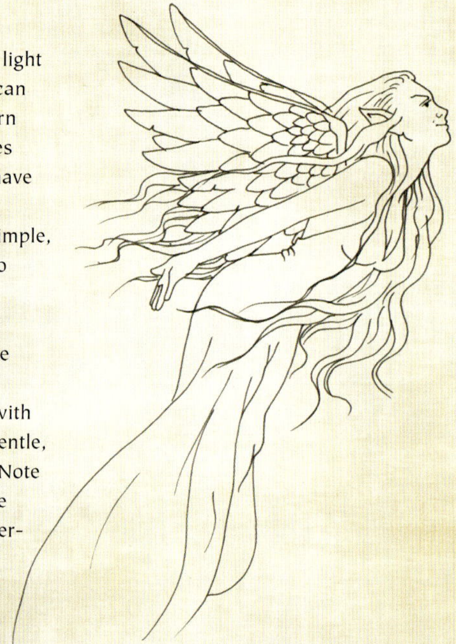

MAIN COLOR PALETTE

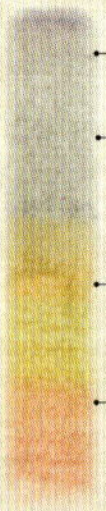

- Payne's gray: clouds, wings, and gown
- Raw umber: pale wash over whole drawing; used for hair and skin tones
- Yellow ocher pencil: parts of the gown and cloud formations
- Rose madder pencil: add blush to skin on the hand, shoulder, and cheeks
- White colored pencil: dress and wings; highlights to clouds

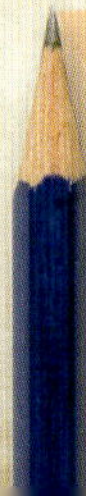

Copy it!

Copy or trace the drawing or scan it into your computer. Then color it.

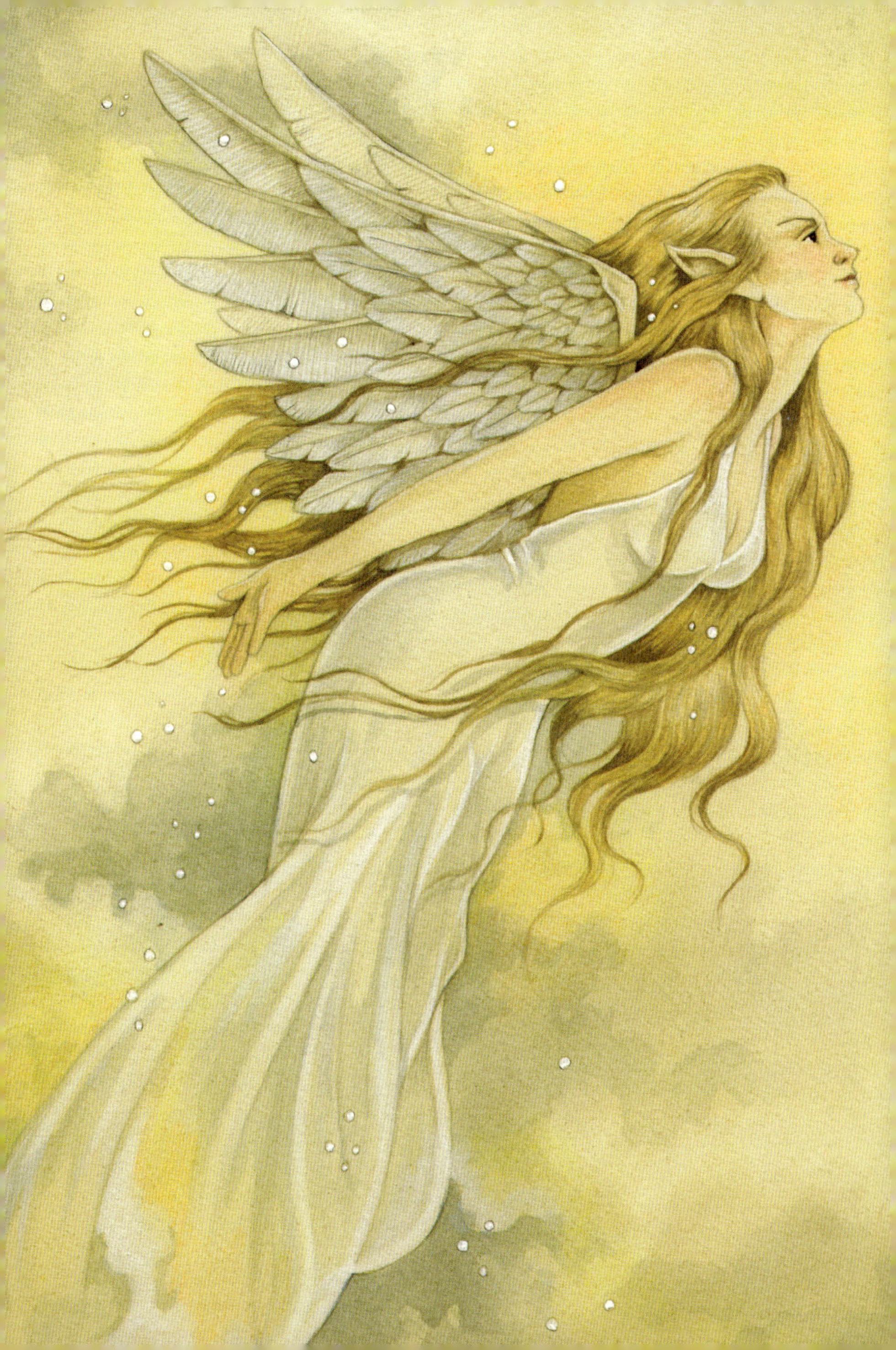

Constructing the figure

Sylphs are often semi-transparent or invisible. Note how the lower part of the body blends into the surrounding air. This gives a sense of impermanence—she has materialized out of the air but may disappear again at any moment. In this figure, the energy is all in the upper part of the body, so concentrate on this area.

See also: Fairy poses, page 60.

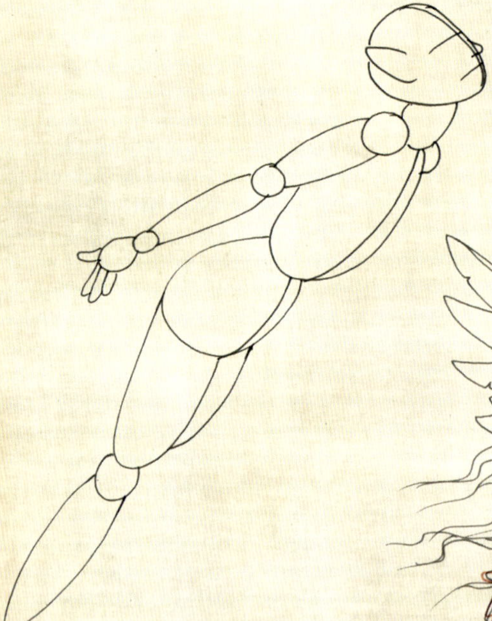

Basic forms help to construct the upward thrust of the figure in flight. The lower legs and feet are left as generalized shapes that will be concealed beneath floating fabric.

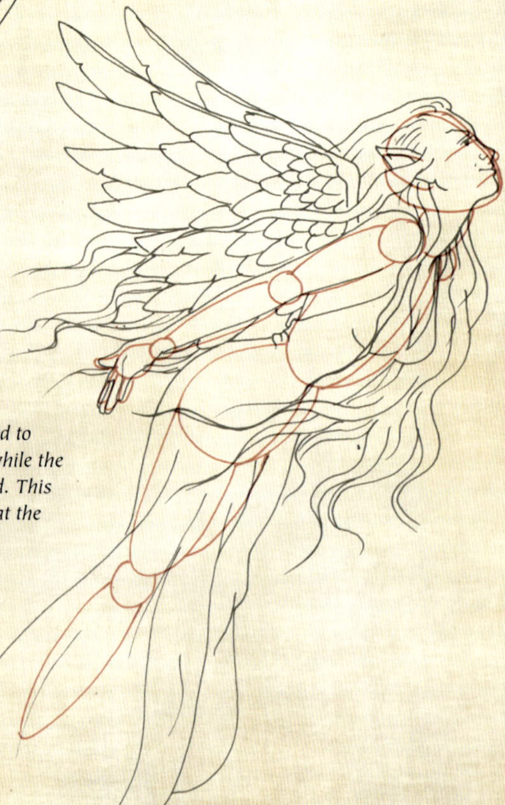

All the added detail is confined to the upper part of the figure, while the lower half is merely suggested. This helps to create the illusion that the figure is lighter than air.

Alternative flying poses

Sylphs are always pictured in midair, so flying poses are important to master. The energy for flight is generated in the upper body by the arms and wings, but the lower limbs must carry the movement through gracefully.

IN FULL FLIGHT
Here, the fairy flies toward and slightly above the viewer. From this angle, perspective distorts familiar proportions. Imitate the resulting foreshortening in the body, legs, and arms to give your drawing three-dimensional realism.

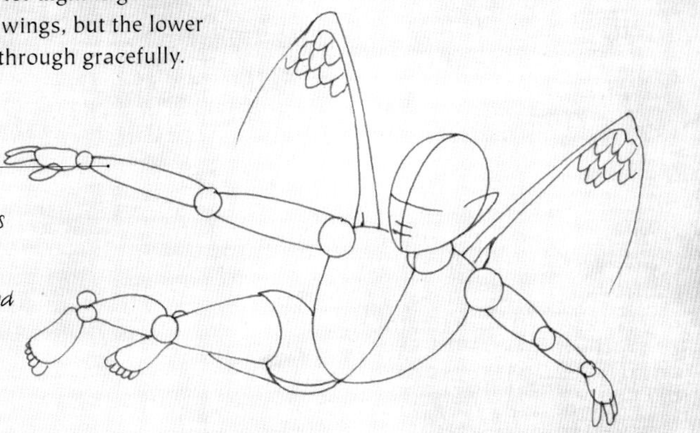

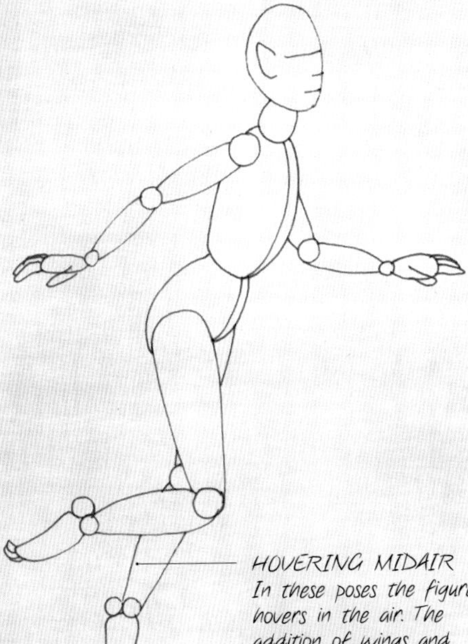

HOVERING MIDAIR
In these poses the figure hovers in the air. The addition of wings and floating garments will suggest weightlessness. Make sure your drawing technique is suitably light and delicate.

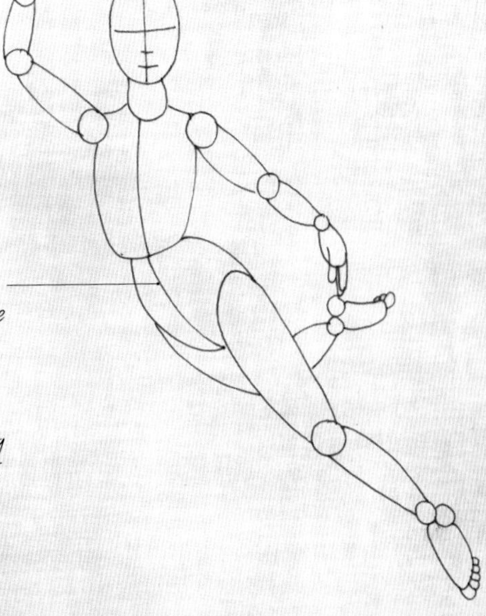

Drawing a feathered wing

Feathered wings may seem daunting to draw but, as with figures, you can approach them with the basic structure first, then "clothe" them with feathers. Once mastered, this simple formula can be adapted to create feathered wings to suit all kinds of characters, from the soft white wings of a gentle Sylph to the black raven's wings of a Gothic Fairy. As always, nature is the best source of inspiration.

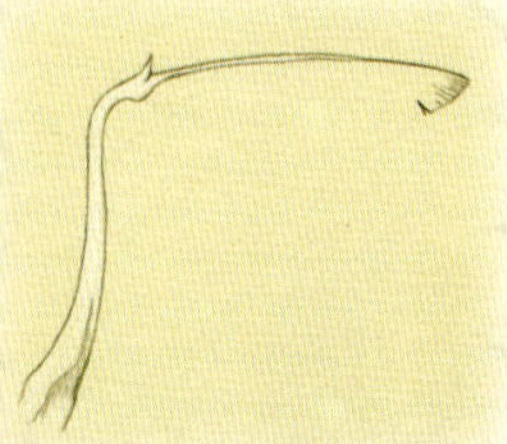

1 Using a graphite pencil, draw a simple, slightly curved and tapered upside-down L shape. This represents the skeletal structure of a bird's wing.

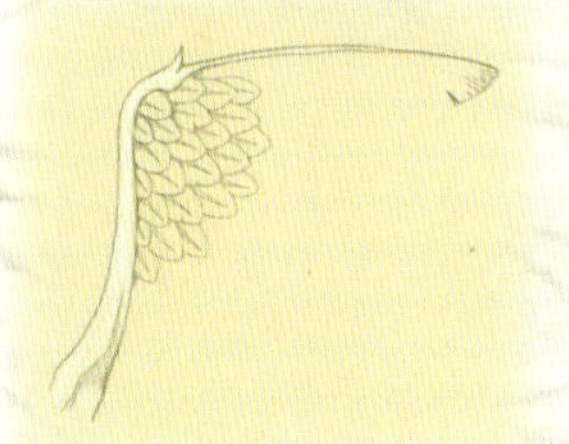

2 In this position the underside of the wing is seen. First add the small downy under feathers, arranging them in three or four overlapping layers.

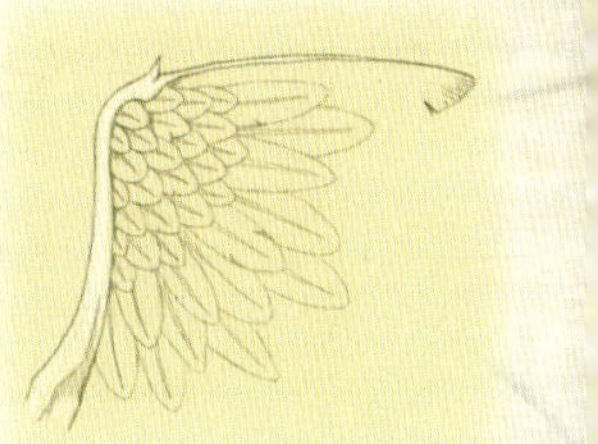

3 Begin to fill out the wing shape with two rows of longer feathers, overlapping them as before. Draw in the central quill of each feather.

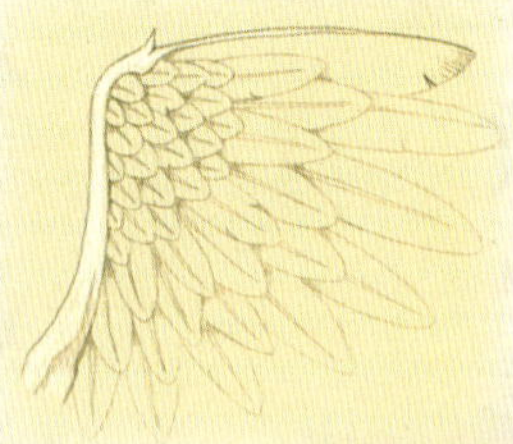

4 Now add a single row of large, strong flight feathers. Note that these are largest at the top edge of the wing, gradually getting smaller as they fan downward.

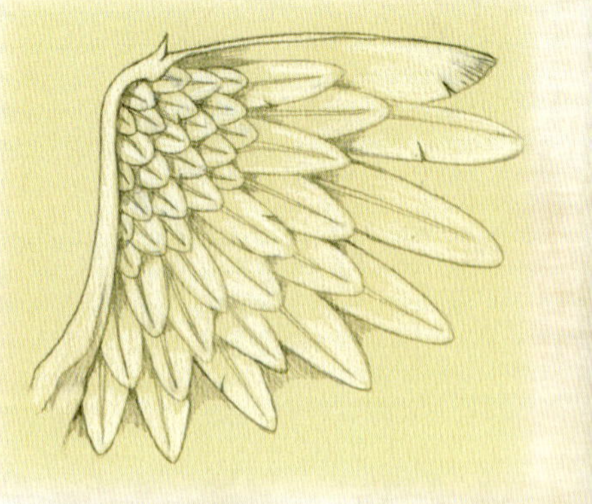

5 Add some shading with gray and white pencils to separate out the layers of feathers and add realistic three-dimensional form.

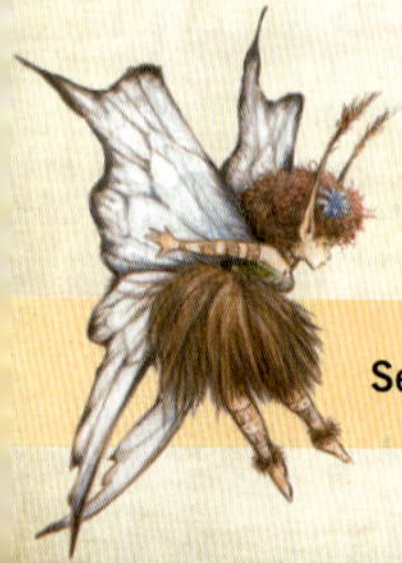

See also: Constructing the wings, page 70.

Creating atmosphere

Weather affects light and light affects atmosphere. Fairies are creatures of the atmosphere, so you'll often want to depict natural effects. This can be achieved in a variety of media and techniques, as shown below.

MONOCHROME TECHNIQUES

CROSS-HATCHING
With a 2B graphite pencil, draw diagonal lines across pastel paper. Leave some areas blank for the white clouds.

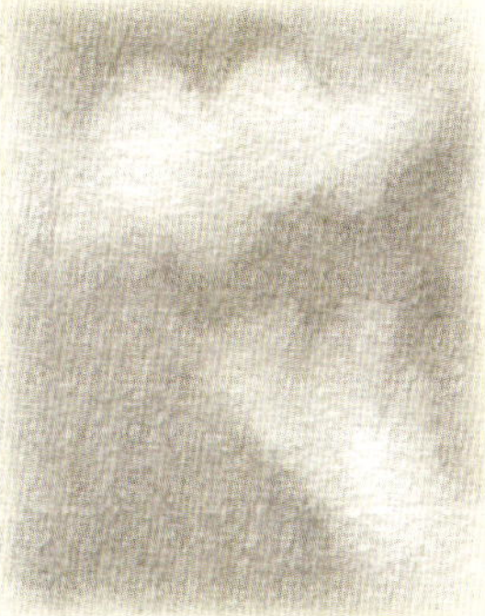

BLENDING
Gently blend graphite pencil lines together using a clean tissue or cotton ball, trying not to smudge the graphite across too much of the white area.

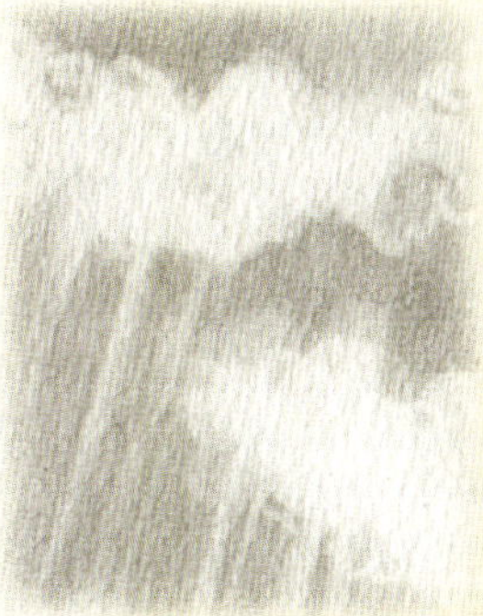

ERASING
Using an eraser, gently remove some of the graphite in diagonal sweeps across the sky. This creates the illusion of driving rain.

COLOR TECHNIQUES

COLORED PENCIL
Apply swathes of blue colored pencil and blend the strokes of color together to soften the reserved cloud shapes, leaving some areas white.

WATERCOLOR WASH
Apply a loose cobalt-blue wash to watercolor paper. While still wet, lift out the clouds by dabbing the wash with dry tissue for a dusk sky.

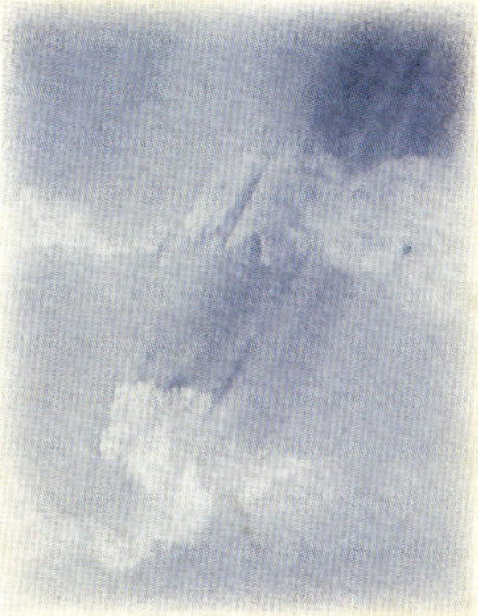

DRY WATERCOLOR
Use tissue as before to lift out clouds from a wet cobalt-blue wash. Then stroke diagonally over the wet wash with a soft, dry fan brush to drag paint across the paper.

Water Fairy

WATER FAIRIES ARE BEGUILING AND UNPREDICTABLE LIKE THE SEA ITSELF, WITH AN ALLURING BEAUTY THAT IS SAID TO BE THE DOWNFALL OF MANY A MISGUIDED MARINER.

Character and appearance

Wherever there is natural water—fresh or salt—there is a fairy who will protect it passionately to ensure its purity. If you pollute the water, her anger is aroused and she will deceive you with her beauty, enticing you to a watery grave. Indeed, legend has it that many ships are lured onto the rocks by the beautiful fairies of the deep, or "Sirens" as they are famously called in Homer's *Odyssey*.

Water Fairies have the lower bodies of fish, with fins and tails that enable them to navigate the water with ease. The creature in this piece has a magnificently elaborate tail and wing fins that give a sense of the exotic. To express the dark and dangerous aspect of the character, the image was drawn first in waterproof sepia ink, then watercolor washes were added.

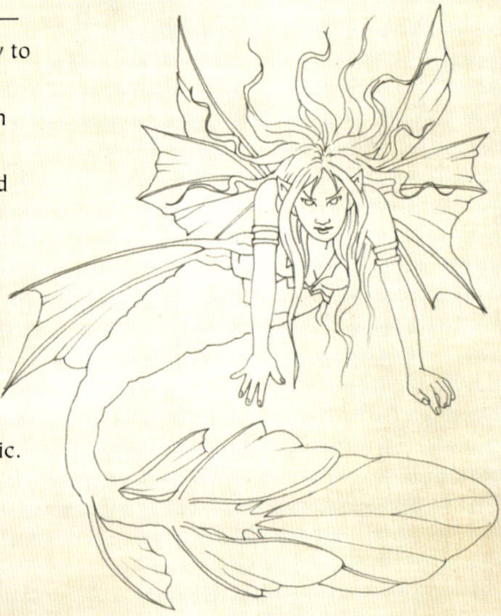

MAIN COLOR PALETTE

- Payne's gray: hair and any dark shadows or shading
- Cobalt green: for the rounded bumps on the fairy's tail
- Sap green: very pale wash for tail section and bikini top
- Olive green: base coat for fins
- Deep red: very pale wash for skin; stronger wash added to fin and tail tips

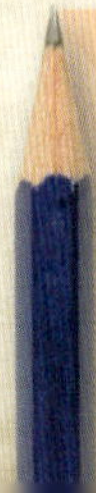

Copy it!

Copy or trace the drawing or scan it into your computer. Then color it.

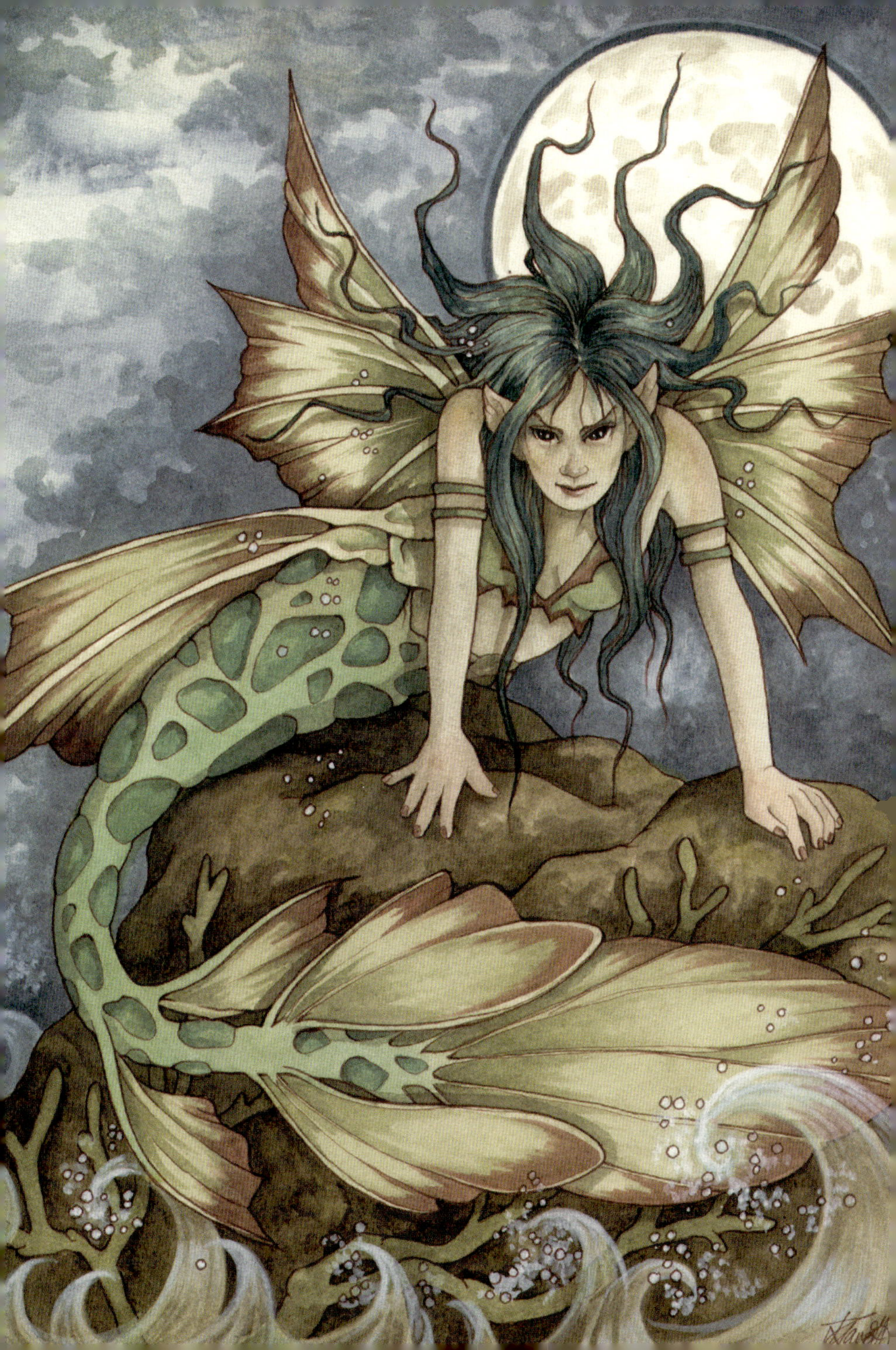

Constructing the figure

Like the legendary mermaid, a Water Fairy is a beautiful and voluptuous female from the waist up. The lower body, however, is that of a lithe fish, with a long, strong tail instead of legs, and wings that resemble elaborate fins.

See also: Figure construction basics, page 58.

The leaning upper body is constructed from basic geometric shapes, with the weight fully supported by the braced arms. Note the foreshortening of the torso when seen from this angle. The lower body sweeps into a long, fish-like tail.

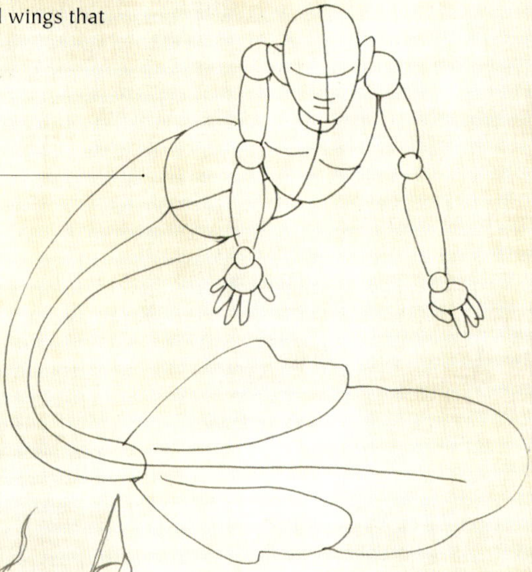

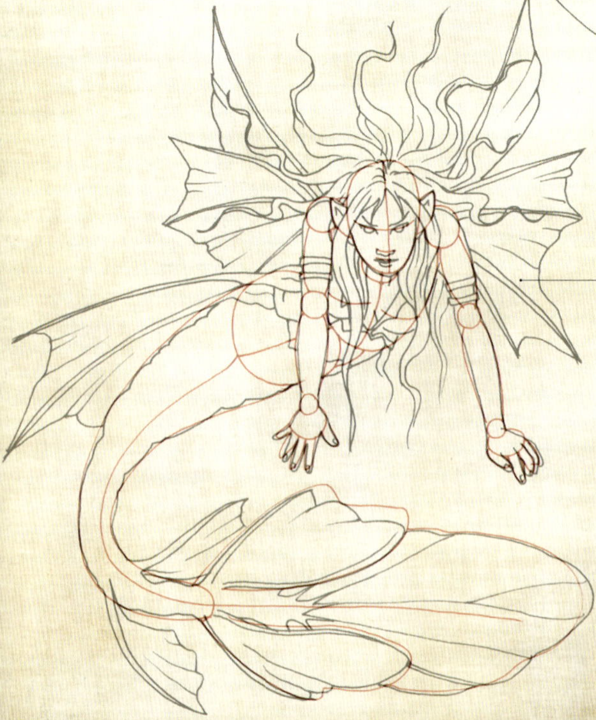

When the pose and proportions are correct, flesh out the figure with details of hair and add an elaborate set of fin-like wings.

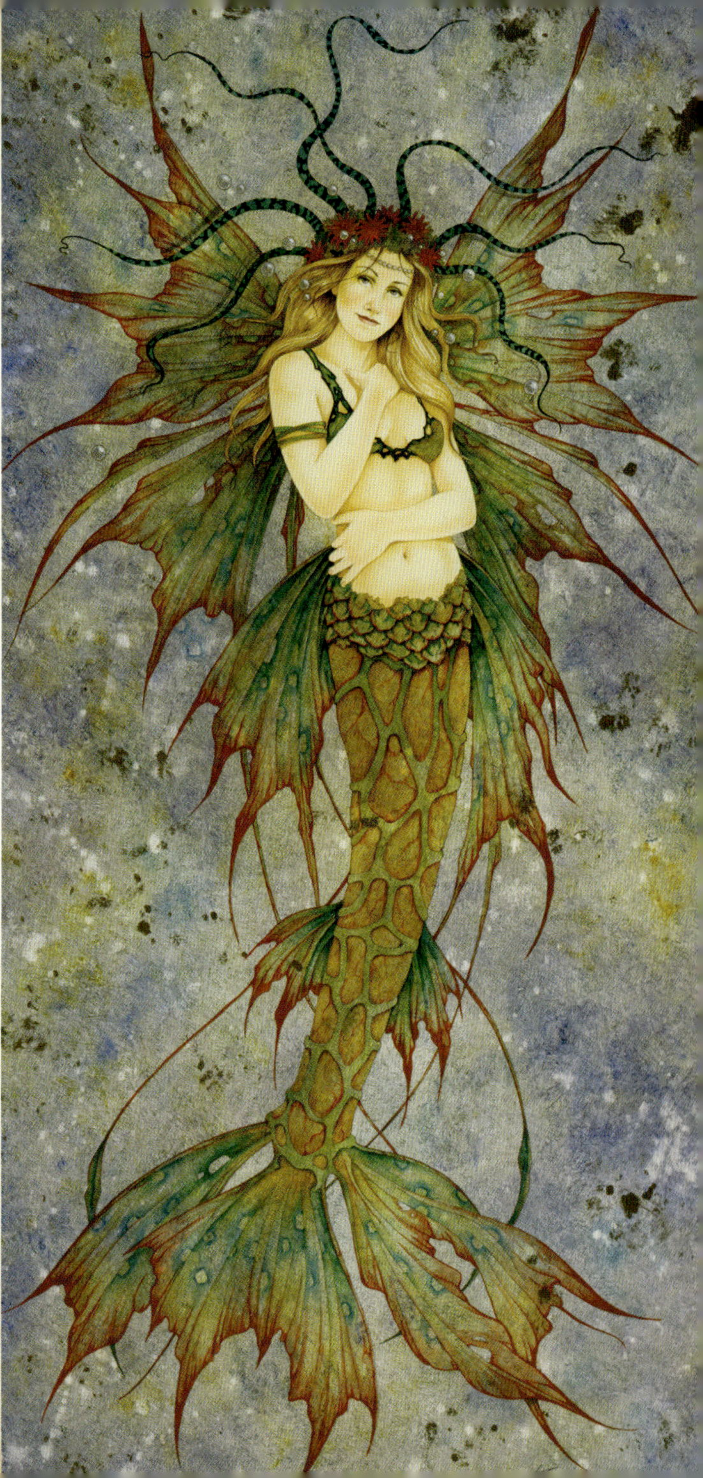

UNDERWATER BEAUTY
This Water Fairy appears beguilingly gentle. Ornate wings like the elaborate fins of exotic fish frame her pale body, and her hair resembles a sea anemone. Writhing, snake-like tendrils introduce a sense of menace to an otherwise tranquil image. The delicate drawing is enhanced by subtle watercolor washes, mottled in places for a watery effect.

Drawing tails and fins

Tails and fins enable the Water Fairies to move about with ease in their watery element. The larger shoulder fins also function as wings, allowing them to undertake short flights just above the surface of the water. Consider the habitat of your characters—sea, river, lake, pond—and research the fish that live in these waters for ideas.

Shape, size, and color

Choose fin colors to coordinate with the tail, and design the shape to suit the character. They can be small, subtle, and delicate, or large, elaborately shaped, and flamboyant.

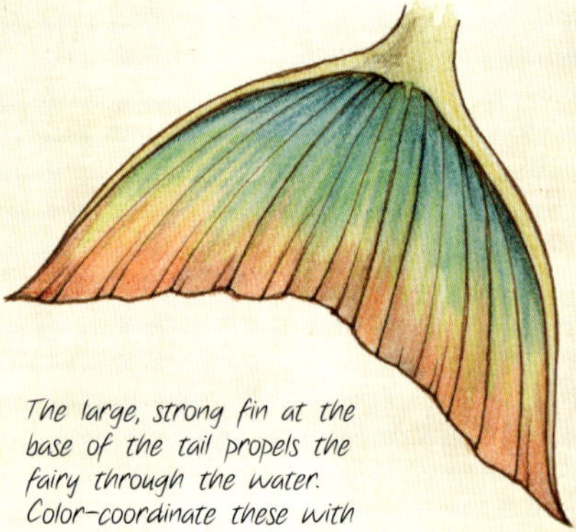

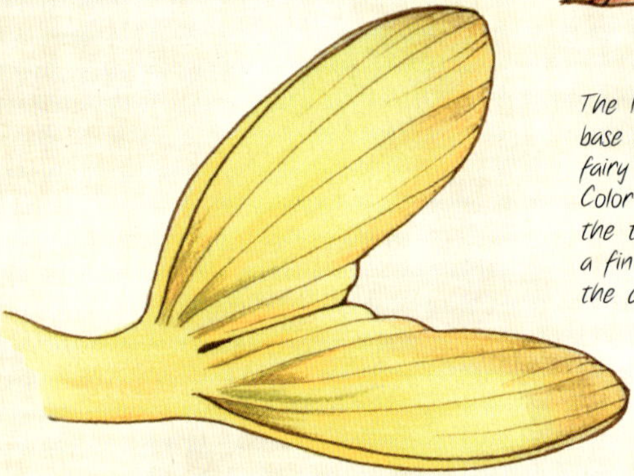

The large, strong fin at the base of the tail propels the fairy through the water. Color-coordinate these with the tail design and develop a fin shape according to the character.

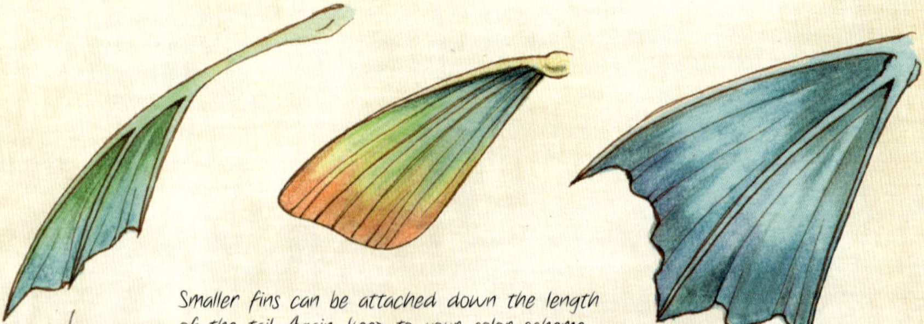

Smaller fins can be attached down the length of the tail. Again, keep to your color scheme and develop the shapes to express the character and enlarge some to create wings.

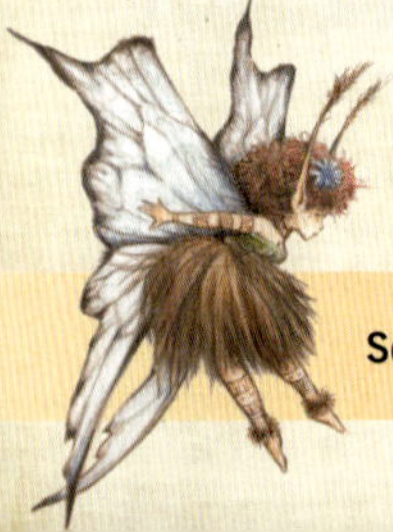

See also: Fairy wings, page 70.

Drawing scales

Fish scales can be so small that the skin appears smooth and glistening. Larger scales create visible patterns that you can imitate for interesting surface texture.

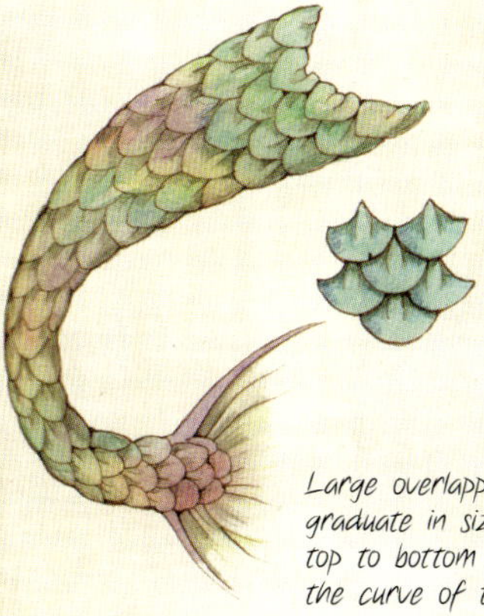

Large overlapping scales graduate in size from top to bottom and follow the curve of the tail. You can use variegated color to enhance the textural effect.

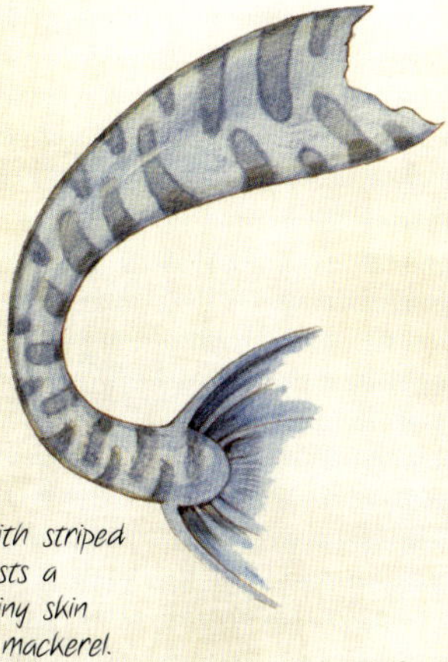

A silver tail with striped markings suggests a smooth and shiny skin like that of a mackerel. There are no visible scales to disturb the gleaming surface.

Adding texture

Think laterally when you design water fairies—you can depict the fish tails in any way that suits both character and habitat. Try this alternative to scales for adding texture, as used in the main image.

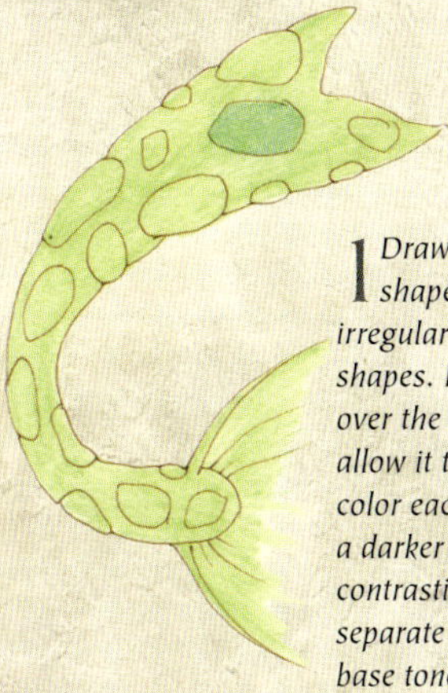

1 Draw a simple tail shape and add irregular rounded shapes. Paint a wash over the entire tail and allow it to dry. Then color each shape with a darker tone or a contrasting shade to separate them from the base tone.

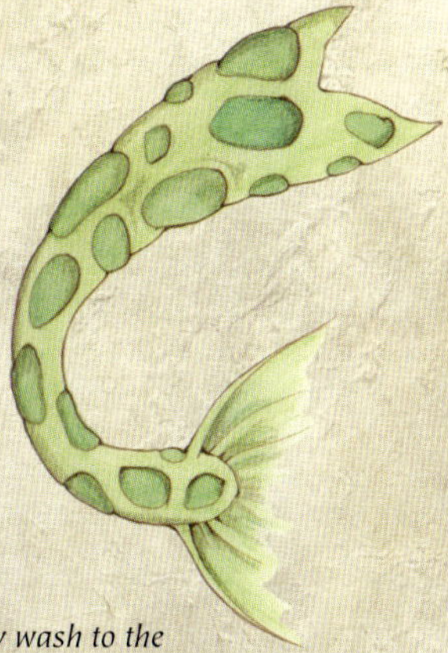

2 Add a gray wash to the top corners of each shape, creating a three-dimensional effect so they appear to protrude from the surface of the skin. Add gray shading to the edges of the tail to further enhance the rounded form.

Boogie

BOOGIES ARE THE ILL-TEMPERED COUSINS OF BROWNIES. ALSO KNOWN AS HOBGOBLINS, BOGGARTS, HOBBERS, AND PADFOOTS, THEY DELIGHT IN INFESTING THE HOMES OF HUMANS TO INSTIGATE UNSPEAKABLE MISCHIEF.

Character and appearance

Boogies are twisted, ugly, and generally miserable creatures with dirty, tattered clothing. Once they invade a home they are virtually impossible to remove. They spill milk, slam doors, upset the dog, pinch and poke children in their beds, and steal their food. And they don't confine their mischief indoors. Outside, they enjoy frightening travelers and opening farmers' gates so their animals escape.

This detestable Boogie is depicted in a night setting using a muted palette of dark blues and grays that reflects his mean personality. The figure is hunched over and on the prowl, his twisted grimace conveying his nasty nature. Wet washes are mixed together on the paper to create blotched and mottled skin tones that amplify his repellent appearance and disagreeable character.

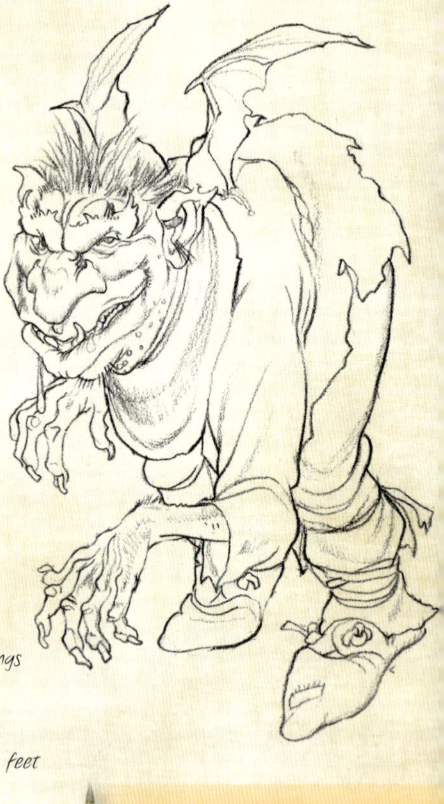

MAIN COLOR PALETTE

- Winsor blue: background washes, clothing, wings
- Permanent green: background washes
- Burnt umber: background washes and under feet
- Cadmium scarlet: skin tones and clothes
- Yellow ocher: skin tones and clothes
- Alizarin crimson: added to outlining mix
- Cerulean blue (not shown): background washes

Copy it!

Copy or trace the drawing or scan it into your computer. Then color it.

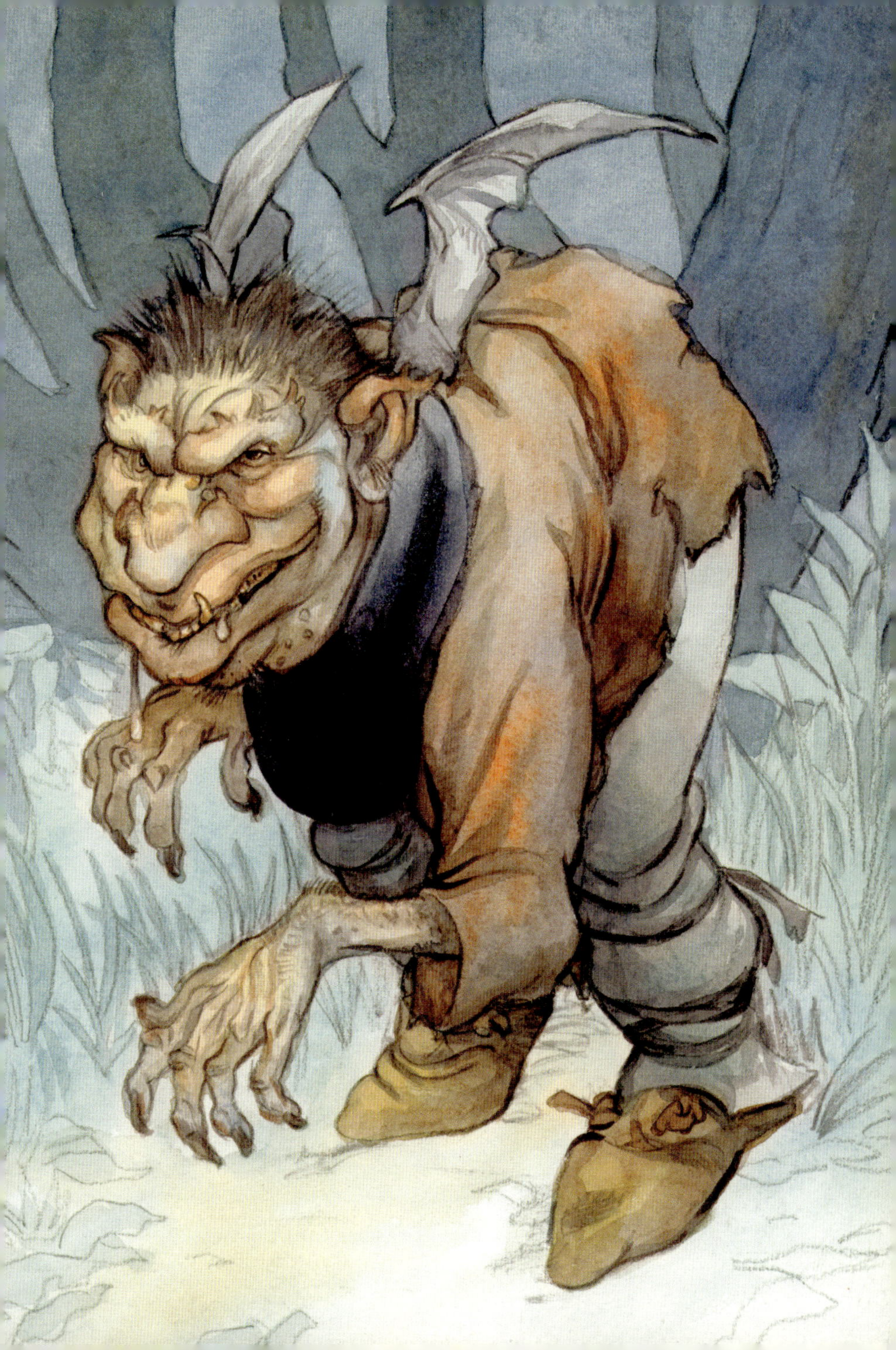

Constructing the figure

This figure is drawn in basically the same hunched, prowling position as the main image, but seen this time from the side. To make things utterly convincing, start as always with the basic shapes—you'll see clearly how the posture is created and balanced, and this will help you understand the pose from the three-quarter viewpoint of the finished image.

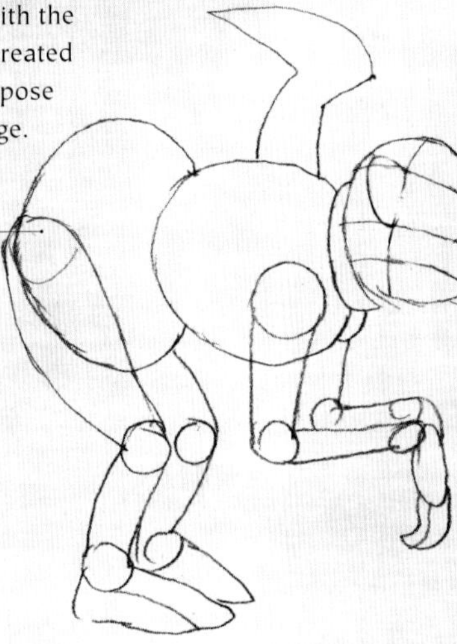

1 Draw the three basic body masses: head, torso, and lower body. Divide the head into three sections, add a dot for the eye, and indicate protruding nose and lips. Add arms and legs. Notice how the legs bend for balance.

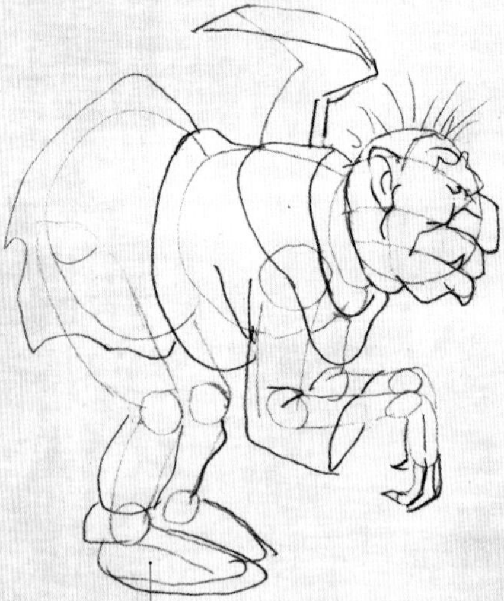

2 Add clothes lightly, making sure they wrap around the body forms, and add creases at elbows and armpits. Develop the facial details on the initial section lines, and establish the chin and brow. Add hair, wings, and finger details.

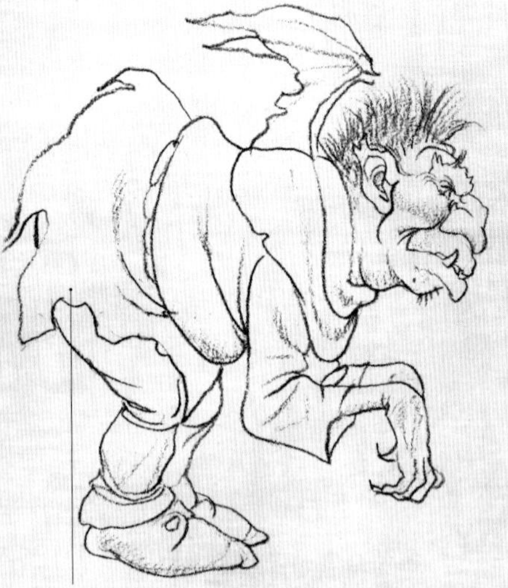

3 Use a stronger line to define the drawing. Establish the boots and ragged clothing edges. Add more hair, and work up the facial features including chin stubble. Emphasize the finger joints and claws, and give the wings ragged edges.

Drawing the head

An artist needs to generate drawings quickly and easily in order to try out character variations. To develop versatility, try using the same simple construction shapes to create several faces—pushing and pulling the features enables the artist to exploit his imagination and explore different possibilities. Try these simple examples.

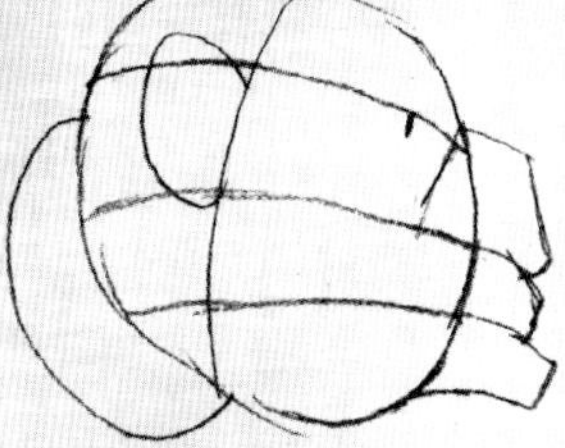

Basic head construction

These examples are based on the head shape shown above—a basic ball shape divided into three sections, with a simple nose and lip form added.

GIANT

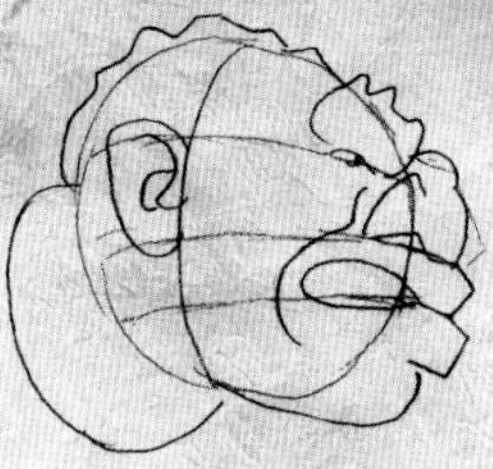

1 Here, the nose is pushed back a little and a loop is added to the mouth to show teeth. Add bumps on top of the head.

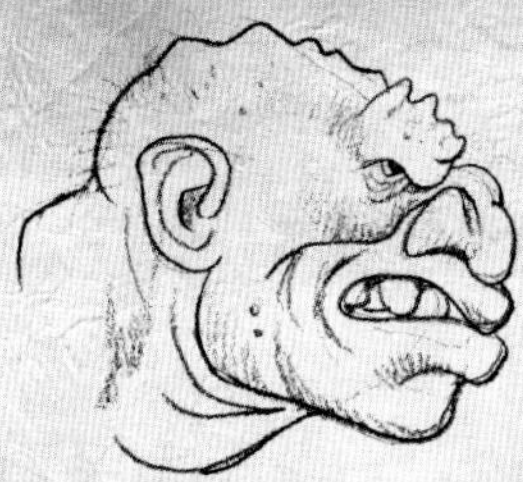

2 Develop the ear. Add shading to round out the fleshy folds. Draw in the large teeth and add stubble to create a perfect giant-like character.

DEMON

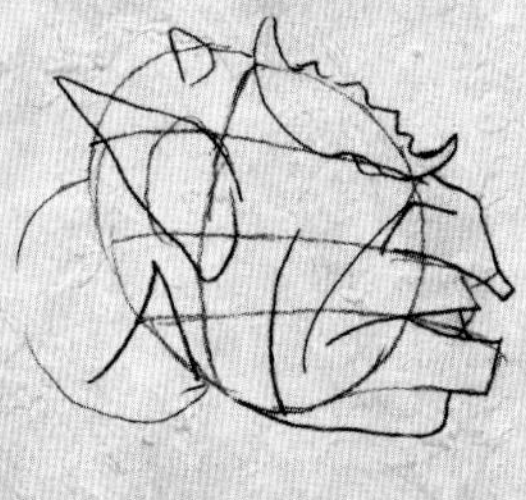

1 Draw a pointed ear and hook the nose. Turn the mouth down and build out the chin. Develop the brow into a horn.

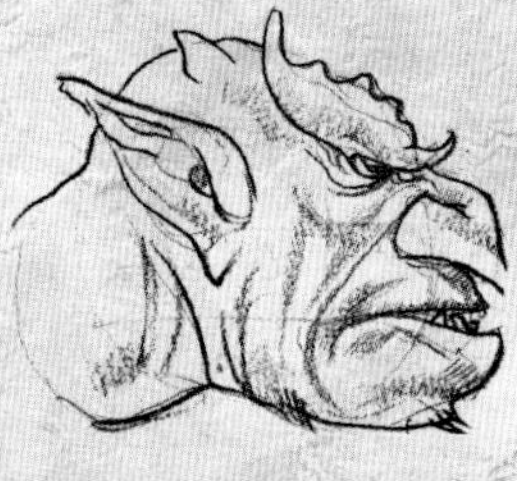

2 Add shading to show the folds of the face and the bulbous lower lip. Add another horn on the head and suggest a small goatee beard.

ANIMAL

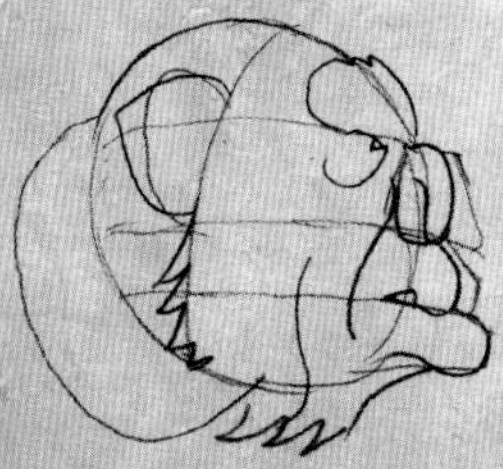

1 Push back the nose into a snout, and point the ear. The brow is similar to the giant's. Add jagged lines beneath the chin to suggest fur.

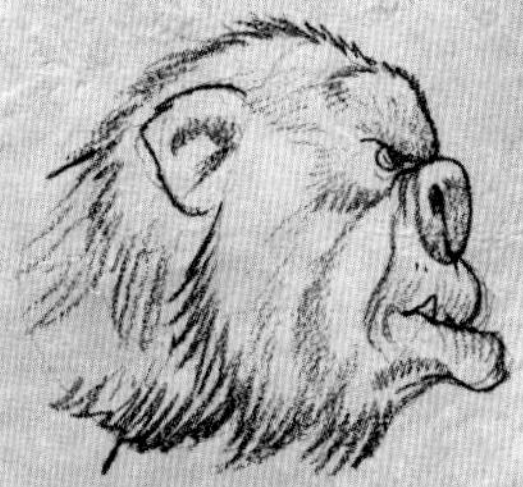

2 Developing the fur takes this character right away from its human aspect. Shade in suggestions of shaggy hair all over the head and below the jaw.

Creating character

Before deciding on the final creature, investigate a variety of facial characterizations. Boogies are malicious, repellent individuals, so twist and distort the features, and add facial growths and ugly teeth. Use different color schemes to see which best conveys the fairy's dark spirit. Never destroy rejects—these may be perfect as future designs for other creatures.

HOBGOBLIN

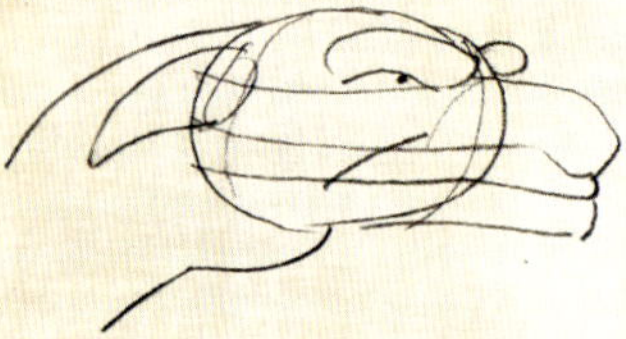

1 Start with a simple circle. Then elongate the nose and mouth and add flattened, pointed ears for an animal-like look. Draw a heavy brow bulge.

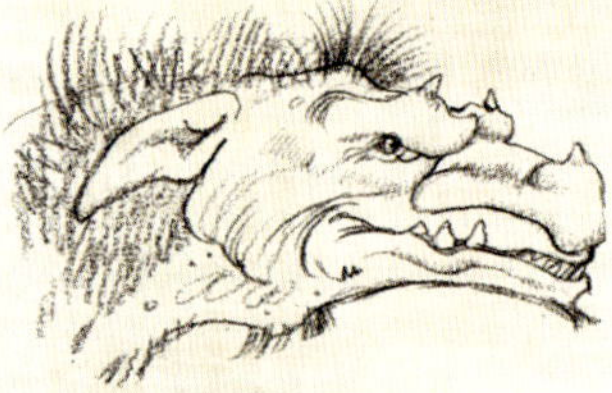

2 Increase the unpleasantness with small horns and protruding teeth that distort the lower lip. Add some bristly hair and some pencil shading to give form.

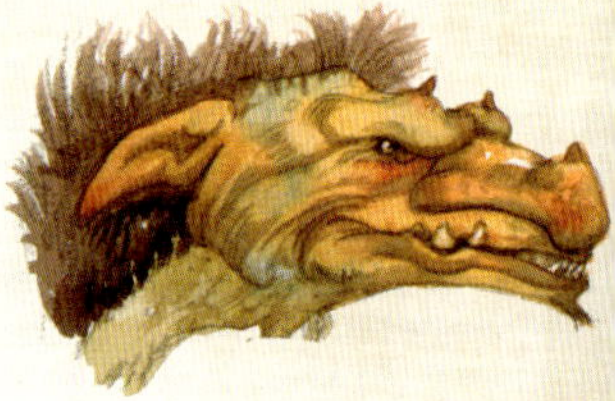

3 Color with warm ocher washes combined with cool greeny-blues to give the face a weird amphibian aspect. Add plenty of unkempt hair to increase the wild look.

GOBLIN

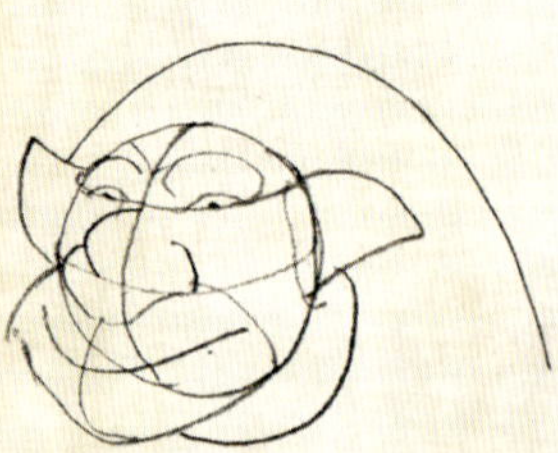

1 Start with a basic circle. To exaggerate features, add a large semicircle to the mouth area. Sketch in the broad nose and big mouth.

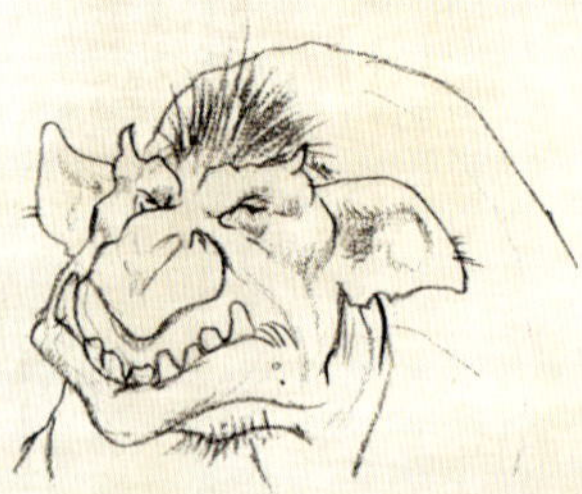

2 Develop the mouth into a sinister, toothy grimace. Refine the broad nose and mean eyes and add hair. Point the ears in opposite directions for extra weirdness.

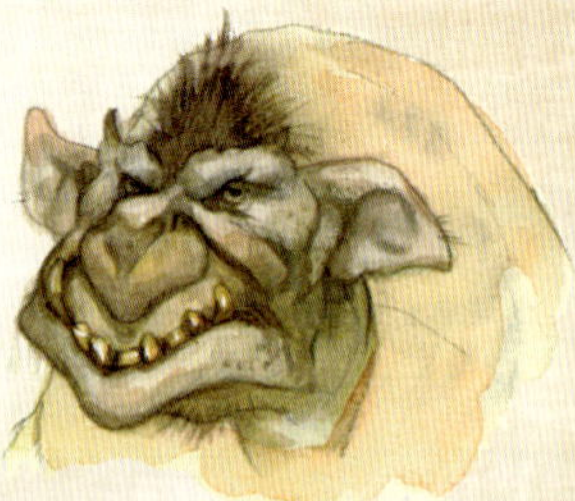

3 This time, render the face with a chilly gray-blue palette to suggest the disgusting, clammy skin of an underworld creature. Paint the teeth a rotting yellow.

BOGEY MAN

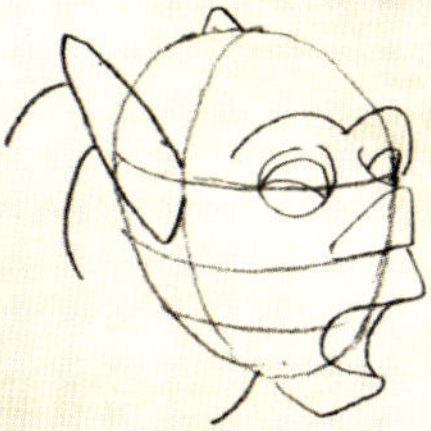

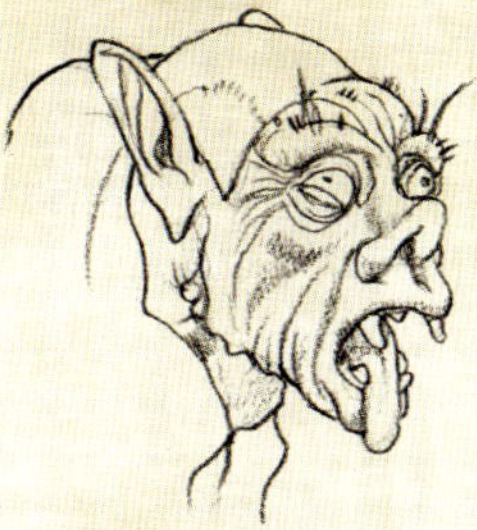

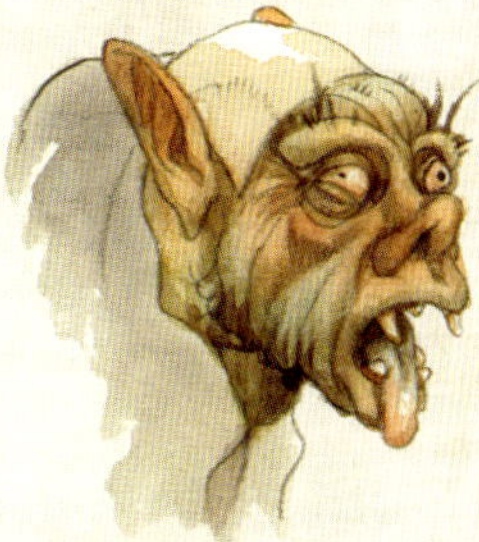

1 Develop the basic circle into a ghastly face with tall pointed ears, heavy overhanging brows, large eyes, pushed up pig-like nose, and sagging lower jaw.

2 Add descriptive shading and refine the facial detail: long eyebrow hairs, eyes looking in different directions, and tongue lolling over disgustingly misshapen teeth.

3 Render the hideous face in pale, beyond-the-grave colors. The top of the head is skull-like, the eyes ghoulish, and the wizened face tinged with rotting green.

BOGGART

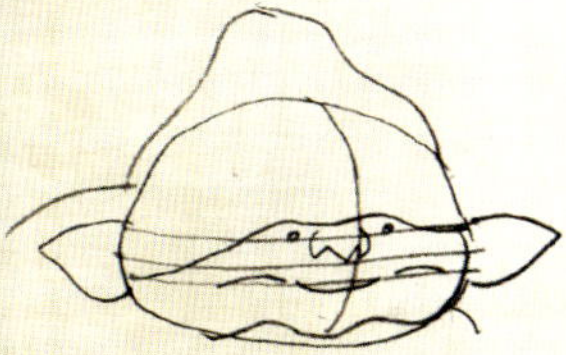

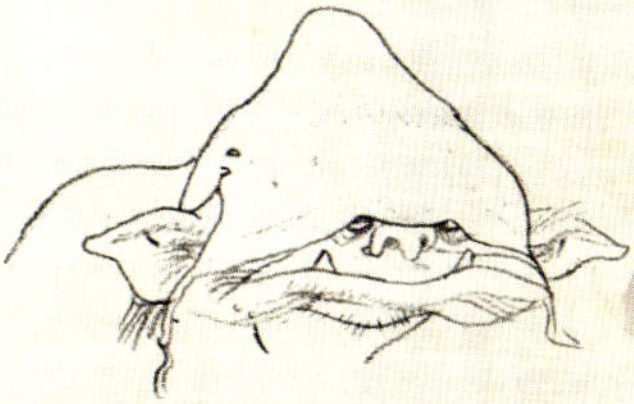

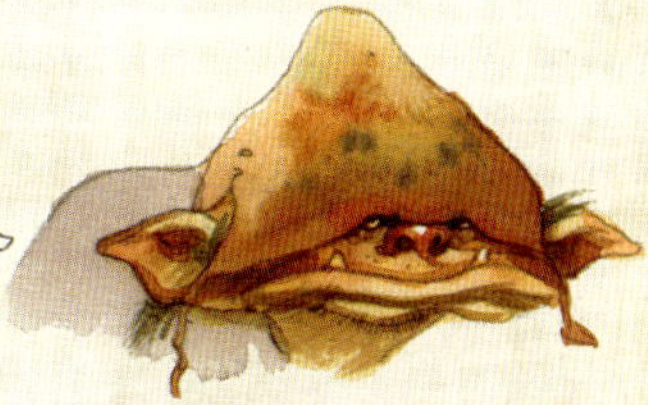

1 Begin with a flattened circle divided into three. Add the large hat and sticking-out ears and plot the facial features; a simple "M" shape creates the nose.

2 Develop the sagging lip that hides the chin, the over-large mouth, and mean, beady eyes. The hat sits over the eyes like eyebrows for a menacing look.

3 Color this creature with a warm palette. Notice that the dirt-spattered hat becomes almost as important as the facial features in defining his unnerving and sinister character.

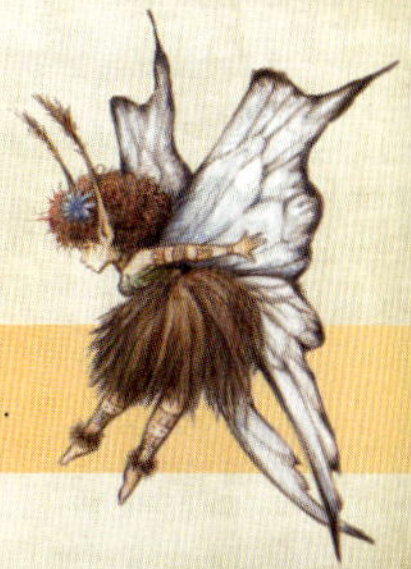

See also: Facial expressions, page 66.

Boogie: from sketch to finished painting

This figure, in true skulking Boogie fashion, is bent on perpetrating some unspeakable mischief. The sinister nighttime setting enhances the sense of menace, while the background trees focus the attention on the figure and prevent the eye escaping the horror. Skillfully applied wet-in-wet watercolor washes create the unpleasant mottled appearance of this disgusting creature.

See also: Rendering, page 52.

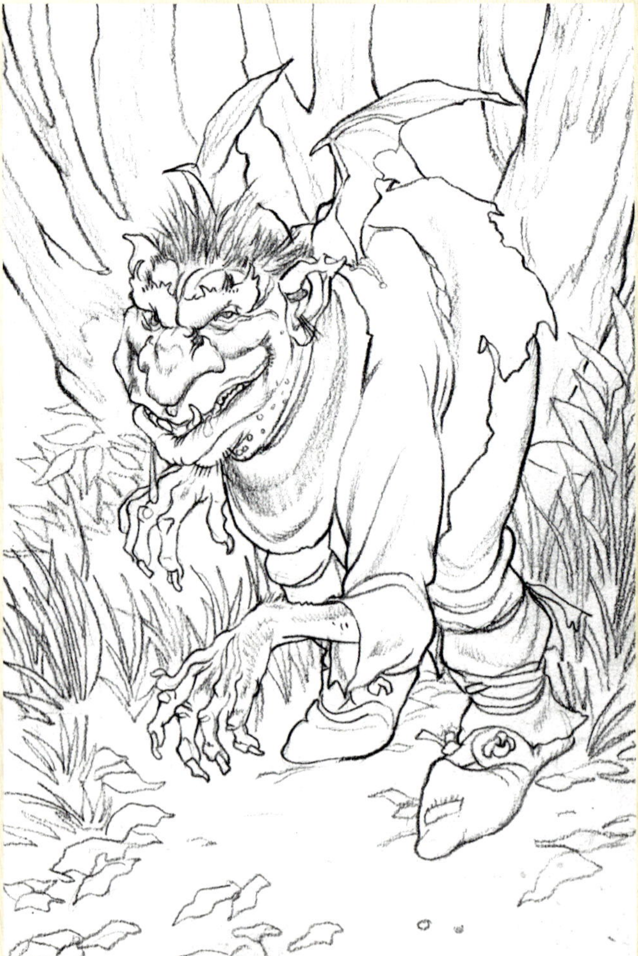

The initial drawing

- *Construct the figure using basic shapes to create a solid and balanced image.*
- *Work lightly at first, using a graphite pencil.*
- *Place the figure in the upper center of the picture area, framed by the trees and foreground textures.*
- *Use a black colored pencil to complete the drawing, refining the basic shapes and adding clothing and character details.*

Painting the background

- *Flood a wash of Winsor blue, burnt umber, and a little permanent green over the background down to the undergrowth.*
- *Use a graduated wash of cerulean blue and permanent green over the remaining area.*
- *Add burnt umber beneath the feet.*
- *Using stronger mixes, paint the trees with a Winsor blue and burnt umber wash, and stalks with a cerulean blue and permanent green mix.*

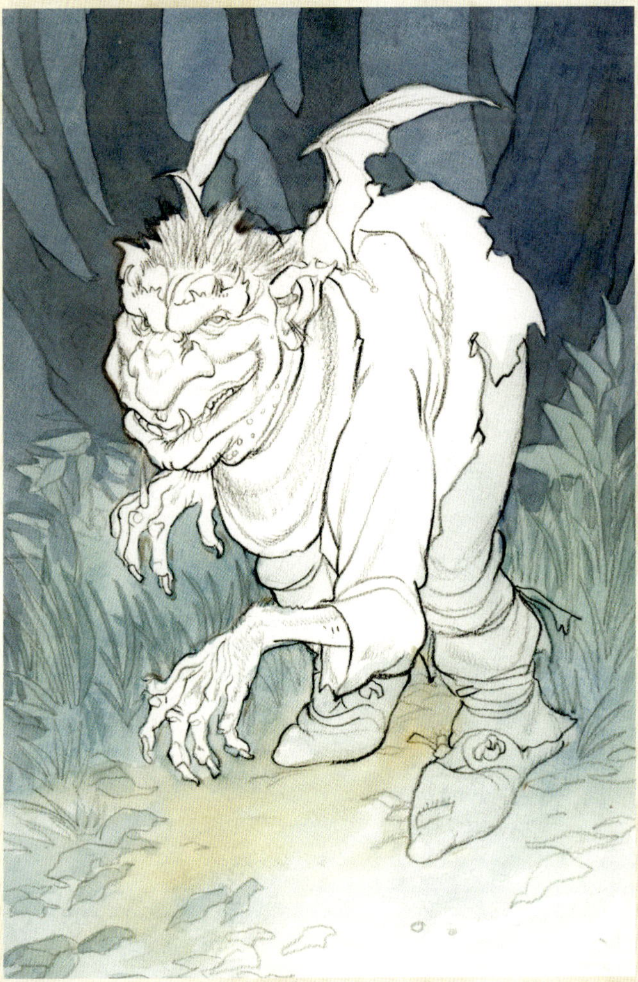

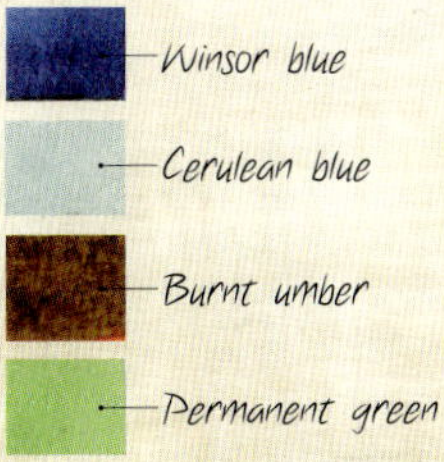

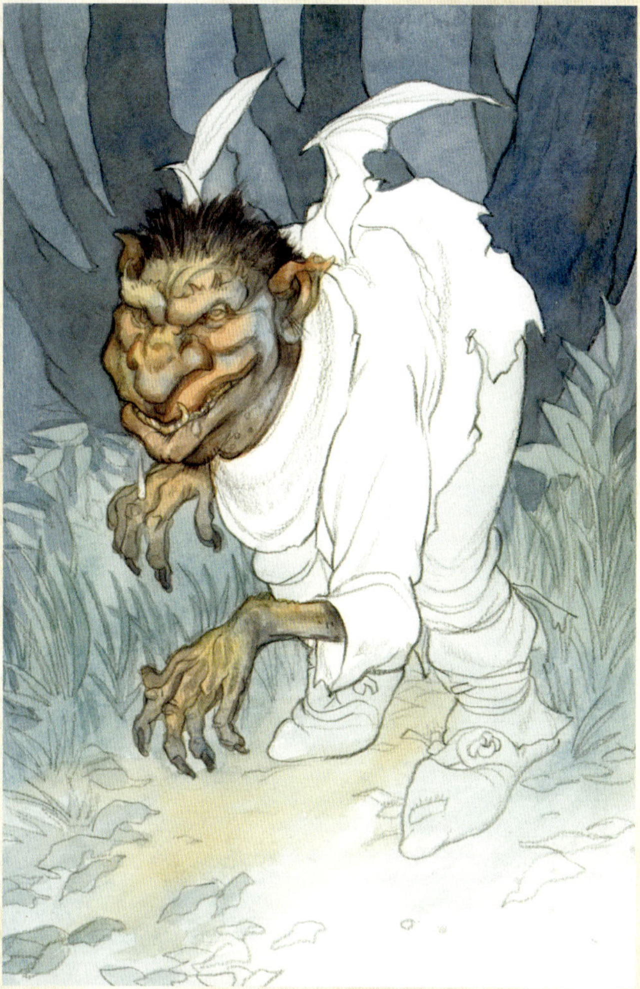

Adding skin tones

- *Apply a light cerulean blue wash to the right side of the face.*
- *While wet, blend in a cadmium scarlet and yellow ocher wash to the left side.*
- *Define mouth, cheeks, and ear with stronger mixes.*
- *Paint arms and hands with a watery wash of cerulean blue with a touch of cadmium scarlet, adding yellow ocher wet-in-wet.*
- *Use cadmium scarlet and cerulean blue for the hair.*

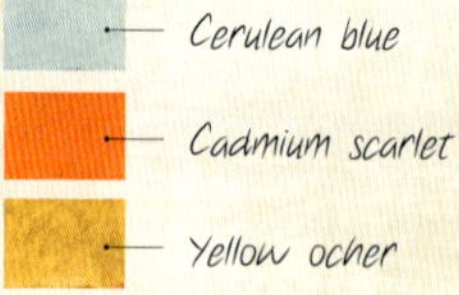

See also: Basic watercolor techniques, page 50.

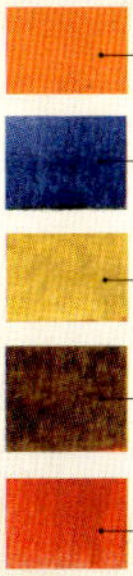

Cadmium scarlet

Windsor blue

Yellow ocher

Burnt umber

Alizarin crimson

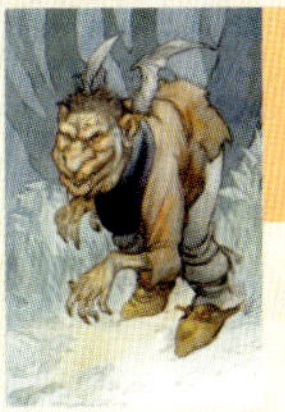

See also: Finished Boogie image, page 177.

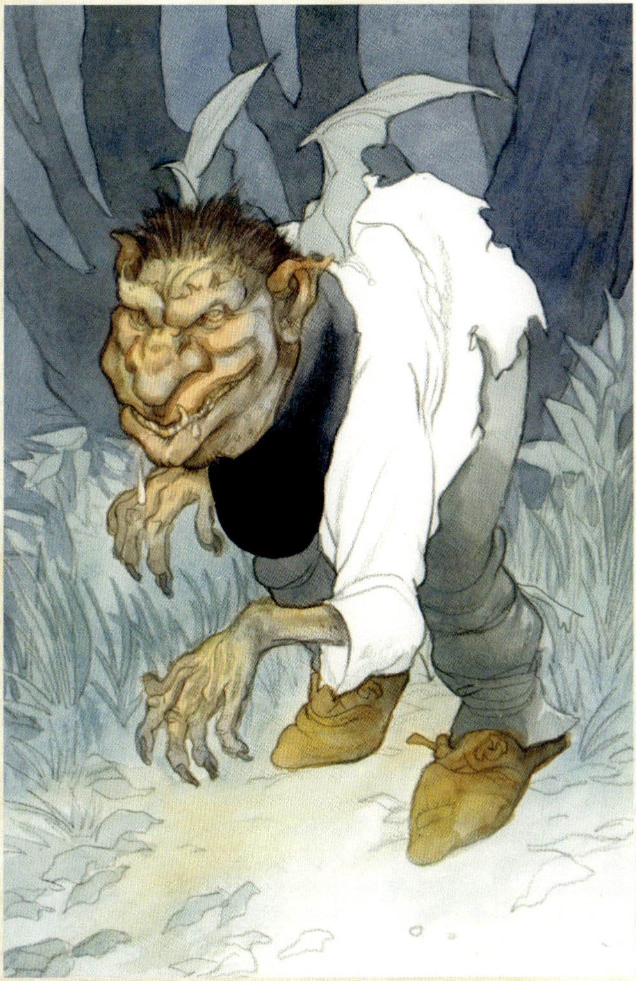

Adding clothes to finish the piece

- *Paint the neck cowl with a cadmium scarlet and Winsor blue wash.*
- *Add yellow ocher to this mix for the boots.*
- *Paint the tunic with a light Winsor blue wash, then run in a yellow ocher and cadmium scarlet wash wet-in-wet, followed by stronger Winsor blue.*
- *Paint the pants in a graduated wash of yellow ocher, Winsor blue, and a hint of cadmium scarlet, thinning it as it goes up the leg.*
- *Tone the wings lightly with a mix of Winsor blue and cadmium scarlet.*
- *As a final touch, strengthen some outlines with a concentrated Winsor blue, alizarin crimson, and burnt umber mix applied with a fine brush.*

Gothic Fairy

GOTHIC FAIRIES ARE SINISTER, BEAUTIFUL, AND DISTURBINGLY COMPELLING CREATURES OF THE NIGHT WHO WILL USE ALL KINDS OF DEVIOUS MEANS TO LEAD PEOPLE ASTRAY.

Character and appearance

Commonly associated with disturbing nocturnal creatures such as bats, Gothic Fairies can be portrayed in many ways. They are seen as solitary creatures, dark and treacherous but not deeply malevolent. The traditional Gothic Fairy is vamp-like, cloaking her menacing nature in elegant but modest Medieval gowns of dark velvet.

By contrast, modern Goth fashions have inspired a whole new take on Gothic Fairies, creating characters with serious attitude and funky clothes, hairstyles, and makeup to match. This image shows a confrontational character with an unmistakable no-messing stance. She has the pale skin of a night creature and wears quirky garments painted with strong black and red watercolor washes. Bat wings complete the sinister impression, while the graveyard setting adds to the sense of menace.

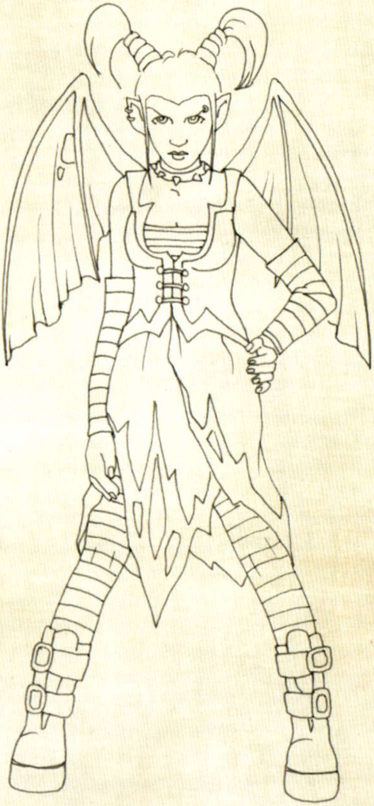

MAIN COLOR PALETTE

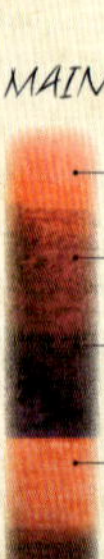

- Rose madder: hair color and wing tips
- Cadmium deep red: under-bodice
- Blue-black: varying washes on socks, wings, clothing, and boots
- Scarlet: for socks, arm warmers, and dress trims
- Alizarin crimson: for varying washes on the wings

Raw umber (not shown): very pale washes on skin

Copy it!

Copy or trace the drawing or scan it into your computer. Then color it.

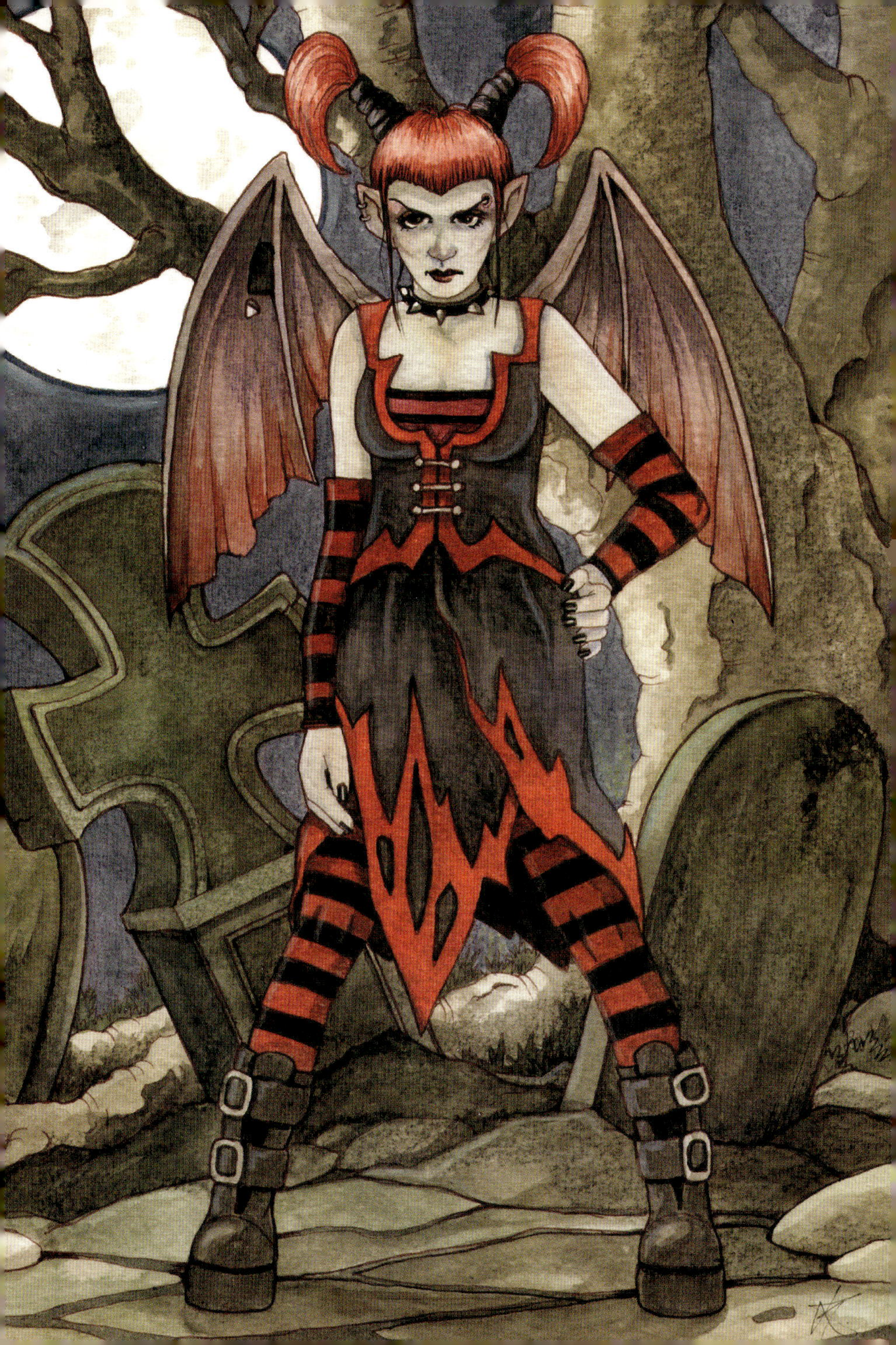

Constructing the figure

This pose is full of in-your-face attitude. Everything about the stance conveys aggressive confrontation. A full frontal view is often enough to create a sense of challenge and hostility. In addition here, the firmly planted legs, the hand on hip, and the insolent stare all say that this fairy means to have things her way. Plot the figure first using the basic shape approach to achieve the powerful image.

See also: Hair and headwear, page 82.

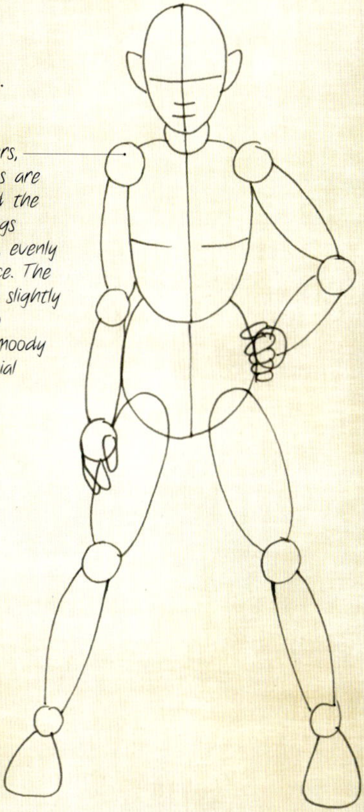

Head, shoulders, torso, and hips are square-on and the widespread legs create a solid, evenly balanced stance. The head is tilted slightly downward to enhance the moody and sullen facial expression.

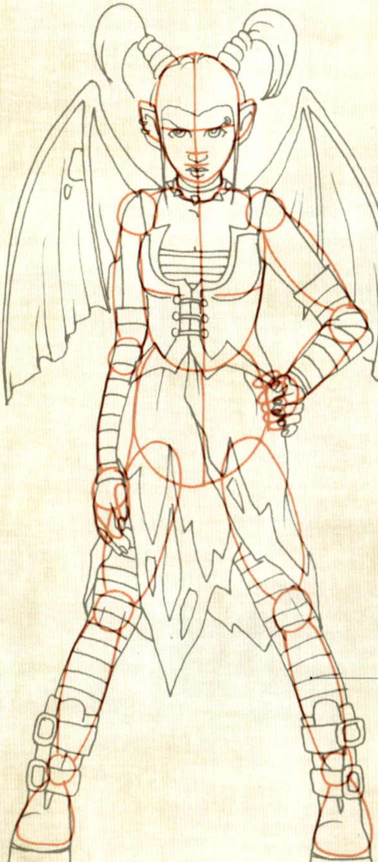

Using the basic construction, flesh out the figure, drawing the clothing and facial details. Add wings, funky hairstyle, and chunky biker-boots for instant character description.

Creating character

Gothic Fairies are usually portrayed in dark clothing, but their characters are richly varied and fun to create. Decide what type you wish to paint and let your imagination do the rest. Traditional, vamp-like Gothic Fairies have understated makeup, neat hair, and flowing velvet gowns. A modern Gothic Fairy might have funky corsets and boots, wild hair, and extreme makeup. What links them is their love of darkness.

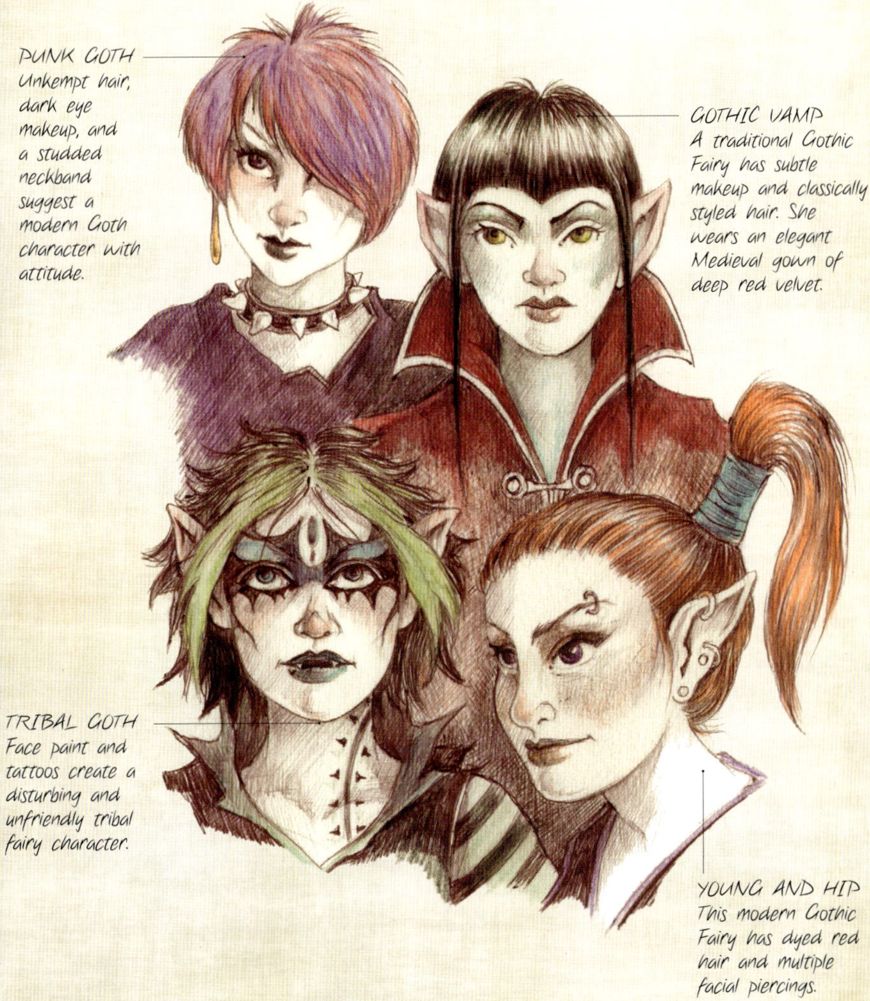

Gothic makeup

The traditional Gothic Fairy wears much less makeup than the modern Goth-style version that owes much to the flamboyant punk-rock era. However, both are characterized by thin sculpted faces, hollowed cheeks, and pale skin that instantly suggests a character that never sees the light of day.

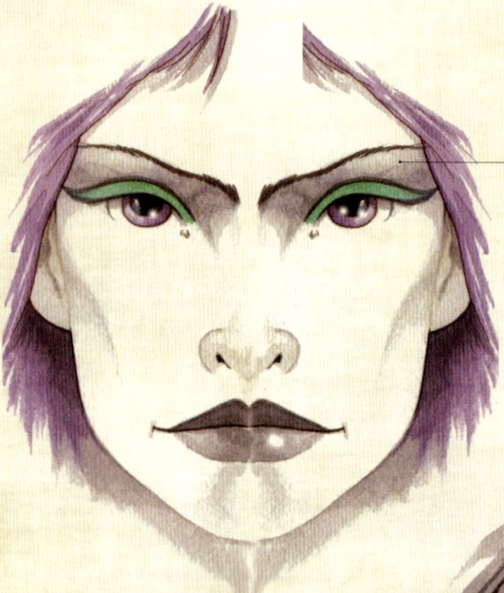

TRADITIONAL GOTHIC FAIRY
The face is white, with smoky eye sockets, wild purple hair, and eyes shadowed with vivid green. For a traditional Gothic Fairy, try sleek black hair and dark eyes to match the black lips.

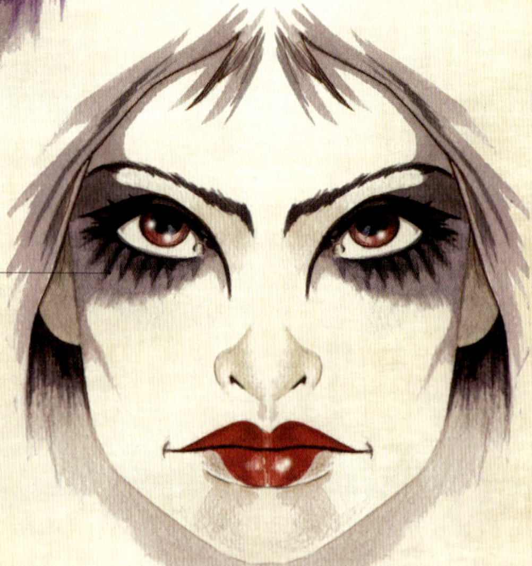

PUNK-STYLE GOTH
Here, the eyes are surrounded by dark, smudged shadow, eyelashes are exaggerated, and strong eyeliner creates a cat-like look. Startling red lips are painted like a doll's mouth.

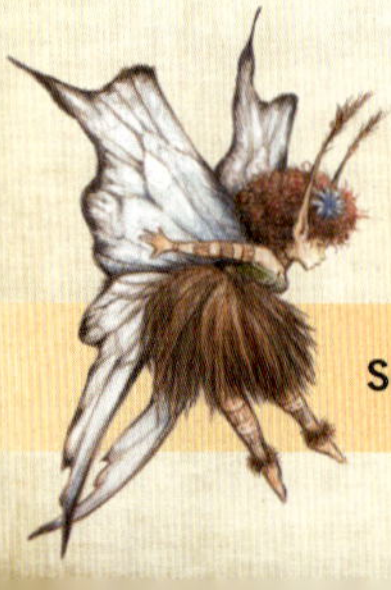

See also: Fairy wings, page 70.

Wing variations

Gothic fairies are generally associated with dark and frightening nighttime creatures such as bats and spiders, ravens, and dragons. Attributes of these creatures are often adapted to characterize the Gothic Fairy. Their wings especially convey an appropriately chilling sense of threat and menace. Try these examples, then look through some natural history books for more inspiration.

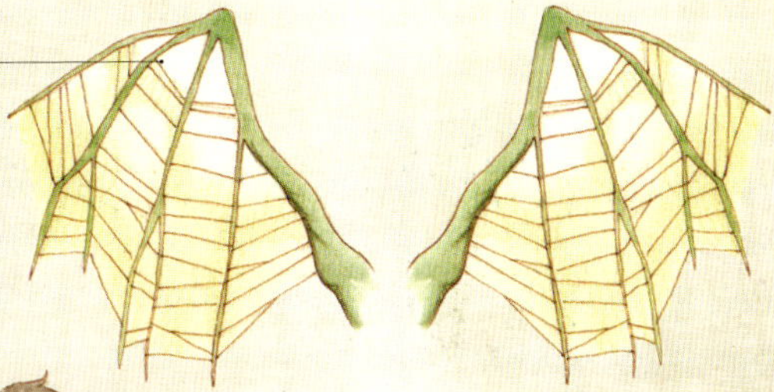

COBWEB WINGS
While not suitable for flight, cobweb wings evoke a creepy sense of terror that fits the disturbing nature of the Gothic Fairy.

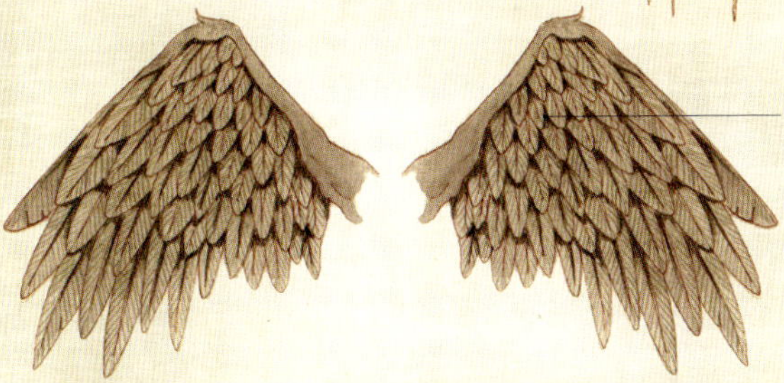

RAVEN WINGS
Glossy black raven-like wings make a menacing statement, very different from the soft feathers of other, gentler birds.

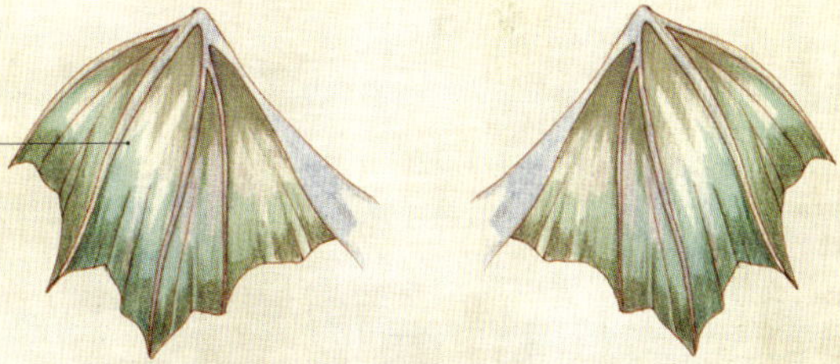

BAT WINGS
Bat wings with their leathery skin stretched between long, claw-like digits instantly evoke all sorts of dark horror stories.

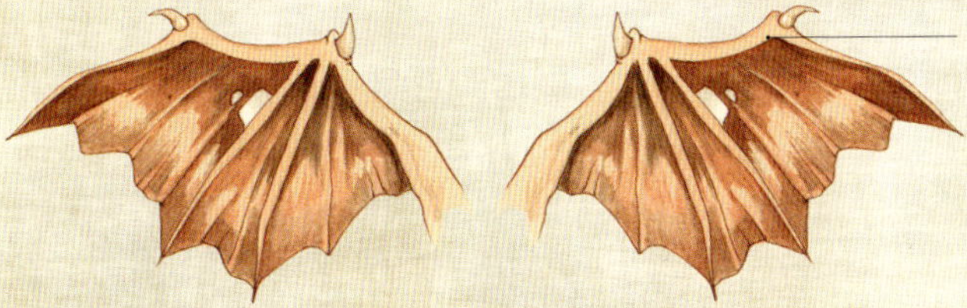

DRAGON WINGS
Dragons are mythical creatures, so you can depict their wings in any way your imagination suggests; perhaps, as here, like larger stronger versions of bat wings.

Tree Fairy

WOODLANDS ARE HOME TO A HOST OF MAGICAL FAIRY FOLK WHO LOOK AFTER THE TREES, PROTECT THEM FROM HARM, AND ENSURE THEIR HEALTH AND FERTILITY.

Character and appearance

The fairy creatures that inhabit woods and forests are similar in nature to the flower fairies. Like them, they are brave, gentle, and benevolent, caring deeply for their trees and the plants and animals that share them. They derive their wisdom and knowledge from the trees and protect them and their habitat at all costs.

Tree fairies can be male or female—like flower fairies, they take their character and appearance from the tree they inhabit. Their clothes echo nature: leaves, blossoms, buds, and fruit all create fairy garments (here, the Oak Tree Fairy wears an acorn-cup cap). Use colors that blend with the surroundings, and remember the importance of body language and facial expression to tell the story. This little character gazes in delight at his acorn, a symbol of nature's cycle.

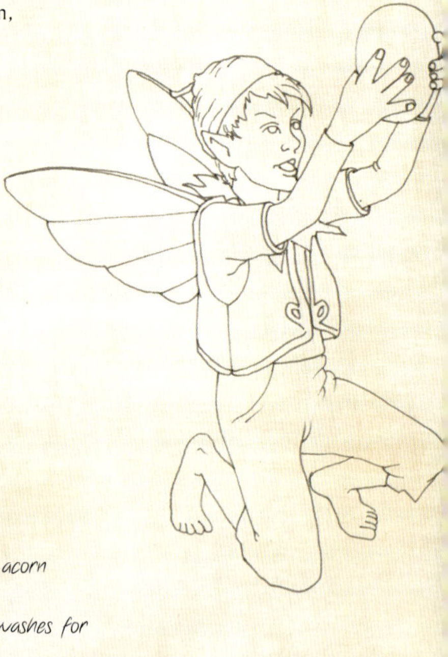

MAIN COLOR PALETTE

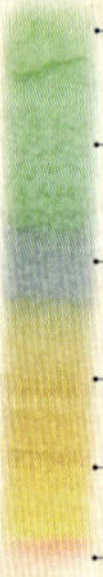

- Yellow-green: sleeves, under-vest, and top of acorn
- Sap green: very pale wash for skin; darker washes for hair, vest, and wing patterns
- Hooker's green: trim on vest and in washes for shading and depth
- Raw umber: for hat and acorn
- Yellow ocher: pants, sleeves, and wings
- Rose madder: for light blush to cheeks and ear tips

Copy it!

Copy or trace the drawing or scan it into your computer. Then color it.

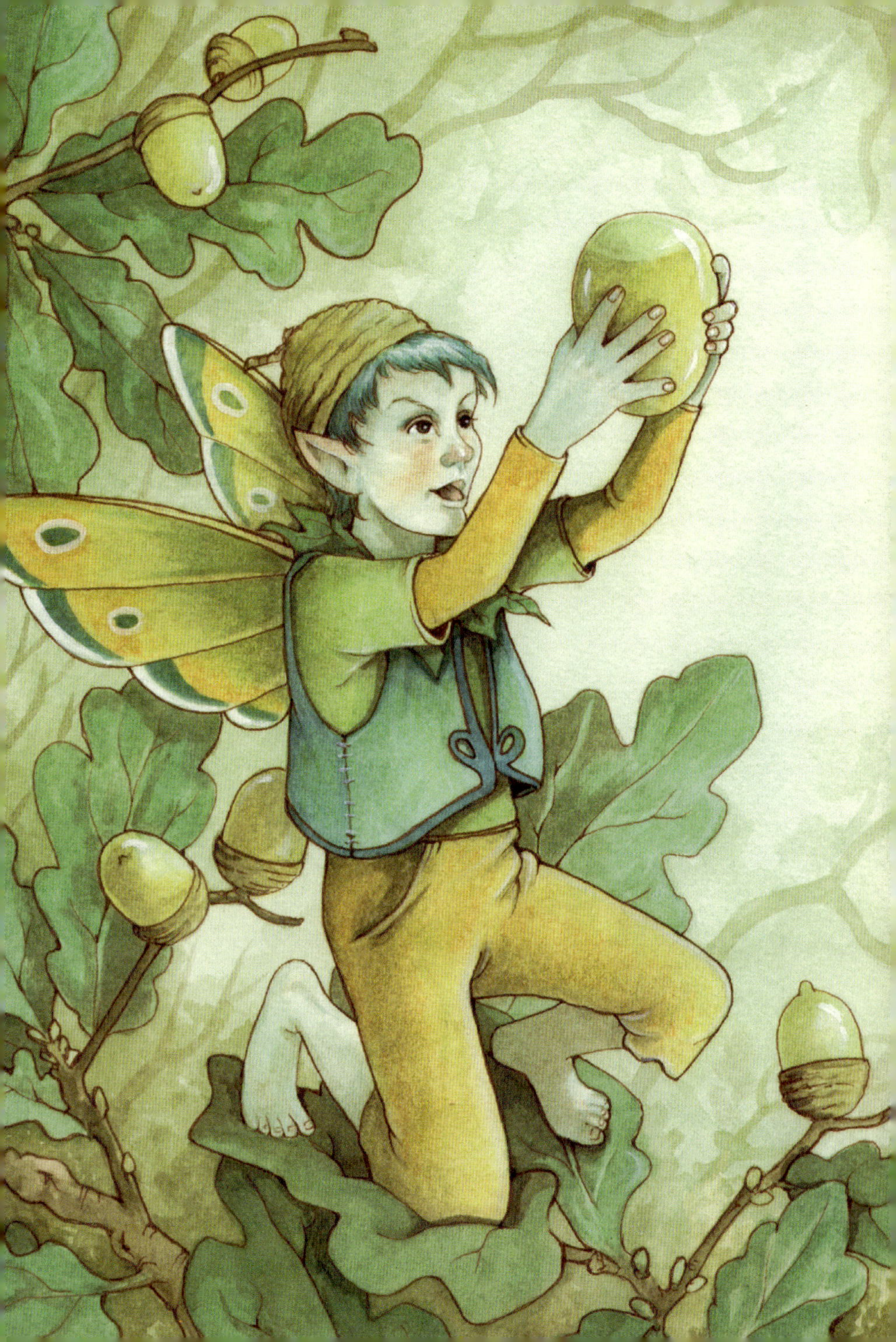

Constructing the figure

A mannequin figure enables you to visualize the positions of the underlying body forms so you can unlock the dynamics of almost any pose. Balance and poise are crucial, even in sitting and kneeling postures like this one—if you don't get this right at the start, your figure will look unstable and unconvincing.

See also: Figure construction basics, page 58.

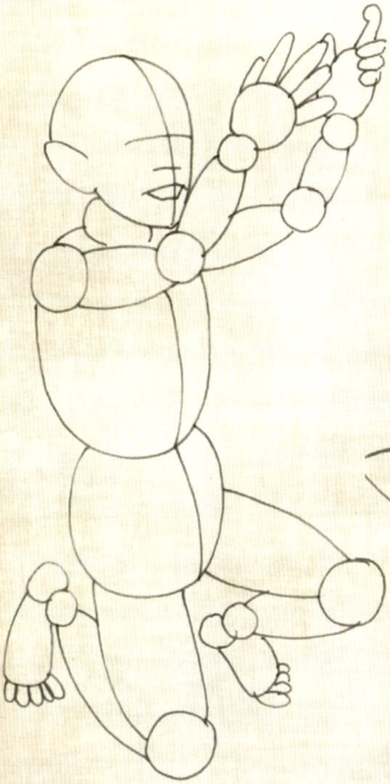

Always start with the basic building blocks to achieve balance and stability. The Oak Tree Fairy's weight is concentrated on one knee, counter-balanced with the other foot.

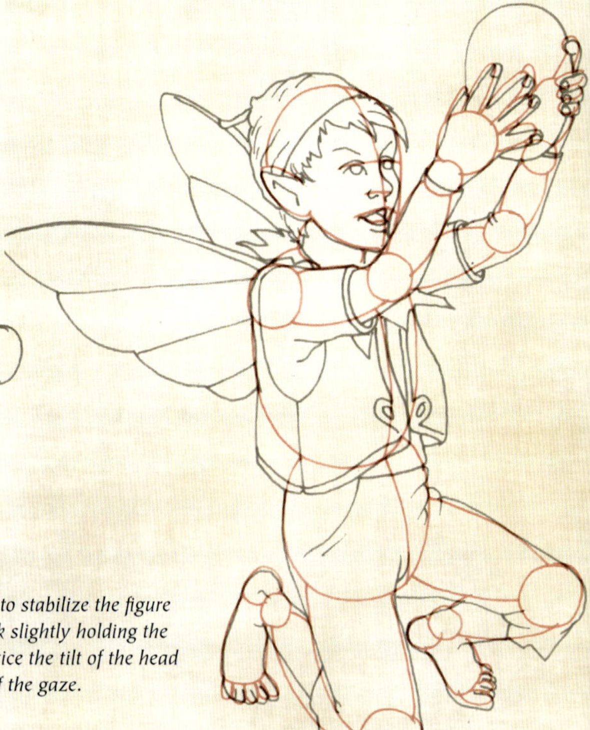

The wings help to stabilize the figure as he leans back slightly holding the acorn aloft. Notice the tilt of the head and the angle of the gaze.

Tree Fairy poses

To give a credible account of your fairy characters, you must first consider their nature and environment. This will help you to visualize their characteristic body language, poses, and activities and give you the narrative for a believable image. Tree Fairies, for example, are typically portrayed with their attention focused on the fruit of their tree, a symbol of fertility and regeneration.

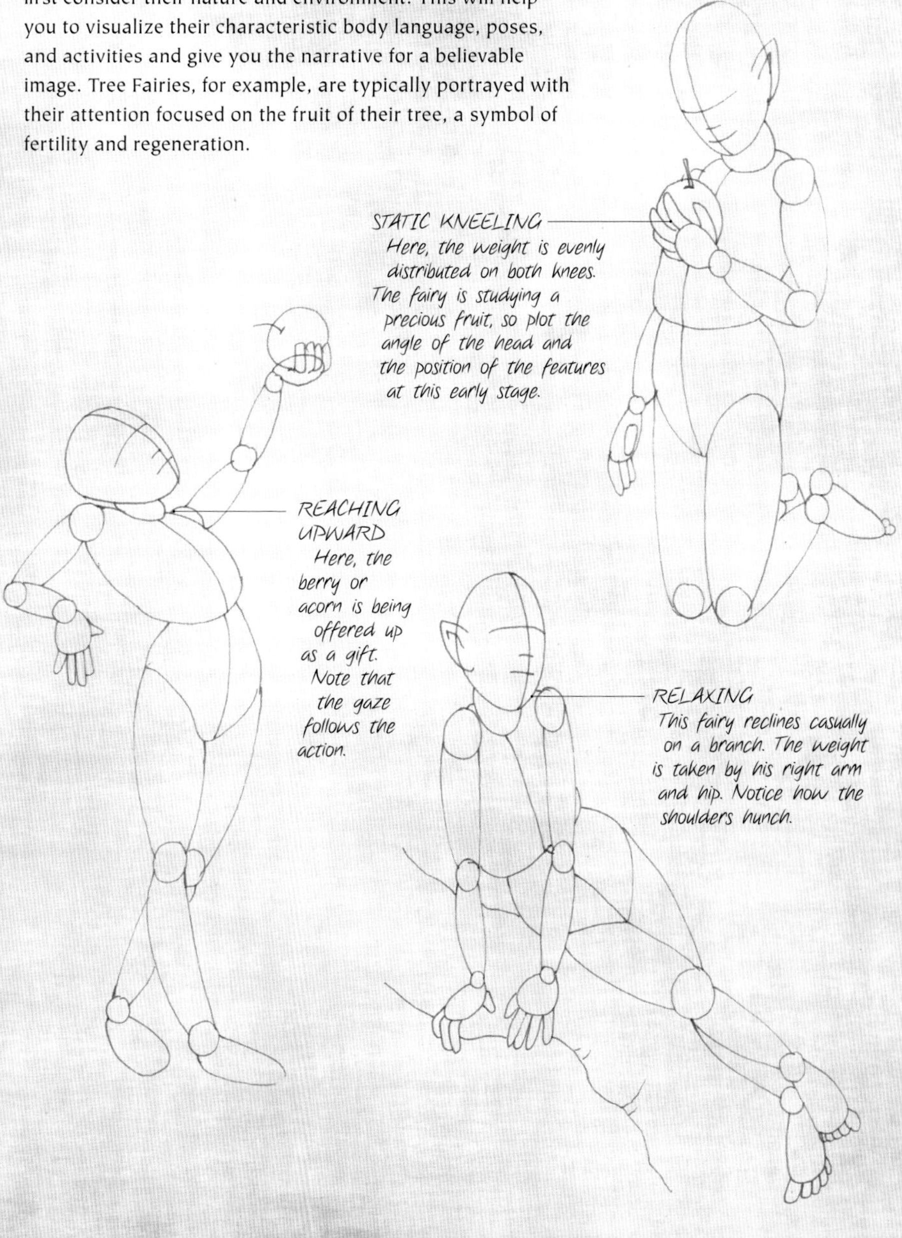

Fairy trees

While every tree has its Guardian Fairy, the flowering and fruiting trees are especially favored homes for these kindly, benign creatures. These include, among others, oak, beech, sycamore, chestnut, hawthorn, and holly. Here is a small selection of favorite trees to start your collection. Make studies from life in your sketchbook, take photographs, or download images from the Internet for instant reference.

BEECH

Beechnuts are a favorite with fairies who use the shells for caps or to collect raindrops. They ripen on the tree in fall, by which time the leaves have turned from bright green to rich, burnished gold to give a sense of season to your image.

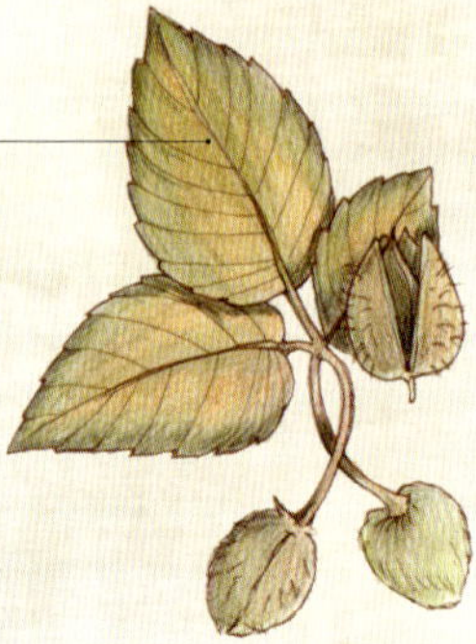

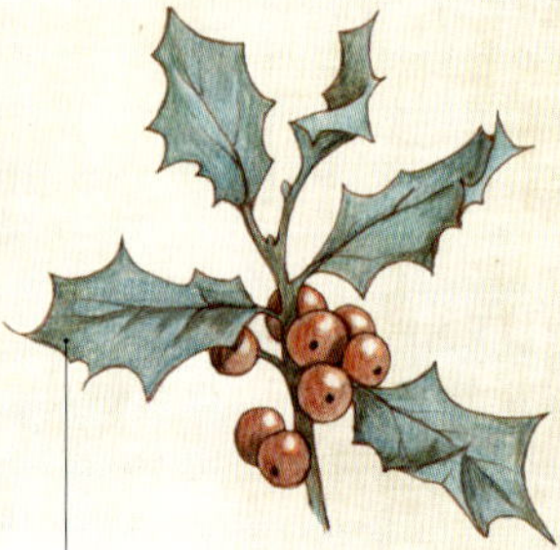

HOLLY

Holly Fairies are winter creatures and their plant is an unmistakable symbol of winter and Christmas. The berries are a deep, rich crimson that sings out from the shiny, prickly, dark green leaves.

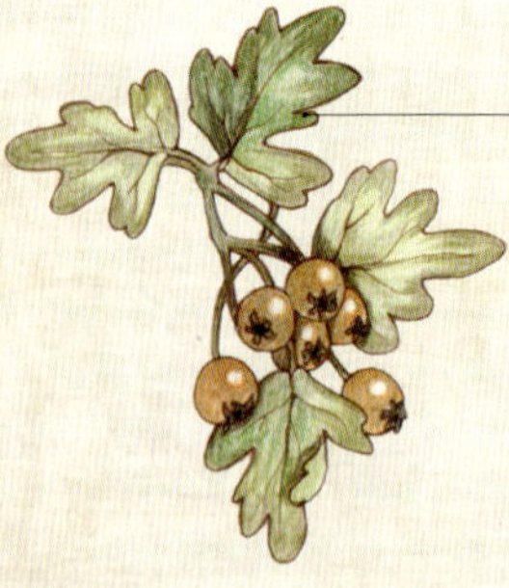

HAWTHORN

The Hawthorn Fairy is guardian of these bright red berries. They make a colorful show against the complementary green of the leaves.

SYCAMORE

The sycamore has large, bright green leaves, and the Sycamore Fairy is often pictured as a little boy with wings fashioned from the distinctive "helicopter" seedpods that children love to play with.

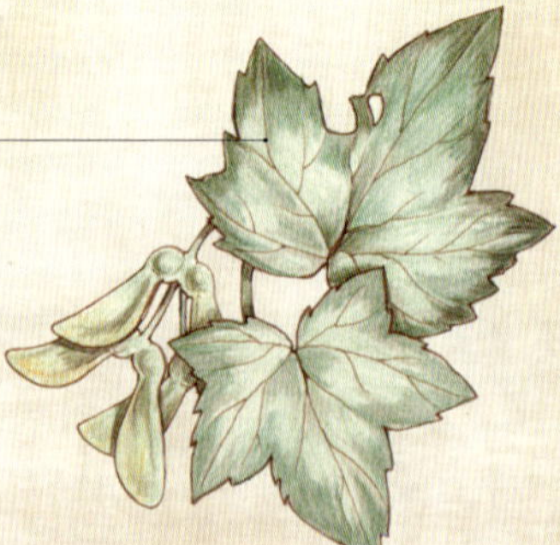

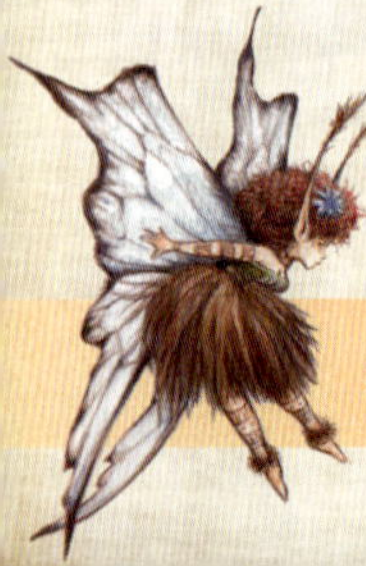

See also: Storytelling, page 34.

Pencil techniques

Pencil work is perfect for recreating natural colors and textures. Try some of the following methods.

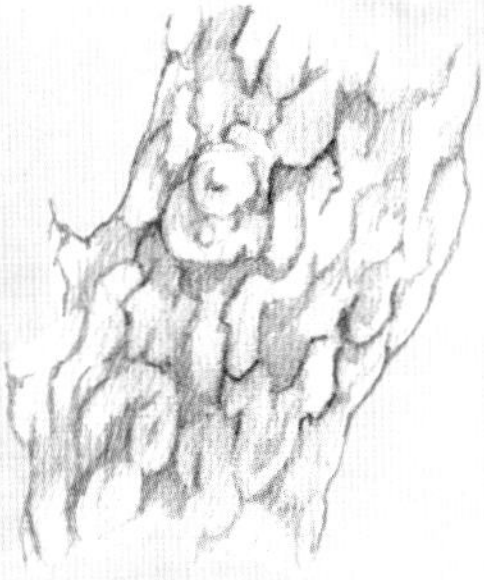

Scales and pits

Using an HB pencil, place shadows between the scales to suggest the scaly effect of the bark. Shadows will appear to protrude from the tree trunk.

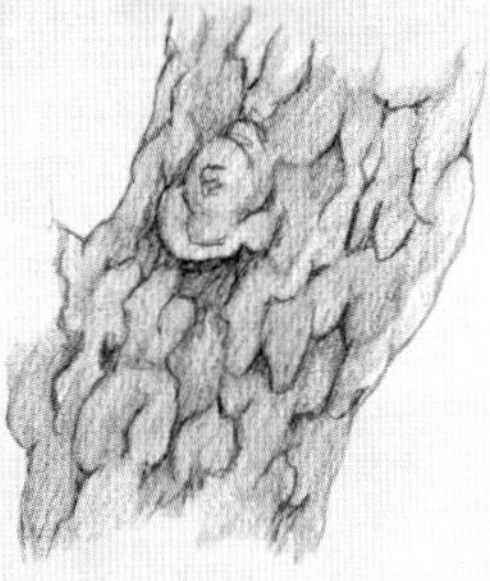

Highlights

Lift the texture of bark further with a little color and more pencil shading. Play with your colored pencils, using ethereal colors reminiscent of fairies.

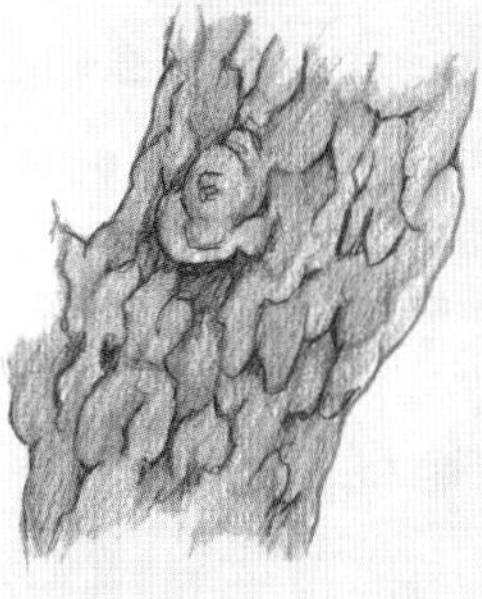

Rough bark

Many tree trunks have a rougher texture and look almost scaly in their appearance.

Pencil on black pastel paper

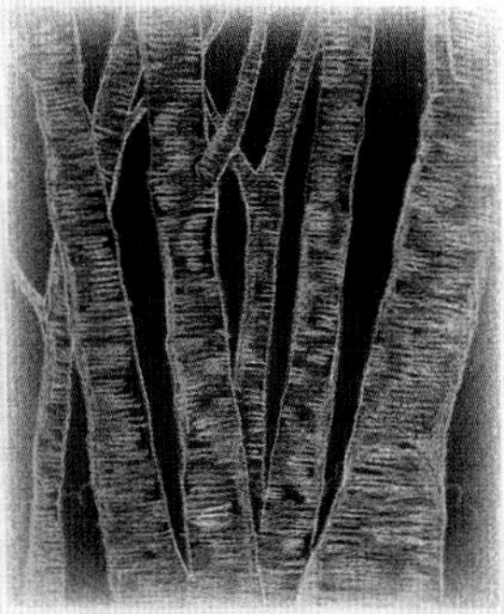

1 Sketch the outline of the trees in bold vertical strokes. Apply a raw umber pencil with horizontal strokes, leaving black to show through.

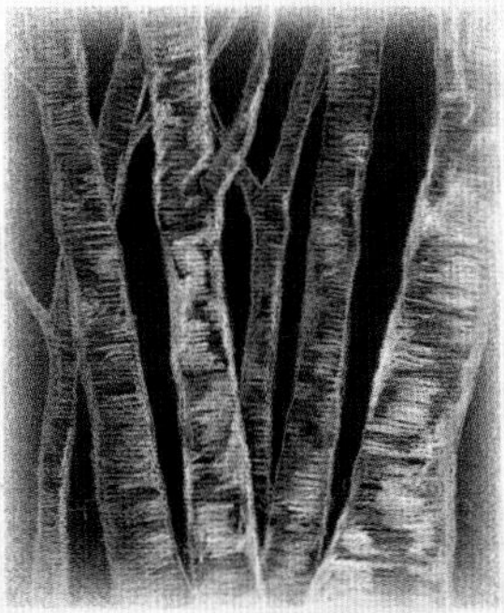

2 Add heavier clumps of white and highlights to the edges of the tree trunks and branches. Don't overdo this—make sure you leave enough of the horizontal strokes showing through.

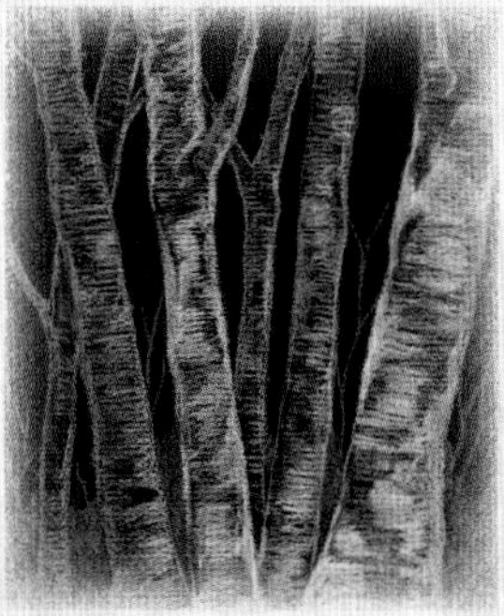

3 Add a few horizontal strokes of raw umber and sepia brown to the trunks as needed. Simply filling in areas between the trees with olive green and viridian creates the optical illusion of foliage growing in the background.

Morgan le Fay

HALF FAIRY AND HALF HUMAN, MORGAN LE FAY IS KNOWN AS A POWERFUL, SEDUCTIVE, AND EVIL SORCERESS AND MISTRESS OF THE DARKEST FAIRY ARTS.

Character and appearance

Morgan le Fay (meaning fairy) appears in the Arthurian legends as Arthur's half-sister. She is a sensual and villainous creature with potent magical skills. An alluring beauty, she uses her powers of seduction to control and destroy her opponents. She is a wonderful character for the fairy artist to visualize—a deliciously dark and bewitching enchantress, intimidating but irresistible.

This image conveys the character of Morgan le Fay instantly. She is a powerfully alluring creature, with a dark heart reflected in her face. The image, including the shadow areas, is drawn first using a black ballpoint pen. This expresses the darkness of the subject, and only minimal color is needed to enhance the drawing—the red and black costume completes the sense of a strong and intimidating creature.

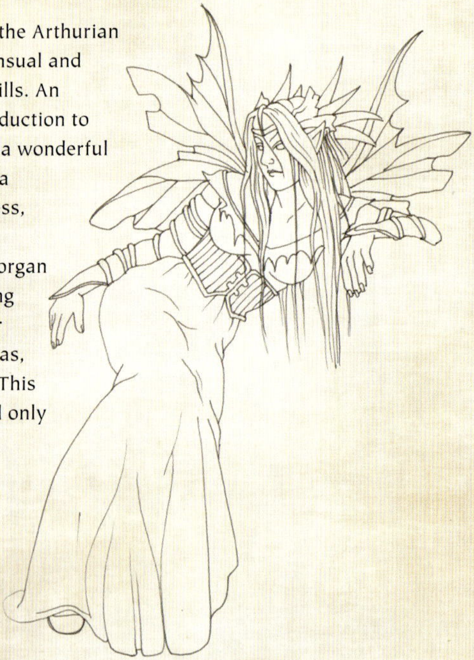

MAIN COLOR PALETTE

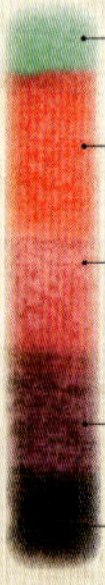

- Cobalt green: very light washes to give skin a green hue
- Scarlet red: corset trim, dress piping, and wing tips
- Alizarin crimson: medium wash on main body of the gown and wings; heavier color added to the bottom of gown and wing tips
- Permanent magenta: sleeves, bodice, and collar trim
- Lamp black: hair, eyes, corset, sleeve stripes, wing patterns

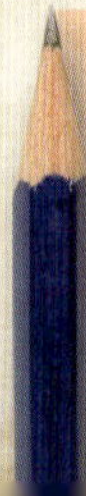

Copy it!

Copy or trace the drawing or scan it into your computer. Then color it.

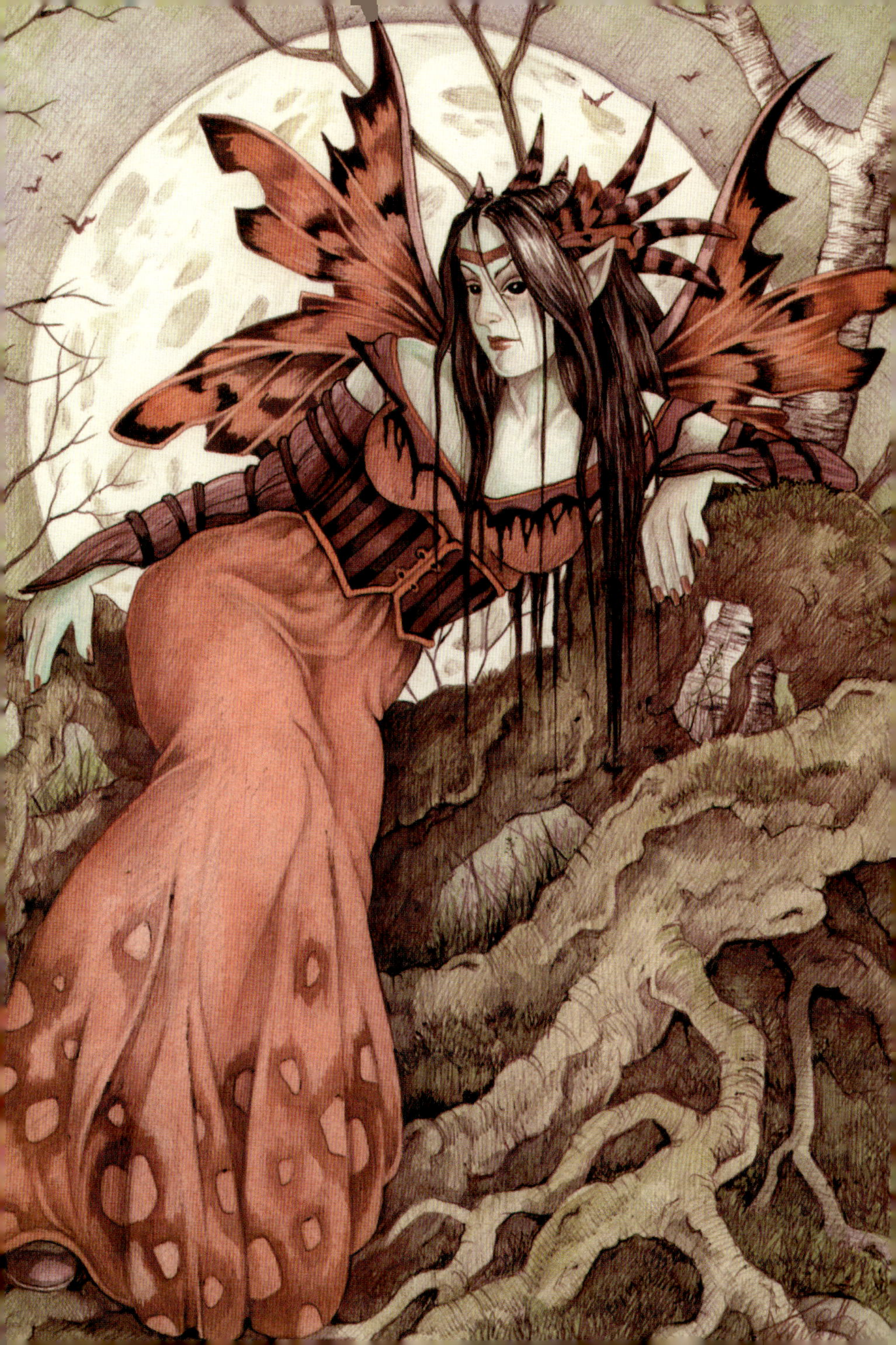

Constructing the figure

Morgan le Fay is a sensual female, and this semi-reclining pose expresses her alluring femininity. She is strong, powerful, and challenging. To draw a reclining pose convincingly, look for the main weight-bearing points—in this case, the left hip and arm. Notice the angles of the torso and legs and the tilt of the head that counterbalances the angle of the upper body.

See also: Figure construction basics, page 58.

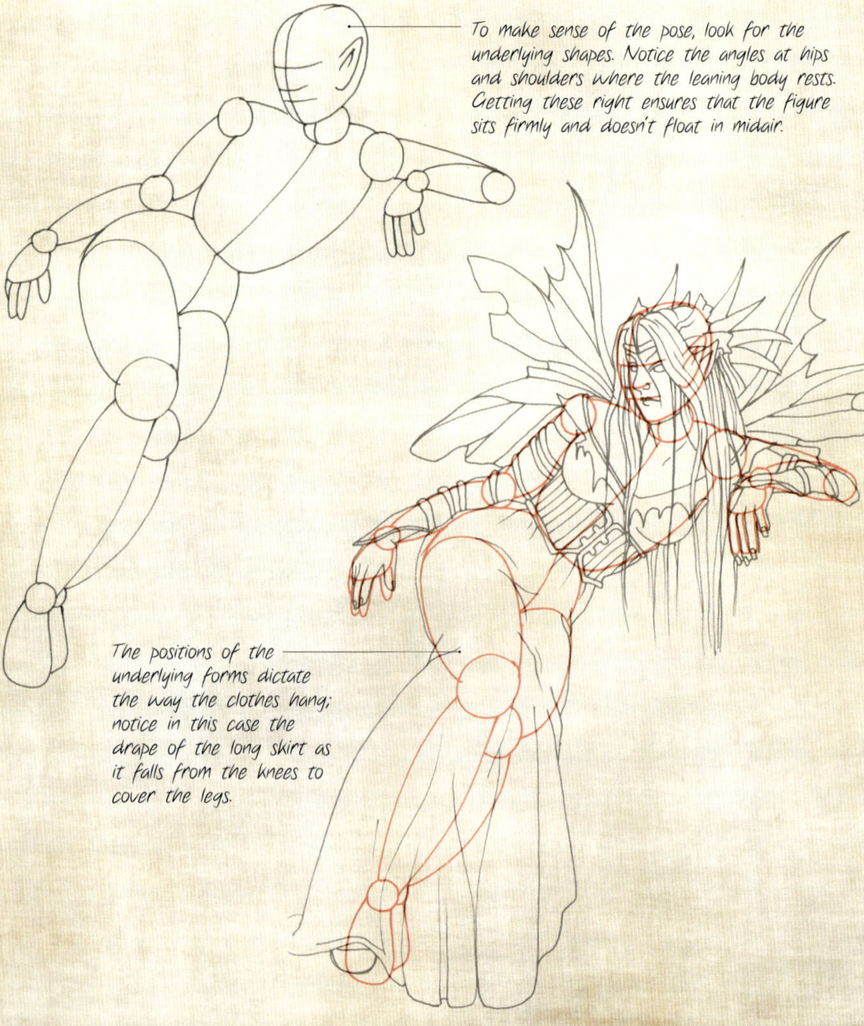

Morgan le Fay poses

The personality of your characters will dictate the poses they adopt. Morgan le Fay is formidable and commanding, sensual and seductive, so go for strong, majestic, and arrogant stances that project these aspects of her nature. These three poses are constructed from basic geometric forms—imagine them "fleshed out" and clothed.

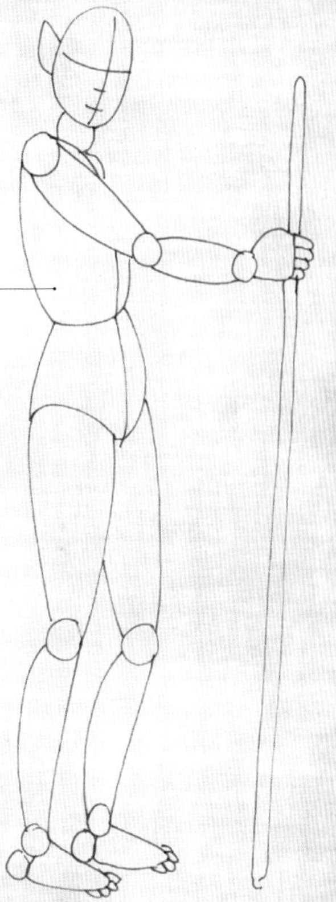

COMMANDING
Here, she stands with her magic staff, looking challengingly over her shoulder with a coy tilt of the head.

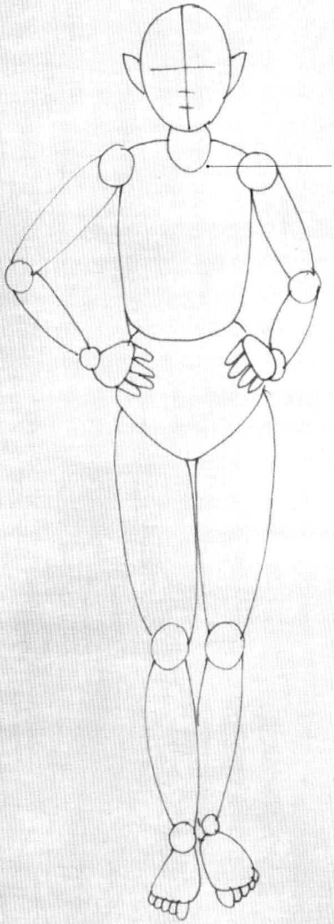

CHALLENGING
Standing front view, hands on hips, she has an arrogant air of bold confrontation.

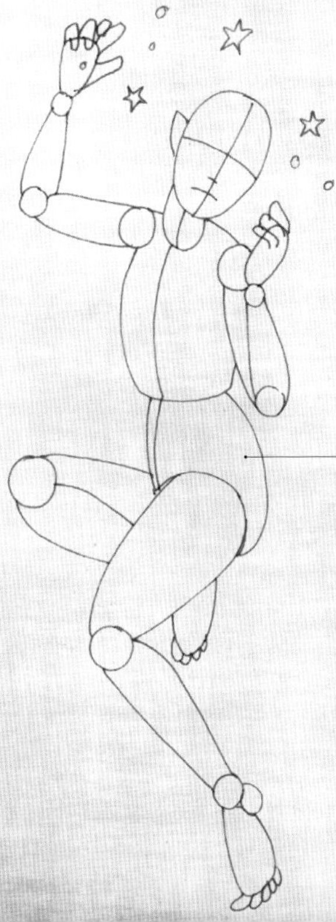

ALLURING
Here, she sits with her arms raised as she casts spells. This is a more delicate, feminine posture than the featured pose.

Spell-casting equipment

Morgan le Fay is one of the most powerful characters of legend and fairy tale, a highly accomplished sorceress with a malevolent personality. To add telling detail to a painting of this dark character, include items of spell-casting paraphernalia that she would use to make her evil magic.

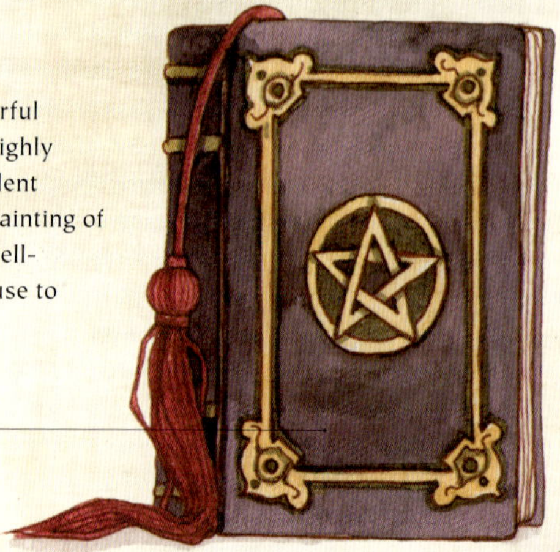

An ancient book of spells with a magic pentagram would hold all sorts of dark secrets.

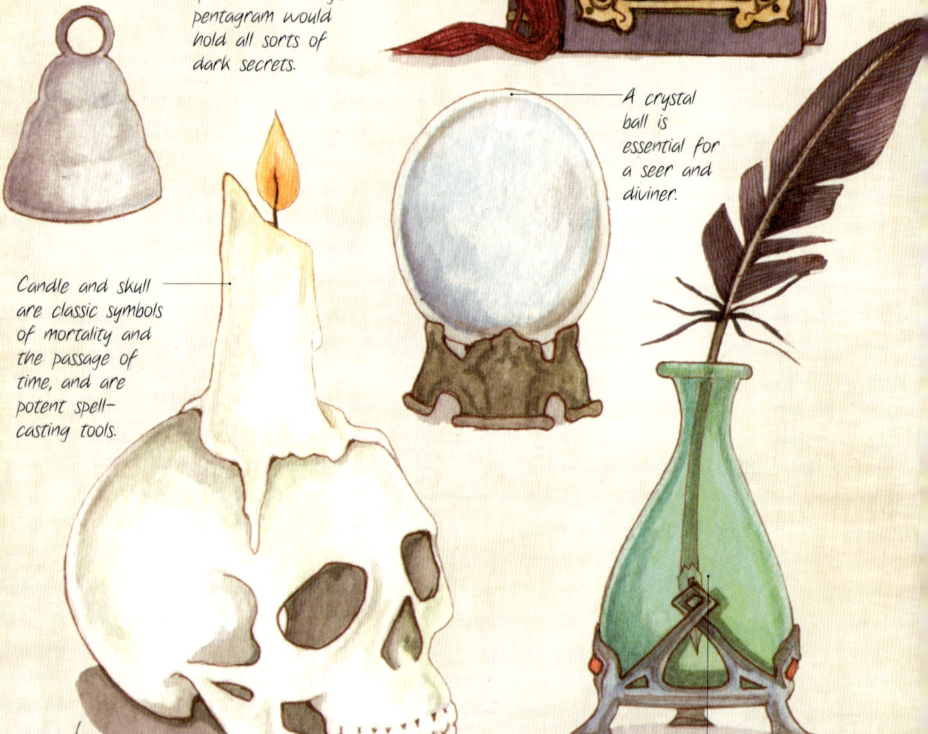

A crystal ball is essential for a seer and diviner.

Candle and skull are classic symbols of mortality and the passage of time, and are potent spell-casting tools.

A quill pen writes spells with poison ink from a jewel-encrusted bottle.

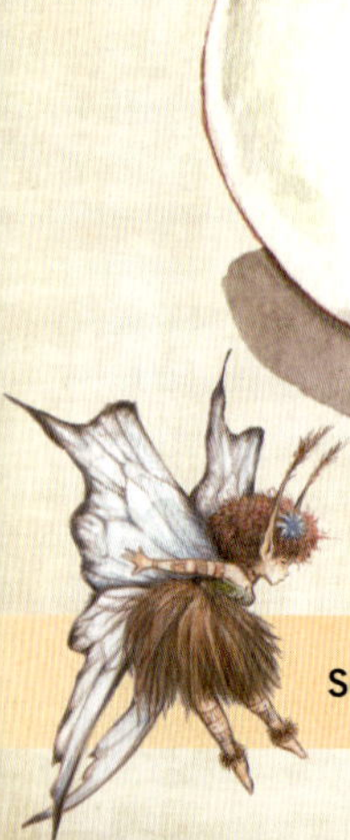

See also: Fairy accessories, page 80.

Eye variations

If eyes are the windows to the soul, then Morgan le Fay must have eyes that reflect her dark personality. Take ideas from animals, especially those that have a sinister or fierce reputation such as the wolf or cat. Experiment with unusual colors and shapes—elongated, oval shapes have a more evil appearance. Here are a few ideas.

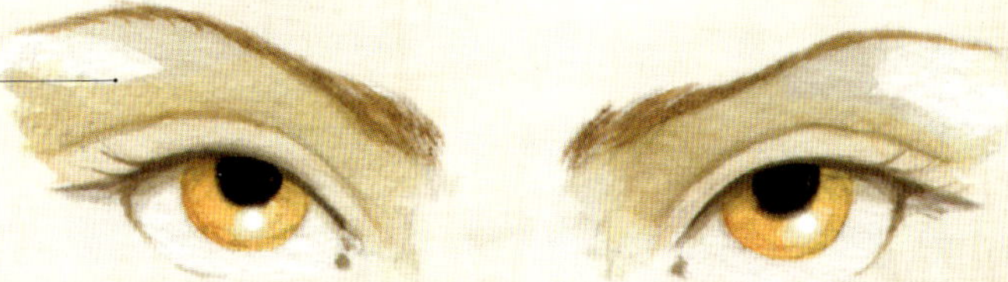

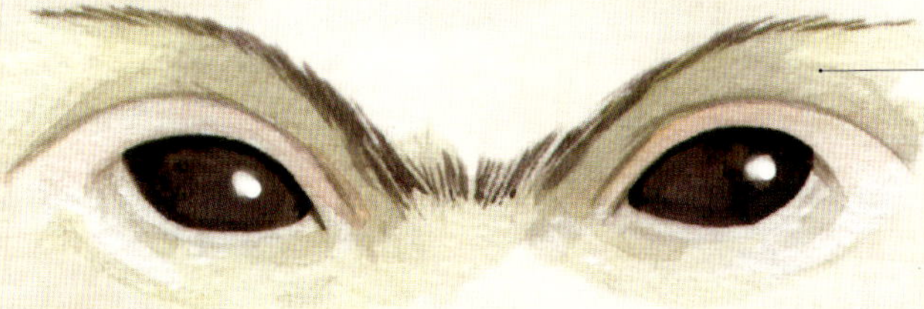

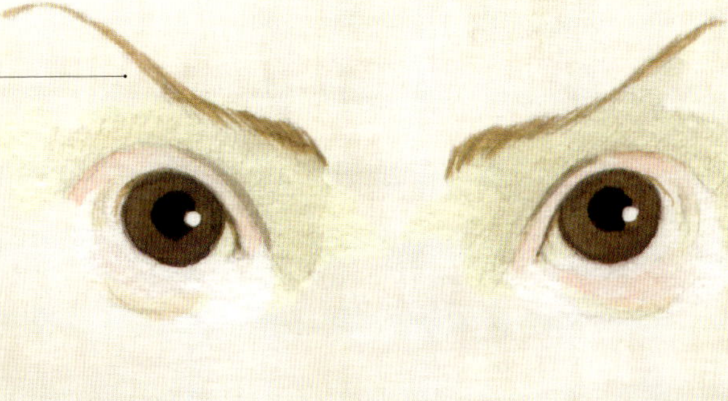

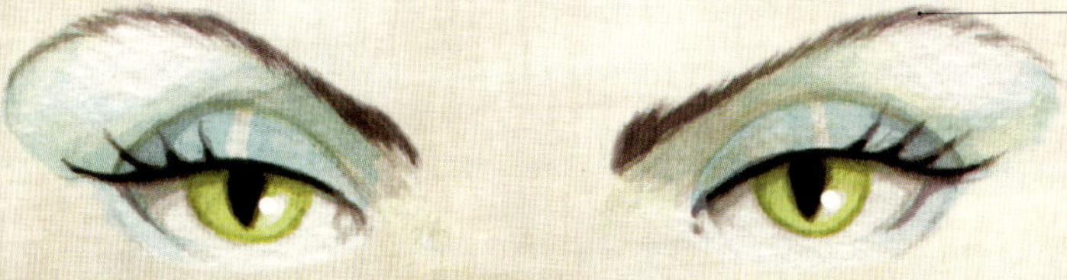

Goblin

MEAN, GREEDY, BAD-TEMPERED, AND SELF-SERVING, GOBLINS ARE AMONG THE MORE EVIL ELEMENTS IN FAIRYLAND AND WILL STOP AT NOTHING TO ACHIEVE THEIR SELFISH ENDS.

Character and appearance

Goblins are cunning, selfish, and notoriously disloyal. They use any devious method to cheat their adversaries, and delight in the suffering they cause. They are cowardly, preferring the secrecy of darkness, but fight savagely to the death if cornered. They feed on dead carcasses, sometimes wearing red caps stained with the blood of their victims.

Goblins are depicted as grotesquely ugly characters, often, as shown, with green skin to denote their slimy nature. Though not human, they walk upright. This nasty creature is typically thin-limbed and misshapen, with unmistakably evil intent in his eyes. Light watercolor washes add subtle hints of tone to the sepia underdrawing and create a brooding image that befits the evil character skulking in the shadows.

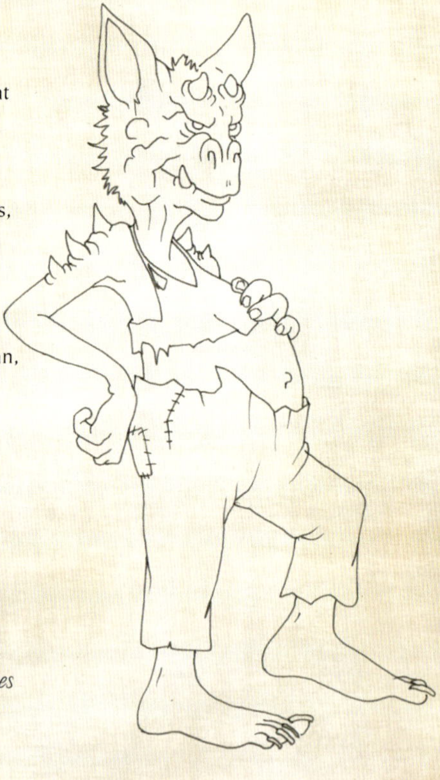

MAIN COLOR PALETTE

Cadmium red: light washes over clothing; highlights added to the dry green washes on skin

Lamp black: for shadows and patches on pants

Cobalt green: used in thin washes to add green hue to skin

Sap green: background wash

Copy it!

Copy or trace the drawing or scan it into your computer. Then color it.

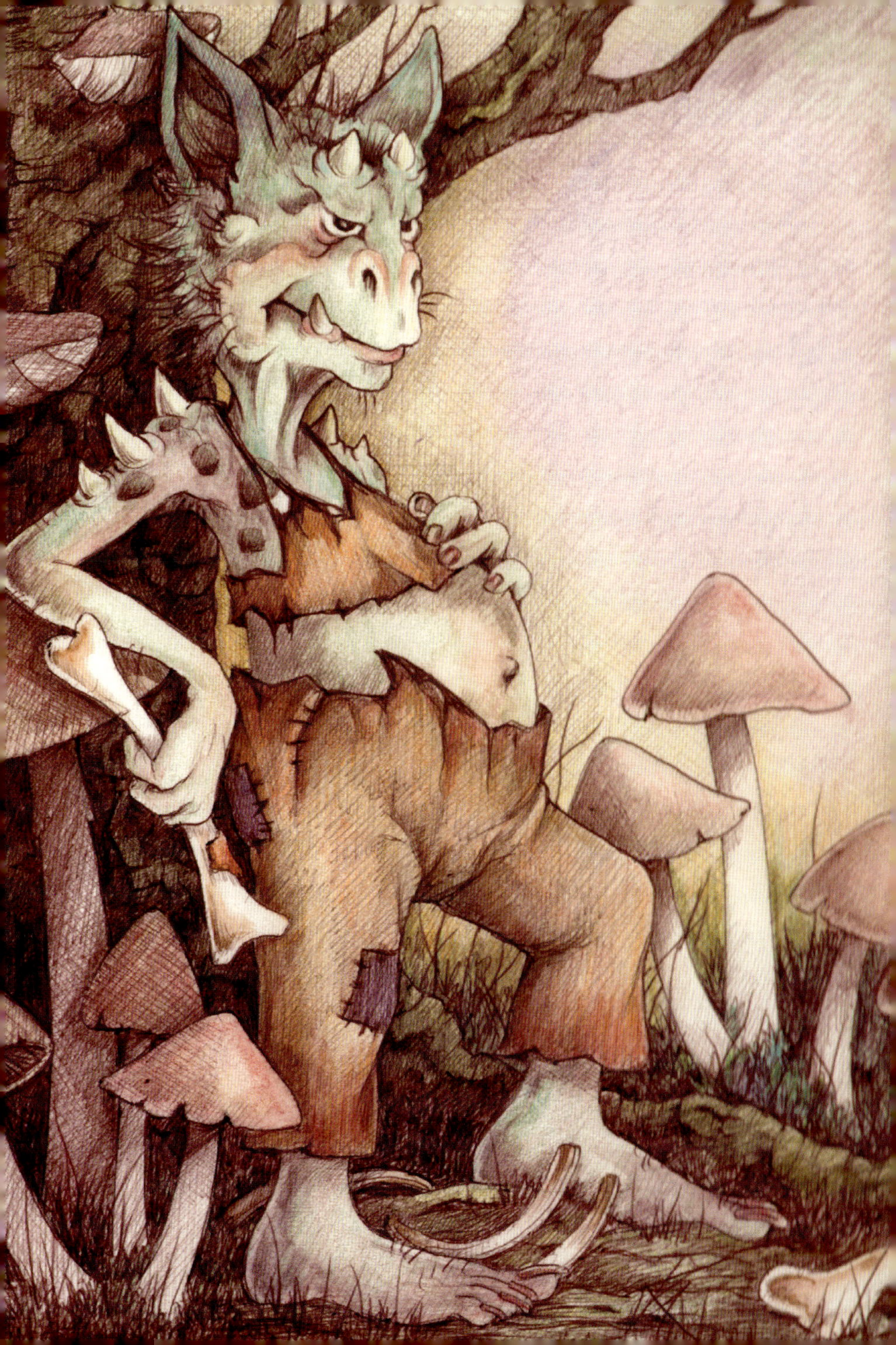

Constructing the figure

Take a slightly different approach here. Start with the same basic underlying shape technique to help you construct a firm and balanced figure. However, while Goblins have the human attribute of walking upright, there's no need to consider proportions in the same way as with a normal human figure. Distortion and exaggeration will help you to convey the inherent evil of the Goblin character.

See also: Figure construction basics, page 58.

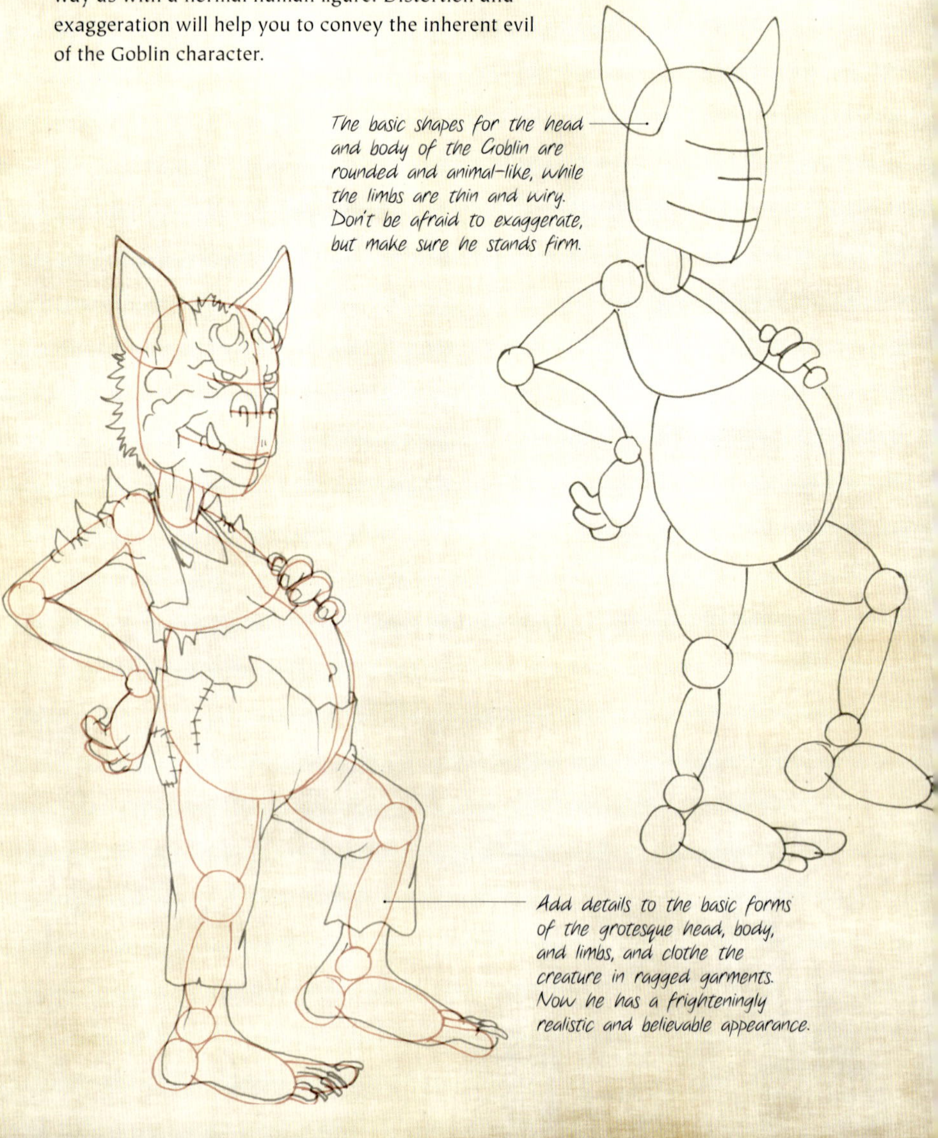

Creating character

When creating Goblin characters, you can ignore the conventional rules of life drawing and use your imagination. These nasty creatures are generally portrayed as ugly hybrids, so you can have great fun with their heads and faces as well as their bodies, combining animal and human features to really disturbing effect—the possibilities are endless.

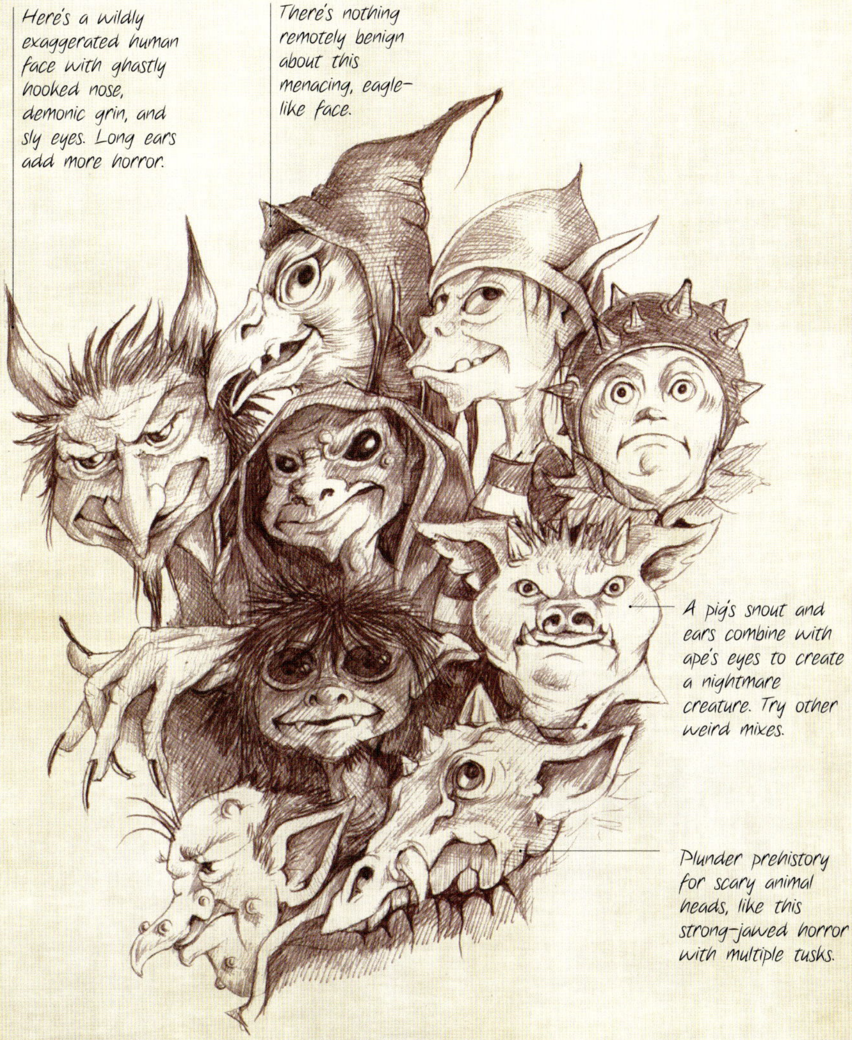

Hand and feet construction

A Goblin's hands and feet are often a mixture of human hands and animal paws. If you reduce the number of digits and play around with proportions, you'll find lots of ways to express the unpleasant nature of your Goblin. Look to nature for inspiration, and use your sketchbook to experiment.

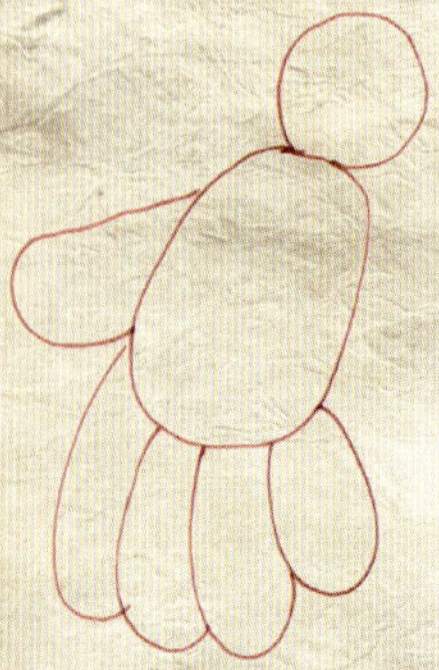

1 Start with the basic shapes of a human hand, but make the digits shorter and fatter, and the palm more rounded.

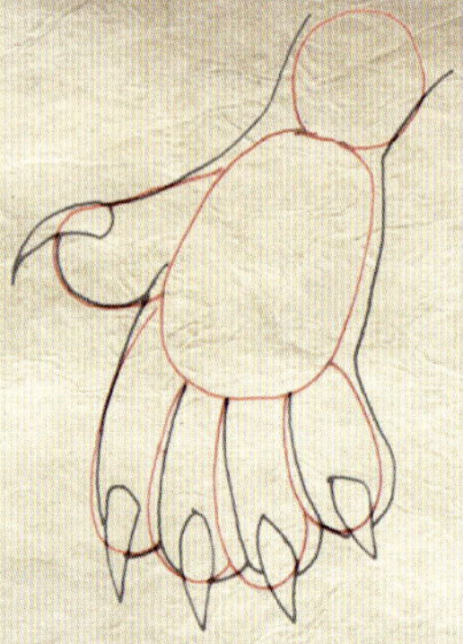

2 Refine the shapes to join fingers to palm, and add long animal claws.

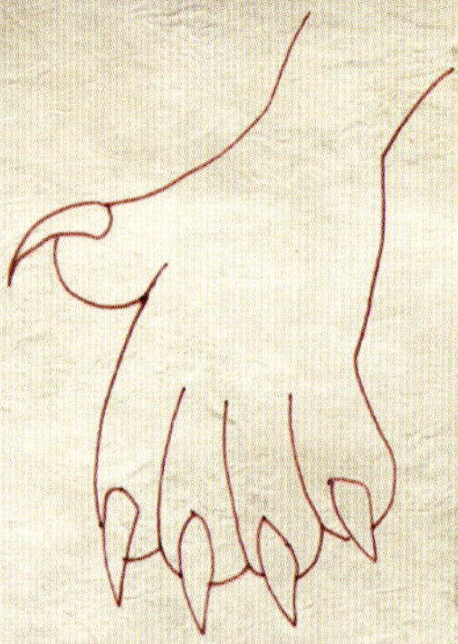

3 Erase the basic shapes, leaving an animal-like paw—only the thumb suggests a vaguely human connection.

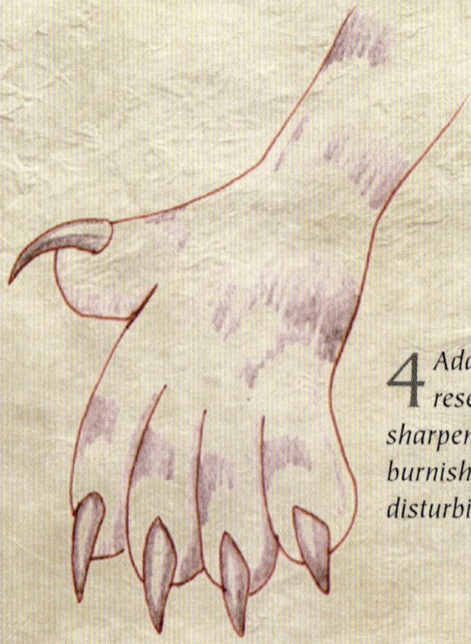

4 Add shading—you can make it resemble tufts of hair—and sharpen the evil claws to a burnished steely sheen for a disturbing sense of the abnormal.

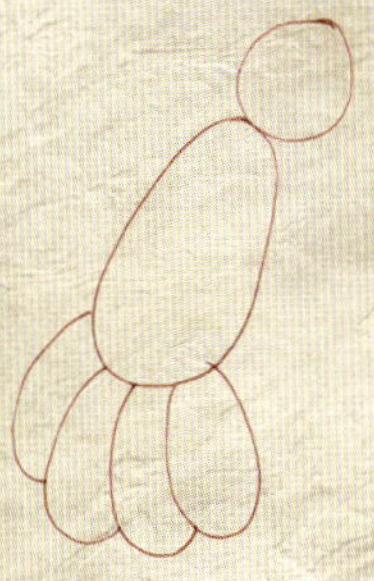

1 Draw an elongated humanoid heel and foot with large toes splayed out at the end. Note that having only four digits adds to the weirdness.

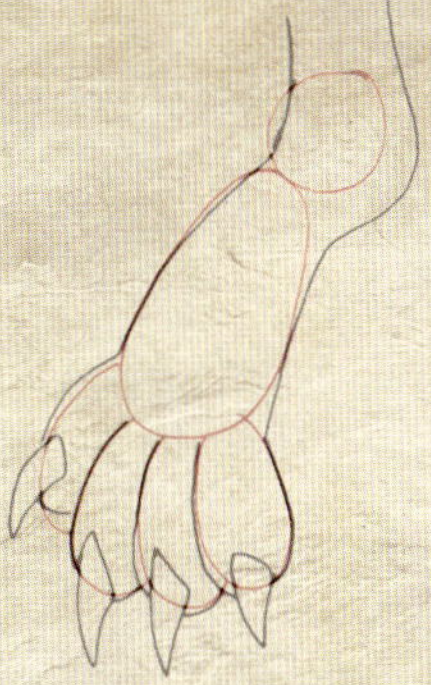

2 Refine the curved outline of the foot and toes, and represent the nails as long, sharp animal claws.

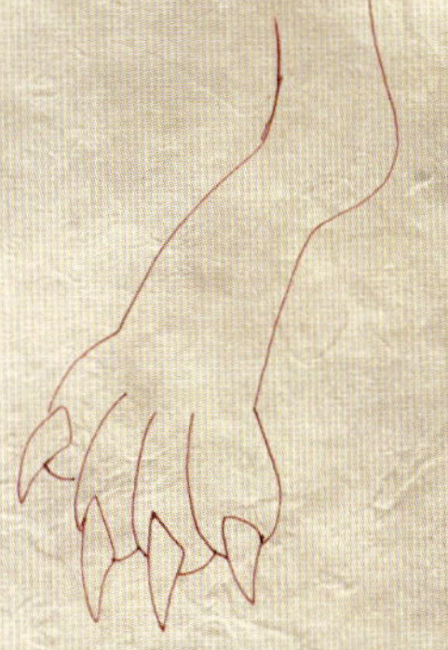

3 Remove the outlines of the underlying basic shapes to reveal a disturbing foot, half human, half animal.

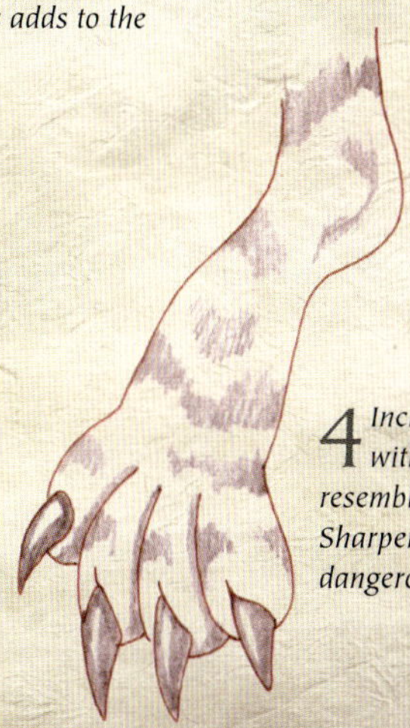

4 Increase the animal look with striped shading that resembles fur markings. Sharpen and shine the nasty, dangerous claws.

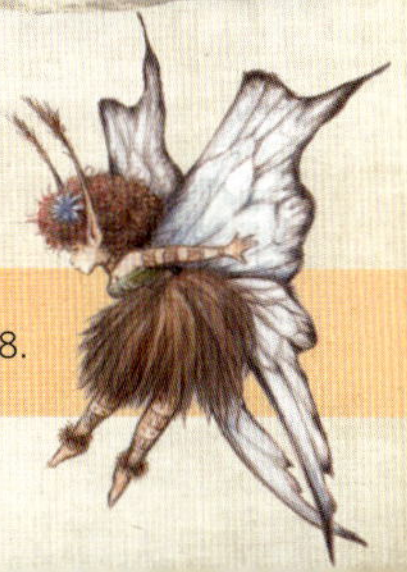

See also: Constructing hands and feet, page 68.

Butterfly Fairy

BUTTERFLY FAIRIES ARE FLIGHTY, GENTLE, AND SHY, AND LOOK SO MUCH LIKE ACTUAL BUTTERFLIES THAT THEY CAN BE DIFFICULT TO SPOT AS THEY FLIT FROM FLOWER TO FLOWER.

Character and appearance

Butterfly Fairies live in gardens and hedgerows where they enjoy visiting the myriad of colorful flowers. However, since they take on the appearance of wild butterflies with their distinctive and brightly colored wings, they can flutter at will among the different blooms without being detected.

This image is created with a sensitive pen outline and colored with layers of translucent watercolor washes. The wings imitate the vivid peacock butterfly—notice how the vibrant scarlet stands out boldly against the complementary green of the leaves. Delicate linear brush strokes on the fairy's bodice imitate the downy covering of a butterfly's body, while opaque white gouache is added over dry washes to pick out the wing markings and to paint the daisy petals.

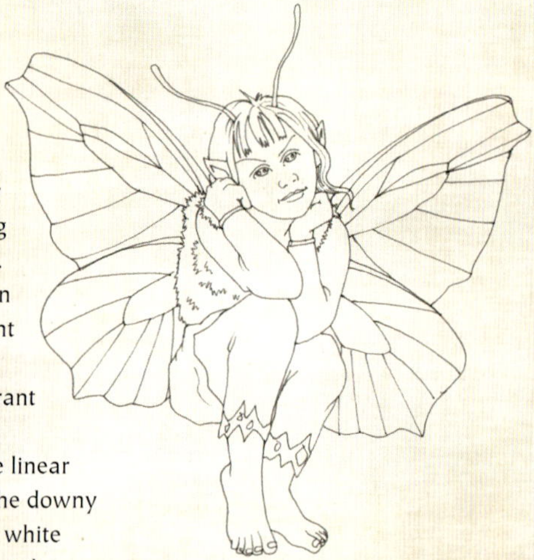

MAIN COLOR PALETTE

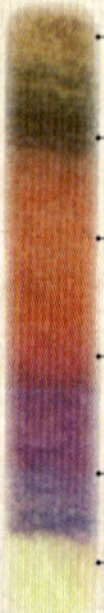

- Raw umber: thin washes for skin; darker mix for hair and clothing
- Sepia: bodice and dark parts of wings
- Vermilion: main part of wings
- Alizarin crimson: peacock eyes on wing tips
- Mauve and ultramarine: peacock eyes on wings
- Cadmium yellow: spots on wing edges; daisy flower centers
- Opaque white gouache (not shown): for peacock eyes and flower petals

Copy it!

Copy or trace the drawing or scan it into your computer. Then color it.

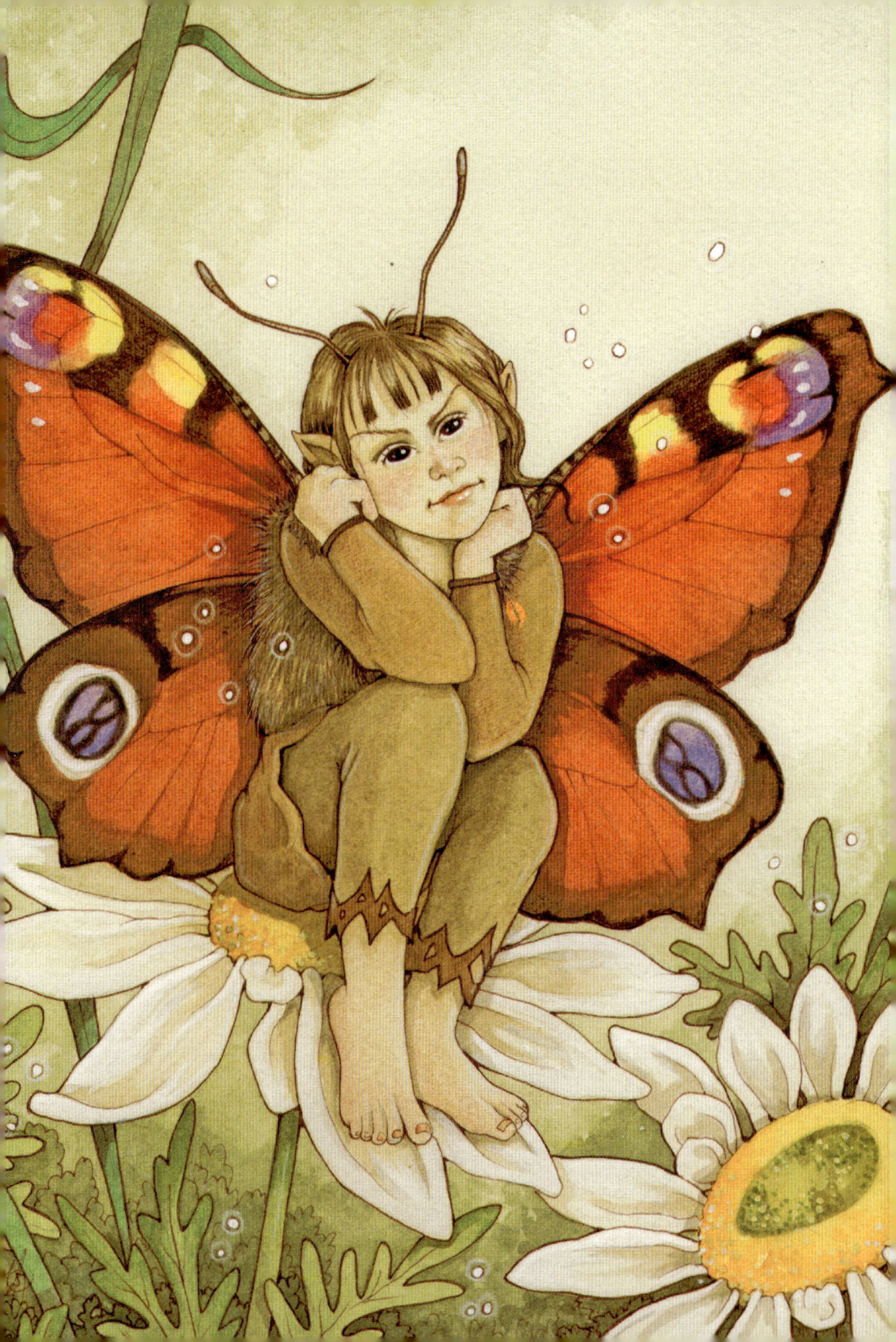

Constructing the figure

The Butterfly Fairy on page 211 is captured in a rare pensive moment, poised lightly on a daisy head. She might be startled into flight at any moment, but for the moment she is still. In this position her body is completely folded up and would be hard to draw convincingly without the basic shape approach.

See also: Figure construction basics, page 58.

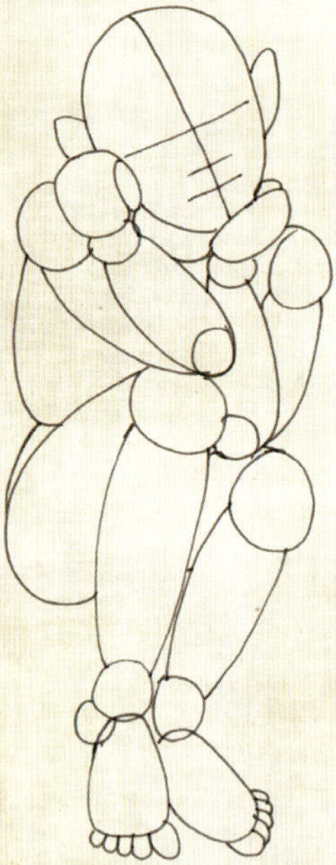

This collection of shapes clearly shows how the figure is composed using simple shapes based on a mannequin model. This provides a strong "scaffolding" on which to draw a convincing and well-balanced finished figure.

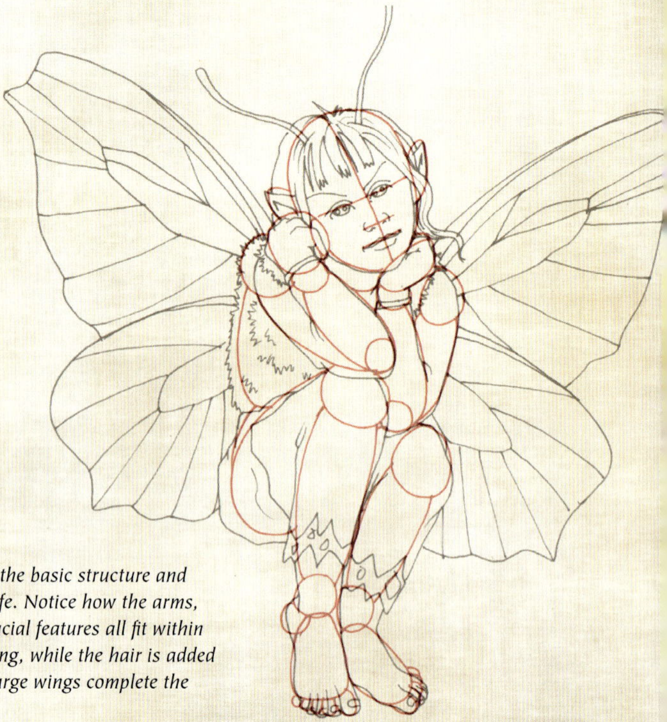

Add details to flesh out the basic structure and bring the character to life. Notice how the arms, hands, legs, feet, and facial features all fit within the underlying scaffolding, while the hair is added onto the head shape. Large wings complete the Butterfly Fairy.

Butterfly Fairy poses

Like their real counterparts, Butterfly Fairies are constantly on the move, flitting from place to place. They are seldom still for long, only pausing to sun themselves for a second or two. Always try to convey this character's alertness and sense of imminent movement in your drawing—use an artist's mannequin to experiment with different poses.

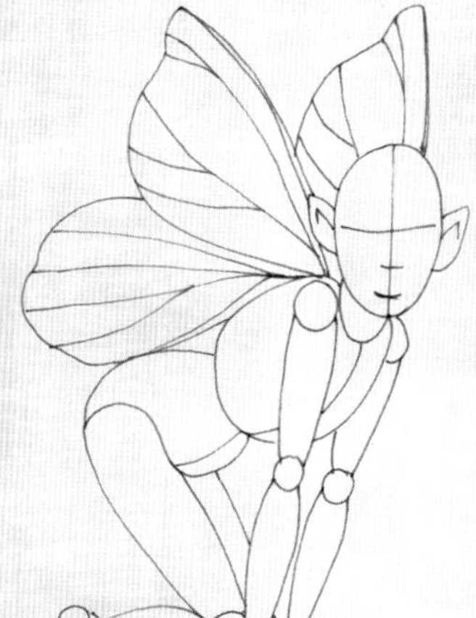

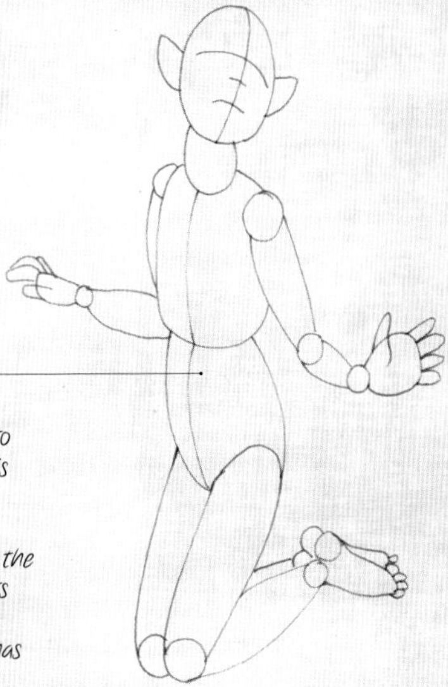

STARTLED
This fairy is taken by surprise and startled into action. The arm position is expressive, the bent legs suggest she has shot quickly into the air, and the tilt of the head suggests there is something over her left shoulder that has made her nervous.

WATCHFUL
The fairy perches watchfully on a flowerhead, balancing equally on both knees, and takes the weight of her upper body on her arms and hands. Notice how the shoulders hunch as she does so.

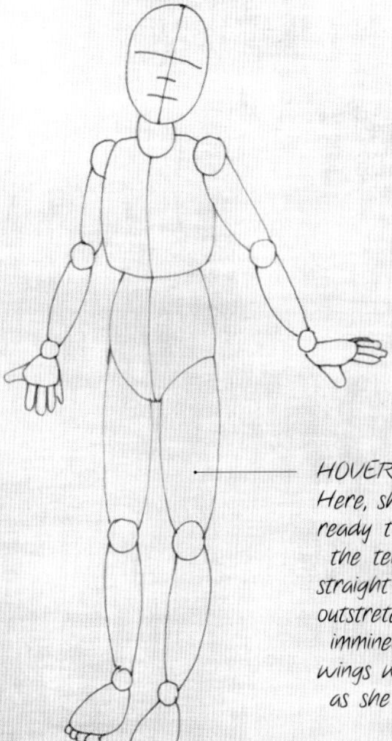

HOVERING
Here, she is poised in midair, ready to take flight. Notice the tension in the pose; straight legs and stiffly outstretched arms suggest imminent departure. Her wings will be beating rapidly as she hovers.

Drawing inspiration from nature

A quick look at the breathtaking variety of butterflies and moths will inspire you with plenty of ideas for colorful wings of all shapes, sizes, and patterns.

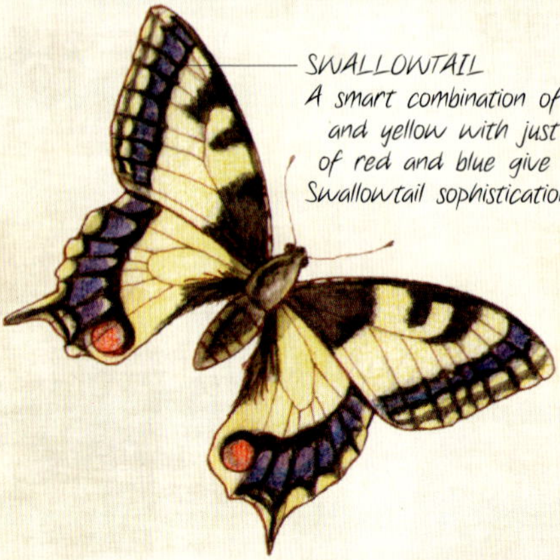

SWALLOWTAIL
A smart combination of black and yellow with just a touch of red and blue give the Swallowtail sophistication.

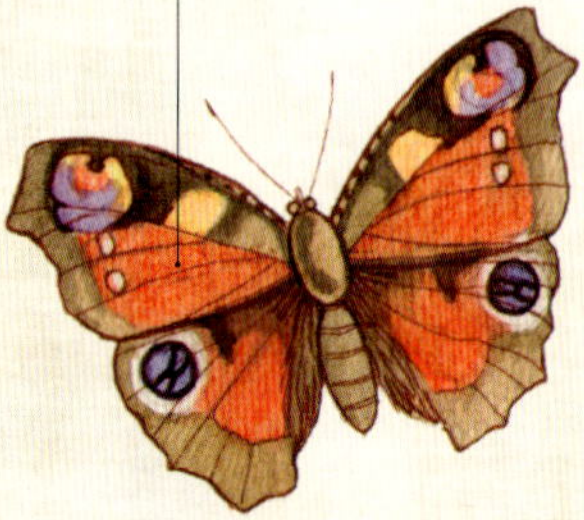

PEACOCK
The Peacock butterfly is as showy and colorful as the bird it's named after, with its distinctive eye pattern on the wings.

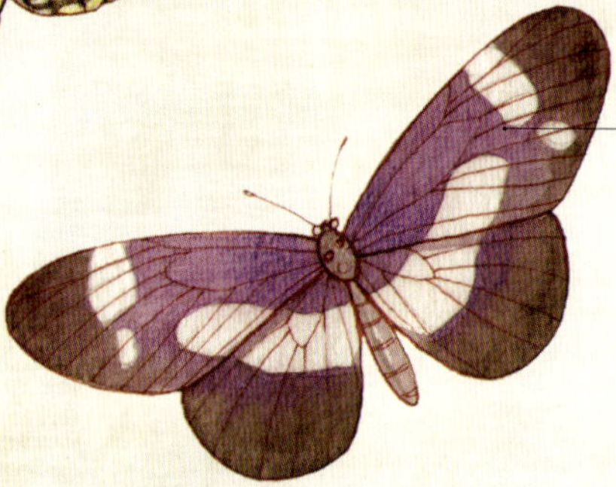

PURPLE EMPEROR
Large, wide wings colored a regal purple give an appropriate sense of majesty to the Purple Emperor.

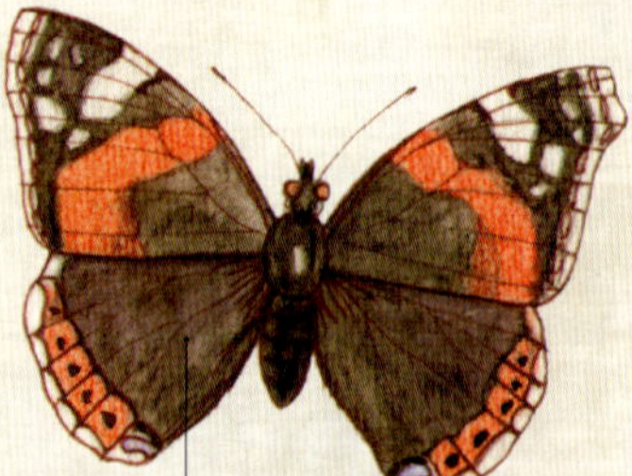

RED ADMIRAL
The eye-catching Red Admiral butterfly demands to be noticed in its red, black, and white uniform and complex markings.

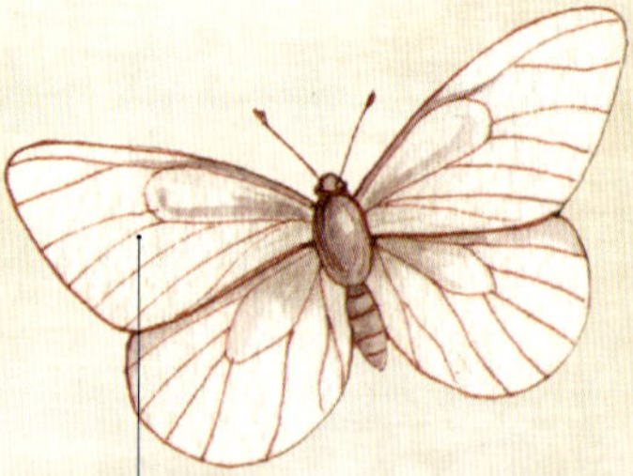

MARBLED WHITE
Though not colorful, the Marbled White butterfly is delicate and dainty, clothed all in white, and is easily spotted fluttering among green leaves.

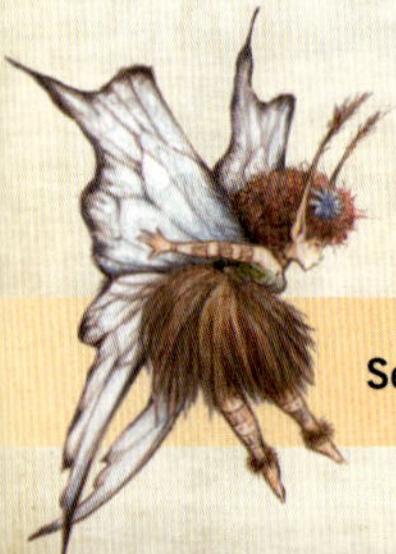

See also: Fairy wings, page 70.

Wing shapes

They may be impressive, beautifully rendered, and majestic, but excessively large, ornate wings may dwarf your fairy character and compromise credibility. However, make sure that you draw wings that are large enough to carry the weight of your Butterfly Fairy as she swoops and dives in the sky.

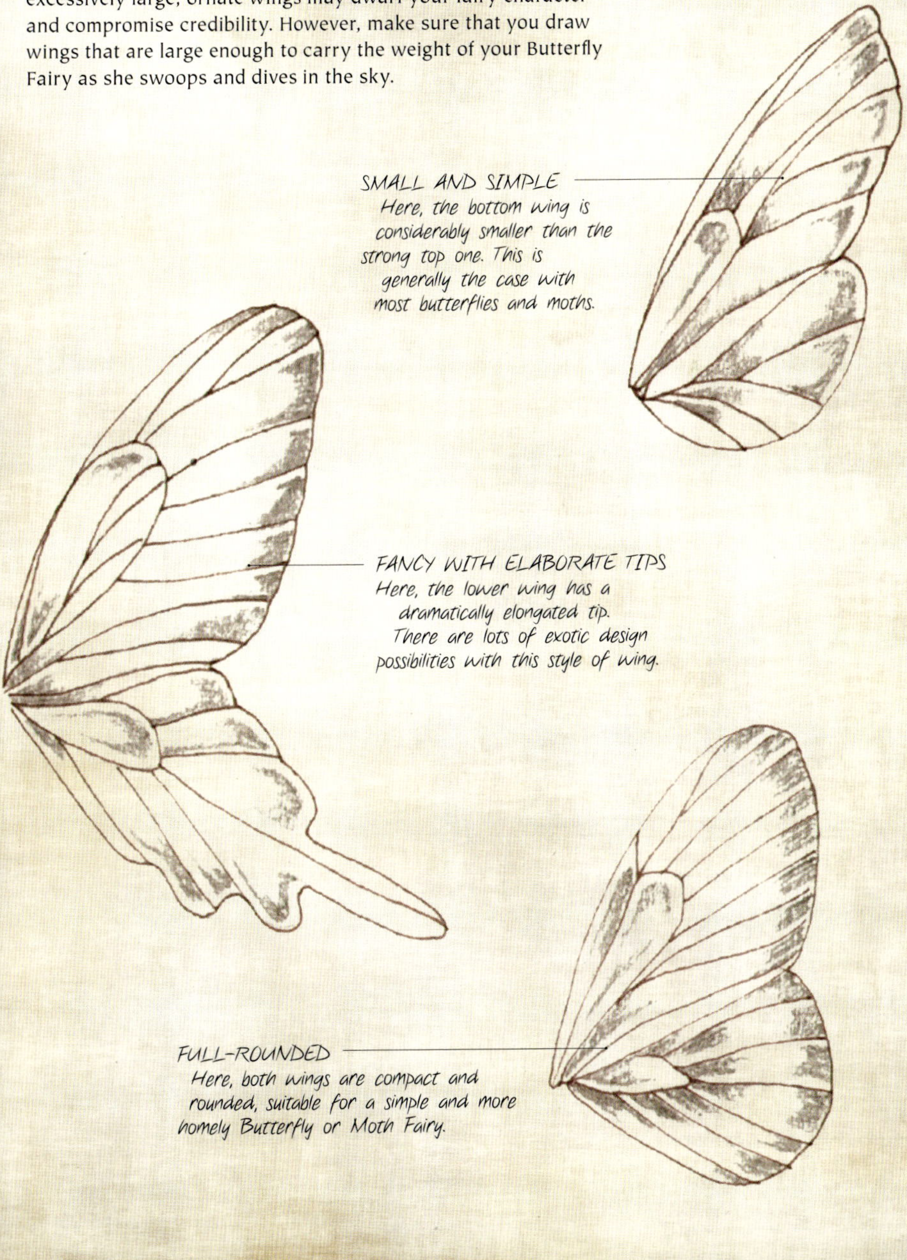

Pixie

PIXIES ARE JOVIAL AND GENERALLY HARMLESS LITTLE PRANKSTERS WHO ARE FRIENDLY AND HELPFUL TO HUMANS AND BRING BLESSINGS TO THOSE WHO TREAT THEM KINDLY.

Character and appearance

Usually diminutive in stature, Pixies are often childlike in both appearance and behavior. They are jolly, mischievous creatures who love to play tricks on other fairy folk as well as humans, delighting in the resulting mayhem. However, they do so without malice and can be just as helpful as they are troublesome, completing household chores and other work while humans sleep.

Pixies are creatures of the forest, often clothed in green to keep them hidden in the undergrowth. In this image, four different shades of green create the Pixie's costume. Habitat is important in creating light effects that help to give a sense of place to any character study. Here, the Pixie's forest home creates dappled light filtered through foliage. Note the resulting downward shadows, especially on the face.

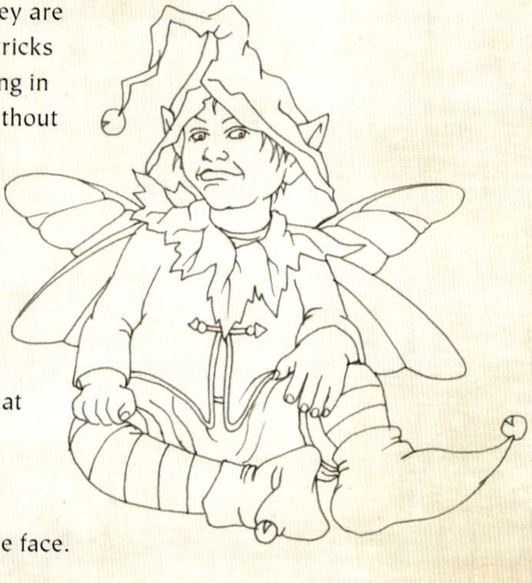

MAIN COLOR PALETTE

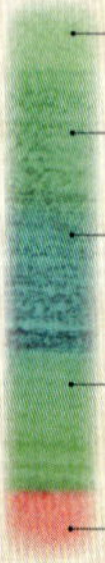

- Yellow-green: wings, leaf collar, hat, stockings, and jacket trim
- Hooker's green: base coat for trousers and shading under the hat
- Winsor green: adds shadow and depth to clothing, wings, and hat
- Olive green: for jacket and boots and to deepen tone on collar and wings
- Rose madder: a touch added to skin washes, then stronger for nose, cheeks, and lips

Copy it!

Copy or trace the drawing or scan it into your computer. Then color it.

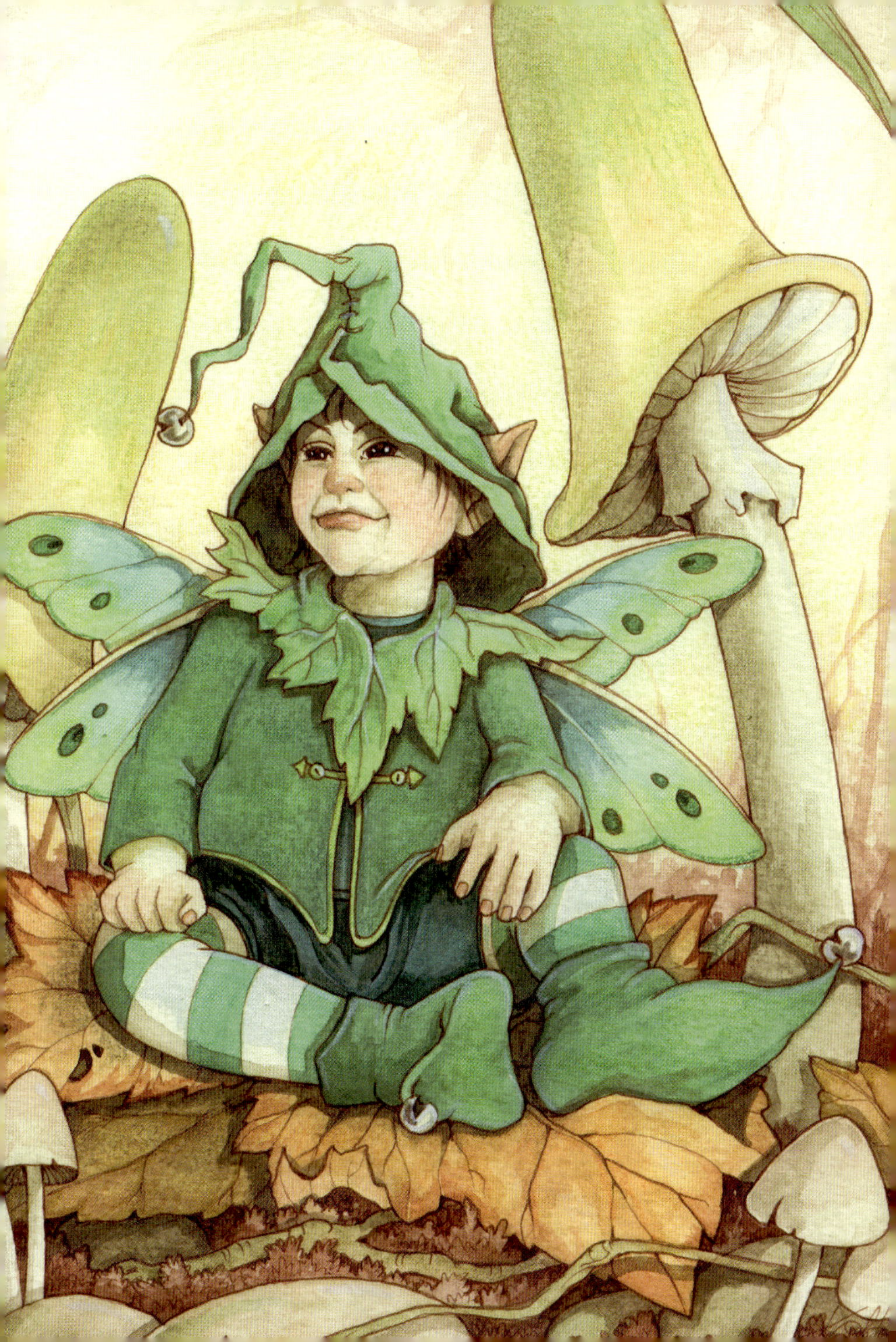

Constructing the figure

Though of indeterminate age, Pixies are always small. Sometimes they simply resemble miniature adult humans. Often, however, they are represented as cuddly little children. This Pixie, for example, is deliciously plump and solid, with the chubby arms and legs of a toddler. Plot the underlying shapes first to help you visualize the final character—adjustments are easy to make at this stage.

See also: Figure construction basics, page 58.

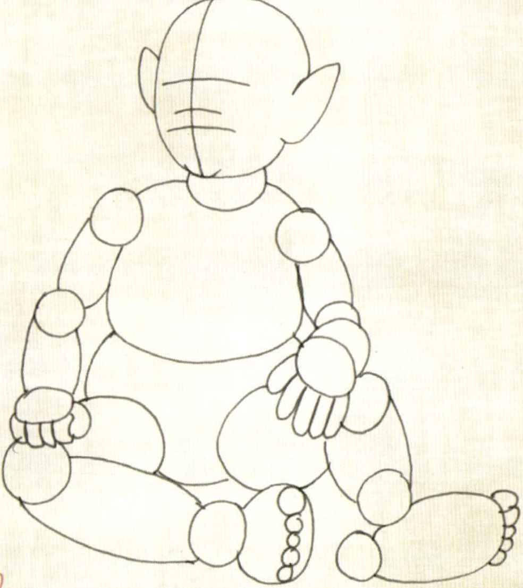

This little figure, composed entirely of simple rounded forms, sits solidly on the ground in a typical toddler position. Assess whether this posture and figure works with the character you visualize. If necessary, slim the shapes and adjust the posture now.

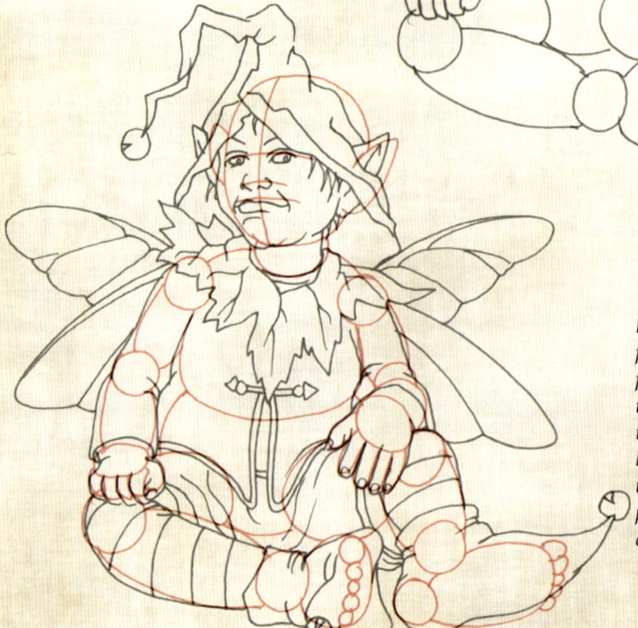

If you are satisfied with the figure, clothe it and add facial features and wings to create the final character. Notice that the face appears older, less babyish, and more "resolved" than that of a toddler, and perfectly projects the character of the little Pixie.

Pixie faces and expressions

Facial expressions are vital in telling the story of any character. In keeping with their love of childish tricks and naughty pranks, Pixies often have the faces of cheeky children, with chubby cheeks, big expressive eyes, and ready smiles that reflect their fun-loving nature.

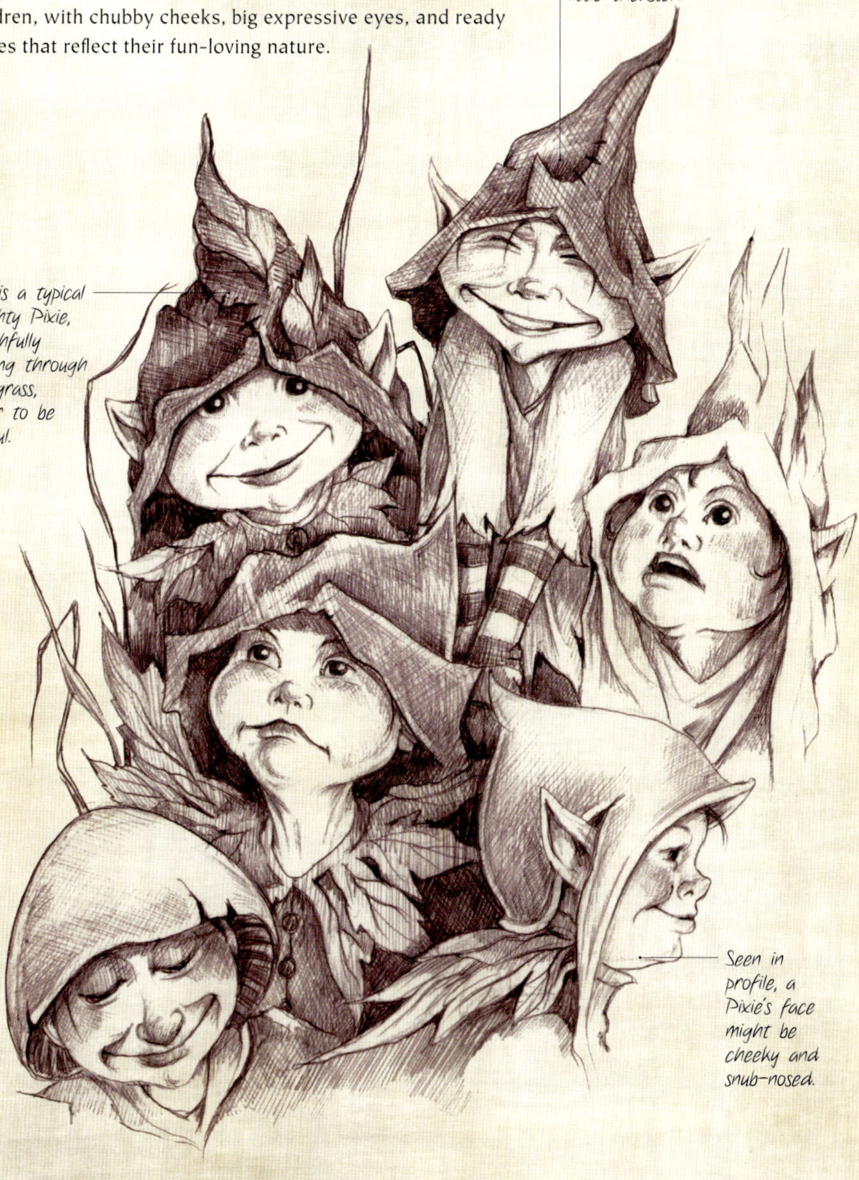

Pixie hats

Images of pixies invariably show them wearing pointed hats that come low over their faces—the archetypal Pixie hat, in fact. These are often simply fashioned from fresh green leaves sewn together into a conical shape. A variety of natural items, from flowers and petals to toadstools and acorn cups, make perfect ready-to-wear hats, while other "found" objects such as scraps of fabric can also be used. Here are a few ideas, and natural history books will suggest many more.

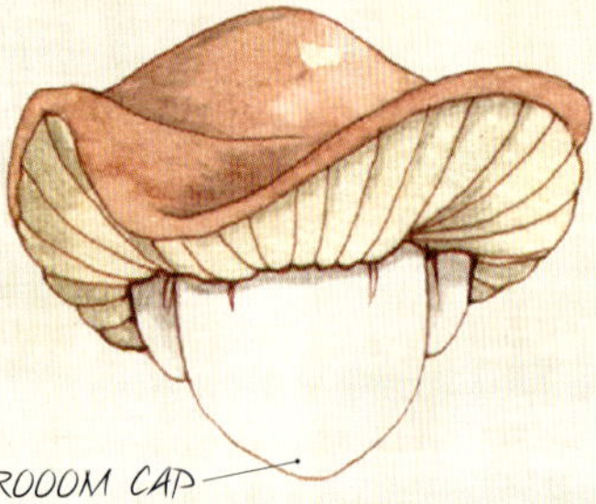

MUSHROOOM CAP
Small mushroom caps make instant Pixie headgear.

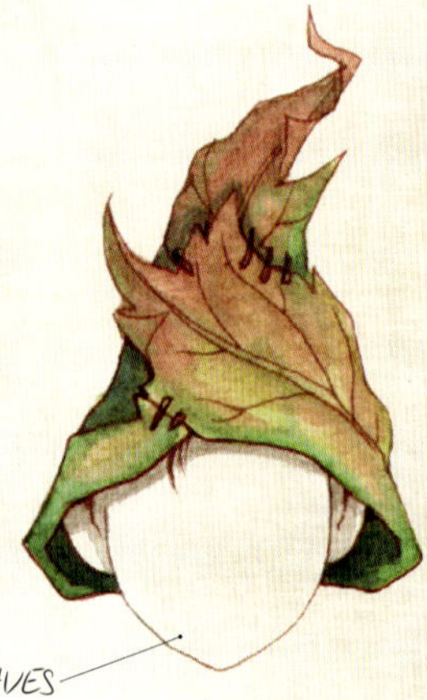

FALL LEAVES
This hat is made from multi-colored fall leaves, curled into a simple conical hat and stitched together, perhaps with hair for thread.

SPRING LEAVES
This pretty hat is simply a fresh green leaf folded around into the favored cone shape and secured at the point with tied grasses.

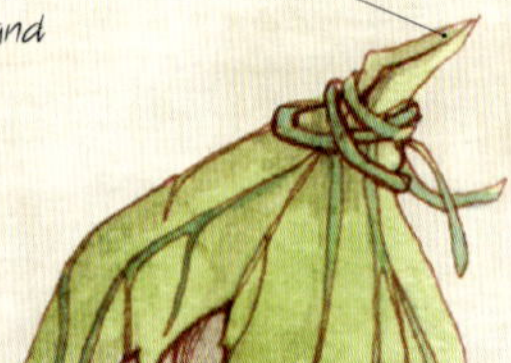

ACORN CUPS
Acorn cups and halved nutshells make instant, ready-to-wear hats that are a perfect fit for tiny Pixie heads.

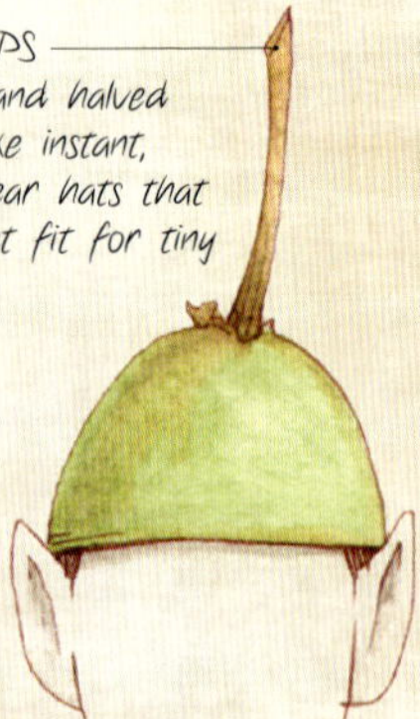

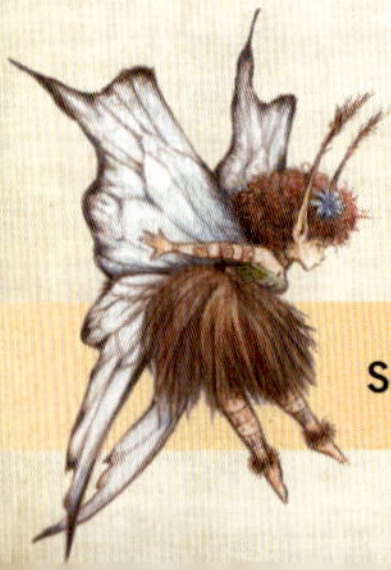

See also: Hair and headwear, page 82.

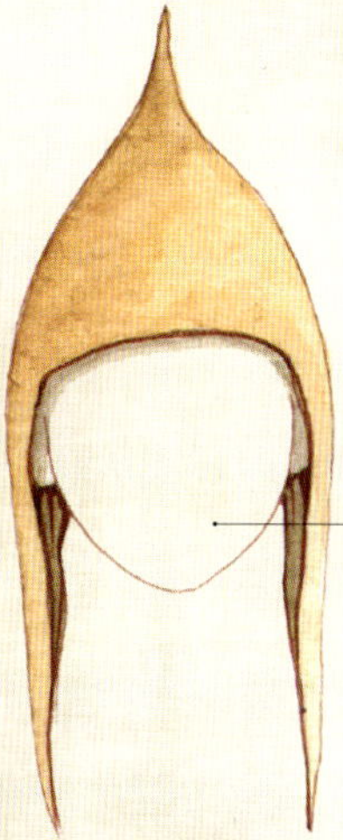

SEEDPODS
Seedpods can be cut to make ideal little hats with protective earflaps. Alternatively, similar styles can be created by resourceful Pixies from found scraps of fabric.

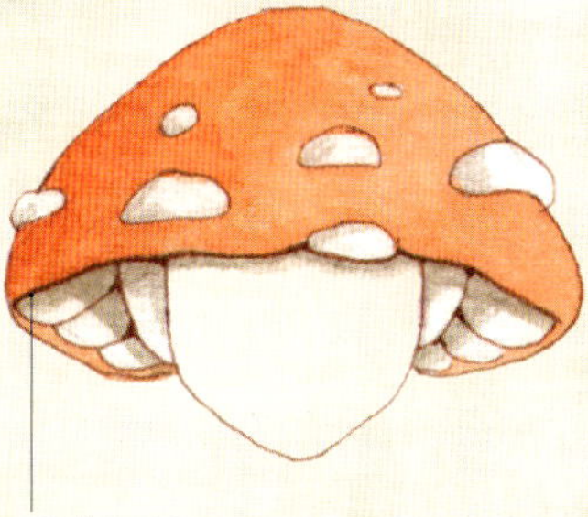

TOADSTOOL
The archetypal red and white toadstool is often a Pixie seat, or a place to take shelter from sun or rain. Here, a small one makes a colorful Pixie hat fashion statement.

This cute, baby-faced character definitely has the Pixie "aaah" factor. He's round and baby-like, sweet and cuddly, with a suitably cheeky little face just asking for some fun. Surrounded by fungi, he wears one as a cap, and on his feet he wears Pixie boots of a type that become popular from time to time as human footwear.

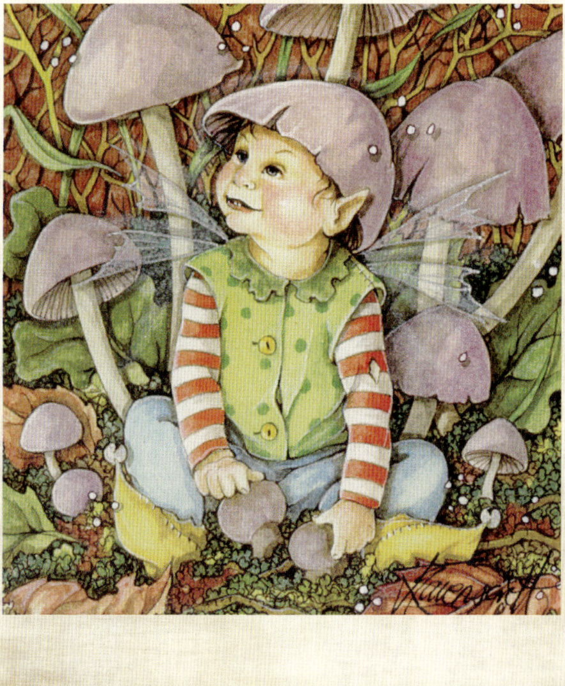

Christmas Tree Fairy

THE CHRISTMAS TREE FAIRY IS A MAGICAL AND TWINKLING CHARACTER, DISPENSING SEASONAL FUN AND HAPPINESS WHILE KEEPING HER TREE HEALTHY AND SPARKLING.

Character and appearance

No Christmas tree is complete without a fairy perched at the top. She has become an essential part of the Christmas tradition and embodies all the magic and excitement of the festive season. A fun-loving creature, she is not averse to the odd bit of mischief—knocking ornaments off the tree or fusing fairy lights—but she is always friendly and full of Christmas goodwill and is never malevolent.

Sometimes the Christmas Tree Fairy has an angelic appearance, but more often she is seen as the archetypal sparkly fairy, complete with short, fluffy skirts, magic wand, and plenty of bling. This little character is painted in watercolor washes of bright gold and yellow, with touches of gleaming white gouache added to create twinkling detail on her dress, hair, and wings.

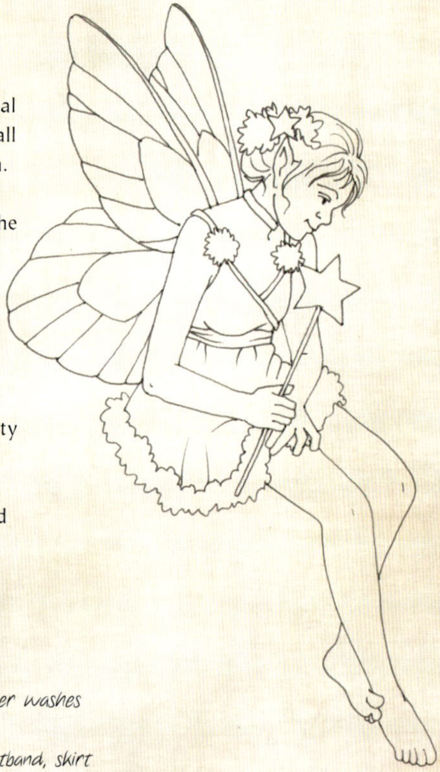

MAIN COLOR PALETTE

- Raw umber: thin washes for skin; heavier washes on hair, wings, and skirt
- Cadmium yellow: deep hue used on waistband, skirt trims, headdress, and wings
- Yellow ocher: washes applied for dress and wings
- Lemon yellow: mixed with white gouache for highlights and patterns on wings

Copy it!

Copy or trace the drawing or scan it into your computer. Then color it.

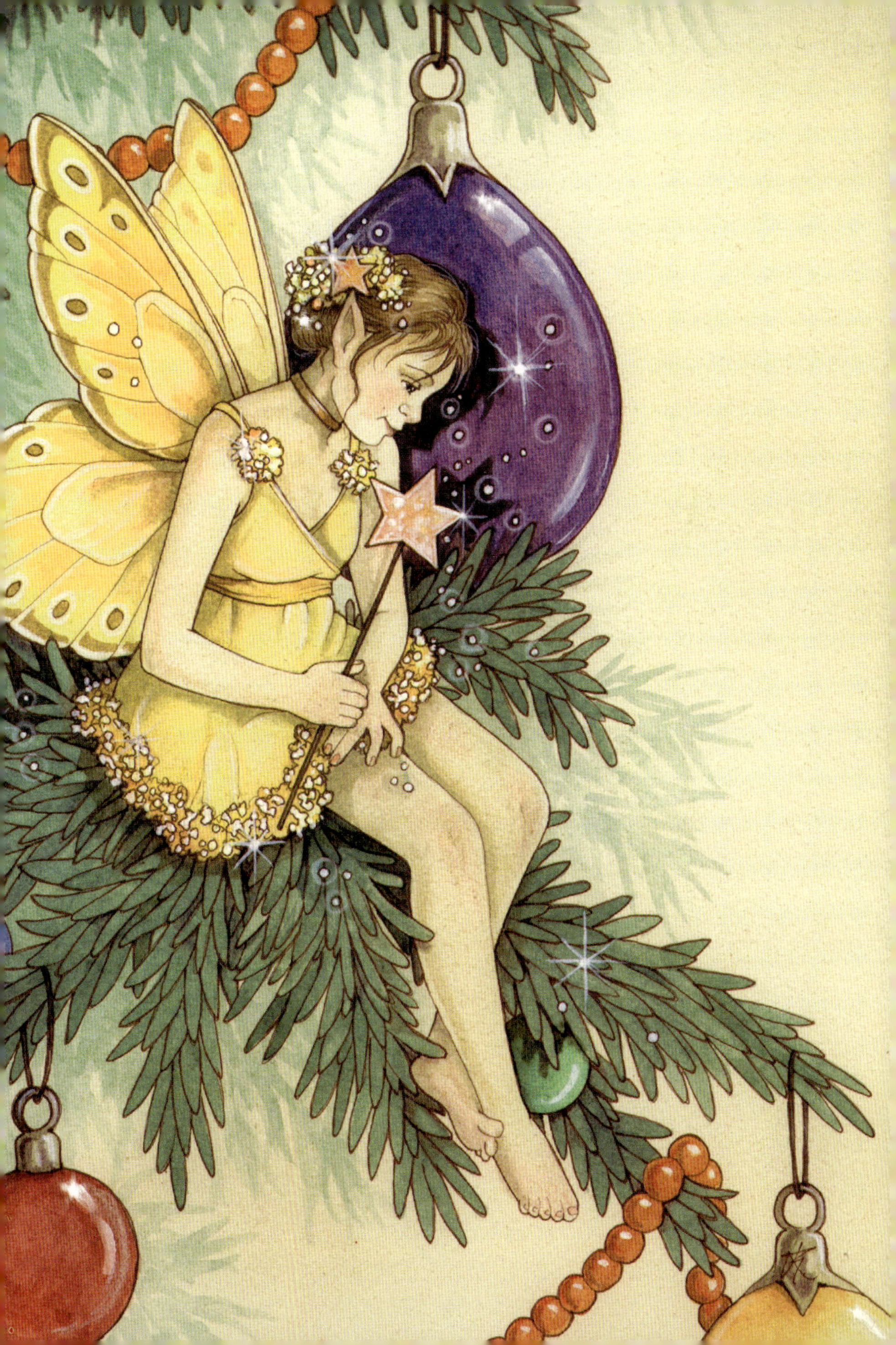

Constructing the figure

Rather than standing at the top of the tree, this Christmas Tree Fairy is seated daintily on a branch. To give a credible account of the figure, use an artist's mannequin to explore the relative positions and angles of the basic underlying forms.

See also: Figure construction basics, page 58.

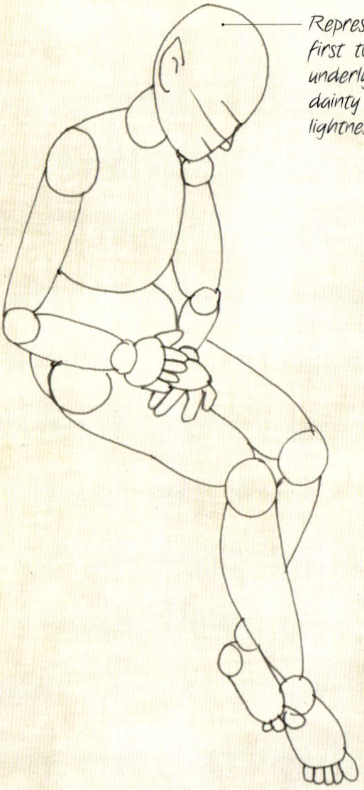

Represent the figure with basic shapes first to explore the pose and get the underlying forms correctly balanced. This dainty pose accentuates the delicacy and lightness of the fairy.

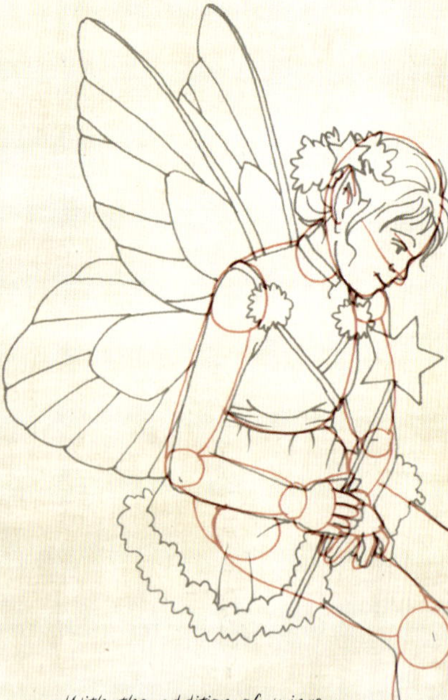

With the addition of wings and gown the fairy figure is complete. She still retains a sense of weightlessness, and her demure, downcast gaze belies her sense of fun.

Posing the Christmas Tree Fairy

The Christmas Tree Fairy is a happy, fun-loving character, so try creating other playful poses that give an immediate sense of her nature. And remember the importance of facial expressions, too.

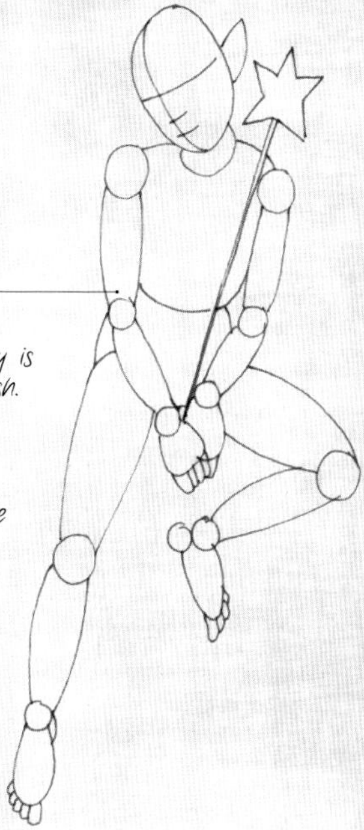

PENSIVE
In an unusually pensive mood, perhaps this fairy is making a Christmas wish. Notice how lightly she perches; the extended right leg and leaning body is balanced by the tilt of the head and the bent left leg.

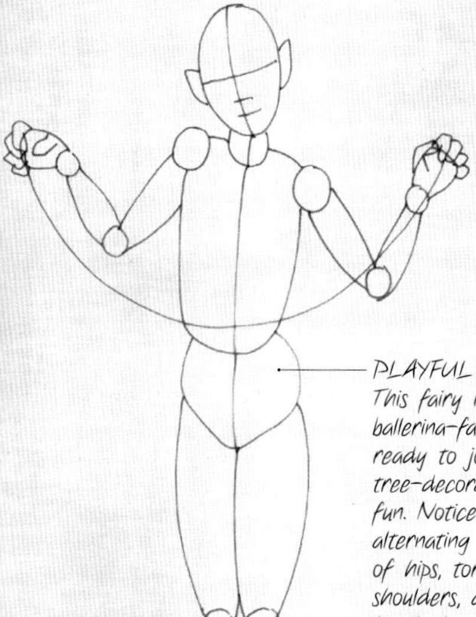

PLAYFUL
This fairy is poised ballerina-fashion, ready to join the tree-decorating fun. Notice the alternating angles of hips, torso, shoulders, and head that create the pose.

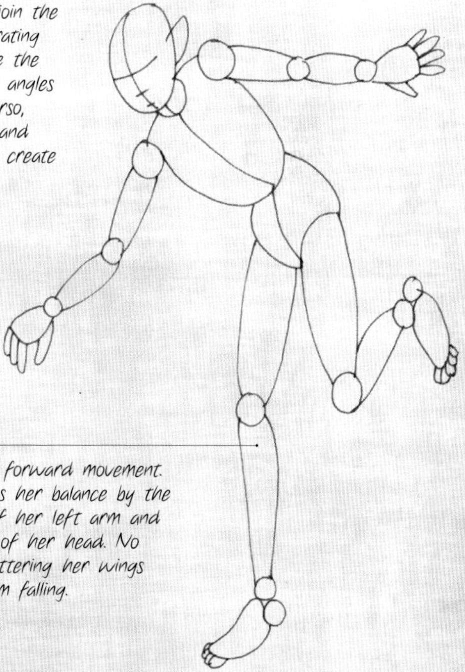

PRECARIOUS
This pose is full of forward movement. The fairy just keeps her balance by the backward thrust of her left arm and the opposing angle of her head. No doubt she's also fluttering her wings to stop herself from falling.

Costumes and accessories

Christmas Tree Fairies often have the gowns, halos, and feathered wings with which the angels in the Christmas story are usually depicted. Another characterization of the Christmas Tree Fairy is as a bold little Pixie dressed in red, fur-trimmed garments. As a fairy artist you can visualize the character as you wish, but make sure you tell the story clearly.

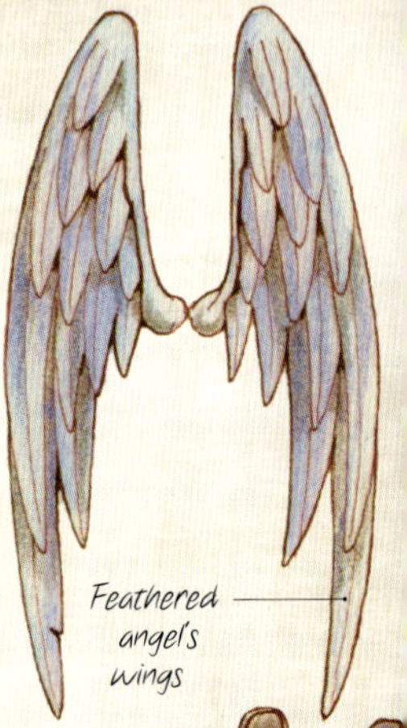

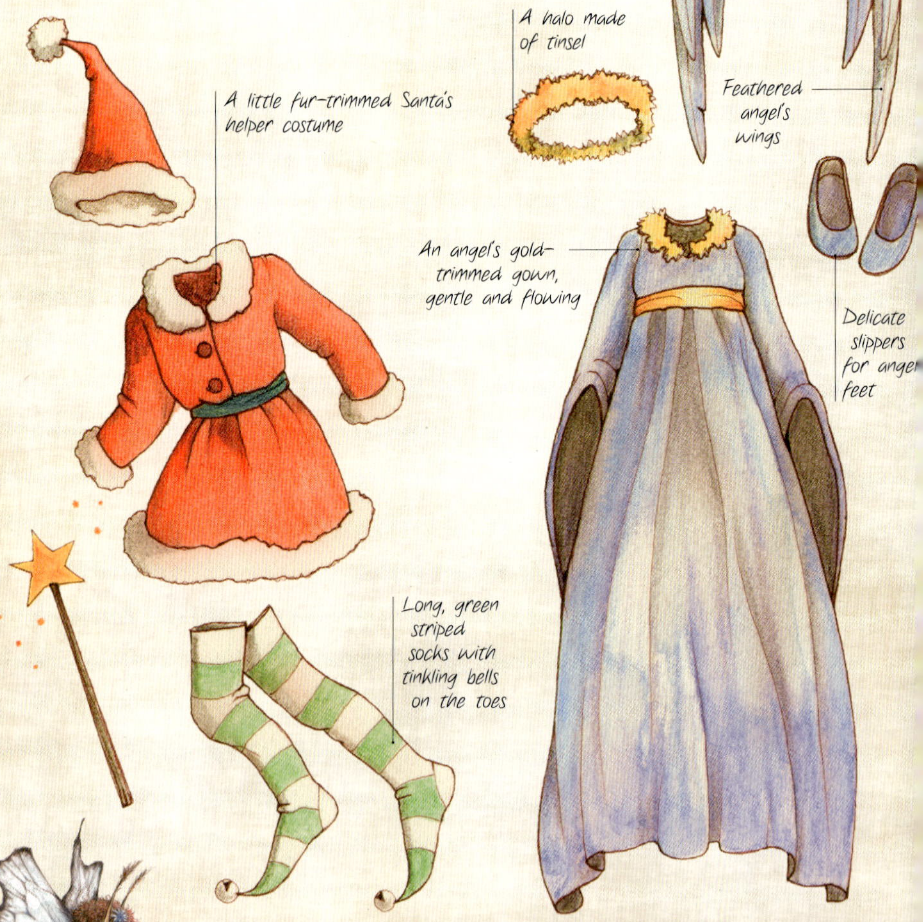

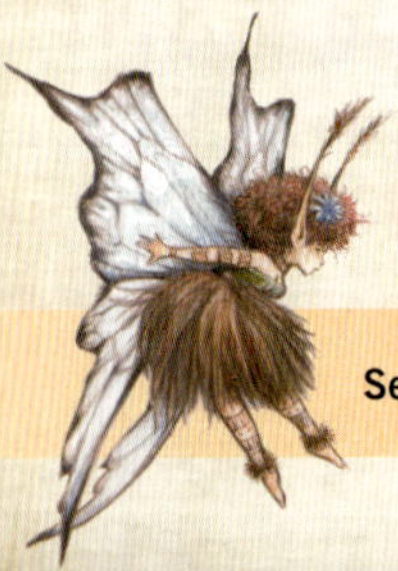

See also: Dresses and robes, page 76.

Adding glitz and shine to beads

The ornaments and beads on the tree will twinkle and add seasonal glamor to the image. These starbursts of light are added with opaque white gouache to a dry painting using a fine 0 or 1 watercolor brush. The simple technique works for any kind of shiny object.

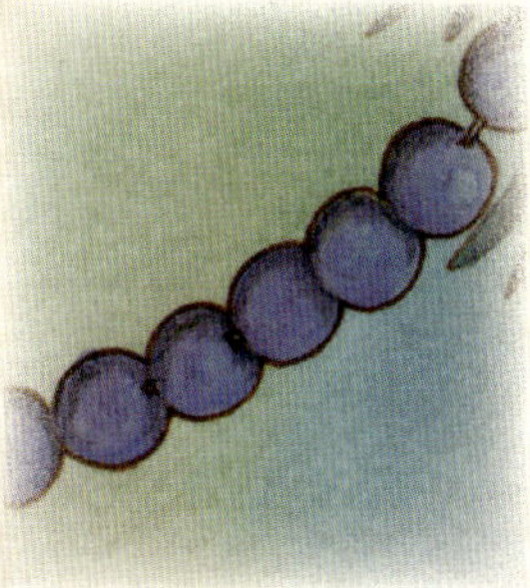

1 First paint your beads and ornaments. Let the painting dry completely.

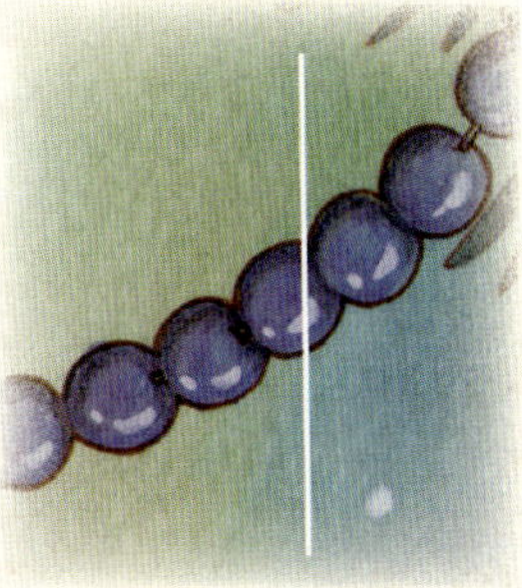

2 Apply white gouache spots to one side of each bead, and a few in the background. When dry, start to add starbursts here and there. First paint a thin vertical line through the dot of light.

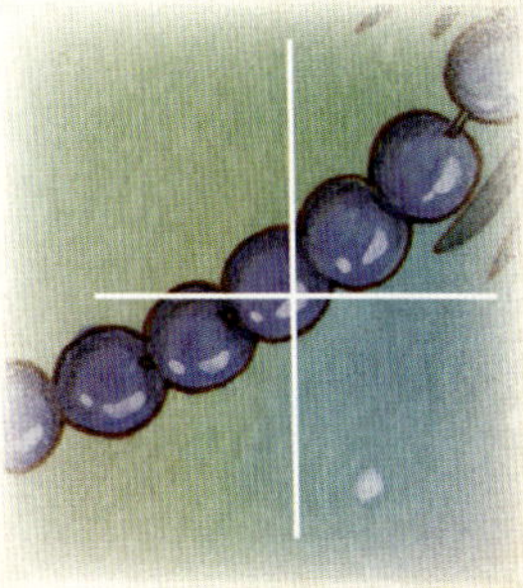

3 Carefully paint a fine horizontal line through the white dot.

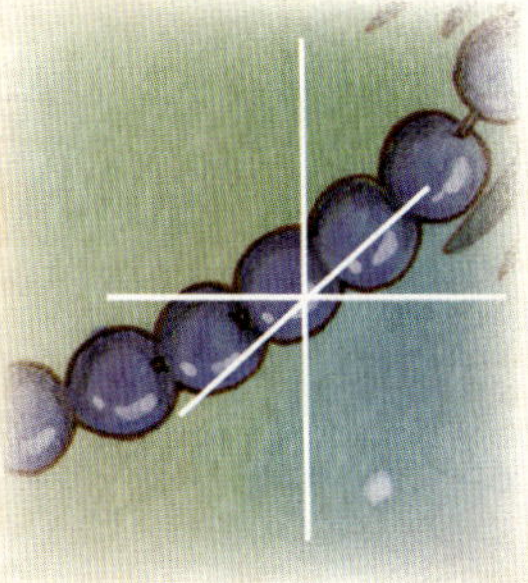

4 Add a diagonal line through the same center point.

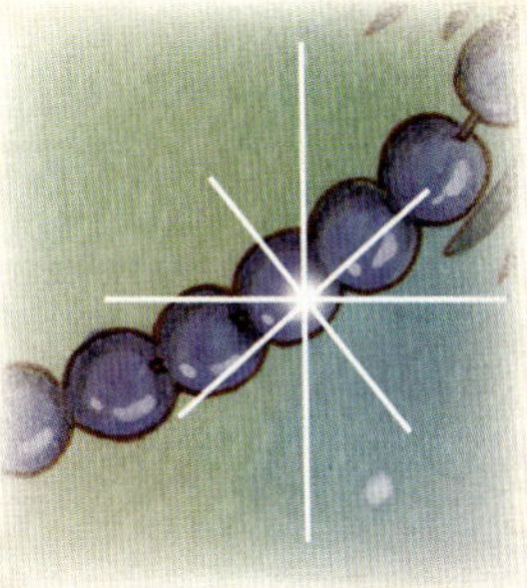

5 Complete the starburst with a second diagonal line. Add a single dot of white gouache in the middle to create a dazzling center. This will also hide any mistakes if the lines don't quite cross in the center.

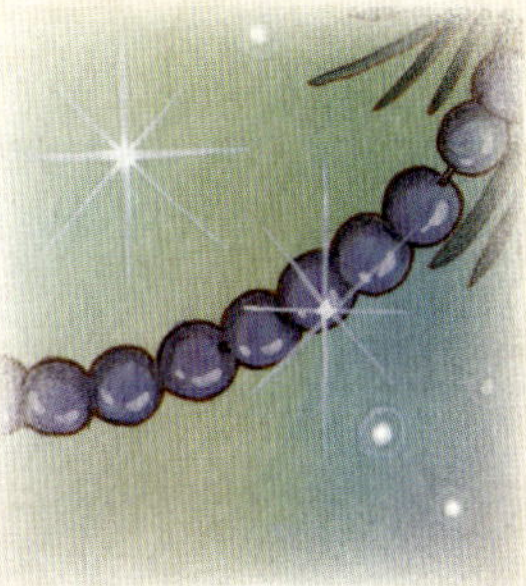

6 Repeat the effect in a few places. Keep it subtle; don't overdo it or you will spoil the effect. The finished image is brought to life with magical bursts of shining light.

Fairy of the Unseelie Court

FAIRIES OF THE UNSEELIE COURT ARE THE WICKED COUSINS OF THE FAIR FOLK OF THE SEELIE COURT. THEY ARE UGLY, DARK, AND SPITEFUL, AND THEY HATE HUMANS.

Character and appearance

Fairies of the Unseelie Court have many guises but all of them are wicked. Some have bat- or insect-like wings; others have no wings. Those that fly, sometimes called "The Host," flock together to wreak havoc on the countryside and swarm around their human prey, who they bite and batter and then take by force on their foul nocturnal adventures.

This image, painted in watercolors, depicts a malicious Fairy of the Unseelie Court waiting to pounce on an unsuspecting passerby. The day is sunny and bright, but the fairy is dark and colorless to convey his evil spirit. The humanoid form is given a disturbing twist with vicious talons, while dark butterfly wings and long antennae reveal his fairy identity.

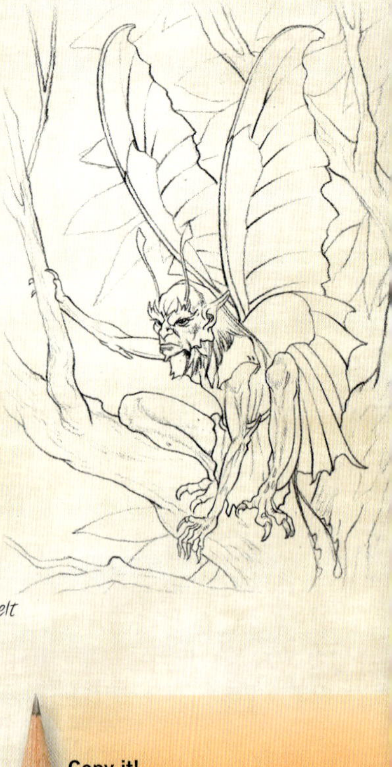

MAIN COLOR PALETTE

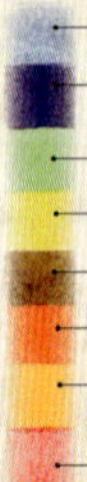

- Cerulean blue: skin tones, wings
- Ultramarine blue: leaves, tree, tunic, hair, wings
- Permanent green: in washes for background, leaves, belt
- Cadmium yellow: skin tones, belt
- Burnt umber: washes and line work on tree, wings
- Cadmium scarlet: skin tones, tunic, belt, hair, wings
- Cadmium yellow deep: background, leaves, tree
- Permanent rose: antennae, wings
- Cadmium red: hair and wing detail
- Payne's gray: face and hands

Copy it!

Copy or trace the drawing or scan it into your computer. Then color it.

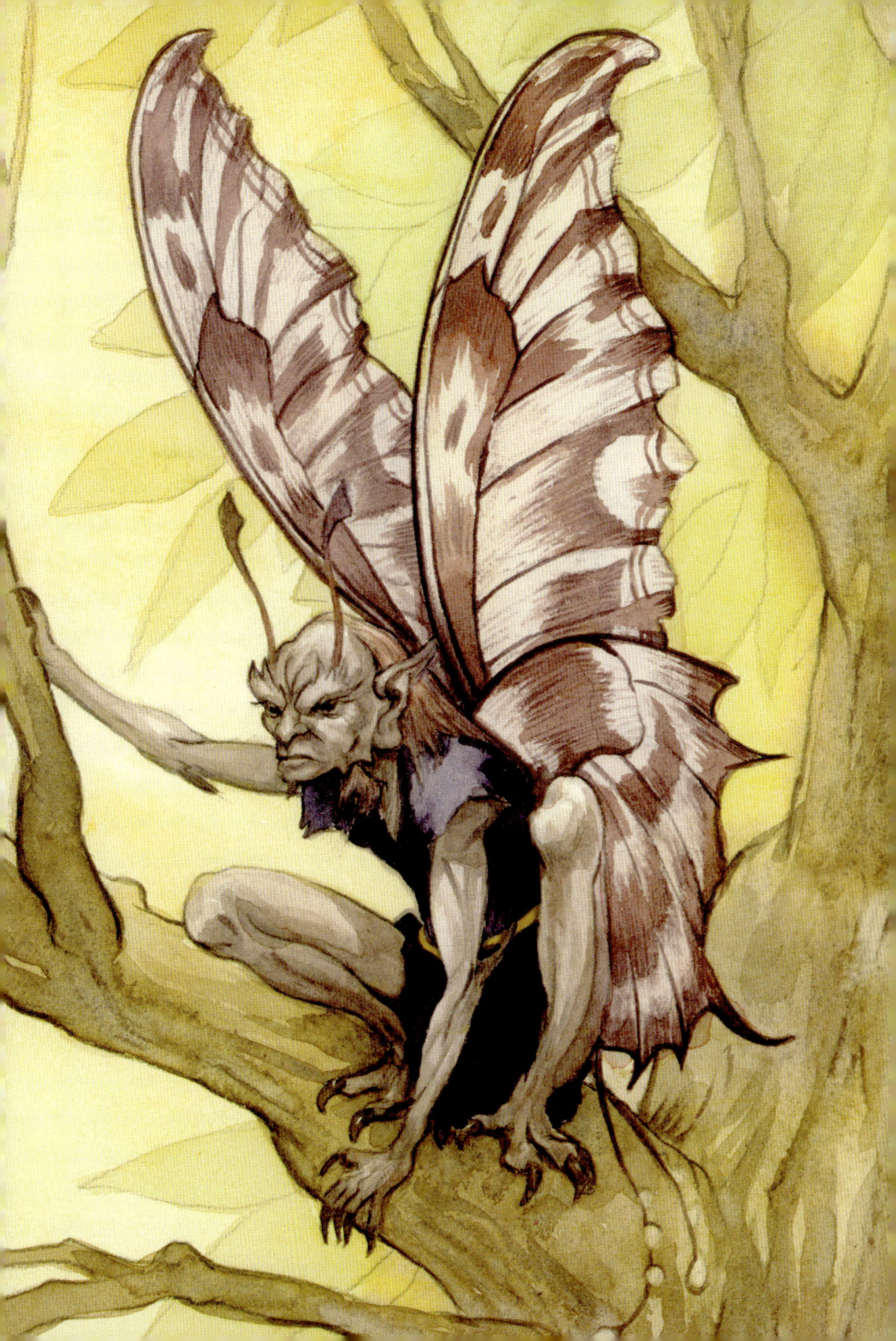

Constructing the figure

This Unseelie Court Fairy is deliberately emaciated to convey the sense of a mean and sinister character with unmistakably evil intent. Approach the figure in the usual way with the basic shape technique, only this time use underlying forms that are skeletal forms instead of full and rounded.

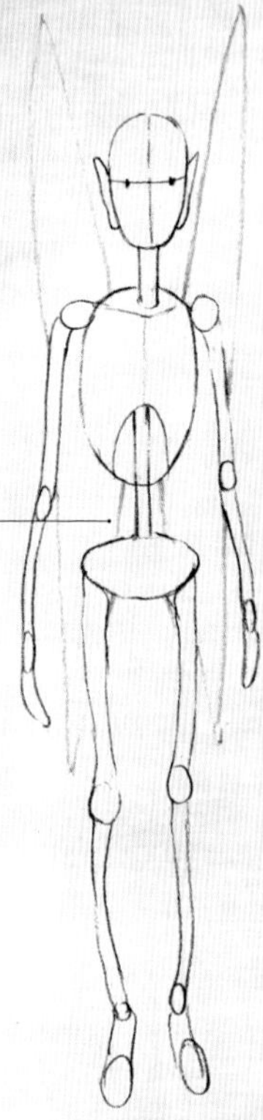

1 Simple skeleton shapes can adapt to any human form. Head, torso, and hips are modified ovals; limbs are thin tubes. Note that the arms hang from the shoulders without touching the torso, and there is space between torso and hips.

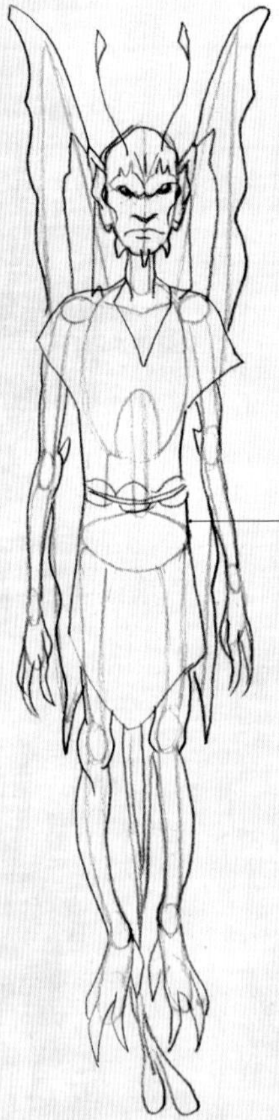

2 Add simplified facial features and enlarge the ears. Indicate the garments, making sure they hang convincingly around the skeletal form. Define the hands and feet with clawed digits. Sketch in the wings.

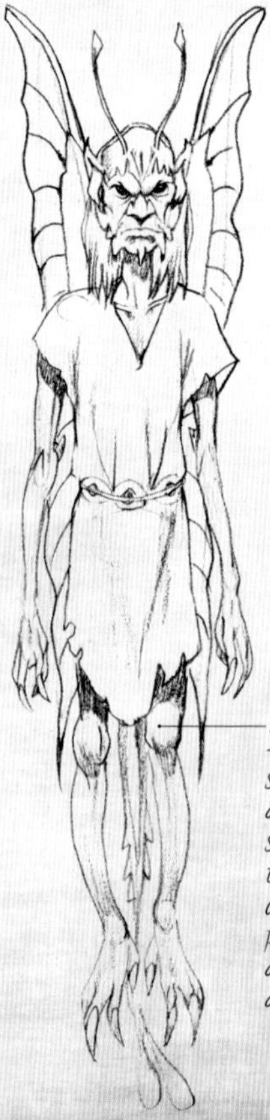

3 Continue refining the face, deepening the scowl and adding hair and antennae. Darken the shadow areas created by the tunic and add the creases. Define the wing patterns, and shade to add form to the sinewy arms and legs.

See also: Basic figure construction, page 58.

Wing variations

The Unseelie Court includes many fairies, each with unique characteristics. To draw these variations, start simply and add telling details that change the image. Wings can create totally dissimilar concepts—these two alternatives start with the same basic creature, but the wings suggest very different fairy individuals.

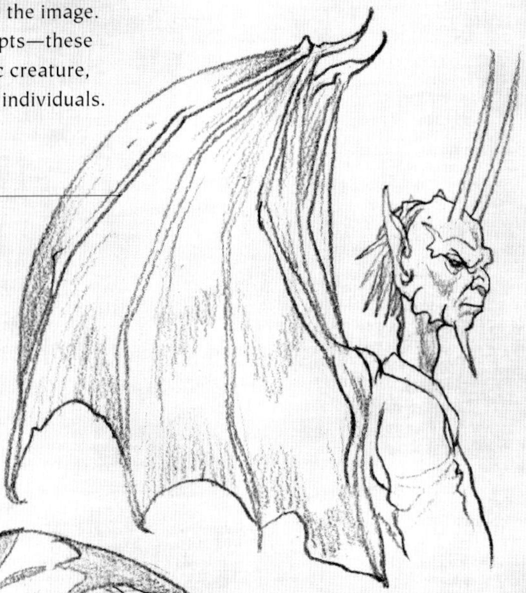

LEATHER WING FAIRY

Sinister dragon or bat wings are based on an arm-like structure that comes from the shoulder and ends in a vicious claw. A leathery membrane stretches between long digits. This nocturnal creature is further characterized by long pointed ears, spiked hair, and dagger-sharp antennae.

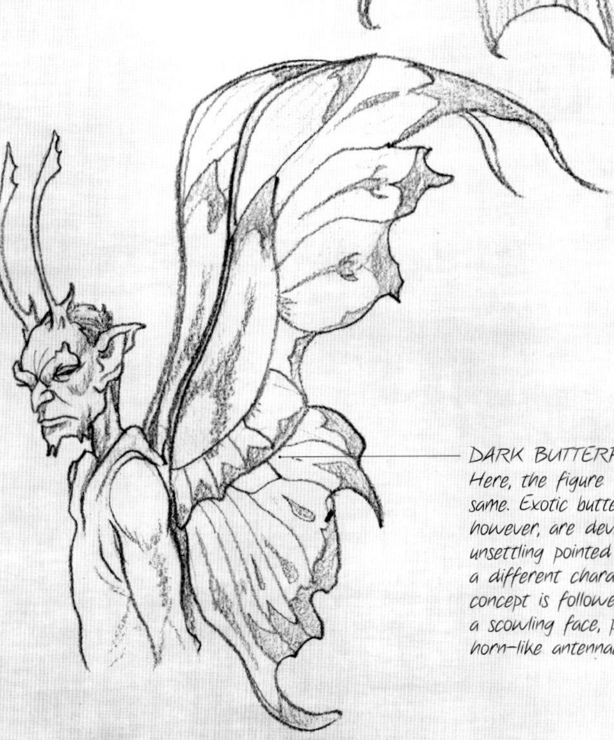

DARK BUTTERFLY

Here, the figure is basically the same. Exotic butterfly wings, however, are developed into unsettling pointed shapes to create a different character. The evil concept is followed through with a scowling face, pointed ears, and horn-like antennae.

Character variations

You can draw on many resources when crafting the appearance of a fantastic creature. Nature in particular is a rich source of inspiration. It's easy to imagine dark elves blending in with their surroundings, so branch and plant forms can be incorporated into their anatomy. Insect and animal features offer plenty of ideas, as these examples show.

BAT CREATURE

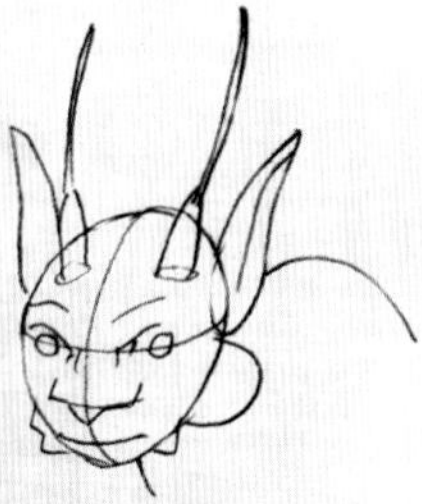

1 Spooky bat faces combine with human features to create a disturbing effect. Start with a simple oval and indicate the position of eyes, nose, and mouth. Add pointed ears and antennae.

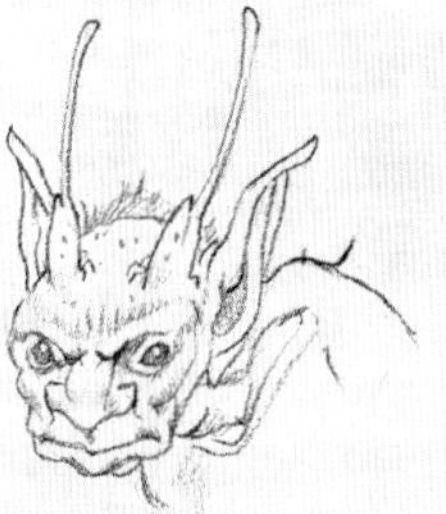

2 Work up the face in more detail, adding furrowed brow ridges and dark animal-like eyes. Develop the nose and mouth, shade the hollow cheeks, and add jowls.

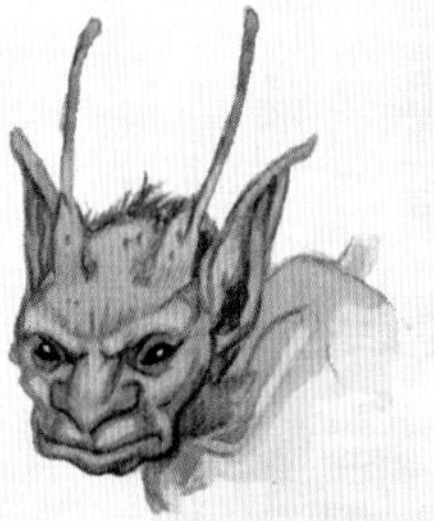

3 Render the face with dark washes for sinister effect. Add sparse tufts of hair and highlights to the glaring animal eyes to complete the half-bat, half-human creature.

GREEN MAN

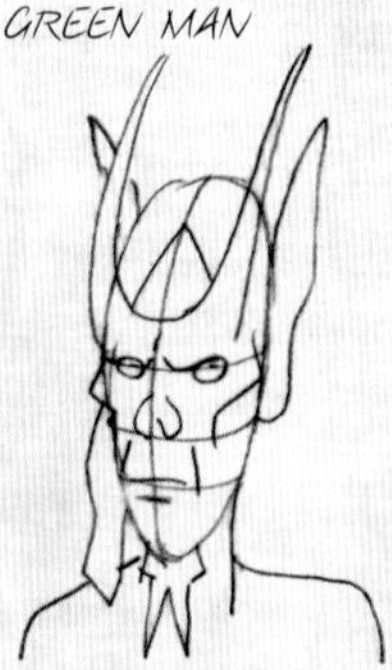

1 Start this grossly elongated face with a long oval. Stretch this further by extending the brow ridges into tall horns and adding spikes to the chin. Plot the features and add long ears.

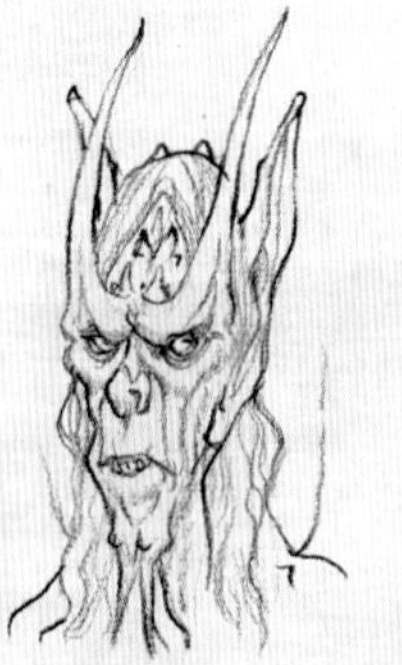

2 For an evil look, add anger lines above the nose and slant the eyes. Use light shading to mold the folds of the gaunt face and add straggly unkempt hair.

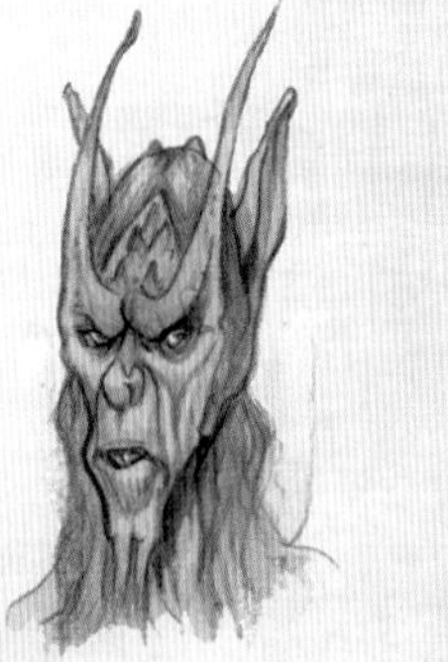

3 Paint the face and head with varied sickly gray-green washes to further reinforce the fairy's nasty lineage and cold, malicious nature.

CATFISH FACE

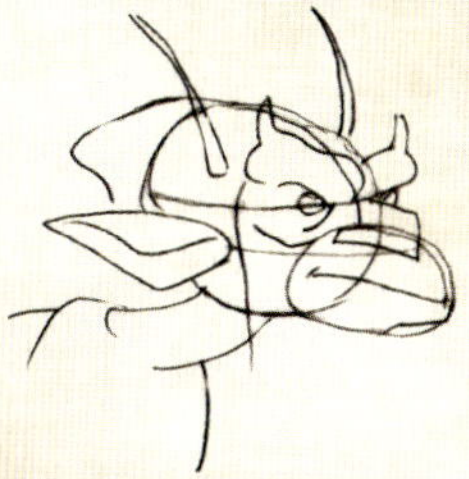

1 This face combines wickedness with a sly smile. Start with an oval, and add another oval to extend the mouth area. Add horns to the heavy brow and indicate the ears.

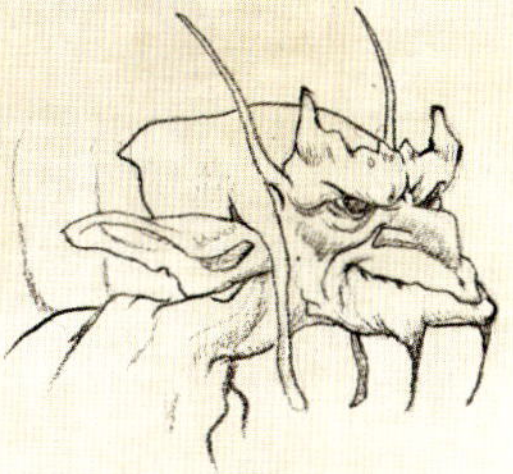

2 Develop the flattened nose, the eyes, and the evil smirking mouth. Add catfish-inspired chin whiskers and antennae growing from the back of the eye sockets.

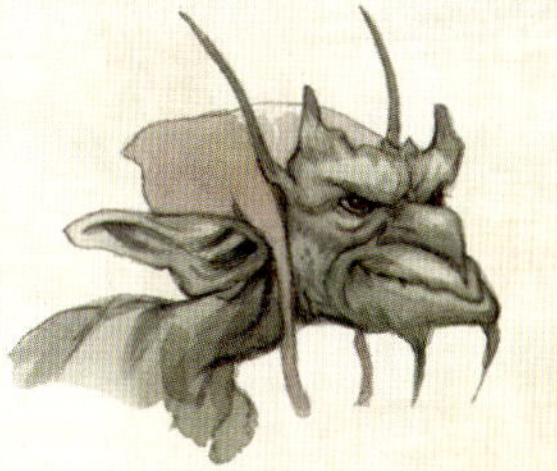

3 Render the fairy with somber monochromatic gray-greens and blues to bring a sinister air to this wicked and unsavory creature.

HORNED FAIRY

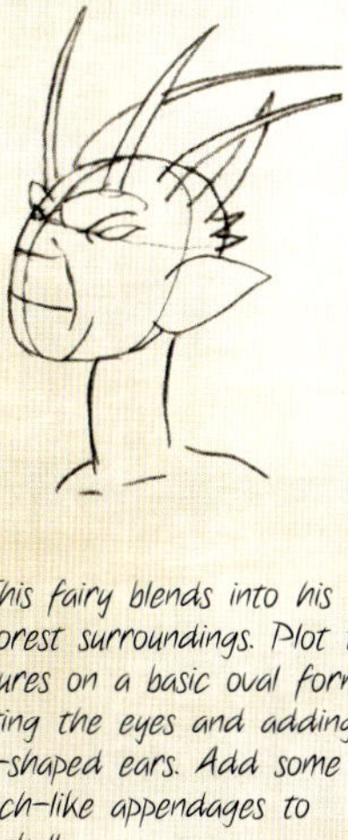

1 This fairy blends into his forest surroundings. Plot the features on a basic oval form, slanting the eyes and adding leaf-shaped ears. Add some branch-like appendages to the skull.

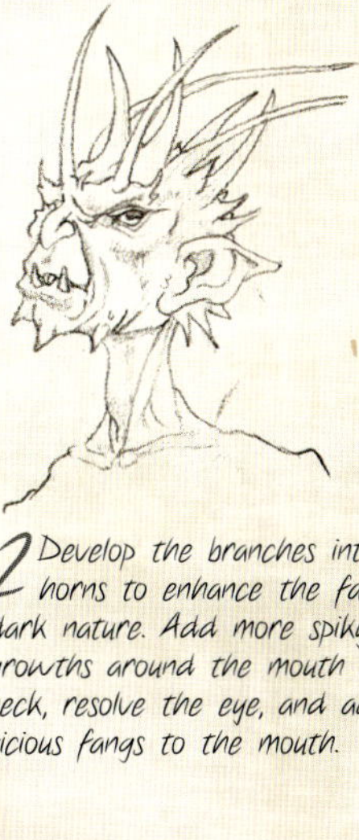

2 Develop the branches into horns to enhance the fairy's dark nature. Add more spiky growths around the mouth and neck, resolve the eye, and add vicious fangs to the mouth.

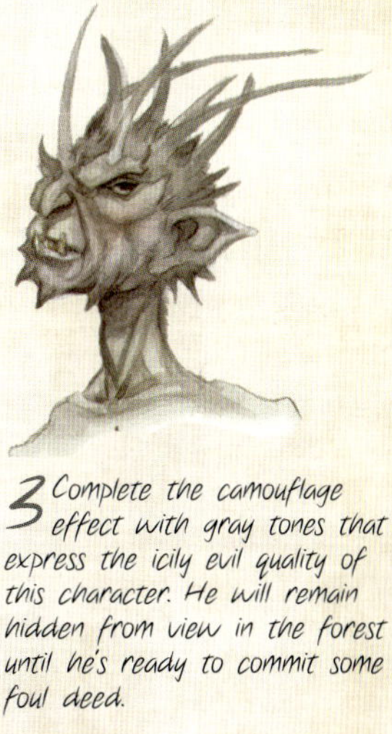

3 Complete the camouflage effect with gray tones that express the icily evil quality of this character. He will remain hidden from view in the forest until he's ready to commit some foul deed.

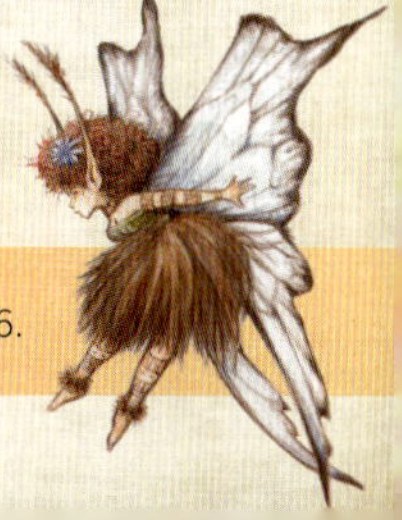

See also: Facial expressions, page 66.

Fairy of the Unseelie Court: from sketch to finished painting

This evil predatory creature is poised to attack his human prey. His coloring and wing markings provide him with camouflage so that he can take his victim by surprise. The crouching pose and large wings fill most of the picture area, while the tree and leaf shapes are used to focus the eye on the central figure.

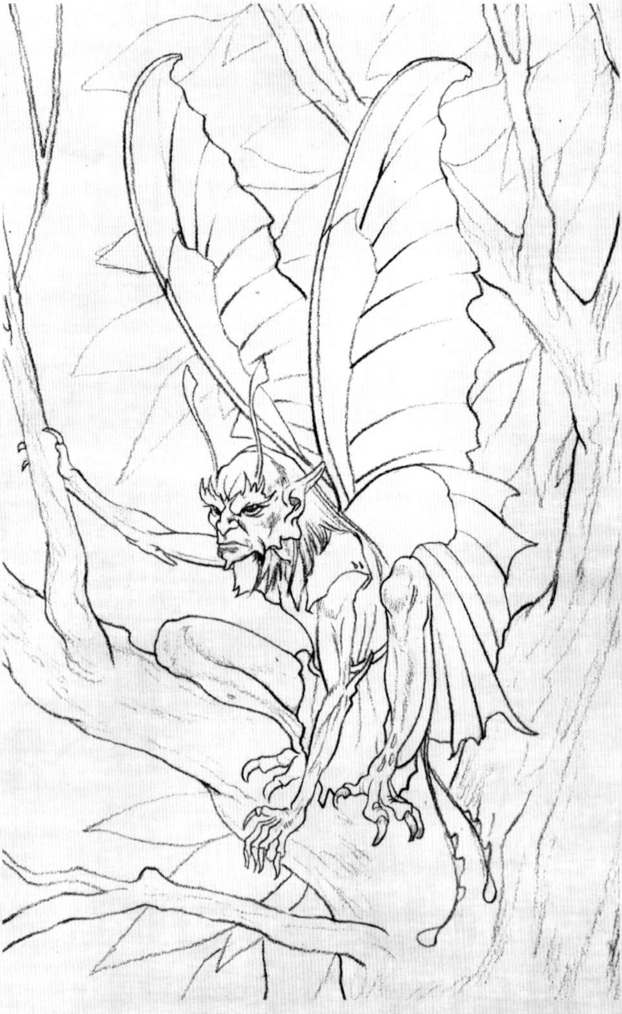

The initial drawing

- *Make a light graphite pencil underdrawing first, constructing the figure with basic shapes to create a credible image.*
- *Make sure the crouching pose balances well.*
- *When the basic structure is established, use a black colored pencil to flesh out the figure with more details and create a fully resolved image ready for color to be added.*
- *Erase the original pencil construction lines.*

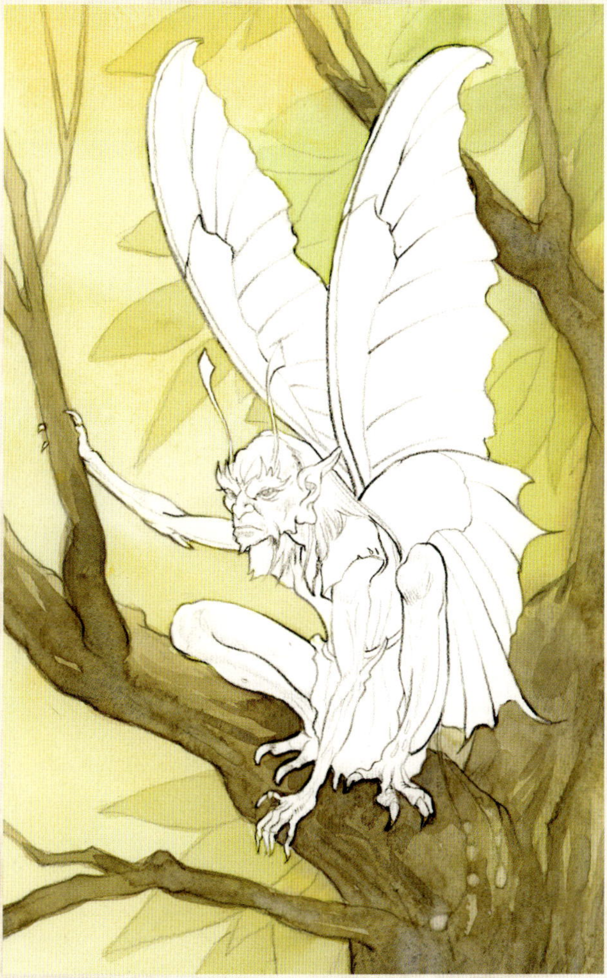

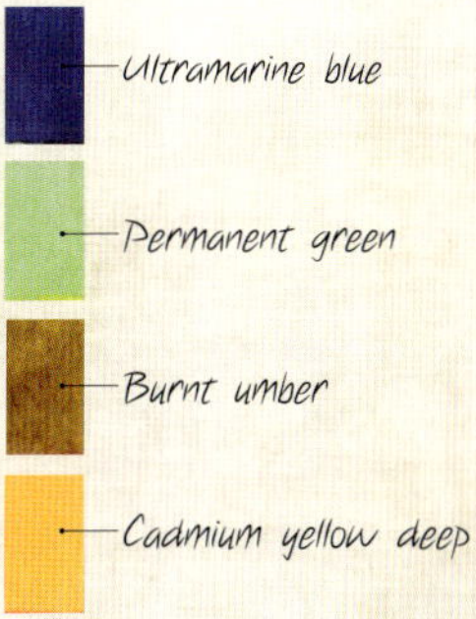

Painting the background

- *Flood a wash of cadmium yellow deep with a touch of permanent green over the entire background, painting around the fairy.*
- *Dilute this wash, adding ultramarine, to paint the leaves.*
- *Block in the tree with a wash of burnt umber, ultramarine, and cadmium yellow deep. While it's still wet, blend in a more concentrated mix to create shadows and texture.*
- *Reinforce some of the drawn lines with a fine brush using an even stronger blend of the same colors.*

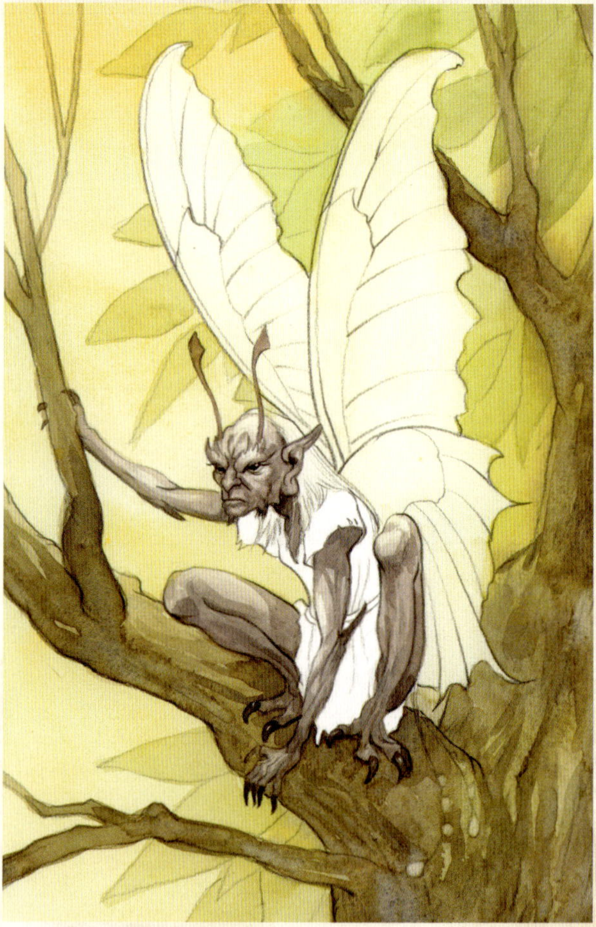

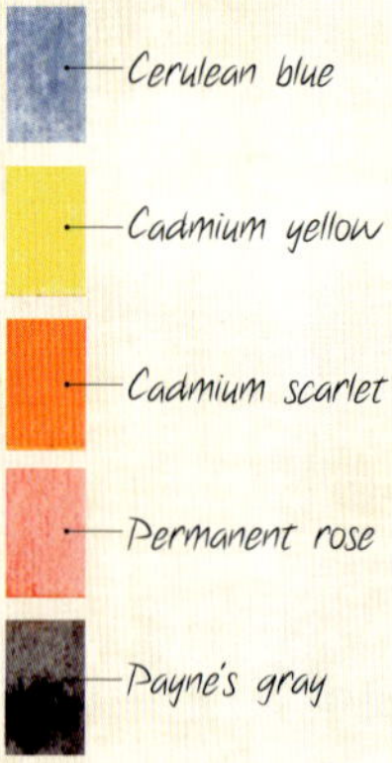

Adding skin tones

- *Wash over the entire figure, including the wings, with a dilute cadmium yellow mix.*
- *Apply various washes of cadmium scarlet and cerulean blue to the skin, laying successive layers on top of each other to create shadows, and define the musculature and facial contours.*
- *Add a touch of permanent rose to the mix for the antennae.*
- *Using a fine brush, enhance the fine lines of the face and fingers with a wash of Payne's gray and cadmium scarlet.*

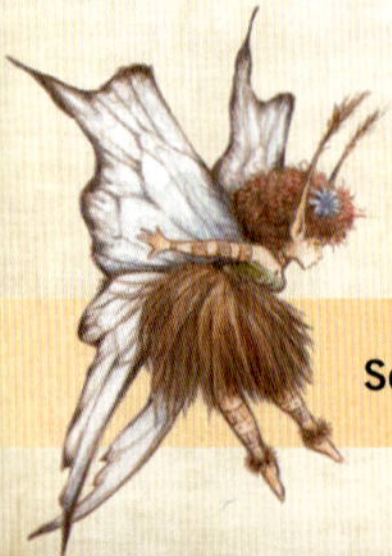

See also: Basic watercolor techniques, page 50.

See also: Finished Fairy of the Unseelie Court image, page 229.

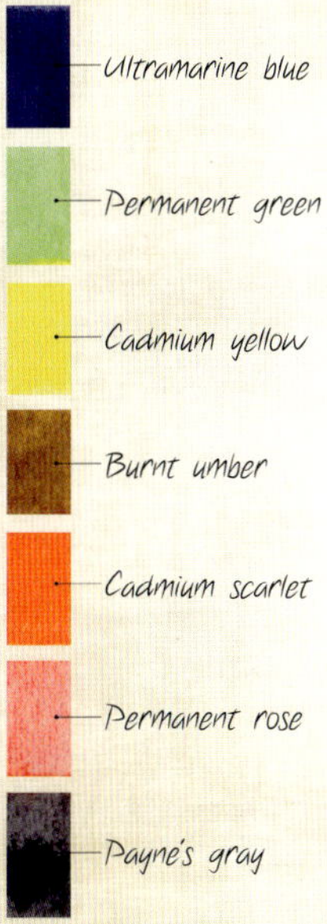

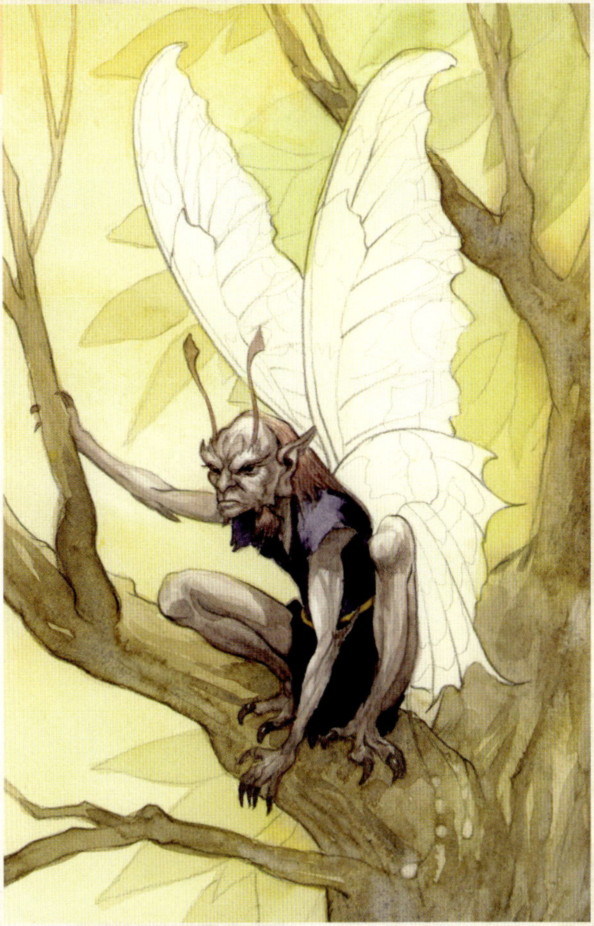

Painting tunic and wings to finish the piece

- *Paint the tunic with a concentrated wash of ultramarine and cadmium scarlet.*
- *Add more scarlet for the hair.*
- *Paint the belt with cadmium yellow, permanent green, cadmium scarlet, and ultramarine.*
- *Use a pale wash of cerulean blue, cadmium scarlet, and a touch of permanent rose for the wings.*
- *Paint the wing patterns with a mix of Payne's gray, cadmium scarlet, and permanent rose, then enhance the lines on the wings with a mix of ultramarine, cadmium scarlet, and burnt umber using a fine brush.*

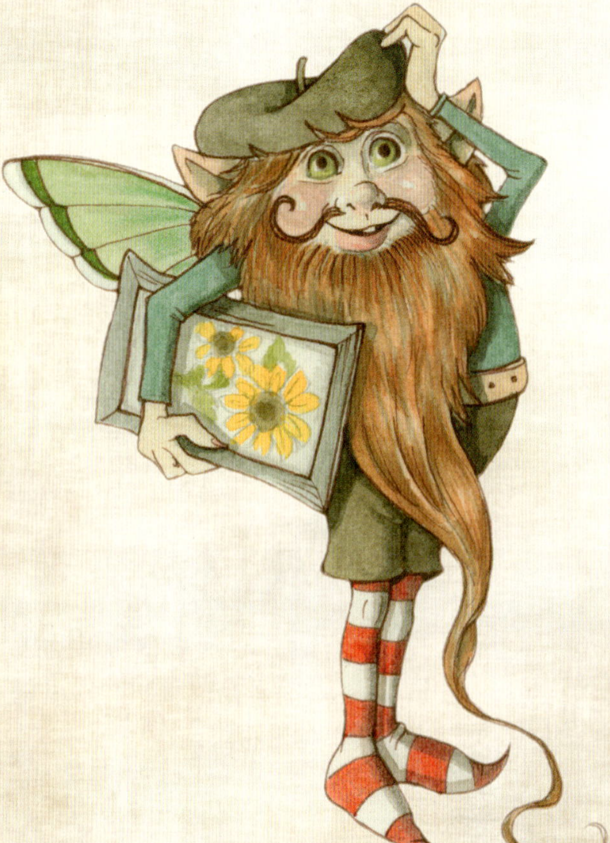

Part 6

The gallery

The range of disciplines, styles, and media used in fairy art today is rich and varied. This selection of fairy art, by contemporary artists working around the world, will get you thinking creatively, and may provide inspiration for masterpieces of your own.

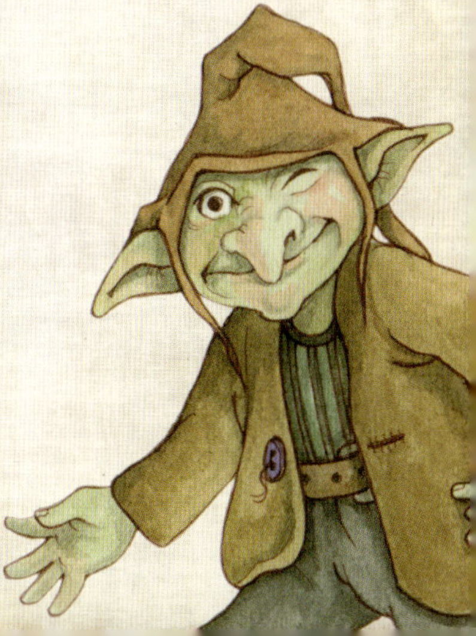

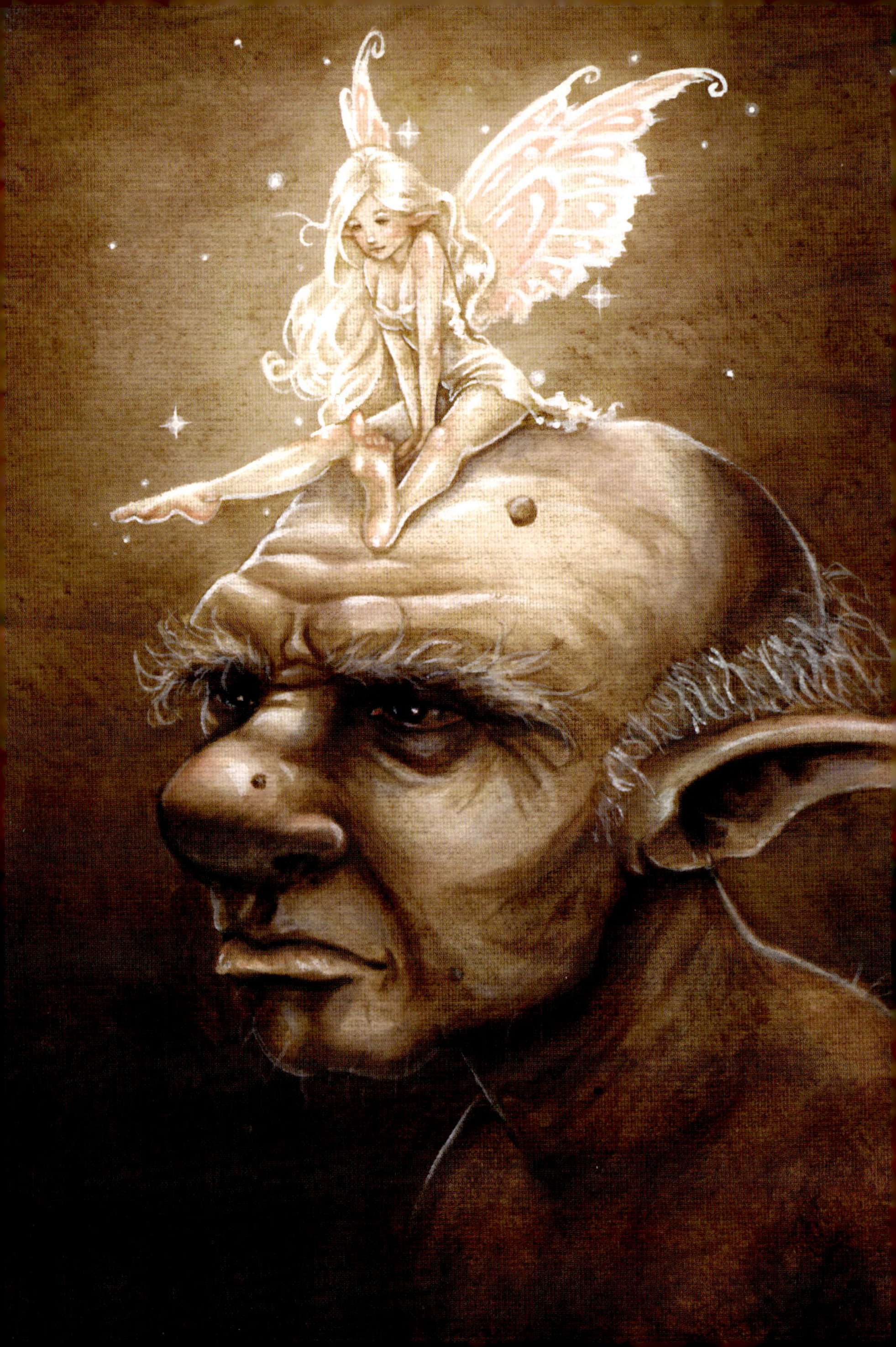

Working with light

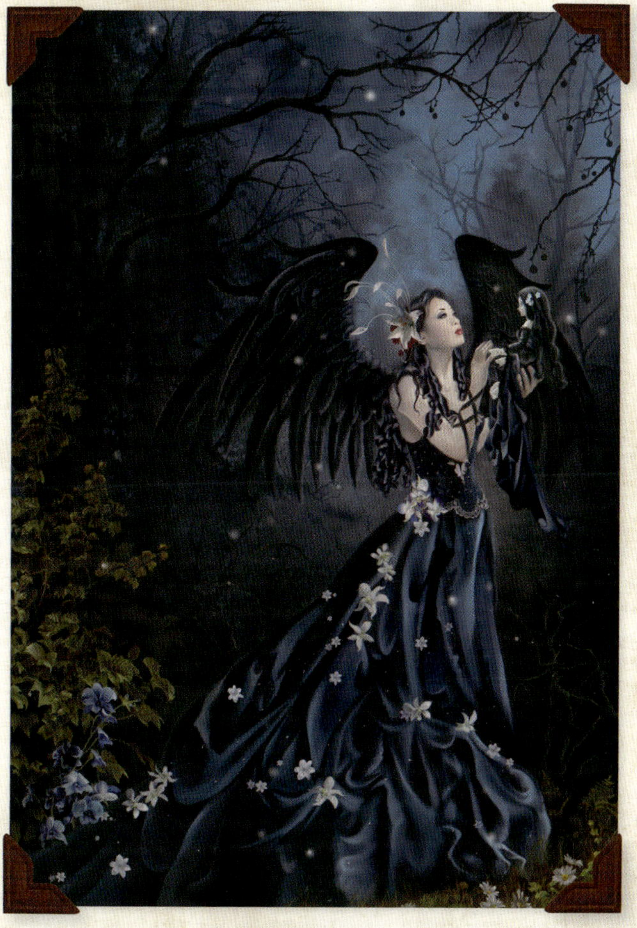

Light the darkness

Selina Fenech

The light that emanates from the fairy in this piece gives her a suitably ethereal glow, and helps define the form of the Goblin's wrinkled head. Highlights—achieved by overpainting with white gouache—flesh out the Goblin's nose, lower lip, and whiskers, and are accentuated by the rich, textural buildup of dark, earthy tones in the background.

Whispers

Nene Thomas

Great atmosphere is suggested by the digital rendition of moonlight in this moody nighttime scene. The branch details create a soft backdrop to the foreground foliage flowers and central figure, while the upward tilt of the fairy's illuminated face leads the viewer's eye to the tiny doll she holds in her hands.

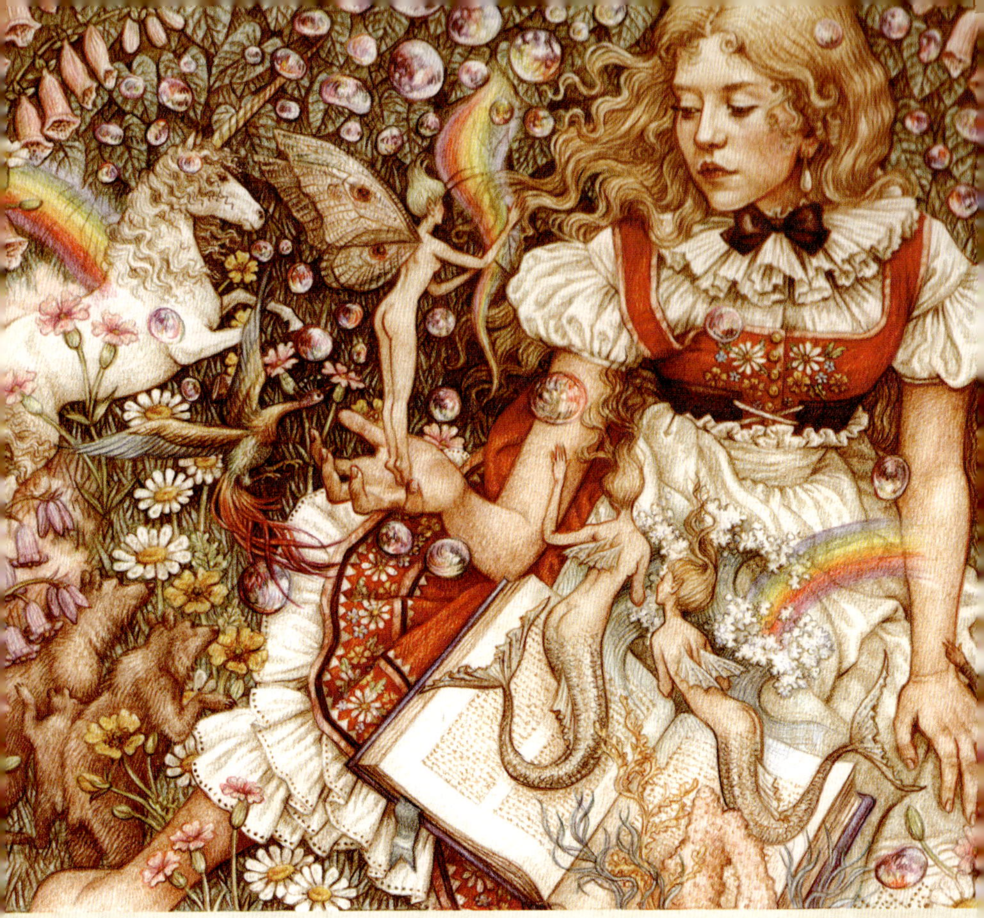

The intricacies of pencil detail

The Magic Book

Yvonne Gilbert

The magic book owned by the heroine of Hans Christian Anderson's *The Wild Swans* brought fairy tale favorites, including Anderson's *Thumbelina* and *Little Mermaid*, to life. The magical details and multi-layered patterns of this painting result from a different kind of wizardry—a masterful understanding of form and structure combined with the precision control of colored pencils.

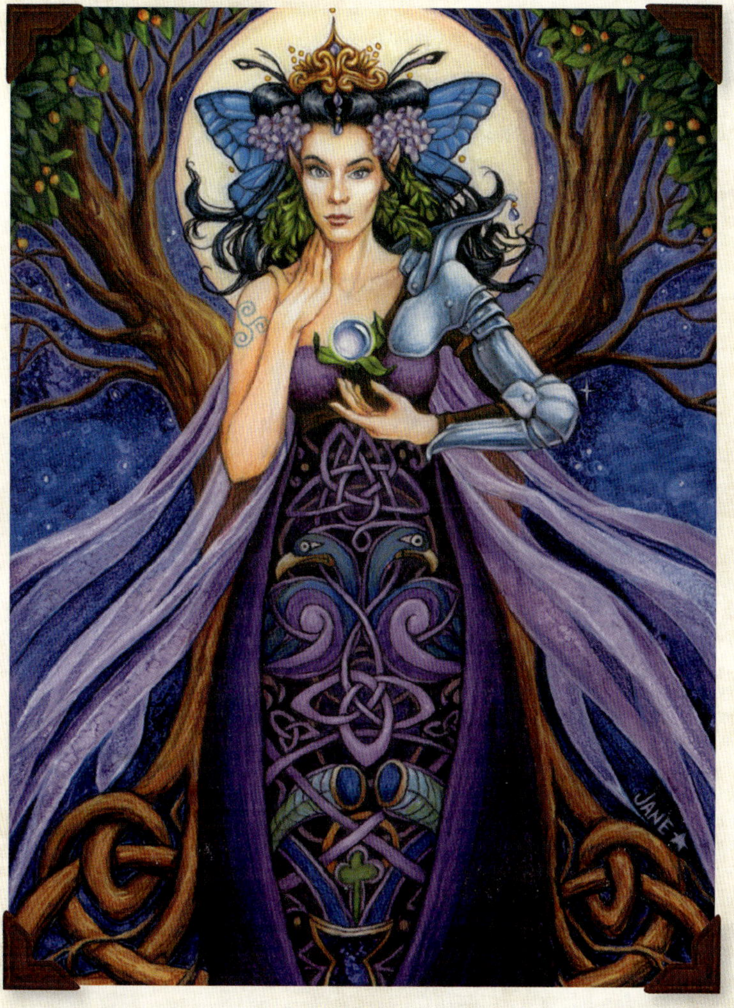

Enchantress

Jane Starr Weils

Composed of layers of colored pencil built up over many layers of watercolor, "Enchantress" translates the transformative instant of twilight into visual images. The magic that turns a tree into a fae is defined by the details: roots become Celtic knots, leaves grow into hair, fog trails into veils, and a flower transforms into a crystal orb.

Coloring effects

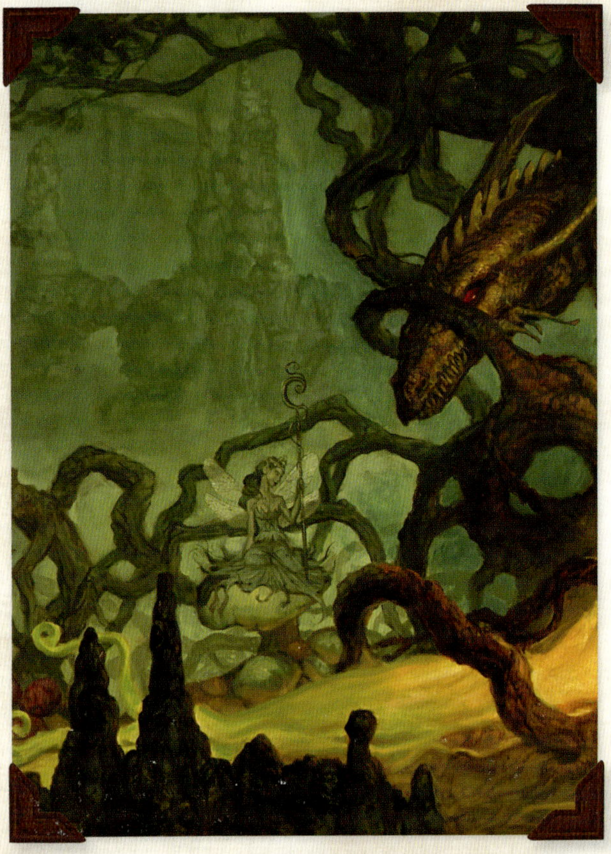

Dragon Fairy

Tom Kidd

Poised over a fiery stream, this fairy's position in this oil painting appears precarious. But the cool colors used to portray her, coupled with the way her pose and scepter mirror the rocks in the foreground and the massive formations in the distance, suggest she has nothing to fear from the dragon entangled in the gnarled runners of the tree to her left.

Barnabus and the Prince

Selina Fenech

White acrylic highlights frosted over a watercolor palette largely limited to browns and cool blues lend a wintry feel to this painting. The impression of iridescence on the skin of Barnabus and the pebble-crusted rock was created by applying small amounts of bright aqua colored pencil, which contrasts sharply with the browns.

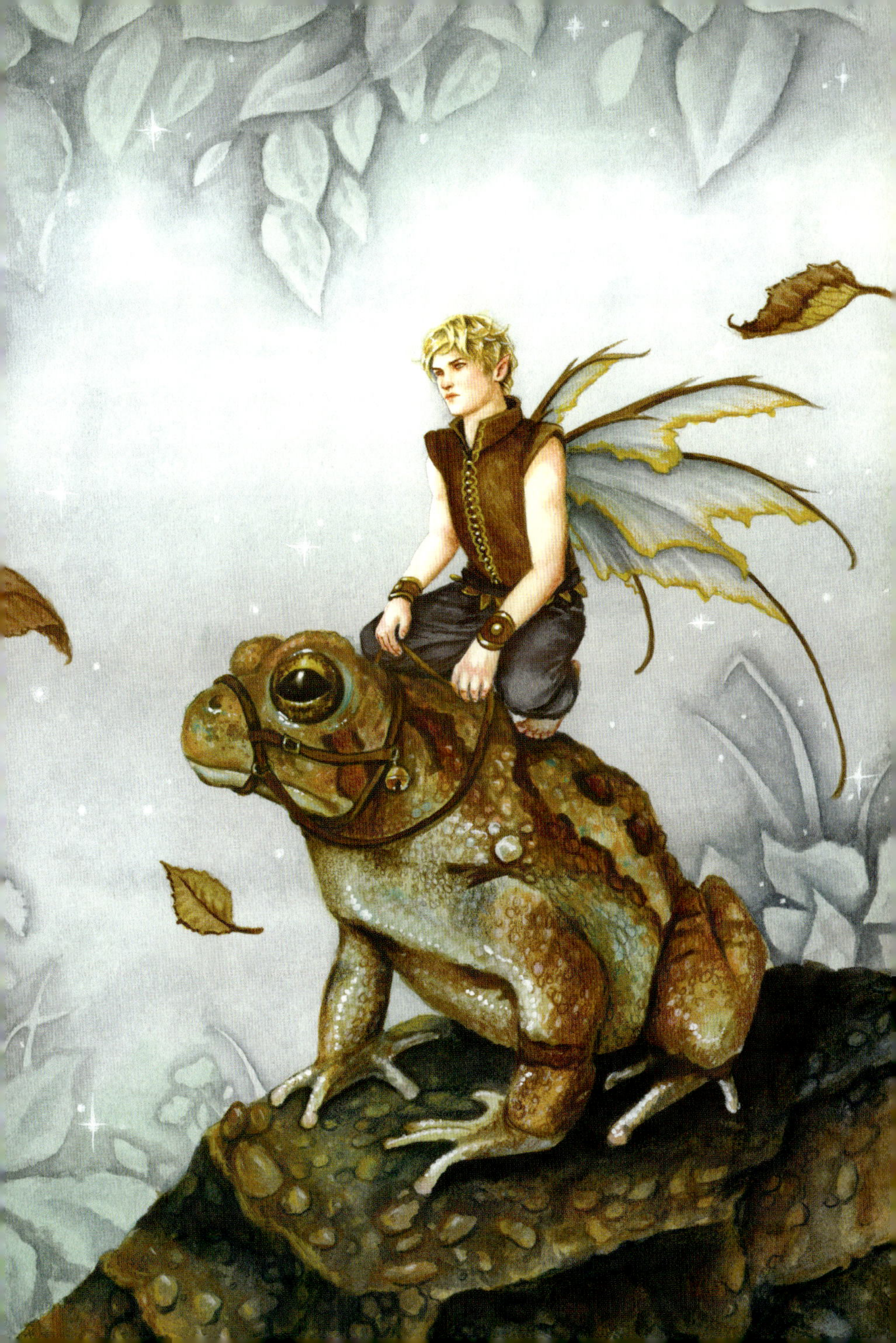

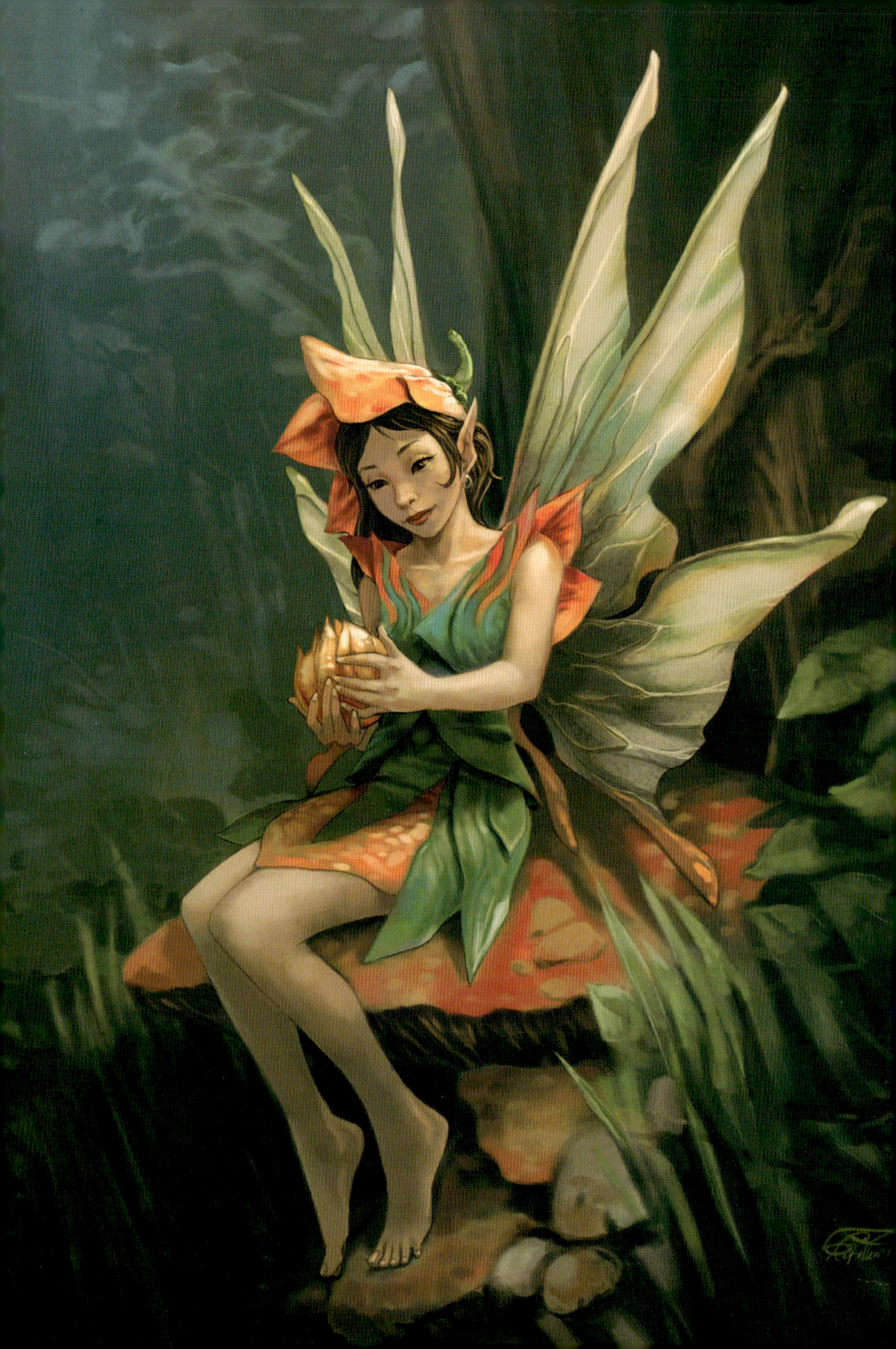

Digital effects

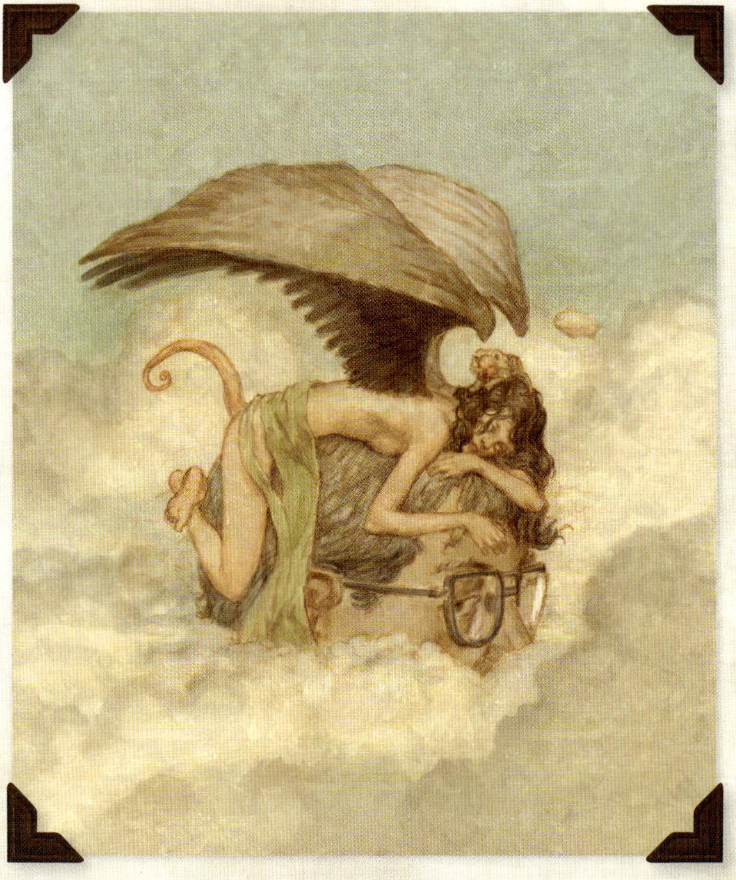

Honeybell the Tree Fairy
Rafi Adrian Zulkarnain

This charming fairy's delicately shadowed face and softly modeled limbs, the gleaming leaves of her dress, and the diaphanous wings are all products of digital coloring techniques. The play of light, opacity, and transparency lend the figure a vivid three-dimensional quality emphasized by the looser, impressionistic rendering of the surrounding plants.

Fairy Muse
Tom Kidd

This digital painting began life as a sketch of the artist and his exhausted fairy muse moving through a miasmal fog of vague thoughts that may never amount to anything. To create the delicate, watercolor-like effect, the artist scanned the drawing and colored it digitally using scans of painterly sections of other works.

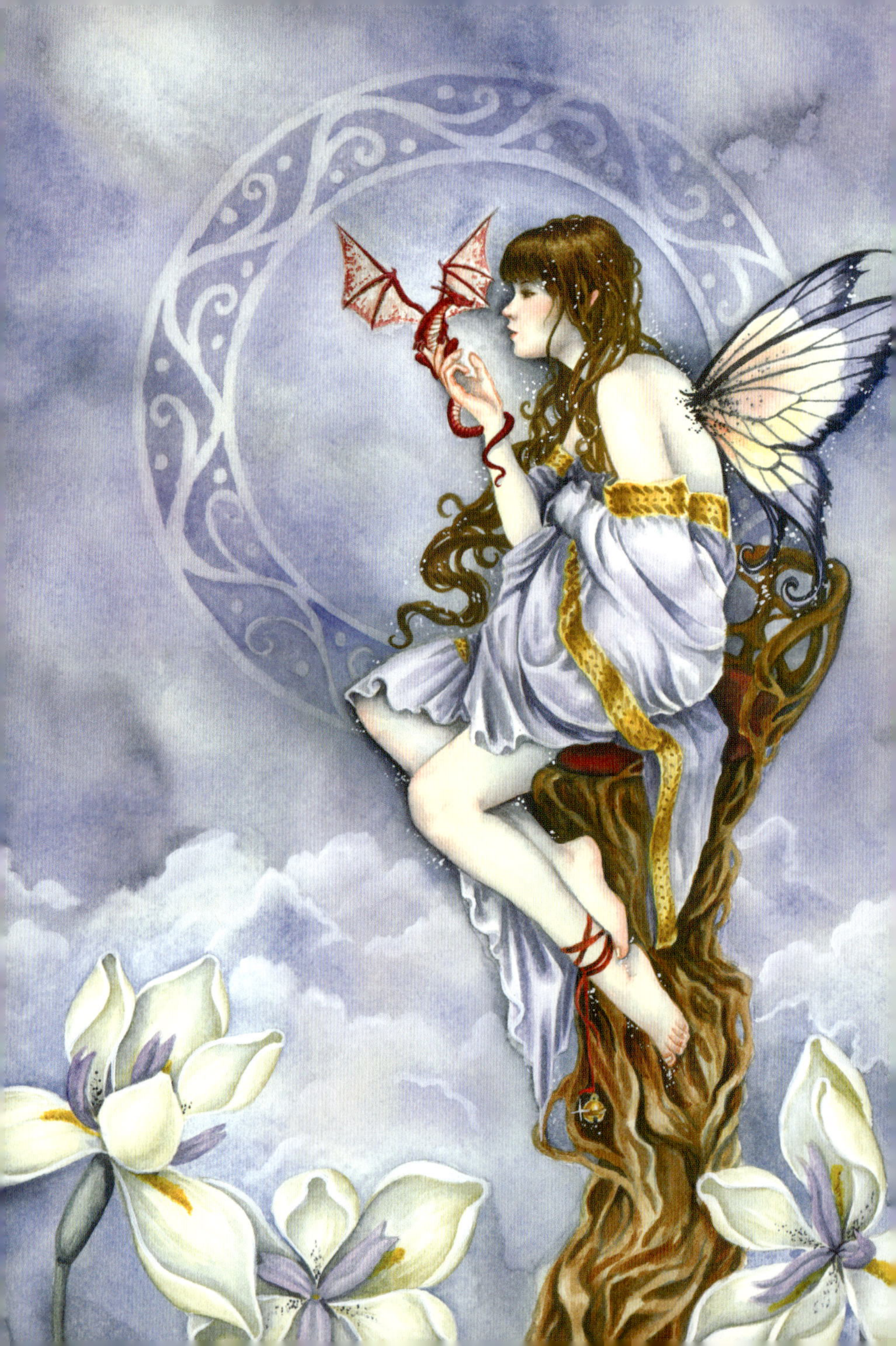

Mixing media

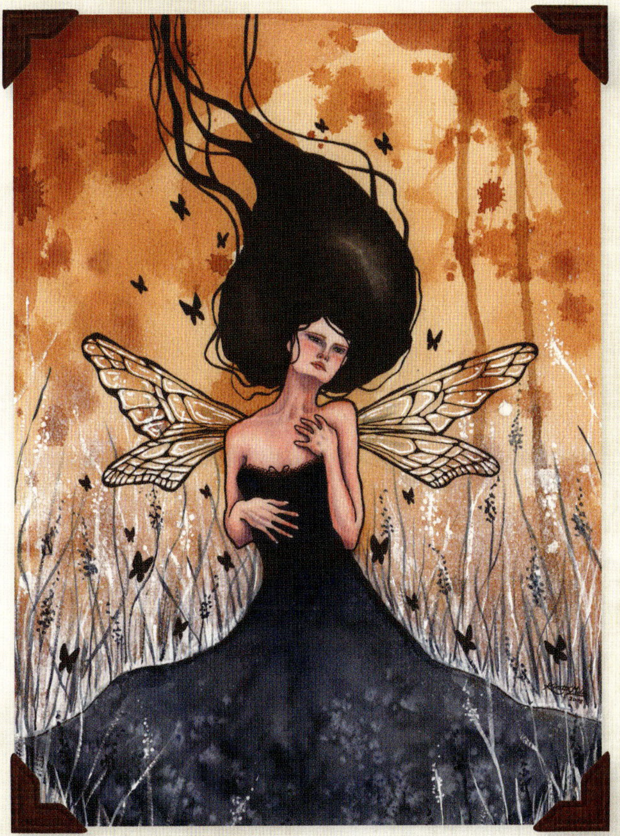

Dragon's Pet

Selina Fenech

The use of white acrylic over watercolor on smooth watercolor paper provides an opacity, brightness, and even application perfect for fluffy white clouds. The circular background design was developed by covering the first color wash of the sky with masking fluid, then building up the blue and light pink color around it.

Lost in Memories

Kirstin Mills

This painting combines a variety of media—a graphite under-sketch, layers of watercolor, dripped and pooled ink, and gouache—to depict a fairy reverie. Tall, waving grasses and black butterflies pull the viewer's gaze upward to the flowing hair, evoking the movement of a breeze through the field as well as the memories flowing over the fairy.

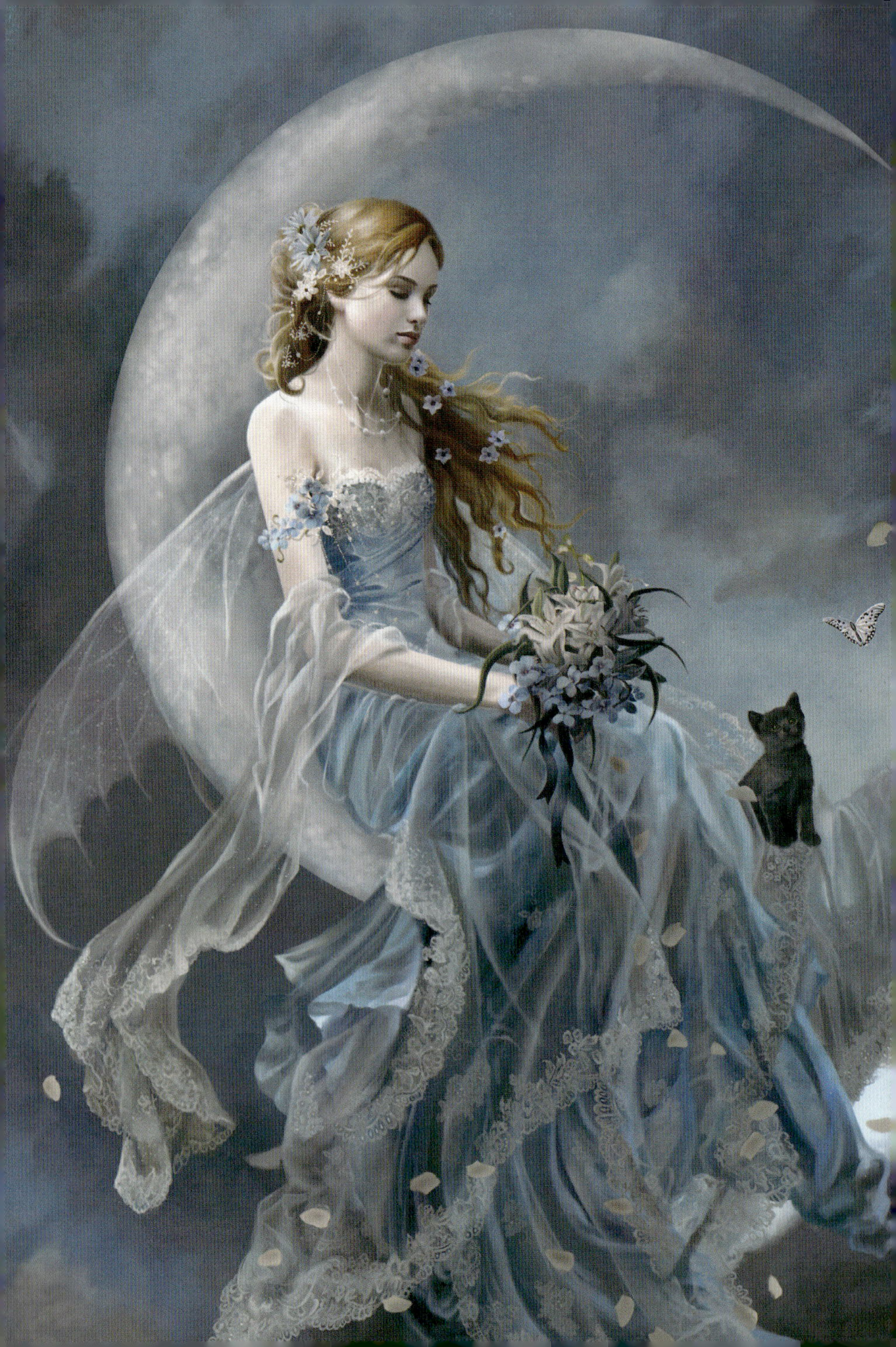

Depicting the ephemeral

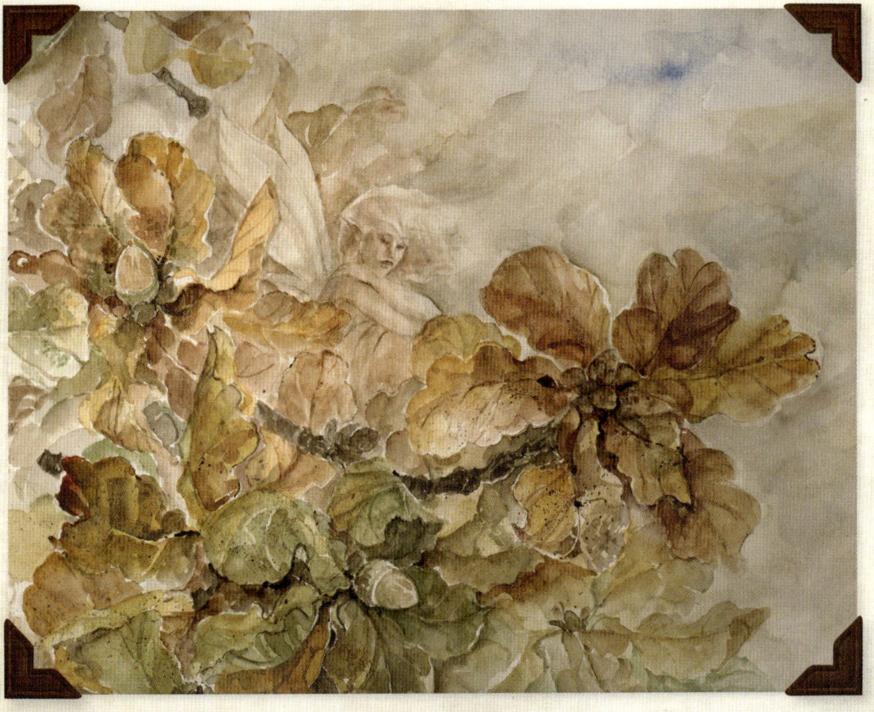

Wind Moon

Nene Thomas

The easiest way to paint invisible forces—such as wind or magic—is to show their effects, but accessories play a role, too. The fairy's fluttering hair and gown, and the petals tossed on the breeze in this digital rendering are neatly complemented by her diaphanous wings and sheer, lacy overdress.

Autumn Fairy

Wenche Skjöndal

Watercolor is uniquely suited to depicting ephemeral creatures of air and magic. Without hard outlines, the different elements of a painting flow into each other, causing the viewer to wonder whether the face lurking amid the acorns and fall foliage belongs to a shivering fairy or the gathering clouds of winter.

Index

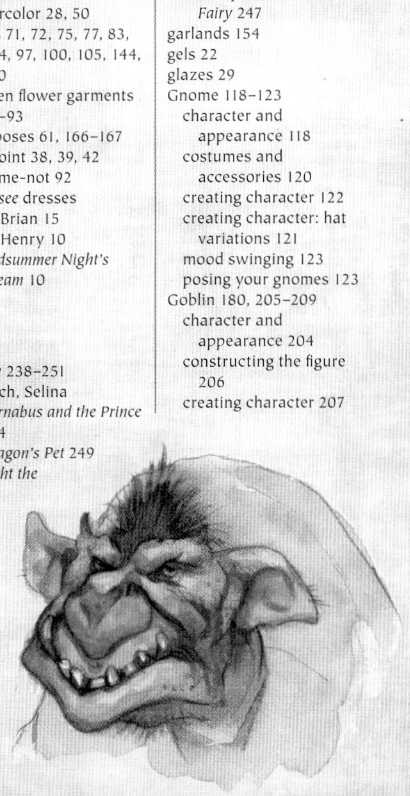